Tenth Edition

Instructional Technology and Media for Learning

Sharon E. Smaldino
Northern Illinois University

Deborah L. Lowther
University of Memphis

James D. Russell
Purdue University

PEARSON

Boston   Columbus   Indianapolis   New York   San Francisco   Upper Saddle River
Amsterdam   Cape Town   Dubai   London   Madrid   Milan   Munich   Paris   Montreal   Toronto
Delhi   Mexico City   Sao Paulo   Sydney   Hong Kong   Seoul   Singapore   Taipei   Tokyo

Senior Acquisitions Editor: Kelly Villella Canton
Senior Development Editor: Max Effenson Chuck
Editorial Assistant: Annalea Manalili
Senior Marketing Manager: Darcy Betts
Production Editor: Gregory Erb
Editorial Production Service: Omegatype Typography, Inc.
Manufacturing Buyer: Megan Cochran
Electronic Composition: Omegatype Typography, Inc.
Interior Design: Omegatype Typography, Inc.
Photo Researcher: Annie Pickert
Cover Designer: Elena Sidorova

Credits and acknowledgments borrowed from other sources and reproduced, with permission, in this textbook appear on the appropriate page within text or on page 334.

Library of Congress Cataloging-in-Publication Data

Smaldino, Sharon E.
  Instructional technology and media for learning / Sharon E. Smaldino,
Deborah L. Lowther, James D. Russell. — 10th ed.
       p.   cm.
  Includes bibliographical references and index.
  ISBN-13: 978-0-13-800815-4 (pbk.)
  ISBN-10: 0-13-800815-9 (pbk.)
  1. Educational technology.   2. Audio-visual education.   I. Lowther,
Deborah L.   II. Russell, James D.   III. Title.
    LB1028.3.H45   2012
    371.33—dc22
                                        2010051005

10 9 8 7 6 5 4 3 2 1   CIN   15 14 13 12 11

www.pearsonhighered.com

ISBN-10: 0-13-800815-9
ISBN-13: 978-0-13-800815-4

About the Authors

Sharon E. Smaldino   Sharon holds the L. D. and Ruth G. Morgridge Endowed Chair for Teacher Education in the College of Education at Northern Illinois University (NIU). She was a professor of educational technology at the University of Northern Iowa for many years prior to moving to NIU. Sharon received her PhD in 1987 from Southern Illinois University, Carbondale. Prior to that she received an MA in elementary education and served for more than a dozen years as teacher, speech therapist, and special educator in school districts from Florida to Minnesota. At Northern Iowa she taught educational media courses for undergraduates and graduate majors and served as coordinator of the educational technology program. Sharon also taught graduate courses in instructional development, technology integration, distance education, and professional standards and ethical practice. She has received several awards for her outstanding teaching. In her current role, she is focused on working with faculty and PK–12 teachers to integrate technology into the learning process. Presenting at state, national, and international conferences, Sharon has become an important voice on applications of technology in the classroom and in distance education. In addition to her teaching and consulting, Sharon has written articles for state and national journals on her primary research interest—effective technology integration in learning. She worked on a teacher quality enhancement grant that identified technology as an important aspect of ensuring quality learning environments. She also served as the editor of *TechTrends,* an AECT publication.

Deborah L. Lowther   Deborah has been an educator for 30 years. For the first seven years of her career she taught middle school science and was highly engaged with providing professional development to teachers within and beyond her district. Because of her desire to work with teachers, she received her PhD in educational technology in 1994 and accepted a faculty position at the University of Memphis in 1995. At the University of Memphis, Deborah serves as the senior technology researcher for the Center for Research in Educational Policy, through which she investigates PK–12 technology integration issues. She has personally conducted observations in PK–12 classrooms and interviewed students, teachers, and principals in numerous schools across the country. She has used the knowledge and experiences gained through engagement in applied research to develop the iNtegrating Technology for inQuiry (NTeQ) Model with Dr. Gary Morrison. This model has been the foundational approach for several high-profile technology initiatives, including Michigan's Freedom to Learn program and Tennessee's EdTech Launch program. With regard to scholarship, Deborah has coauthored several books, chapters, and refereed journal articles; presented at numerous national and international conferences; and has provided professional development to educational institutions across the nation.

James D. Russell   Jim is professor emeritus of Educational Technology at Purdue University, where he taught for 38 years. Jim also worked part time for Purdue's Center for Instructional Excellence, where he conducted workshops on teaching techniques and consulted on instructional improvement. During fourteen spring semesters he was Visiting Professor of Educational Psychology and Learning Systems at Florida State University. There he also worked part time for the Center for Teaching and Learning. A former high school mathematics and physics teacher, Jim's teaching career spans 45 years. He has won numerous honors for his teaching at Purdue, including his department's Outstanding Teacher Award and the School of Education's Best Teacher Award. He is also the recipient of AECT's Diamond Mentor Award. He was selected as a member of Purdue's Teaching Academy and has been inducted into the Purdue Book of Great Teachers. His specialty areas, in which he has achieved national prominence through his writings and presentations, are presentation skills and using media and technology in classrooms. Through his teaching, workshops, consulting, and this textbook, Jim has made a significant impact on classroom teaching practice.

Award-Winning Book

Instructional Technology and Media for Learning has received the following recognition in past editions:

- Outstanding Book in Educational Technology and Teacher Education from the Association of Educational Communications and Technology (AECT) Teacher Education Division
- The James Brown Award for the Best Non-Periodic Publication in the Field of Educational Technology from AECT
- The Outstanding Instructional Communication Award from the International Society for Performance Improvement (ISPI)
- The Visual Design and Layout Award from the Design Society of America

Brief Contents

Contents

3 INTEGRATING TECHNOLOGY AND MEDIA INTO INSTRUCTION: THE ASSURE MODEL 36

4 ACHIEVING 21ST CENTURY LEARNING ENVIRONMENTS   68

5 ENGAGING LEARNERS WITH COMPUTERS   96

6 CONNECTING LEARNERS USING WEB 2.0 TOOLS   124

7 CONNECTING LEARNERS AT A DISTANCE   144

8 ENHANCING LEARNING WITH VISUALS 174

9 ENHANCING LEARNING WITH AUDIO 208

A   LESSON SCENARIO CHART   297

B   EQUIPMENT SAFETY AND SETUPS   299

Special Features

TAKING A LOOK at TECHNOLOGY INTEGRATION

TECHNOLOGY for DIVERSE LEARNERS

USING _____ IN THE CLASSROOM

WHEN to USE

Preface

Instructional Technology and Media for Learning, Tenth Edition, shows how a complete range of technology and media formats can be integrated into classroom instruction using the ASSURE model for lesson planning. Written from the viewpoint of the teacher, the text shows specifically and realistically how technology and media enhance and support everyday teaching and learning. This book is intended for educators at all levels who place a high value on learning. Its purpose is to help educators incorporate technology and media into best practice—to use them as teaching tools and to guide students in using them as learning tools. We draw examples from elementary and secondary education because we know that instructors in these PK–12 settings have found previous editions of this book useful in their work.

This new edition is necessitated by the amazing pace of innovation in all aspects of technology, particularly in those related to computers, Web 2.0, social networks, and the Internet. The text has been updated to reflect the accelerating trend toward digitizing information and school use of telecommunications resources, such as the Web, wikis, and blogs. The tenth edition also addresses the interaction among the roles of teachers, technology coordinators, and school media specialists, all complementary and interdependent teams within the school.

OUR APPROACH

We share a number of convictions that underlie this edition. First, we believe in an *eclectic* approach to instruction. Advocates cite an abundance of theories and philosophies in support of different approaches to instruction—behaviorist, cognitivist, constructivist, and social–psychological. We view these theoretical positions as differing *perspectives*—different vantage points—from which to examine the complex world of teaching and learning. We value each of them and feel that each is reflected in the guidance we offer.

Second, we have a balanced posture regarding the role of technology in instruction. Because of this perspective we consider each technology in light of its advantages,

limitations, and range of applications. No technology can be described solely as being either "good" or "bad," so we strive to provide a balanced treatment to a range of technologies and media resources.

Third, we believe that technology can best be integrated into instruction when viewed from a teacher's perspective. Therefore, throughout the book we attempt to approach technology and media solutions in terms of a teacher's day-to-day challenges and to avoid technical jargon. Our examples deal with everyday teaching issues in a range of content areas.

NEW TO THIS EDITION

The nature of shifts and changes in technology requires us to continually look at new trends and resources that impact learning with technology. Because of these changes, we found the need to add new information and features to this edition of the book.

▶ **Focus on 21st Century Learning.** With the advent of the 21st century, it is important to focus on the new directions that impact today's students. The chapters focus on 21st century learners and how to best use technology and media to address their interests and needs.

▶ **Chapter 2, Understanding 21st Century Learners.** This heavily revised chapter brings the reader into the 21st century classroom where there are new challenges as well as new tools available to enhance teachers' classroom instruction and strategies.

▶ **Web 2.0.** Web 2.0 resources and tools are provided throughout the text. In addition, we have devoted an entire chapter, Chapter 6, to the types of Web 2.0 tools available to use as part of the extension beyond the computers in the classroom. Many open-source and online resources are identified as examples of Web 2.0 tools.

▶ **Websites and Online Resources.** More websites and online resources are featured in each chapter. A balance of student use and teacher support websites have been identified for the many technology and media topics discussed throughout the book.

3D INTERACTIVE CUBE DISPLAY

Tabletop Display Gets Rid of the Glasses

A cube-shaped device offers all the thrills of 3D without those annoying glasses. The device, called "pCubee," has five LCD screens—one on each side and another on the top of the cube. The viewer can pick it up and see virtual objects from four sides and the top. The viewer can shake the cube, tilt it, and even interact with objects in the cube using a virtual stylus. Just think of the advantages of using the 3D cube in the classroom to show different objects without having to store the many objects between uses.

Innovation on the Horizon. The features, which appear toward the end of each chapter, highlight new developments in technology that can impact teachers and students.

Updated ISTE NETS-T. At the beginning of each chapter, the ISTE NETS-T are aligned with chapter Knowledge Outcomes. At the end of each chapter, the professional skills activities have been updated to reflect the ISTE NETS-T. For each end of chapter activity at least one standard has been identified. Students who successfully complete the skills activities will demonstrate that they have accomplished the standards.

Knowledge Outcomes

This chapter addresses ISTE NETS-T 2, 4, and 5.

1. Describe the characteristics of the 21st century learner.
2. Discuss the learning theories described in this chapter.
3. List principles of effective instruction for the 21st century learner.
4. Discuss the principles of effective technology and media utilization.
5. Discuss the concept of text literacy.
6. Compare and contrast the advantages and limitations of integrating text into learning.

Taking a Look at Technology Integration. These miniature case studies of technology and media applications demonstrate how teachers are using technology in a variety of settings. Like the ASSURE Classroom Case Study, they show technology and media use *in context*.

TAKING A LOOK
AT TECHNOLOGY INTEGRATION

New Tech High

Started in California, the New Tech Network is a national initiative to develop innovative high schools. It is an outgrowth of the philosophy that empowering students through an alternative instructional approach will help them to become creators, leaders, and tomorrow's productive citizens. New Tech Network advocates learning environments that provide student-centered settings where

• Problem-based learning engages learners
• Students and teachers have ownership of their learning experiences
• Technology is integrated throughout the entire learning experiences

The goal is to provide students with an integrated curriculum that focuses on critical thinking, collaboration, and problem solving as vehicles to learning. And they have the data to demonstrate that their ideas are working, with graduation rates that are significantly higher than the national averages. Also, more of the graduates from New Tech high schools pursue careers in mathematics, science, and engineering than their regular high school peers.

Shutterstock

Mrs. Roman, a third-grade teacher, noted that her students' test scores indicated problems with visualizing mathematical figures. She especially noted their difficulties with mentally converting a two-dimensional picture on the test into the three-dimensional image that it represented. She spoke with Mrs. Edlund, the art teacher, to seek ways of helping her students understand visualization of ideas. Mrs. Edlund also wanted to find ways to use art to assess learning due to the school's interest in using art and technology in the learning process. She was trying to find a way to bring technology into the art classroom. Both teachers have noted that the children have difficulty thinking about their learning and expressing themselves.

To view the ASSURE Classroom Case Study Video for this chapter, go to the MyEducationKit for your text and click on the ASSURE Video under Chapter 8 to explore how Mrs. Roman works with the art teacher, Mrs. Edlund, to seek ways of using art and technology to help her students understand the visualization of ideas.

Throughout the chapter you will find reflection questions to relate the chapter content to the ASSURE Classroom Case Study. At the end of the chapter you will be challenged to develop your own ASSURE lesson that incorporates use of these strategies, technology, media, and materials, for a topic and grade level of your choice.

The ASSURE Model for Technology Integration.

The presentation of the ASSURE model has been moved forward to Chapter 3 and related features have been substantially revised. In this edition the explanation of the ASSURE model has been revised to be more clear, practical, and focused on PK–12 teaching and learning. Chapter opening ASSURE Classroom Case Studies (in Chapters 3 through 11) each present a video clip of a specific classroom that will be revisited periodically throughout the chapter in the ASSURE Case Study Reflections. These are brief notes and reflection questions that extend the opening case study by addressing the questions that a teacher may face when considering technology integration in the context of specific chapter content. At the end of the chapter the ASSURE Lesson Plan provides a fuller version of the instructional or classroom situation outlined at the beginning of the chapter and offers a possible solution.

ASSURE Case Study Reflection

Review the ASSURE Classroom Case Study and video at the beginning of the chapter. Consider the benefits for Mrs. Roman in using PowerPoint when teaching math concepts? How can she get students to explain their ideas? How might Mrs. Edlund use PowerPoint as part of her art lessons? What can she do to have children connect what they are learning in art class with their math lessons?

ASSURE Lesson Plan

The following ASSURE Lesson Plan provides a detailed description and analysis of the lesson in the ASSURE Classroom Case Study and video at the beginning of the chapter. To review the video again, go to the MyEducationKit for your text and click on the ASSURE Video under Chapter 8. The video explores how Mrs. Roman, a third-grade teacher, and Mrs. Edlund, an art teacher, help students learn through the use of digital images and electronic portfolios.

A nalyze Learners

General Characteristics. The audience consists of 23 third-graders who have recently completed state tests to assess their mathematics knowledge and skills. Because the school is new, they have not had many opportunities to know each other prior to this year. Some come from the same neighborhood, whereas others are from surrounding small communities. All of the students like to play at recess and enjoy movies and video games. Many of the boys are interested in sports, especially baseball. Most of the girls are interested in reading and watching television.

Entry Competencies. A number of the children have scored well on earlier tests in mathematics. A few struggle with some basic mathematics skills they have yet to master. The students have demonstrated difficulty in understanding the concepts of three-dimensional images shown on paper. As their recent test scores reflect, they have difficulty with conceptualizing how to visualize this type of image.

Learning Styles. The class members display a range of learning styles. Most of them have visual and spatial skills and good math ability. The children enjoy drawing and look forward to art classes as they find they can express their ideas in a variety of materials.

S tate Standards and Objectives

Curriculum Standards. National Council of Teachers of Mathematics 3—Geometry and spatial sense: Analyze characteristics and properties of two- and three-dimensional geometric objects. National Standards for Arts Education 5: Reflecting on and assessing the characteristics and merits of their work and the work of others.

Technology Standards. National Educational Technology Standards for Students 3—Technology productivity tools: Students use technology tools to enhance learning, increase productivity, and promote creativity.

Learning Objectives
1. Given art materials, the students will demonstrate their ability to build three-dimensional objects by cutting and shaping construction paper into three shapes: cylinder, cone, and box.
2. Given drawing materials, the students will draw on paper their three-dimensional objects, employing conventions learned in art class.

A Model to Help ASSURE Learning

A nalyze Learners

The first step in planning a lesson is to identify and analyze learner characteristics shown to be associated with learning outcomes. This information will guide your decision making during the design of your lesson. The key areas to consider during learner analysis include (1) general characteristics of learners, (2) specific entry competencies (knowledge, skills, and attitudes about the topic), and (3) learning styles.

S tate Standards and Objectives

The next step is to state the standards and learning objectives as specifically as possible. Begin with the curriculum and technology standards adopted by your district, as these are based on state and national student performance criteria. Well-stated objectives name the learners for whom the objective is intended, the action (behavior) to be demonstrated, the conditions under which the behavior or performance will be observed, and the degree to which the new knowledge or skill must be mastered. For this text, the condition will include the use of technology and media to support learning and to assess achievement of the standard or learning objectives.

S elect Strategies, Technology, Media, and Materials

Once you have analyzed your learners and stated the standards and objectives, you have established the beginning points (students' present knowledge, skills, and attitudes) and ending points (learning objectives) of instruction. Your task now is to build a bridge between these two points by choosing appropriate instructional strategies, technology, and media, and materials to achieve the objectives.

U tilize Technology, Media, and Materials

This step involves planning your teaching role for utilizing the technology, media, and materials to help students achieve the learning objectives. To do this, follow the "5 Ps" process: Preview the technology, media, and materials; Prepare the technology, media, and materials; Prepare the environment; Prepare the learners; and Provide the learning experience.

R equire Learner Participation

To be effective, instruction should require learners' active mental engagement. Provide activities that allow them to practice the new knowledge or skills and to receive feedback on their efforts before being formally assessed. Practice may involve student self-checks, computer-assisted instruction, Internet activities, or group exercises. Feedback can come from the teacher, a computer, other students, or self-evaluation.

E valuate and Revise

After implementing a lesson, evaluate its impact on student learning. This assessment not only examines the degree to which students achieved the learning objectives, but also examines the entire instructional process and the impact of using technology and media. Wherever there are discrepancies between learning objectives and student outcomes, revise the lesson plan to address the areas of concern.

A nalyze Learners

ASSURE Classroom Case Study

General Characteristics

Tiare Ahu is teaching the basic ninth-grade English course geared toward the average learner. The students are 14 and 15 years old. Several students have identified learning disabilities, whereas others are above-average readers and writers. Her students come from primarily moderate to low socioeconomic environments and represent an ethnic population common to an urban setting. Generally, the students are well behaved. However, they show lack of interest and apathy toward learning when activities are textbook and paper-and-pencil oriented.

Entry Competencies

The students in general are able to do the following:
- Create and save word-processed documents
- Navigate the Internet
- Create and save digital video
- Respond via written and verbal communication that ranges from below to above grade-level proficiency

Learning Styles

Tiare has found that her students appear to learn best from activities that incorporate technology and media. Using computers provides intrinsic motivation through the creation of personalized work and the careful reflection of learning. Her students vary in their preferred forms of expression: some favor inputting their thoughts as written text, others choose to capture them with digital video, and still others prefer audio recordings. Tiare has also discovered that most of her students have difficulty working in a completely silent atmosphere and therefore allows the option of listening to music on MP3 players when they work on their digital portfolios.

Visit the Chapter 3 section of MyEducationKit to view the video of Ms. Ahu's ninth-grade English class working on their electronic portfolios.

FEATURES WITH SUBSTANTIAL REVISIONS AND UPDATES

Copyright Concerns.
This feature provides an integrated discussion of copyright issues linked to specific chapter content.

Computer Software

Congress amended the Copyright Act to clear up questions of fair use of copyrighted computer programs. The changes defined the term *computer program* for copyright purposes and set forth rules on permissible and nonpermissible use of copyrighted computer software. According to the amended law, you are permitted to do the following with a single copy of a program:

- Make one backup or archival copy of the program.
- Use a "locksmith" program to bypass the copy-prevention code on the original to make the archival copy.
- Install one copy of the program onto a computer hard drive.
- Adapt a computer program from one language to another if the program is not available in the desired language.
- Add features to a copyrighted program to make better use of the program.
- Adapt a copyrighted program to meet local needs.

Without the copyright owner's permission, you are prohibited from doing the following:

- Make multiple copies of a copyrighted program.
- Make additional copies from an archival or backup copy.
- Make copies of copyrighted programs to be sold, leased, loaned, transmitted, or given away.
- Sell a locally produced adaptation of a copyrighted program.
- Make multiple copies of an adaptation of a copyrighted program even for use within a school or school district.
- Put a single copy of a program onto a network without permission or a special site license.
- Duplicate the printed copyrighted software documentation unless allowed by the copyright-holding software company.

For general information on copyright, see the copyright section on pages 13 through 15 of Chapter 1. Suggested resources (print and web links) on copyright appear at the end of Chapter 1.

Audio

LibriVox
http://librivox.org

Audiobooks from the public domain are available with titles ranging from classics to short stories and poetry. The collection is based on voluntary submissions of audio media, but the entries must all be copyright free. Over 12 languages are available, with native speakers reading familiar books.

Audio Theatre Production Kit
www.balancepublishing.com

Students can create their own audio theatre productions. The kit contains two versions of a script, one with altered vocabulary to meet the needs of below-grade readers, the second for grade-level and above-grade-level readers. In addition, there is a CD with background music and sound effects. Students, working together, record their production for later sharing. They develop technical skills while working collaboratively in a motivating way that helps them with reading and vocabulary competencies.

Joy Stories
www.joystories.com

Available in both English and Spanish, this collection of short stories has been developed to help children gain personal insight and positive self-image. Presenting issues such as diversity, determination, and disappointment, these creative stories are designed to help children view their own personal challenges in a new light.

A Kid's-Eye View of the Environment
www.mishmashmusic.com

Michael Mish based this series of songs, available on CD or as an MP3 download, on his many visits to schools in southern California to talk to children about the environment. He found them to be more aware and concerned about environmental problems than he expected. Mish took the topics that the children were most concerned about (e.g., recycling, water and air pollution, and the greenhouse effect) and put them to music. The songs are engaging, with sing-along choruses. The messages should get primary-age children talking about making this a safer, cleaner world.

Media Samples.
Actual materials in a variety of media formats are highlighted as examples that are commercially available, to make the reader aware of what is available for use in the classroom. The materials referred to are meant to be *typical* of a given format, not necessarily exemplary. No endorsement is implied.

Selection Rubrics.
These updated rubrics, related to each of the technology and media formats, make it easy to preview materials systematically and to preserve the information for later reference. Textbook users have permission to photocopy these for personal use and may also download them from the Book Resources section of MyEducationKit.

W H E N to U S E Text-Based Materials

Use when student learning will be enhanced by …

Guidelines	Examples
… reading text information for which they will be held accountable	High school students read an assigned article from an online source.
… supplementing teacher-presented material	Students use library books, encyclopedias, or newspapers to add to their knowledge of a topic.
… using handouts that guide them through learning activities	Students use a step-by-step guide to write a book report.
… implementing an **SQ3R** method (see Using Text Materials in the Classroom, p. 31)	Students **S**urvey, ask **Q**uestions, **R**ead, **R**ecite, and **R**eview printed information about the Bill of Rights.

When to Use . . . This feature gives specific tips on using technology and media with clarity, flair, and dramatic effect. It goes with the "U" of the ASSURE model (Utilize Technology, Media, and Materials).

TECHNOLOGY for Diverse Learners

Technology for Diverse Learners. Completely revised, this feature describes technology and media that can be used to meet the learning needs of diverse learners, ranging from those with learning disabilities to gifted and talented students.

Text Readers and Digital Books

Students who are poor readers because of learning disabilities or because English is a second language find reading to be slow, inaccurate, and boring. They frequently have to reread passages, struggle to decode unfamiliar words, and suffer from fatigue and stress. On the other hand, gifted learners often find the text materials in the classroom too simple or boring to challenge them.

There are many resources for helping these and other students access information in suitable text formats within the classroom. Audio or digital books allow instant access to any page, chapter, or subheading with the touch of a button. To listen, students need either a portable media player equipped to play the books or a multimedia computer with a CD drive and specialized software. The Kindle, an electronic book device, provides a text-based means to manipulate reading materials.

Students with visual impairments or severe learning disabilities have access to thousands of digital books available for download or on CD from Recording for the Blind and Dyslexic (www.rfbd.org). A collection of over 6,000 digitally recorded educational titles, including popular young adult fiction books, have been added to the nonprofit organization's collection of 91,000 accessible textbooks.

An additional adaptive technology resource for students with limited sight is the Kurzweil Reader (www.kurzweiledu .com), a text-to-speech device that provides a multimedia approach by enhancing printed or electronic text with additional visual and audible cues. It can "read" text to the student who cannot manage that independently. It can even read webpages and email.

$ FREE & INEXPENSIVE

RUBRICS

Rubistar

http://rubistar.4teachers.org/index.php

Rubistar is a free online tool designed to assist teachers in creating a variety of rubrics. The website has numerous examples of rubrics that can be accessed through key word searches. If you are new to rubrics, the site offers a rubric tutorial. When you are ready to try it out, Rubistar provides an easy-to-use template to create and print rubrics. If you complete the registration, you can save and edit rubrics online.

Kathy Schrock's Assessment and Rubric Information

http://school.discovery.com/schrockguide/assess.html#rubrics

This site provides a vast array of links to rubric resources. The links are categorized by Student Web Page Rubrics, Subject-Specific and General Rubrics, Rubric Builders, Educator Technology Skills and Rubrics, and Related Articles.

Rubrics and Evaluation Resources

www.ncsu.edu/midlink/ho.html

This site provides a collection of rubric resources that range from specific rubrics (e.g., book report rubric, multimedia project rubric, and writing assessment rubrics) to generic rubric templates.

Free and Inexpensive. Because many schools have tight budgets, this feature offers a list of practical and valuable resources that are free or inexpensive. They also inform the reader how to obtain the resources. These are listed at the ends of chapters with our all-new web links.

FOCUS ON PROFESSIONAL DEVELOPMENT

To help readers develop their ongoing professional knowledge and skills with regard to effectively using technology and media for learning, we have enhanced the feature at the ends of chapters called Continuing My Professional Development.

The first section, Demonstrating Professional Knowledge, poses questions based on the Knowledge Outcomes at the beginning of each chapter. In the next section, Demonstrating Professional Skills, readers integrate their learning through activities that are aligned with the ISTE NETS for Teachers. Additional activities are also available on this text's MyEducationKit. The final section is Building My Professional Portfolio. In Chapters 3 through 11 readers use the ASSURE model to build lessons using the following three steps:

- **Creating My Lesson** asks readers to select their own topics and settings for developing lessons that integrate the technology and media discussed in the chapter. Chapter-specific questions help readers make decisions to create their own lesson plan using appropriate instructional strategies, technology, and media.
- **Enhancing My Lesson** asks the reader to describe other strategies, technology, media, and materials that could enhance the lesson. The reader addresses how the lesson could be enhanced to meet the diverse needs of learners, including students who already possess the knowledge and skills targeted in the lesson plan.
- **Reflecting on My Lesson** prompts readers to reflect on the lesson, the process used to develop it, and different types of students who could benefit from it. Readers are also asked to reflect on what they learned about the process of matching audience, content, strategies, technology, media, and materials.

INSTRUCTOR SUPPLEMENTS

The following instructor ancillaries support and reinforce the content presented throughout the text. All supplements are available for download from Pearson's password-protected Instructor Resource Center (www.pearsonhighered.com/irc) for instructors who adopt this text. For more information, contact your Pearson Education sales representative.

INSTRUCTOR'S MANUAL

The Instructor's Manual provides chapter by chapter tools to use in class. Teaching strategies, in-class activities, student projects, key term definitions, and helpful resources will reinforce key concepts or applications and keep students engaged.

MYTEST COMPUTERIZED TEST BANK

MyTest Computerized Test Bank (www.pearsonmytest.com) provides multiple-choice and essay questions tied to each chapter. Pearson MyTest is a powerful assessment generation program that helps instructors easily create and print quizzes and exams. Questions and tests are authored online, allowing ultimate flexibility and the ability to efficiently create and print assessments anytime, anywhere! To access Pearson MyTest and your test bank files, simply go to www.pearsonmytest.com to log in, register, or request access.

FEATURES OF PEARSON MYTEST:

Premium assessment content

- Draw from a rich library of assessments that complement your Pearson textbook and your course's learning objectives.
- Edit questions or tests to fit your specific teaching needs.

Instructor-friendly resources

- Easily create and store your own questions, including images, diagrams, and charts using simple drag-and-drop and MS-Word-like controls.
- Use additional information provided by Pearson, such as the question's difficulty level or learning objective, to help you quickly build your test.

Time-saving enhancements

- Add headers or footers and easily scramble questions and answer choices, all from one simple toolbar.
- Quickly create multiple versions of your test or answer key, and when ready, simply save to MS-Word or PDF and print.
- Export your exams for import to Blackboard 6.0, CE (WebCT), or Vista (WebCT).

MYTEST SUPPORT

MyTest questions from instructors are fully supported by Pearson Customer Support, and there are numerous helpful documents posted at www.247pearsoned.custhelp.com and www.pearsonmytest.com/support.html.

POWERPOINT SLIDES

Each slide reinforces key concepts and big ideas presented throughout the text. These are available for download from the Instructor Resource Center.

Dynamic Resources Meeting Your Needs

MyEducationKit is a dynamic website that connects the concepts addressed in the text with effective teaching practice. Plus, it's easy to use and integrate into assignments and courses. Whenever the MyEducationKit logo appears in the text, follow the simple instructions to access a variety of multimedia resources geared to meet the diverse teaching and learning needs of instructors and students. Here are just a few of the features that are available:

- Online study plans, including self-assessment pre- and post-test quizzes, resource material, and flashcards
- Gradetracker, an online grade book
- A wealth of multimedia resources, including classroom video, rubrics, strategies, and lesson plans
- Annotated web links to important national organizations and sites in your field

Study Plan A MyEducationKit Study Plan is a multiple-choice assessment with feedback tied to chapter objectives. A well-designed Study Plan offers multiple opportunities to fully master required course content as identified by the objectives in each chapter:

- *Learning Outcomes* tie to the knowledge outcomes for the chapter and give students targets to shoot for as they read and study. Learning outcomes are aligned with relevant ISTE NETS-S standards.
- *Multiple-Choice Assessments* (*pre- and post-tests*) assess mastery of the content. These assessments are mapped to chapter objectives, and students can take the multiple-choice quizzes as many times as they want. Not only do these quizzes provide overall scores for each objective, but they also explain why responses to particular items are correct or incorrect.
- *Study Material: Review and Enrichment* gives students a deeper understanding of what they do and do not know related to chapter content with text excerpts connected to learning outcomes.
- *Flashcards* help students study the definitions of the key terms within each chapter.

Assignments and Activities Designed to save instructors preparation time and enhance student understanding, these assignable exercises show concepts in action (through video, cases, and/or student and teacher artifacts). They help students synthesize and apply concepts and strategies they read about in the book.

Multimedia Resources The rich media resources you will encounter throughout MyEducationKit include:

- *ASSURE Videos:* These videos tie directly to the ASSURE Lesson Plans in Chapters 3 through 11 of the text.
- *Additional Classroom Videos*: The authentic classroom videos in MyEducationKit show how real teachers handle actual classroom situations. Discussing and analyzing these videos not only deepens understanding of concepts presented in the text, but also builds skills in observing children and classrooms.
- *Selection Rubrics:* The selection rubrics that you find in the chapters are also available in the Book Resources section of MyEducationKit. Although these are available for photocopying from the book, they are also available for printing from the site.
- *Strategies and Lesson Plans*: These teacher-tested, research-based strategies and lesson plans span grade levels K–12 and all content areas.
- *Annotated Web Links:* On MyEducationKit you don't need to search for the sites that connect to the topics covered in your chapter. Here you can explore websites that are important in the field and that give you perspective on the concepts covered in your text.

General Resources on MyEducationKit The Resources section on MyEducationKit is designed to help students pass their licensure exams, put together effective portfolios and lesson plans, prepare for and navigate the first year of their teaching careers, and understand key educational standards, policies, and laws. This section includes:

- *Licensure Exams*: Contains guidelines for passing the Praxis exam. The *Practice Test Exam* includes practice multiple-choice questions, case study questions, and video case studies with sample questions.
- *Lesson Plan Builder*: Helps students create and share lesson plans.
- *Licensure and Standards*: Provides links to state licensure standards and national standards.
- *Beginning Your Career*: Educates and offers tips, advice, and valuable information on:
  - Resumé Writing and Interviewing: Expert advice on how to write impressive resumés and prepare for job interviews.

- Your First Year of Teaching: Practical tips on setting up a classroom, managing student behavior, and planning for instruction and assessment.
- Law and Public Policies: Includes specific directives and requirements educators need to understand under the No Child Left Behind Act and the Individuals with Disabilities Education Improvement Act of 2004.

Visit **www.myeducationkit.com** for a demonstration of this exciting new online teaching resource.

ACKNOWLEDGMENTS

Through each of the editions we have been fortunate to have guidance from the people who teach the courses for which this book is designed. In preparing for this edition, again we surveyed a sample of adopters and other leaders in the field to elicit their advice about content and emphases. We also asked other well-respected colleagues in the field to critique the text. We thank all those who gave their time and expertise to help make this textbook what it is. In particular we want to acknowledge those talented individuals who reviewed the tenth edition and suggested improvements: Gerald Burgess, Albany State University; Donna Goodwyn, Elmhurst College; Kelly Marie Gordon, Durham Technical Community College; Ruth Johnston, Valparaiso University; Mark Jones, Indiana State University; Nicole Kendall, Tennessee State University; Carrilyn E. Long, Stark State College; Sharon Tettegah, University of Illinois at Urbana-Champaign; and Lisa Yamagata-Lynch, Northern Illinois University.

We have been lucky to have Angela Christopher, University of Memphis graduate student, to help with some of the tasks associated with compiling a book of this nature. We wish to thank her for her assistance in updating and expanding the instructional supplements for this edition. We also wish to thank Jean Callary for her work on the Study Plan in MyEducationKit.

We also extend our appreciation to the following teachers for sharing their expertise and allowing us to record their integration lessons: Chapter 3—Tiare Ahu, ninth grade; Chapter 4—Lindsay Kaiser and Jena Marshall, fifth grade; Chapter 5—Kerry Bird, fourth grade; Chapter 6— Vicki Davis, high school; Chapter 7— Jimmy Chun, high school; Chapter 8—Christine Edlund, art, and Mary Roman, third grade; Chapter 9—Aina Akamu, high school; Chapter 10—Scott James, fifth grade; Chapter 11—Phil Ekkers, first grade.

The editorial and production staff of Pearson Education, particularly Kelly Villella Canton and Greg Erb, deserve special commendation. Members of the editorial and production team, Maxine Effenson Chuck and Amy Nelson, development editors; Annie Pickert, photo editor; and Omegatype Typography, designer, greatly enhanced the look of this edition. We also want to thank our copyeditor for valuable editing contributions and for assistance with the content related to computers. Angela Christopher provided valuable assistance in updating the PowerPoint slides and preparing the Instructor's Manual and Test Bank. We have never had such intense and helpful support from any previous publication team.

We are grateful to our colleagues from our own universities—Northern Illinois University, the University of Memphis, and Purdue University—for their many and valued forms of support over the years.

Finally, we thank our families for all they do to make this project possible. Their patience and support have been invaluable in helping us finish this project.

Sharon E. Smaldino
Deborah L. Lowther
James D. Russell

ASSURE Classroom Case Study Video Clips

Chapter 3: Integrating Technology and Media into Instruction: The ASSURE Model

Tiare Ahu has her ninth-grade English students use computers, DreamWeaver, and iMovie software to create electronic portfolios as a way to improve their writing and comprehension skills.

Time: 10:20

Chapter 4: Using Instructional Strategies to Achieve 21st Century Learning

Lindsay Kaiser and Jena Marshall co-teach fifth grade. To enhance their students' limited interest in social studies, they use a WebQuest to guide students' exploration of Lewis and Clark's famous expedition.

Time: 7:17

Chapter 5: Engaging Learners with Computers

The students in Kerry Bird's fourth-grade class increase their understanding of the water cycle by using computers, PowerPoint software, and Internet resources to create individualized presentations of the water cycle.

Time: 6:57

Chapter 6: Connecting Learners Using Web 2.0 Tools

Vicki Davis teaches a technology class comprised of high school students who are interested in exploring new technology applications. The lesson involves students conducting a discussion about helping younger students learn online safety within a student-created virtual world. The students use online tools to record their discussions.

Time: 10:22

Chapter 7: Connecting Learners at a Distance

Jimmy Chun's high school social studies students from Hawaii use two-way audio/video distance education and Blackboard course management software to interact with students from New Hampshire.

Time: 12:23

Chapter 8: Enhancing Learning with Visuals

The third-grade students in Mary Roman's class work with the art teacher, Christine Edlund, to create an electronic art portfolio that demonstrates their understanding of mathematics concepts such as symmetry.

Time: 11:44

Chapter 9: Enhancing Learning with Audio

Aina Akamu's high school advanced speech–communications students use audio recordings and other media to create presentations depicting their impressions of "What It Means to Be Hawaiian."

Time: 11:25

Chapter 10: Enhancing Learning with Video

Scott James has his fifth-grade students use digital video, iMovie, and "green screens" to create student-scripted news broadcasts on natural disasters.

Time: 20:07

Chapter 11: Using Multimedia to Engage Learners

The first-grade students in Phil Ekker's class enhance their reading, mathematics, and writing skills by completing a series of learning center activities that include audio books and drill-and-practice software on fractions.

Time: 12:14

Instructional

Technology

and

Media for Learning

CHAPTER ONE

Exploring
21st Century Learning

Knowledge Outcomes

This chapter addresses ISTE NETS-T 3, 4, and 5.

1. Describe key components of the framework for 21st century learning.

2. Discuss the status of the technology gap in today's PK–12 schools.

3. Differentiate between technology and media.

4. Name and describe the six basic categories of media.

5. Differentiate between teacher and student use of technology and media.

6. Name and describe the eight literacies.

7. Discuss the three types of instruction as described in the classroom continuum.

8. Describe the key concerns regarding copyright law for educational uses.

Goal

Learn about the uses of technology and media to ensure appropriate student learning in the 21st century.

INTRODUCTION

This book offers a systematic approach for using technology and media to facilitate student learning in the 21st century. This approach is based on the ASSURE model, which helps teachers plan effective, integrated lessons by following a six-step process. Exploring both traditional technologies used in PK–12 classrooms today as well as innovative and cutting-edge approaches that may be commonplace in the future, we describe technology and media that teachers can use to promote learning both within and beyond the classroom. The book describes how to select, use, and evaluate technology and media to ensure that learners emerge with the knowledge and skills needed for successful 21st century careers.

This chapter explores the influence of technology and media within the 21st century learning process on the roles of teachers and students in the classroom. No longer are teachers and textbooks the sources of all information. Instead, the teacher has become the facilitator of knowledge acquisition. With a few keystrokes, students can explore the world using boundless online resources and a wide array of digital media to obtain the information they seek and then discuss their findings in real-time conversations with experts and students living in other countries.

These exciting innovations provide unlimited ways to expand educational opportunities for our students, but they also present new challenges to teachers. How will you go beyond the textbook? How will you select the "right" technology and media when so many choices are available? And most importantly, how will you create learning experiences that effectively use these tools and resources to ensure that your students gain new knowledge and skills?

FRAMEWORK FOR 21ST CENTURY LEARNING

As we transition from one century to the next, it is critical that the foundational components of PK–12 education keep pace with evolving societal needs to prepare students for citizenship and successful careers. Today's teachers are challenged to help students achieve mastery of core subjects as well as gain 21st century knowledge and skills. Leaders from business and education as well as other associations and institutions are joining together to recommend new approaches and broader learning expectations for PK–12 students (ISTE, 2007; Partnership for 21st Century Skills, 2008). Foundational to 21st century knowledge and skills is the preparation of students to meaningfully and purposefully use technology and media for creativity and innovation, communication, research, and problem solving. Themes based on global awareness, entrepreneurship, and life-long learning skills such as adaptability, leadership, and responsibility are also recommended for inclusion with core subject area courses. This text will serve as a guide to assist you in integrating 21st century knowledge and skills into your instructional planning and practices.

TECHNOLOGY

Currently when most people hear the word *technology*, they think of products like computers, MP3 players, and web cams. In this text, we will be referring to **instructional**

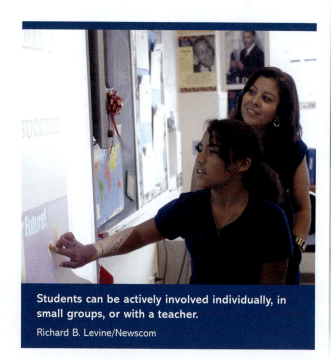

Students can be actively involved individually, in small groups, or with a teacher.
Richard B. Levine/Newscom

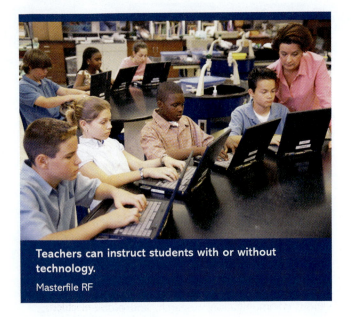

Teachers can instruct students with or without technology.

Masterfile RF

Although some educators view technology as a classroom cure-all, it is important to note that computers and other technology don't automatically make teachers more capable. They need to be versed in best practices for integrating technology into the curriculum. The ASSURE model provides a structure and easy-to-follow steps to guide teachers through the process of creating lessons that achieve the goals of using technology effectively. The model is applicable for all types of technology across all subject areas for different learning conditions.

Current technology offers several benefits for teachers. One is the ability to digitally store and access large amounts of information, whether as text, audio, visuals, games, or movies, in computer files or on CDs or DVDs (Table 1.1). Another unique advantage of current technology is its adaptability to meet the varying needs of students. As seen in the Technology for Diverse Learners box on the following page, teachers can differentiate instruction and access to learning tools with a variety of technology tools. A third advantage of technology is that students are no longer limited to the confines of the classroom. Through the school media center and

technology, which involves the integration of teacher and student use and knowledge of tools and techniques to improve student learning.

Table **1.1** CD versus DVD Comparison Chart		
Format Types	**CD**	**DVD**
Audio (Music)	Yes	Yes
Movie	No	Yes (standard and high definition)
ROM/Read Only Memory	Yes	Yes
R (+ or −)/Record Once	Yes	Yes
RW (+ or −)/Rewritable	Yes	Yes
RAM/Random Access Memory	No	Yes
Mini (3.15 inch/80 mm)	210 MB	1.4 GB
One side, single layer	700 MB	4.7 GB
One side, double layer	Not available	8.5 GB
Two sides, single layer	Not available	9.4 GB
Two sides, double layers	Not available	17 GB
Players	Music CD players only play audio CDs	Newer DVD players can play audio CDs and most DVD formats
Drives	Most CD drives can play all CD formats including audio. They cannot play DVD formats.	Most DVD drives can play all CD and DVD formats except DVD RAM, which needs a specialized drive
Low	1x = 150 KB/sec	1x = 1.35 MB/sec
High	52x = 7.8 MB	24x = 32.4 MB

CD (Compact Disc)—a 4.72 inches (120 mm) optical disc that is used to store audio or data files on one side of the disc.

DVD (Digital Versatile Disc or Digital Video Disc)—an optical disc the same size as a CD that is used for storing movies, interactive media, and data. DVD capacity is much greater than a CD because DVDs are encoded at a higher density and can sometimes be recorded on both sides or on more than one layer on one side.

TECHNOLOGY
for Diverse Learners

Introduction

As a result of inclusion, the number of students with disabilities in the general classroom is increasing. Technology plays an important role in the education of students with exceptionalities. Adapted and specially designed technology and media can contribute enormously to effective instruction of all students and can help them achieve at their highest potential regardless of innate abilities.

Children with disabilities in particular need special instructional interventions. Children with mental disabilities have a greater opportunity to learn when presented with highly structured learning situations. Structure compensates for ill-structured prior knowledge that decreases their ability to incorporate messages into atypical mental constructs. These students benefit from having much more of the message placed within a familiar context.

Students with hearing or visual impairments require different kinds of learning materials. More emphasis should be placed on audio for students with visual impairments and on visuals for those with hearing problems. Adjusting instruction for all exceptional groups requires heavy reliance on technology and media as well as the appropriate selection of these materials to fit specific purposes. Many teachers have found that these assistive strategies for students with disabilities have the added benefit of helping all students.

Assistive technologies can be classified as low tech, medium tech, or high tech. Low tech does not use electricity (neither plug in nor battery). For example, a magnifying glass to enlarge printed material for a visually impaired student would be low-tech assistive technology. Medium tech includes electrical devices. A mini-book light to increase illumination would be representative of medium tech equipment. High tech involves the use of a computer. The Kurzweil reader is an example of high-tech assistive technology.

Diverse learners also include gifted and talented students who, for example, could use newspapers, periodicals, DVDs, or archived documents to explore topics beyond or in addition to regular classroom assignments. They can also use the Internet to search for current information or to engage in a live chat with the author of a book the class is reading or a state senator who will vote on an environmental issue being studied. They can be asked to analyze the information they locate and to synthesize a presentation for the class, perhaps using PowerPoint, or they can post their findings on a class webpage.

For more information, see the Technology for Diverse Learners features throughout this book.

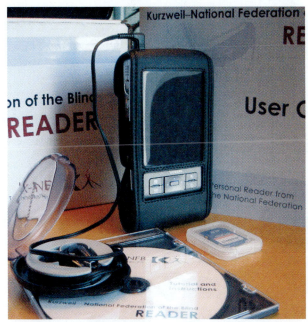

The Kurzweil reading machine allows students who are visually impaired to "read" printed material.

Kurzweil Educational Systems

computer networks such as the Internet, the world becomes each student's classroom.

STATUS OF THE TECHNOLOGY GAP

As you plan different technology integration activities, it is important to stay current on technology issues, such as the "digital divide," that may influence your instructional choices. The digital divide—or technology gap—in PK–12 schools continues to narrow. Students of all economic levels have greater access to high-speed Internet-connected computers at school. The current ratio of about one computer per every four students (Bausell, 2008) helps bridge the gap for students who may not have home computers.

On the other hand, the technology gap varies when examining Internet usage by adults. Even though in 2009 approximately 79 percent of American adults used the Internet at home or work, there were wide gaps in Internet use based on level of education and income (Pew/Internet and American Life Project, 2009). For example, nearly all (94%) adults with a college degree reported using the Internet compared to only 70 percent of those with a high school education. A similar pattern was seen for income level, with Internet use decreasing by level of income. Encouragingly, the report revealed only moderate differences in Internet use by ethnicity. Specifically, 84 percent of English-speaking Hispanics, 79 percent of Caucasians, and 67 percent of African Americans used Internet-connected computers at home or work.

MEDIA

Media, the plural of *medium,* are means of communication. Derived from the Latin *medium* ("between"), the term refers to anything that carries information between a source and a receiver. The purpose of media is to facilitate communication and learning.

Media are discussed in more detail in later chapters, but as an overview, let's look at the six basic types of media used in learning (Figure 1.1): text, audio, visuals, video, manipulatives (objects), and people. Text, the most commonly used medium, is composed of alphanumeric characters that may be displayed in any format—book, poster, whiteboard, computer screen, and so on. Another medium commonly used in learning, audio includes anything you can hear—a

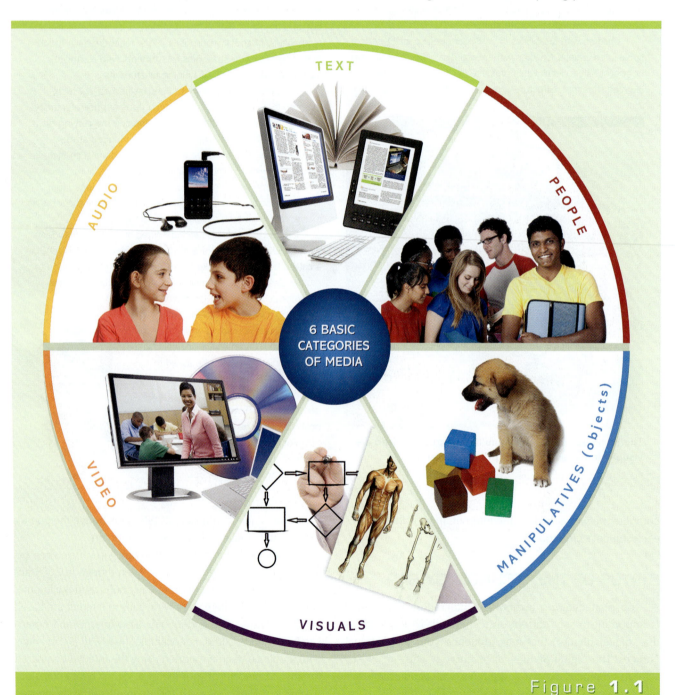

TEXT

AUDIO

PEOPLE

6 BASIC CATEGORIES OF MEDIA

VIDEO

MANIPULATIVES (objects)

VISUALS

Figure **1.1**
Six Basic Categories of Media

person's voice, music, mechanical sounds (running car engine), noise, and so on. It may be live or recorded. Visuals are also regularly used to promote learning and include diagrams on a computer screen, drawings on a whiteboard, photographs, graphics in a book, cartoons, and so on. Video is a visual as well as audio medium that shows motion and can be stored on DVDs, in streamed videos from the Internet, as computer animation, and so on. Although often not considered media, real objects and models are three-dimensional manipulatives that can be touched and handled by students. The sixth and final category of media is people. In fact, people are critical to learning. Students learn from teachers, other students, and adults.

MEDIA FORMATS

Media are very broad categories—text, audio, visuals, video, manipulatives, and people. There are many types of media in each category, which we will refer to as **media formats,** the physical forms in which messages are incorporated and displayed. Media formats include, for example, whiteboards (text and visuals), PowerPoint slides (text and visuals), CDs (voice and music), DVDs (video), and computer multimedia (audio, text, and video). Each has different strengths and limitations in terms of the types of messages that can be recorded and displayed. Choosing a media format can be a complex task—considering the vast array of media and technology available, the variety of learners, and the many objectives to be pursued (Table 1.2). When selecting media formats, the instructional situation or setting (e.g., large group, small group, or self-instruction), learner variables (e.g., reader, nonreader, or auditory preference), and the nature of the objective (e.g., cognitive, affective, motor skill, or interpersonal) must be considered, as well as the presentational capabilities of each of the media formats (e.g., still visuals, video, printed words, or spoken words).

INSTRUCTIONAL MATERIALS

Once you determine the media format, such as a DVD, you must determine which of the appropriate DVDs you will use. The specific DVD becomes the instructional material.

Instructional materials are the specific items used within a lesson that influence student learning. For example, a middle school lesson may focus on adding polynomials with a computer software program that provides virtual manipulatives students use to create "concrete" examples of addition problems in order to reach solutions. The computer software offers feedback and opportunities to continue practicing. The specific math problems and feedback generated by this software are the instructional materials. Another example is the chapter in this text that you are currently reading, which consists of the written information (text), visuals, and learning exercises found at the end of the chapter.

The design and use of instructional materials are critical, because it is the interaction of the students with those materials that generates and reinforces actual learning. If the materials are weak, improperly structured, or poorly sequenced, only limited learning will occur. On the other hand, powerful, well-designed instructional materials are experienced in such a way that they can be readily encoded, retained, recalled, and used in a variety of ways. Learners will remember these materials if they are created, integrated, and presented in a manner that allows them to have the needed impact.

TEACHER USE OF TECHNOLOGY AND MEDIA

When instruction is teacher centered, technology and media are used to support the presentation of instruction. For example, the teacher may use an electronic whiteboard to

Table 1.2 Examples of Media Formats and Instructional Materials

Media	Media Formats	Instructional Materials
Text	Book, computer software	This textbook
Audio	CD, live presenter, podcast	State of the Union address on webcast
Visual	Drawing on interactive white board	Drawing of the musical scale
	Photo in a newspaper	Photo of local building
Video	DVD, IMAX documentary film, streamed video	*Lewis & Clark: Great Journey West*
Manipulative	Real or virtual object	Algebra tiles
People	Teachers, subject-matter expert	The chief officer of NASA

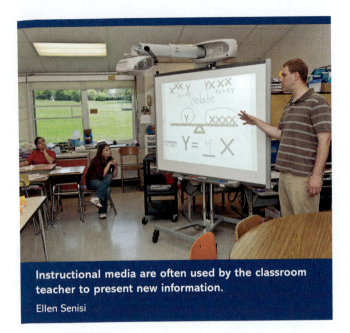

Instructional media are often used by the classroom teacher to present new information.

Ellen Senisi

and audio from Internet-based files that range from short clips demonstrating specific concepts to full-length documentaries. Teachers instantaneously go to a specific section of a DVD and show a segment in slow or fast motion or as a still shot to reinforce targeted student outcomes. PowerPoint presentations integrate animations, sounds, and hyperlinks to digitized information.

Personal Response Systems (PRS). Digital teachers use handheld digital devices, such as **personal response systems (PRS),** to collect and graphically display student answers to teacher questions. The PRS, commonly called a "clicker," is a wireless keypad similar to a TV remote that transmits student responses. Because each PRS is assigned to a designated student, the PRS system can be used to take attendance. However, its main benefit is to allow the teacher to know each student's responses in a variety of circumstances. Using PRS during instruction enhances learner–instructor

display variations of a bar graph as students predict population growth over time. The teacher may also use a pocket chart to show how the meaning of a sentence changes when word cards are rearranged. Projecting a live video "feed" from a zoo can facilitate a teacher's presentation on the feeding habits of birds. Certainly, properly designed instructional materials can enhance and promote learning. This book uses the ASSURE model to assist you in selecting and using instructional strategies, media, technology, and materials. However, their effectiveness depends on careful planning and selection of the appropriate resources, as seen in the next section.

THE DIGITAL TEACHER

Digital tools expand and enhance teacher capabilities to fulfill the numerous roles and responsibilities associated with being an educator. These tools better enable the "digital teacher" to plan for and provide interactive instruction while participating in a global community of practice with fellow educators. The following examples show the potential available in a well-equipped digital environment.

Interactive Instruction. The digital teacher's instruction includes presentations that are media rich and interactive. Live digital videoconferences bring historians, novelists, and content experts into the classroom. Notes and concept maps from brainstorming sessions are captured on electronic whiteboards and instantaneously emailed to students. Instructional presentations seamlessly integrate streamed digital video

Personal response systems provide teachers with immediate feedback from students.

Interwrite Learning

interactivity in whole-class settings, which has been shown to produce better learning outcomes (Flynn & Russell, 2008). Educational uses of the PRS include measuring student understanding of concepts, comparing student attitudes about different ideas, predicting "What if . . ." situations, and facilitating drill-and-practice of basic skills. The PRS graphs student responses to provide teachers and students immediate feedback. Teachers can use this information to guide the pace and direction of a discussion and to make instructional decisions to meet student learning needs.

Mobile Assessment Tools. Advances in mobile computing enable teachers to record student assessment data directly into a handheld device that transfers the data to a computer for report generation. For example, handheld digital devices are used to create running records of primary student reading ability or student performance data observed in presentations, lab experiments, or handwriting (Weinstein, 2005).

Elementary teachers are fast becoming large-scale users of mobile assessment tools to monitor and record the reading abilities of their students. Many use mCLASS:Reading 3D by Wireless Generation, software that provides the text of a book the student is reading and a series of tools to let the teacher easily track performance while the student reads the book (Figure 1.2). The software also offers digital versions of leading reading assessment instruments, such as Dynamic Indicators of Basic Early Literacy Skills (DIBELS).

The mobile devices not only save the teacher time, but the software provides automated timing and scoring of student results. The teacher can continually individualize instruction because of the availability of immediate results. Assessment data are easily downloaded to a secure, password-protected website that offers a variety of reporting options from whole class to individual student.

Special education teachers often use a handheld computer equipped with GoObserve software as a mobile assessment tool. The program can be customized to record designated activities in a student's Individual Education Plan. During an observation of student performance or behavior, the teacher uses the stylus to record the observed strategies from a list of possible choices. The teacher also adds written comments and notes to the student record. After the observation, the teacher transfers the information to her computer to generate reports and graphs of student progress.

Community of Practice. Digital teachers participate in community of practice (CoP) activities, in which groups of educators with common goals from across the nation and around the world share ideas and resources. These Internet-based interactions allow teachers to collaborate and exchange ideas and materials. The CoPs can include educators who are teaching the same subject area and grade level or educators with similar needs, such as technology integration, classroom management, or working with gifted and talented students.

Teachers interested in integrating technology into their instruction can utilize the resources and networks of experts, mentors, and new colleagues supported by a variety of web communities. An example is Tapped In, a virtual community that offers teachers the opportunity to work collaboratively with teachers across the country and around the world. For example, teachers can collaborate to plan and conduct joint learning projects that engage students from both locations in working together to solve a common problem. Teachers can also participate in topical discussions with groups focused

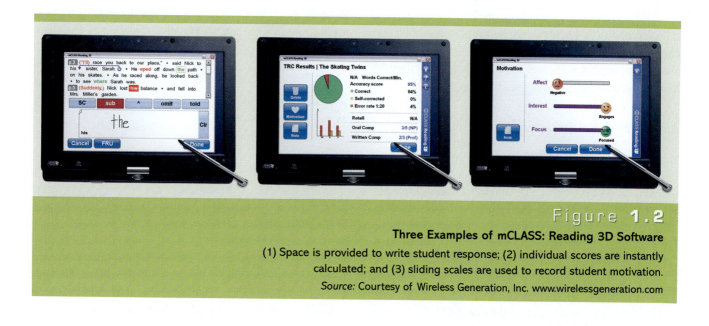

Figure **1.2**

Three Examples of mCLASS: Reading 3D Software
(1) Space is provided to write student response; (2) individual scores are instantly calculated; and (3) sliding scales are used to record student motivation.
Source: Courtesy of Wireless Generation, Inc. www.wirelessgeneration.com

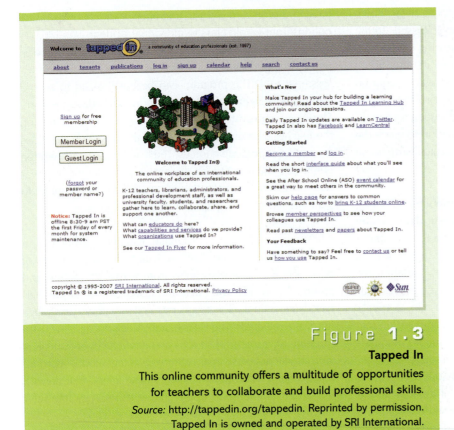

THE ASSURE MODEL

To promote student learning, you need to create an appropriate learning environment. Throughout the book we will describe the decision-making processes that teachers use and the factors they must balance. You will need to know the characteristics of your learners. The expected outcomes (objectives) must be specified. You will need to select the appropriate strategies and materials. The best available technology and media must be used properly to promote optimal learning. You will need to get your learners involved through appropriate practice and feedback. Throughout the process you will be assessing student learning and evaluating the instructional experience as well as its components so you can revise as necessary. We have put all of these steps together in the ASSURE model, which is described in Chapter 3.

Developed as a planning aid to help ensure that technology and media are used to their maximum advantage, not just as interchangeable substitutes for printed or oral messages, the ASSURE model provides a systematic process for creating learning experiences. Indeed, one of the most important roles of technology and media is to serve as a catalyst for change in the whole instructional environment.

The effective use of technology and media demands that teachers be better organized in advance, first thinking through their objectives, then altering the everyday classroom routine as needed, and finally evaluating to determine the impact of instruction on mental abilities, feelings, values, interpersonal skills, and motor skills. However, the shift to the 21st century and increased access to digital resources will change not only how teachers function but student roles as well, as we discuss next.

on key educational issues. Other possibilities include the opportunity to manage or attend online courses, mentor other educators, or try out new ideas in a safe, supportive environment (Figure 1.3).

As members of the Virtual Math Teams (VMT) project at the Math Forum, math teachers can learn to enhance student use of technology in solving nonroutine authentic problems requiring pre-algebra, algebra, or geometry knowledge and skills. Through the VMT, middle and high school teachers can work with peers in special Internet chat sessions with shared whiteboard software, which will then be used by their students.

NETS FOR TEACHERS

The National Educational Technology Standards for Teachers (NETS-T) provide five basic guidelines for becoming what we call a "digital teacher" (ISTE, 2008). As seen in Table 1.3, the NETS-T describe classroom practices, lesson development, and professional expectations. Each chapter of this text includes a Continuing My Professional Development section to help emphasize the importance of the NETS-T and to build your knowledge and skills by providing Demonstrating Professional Skills and Building my Professional Portfolio activities that are directly associated with NETS-T.

STUDENT USE OF TECHNOLOGY AND MEDIA

When instruction is student centered, the primary users of technology and media are the students themselves. Student-centered activities allow teachers to spend more of their time assessing and directing student learning, consulting with

Table **1.3**	National Educational Technology Standards for Teachers (NETS-T)
Standard	**Description**
Facilitate and Inspire Student Learning and Creativity	Teachers use their knowledge of subject matter, teaching and learning, and technology to facilitate experiences that advance student learning, creativity, and innovation in both face-to-face and virtual environments.
Design and Develop Digital-Age Learning Experiences and Assessments	Teachers design, develop, and evaluate authentic learning experiences and assessment incorporating contemporary tools and resources to maximize content learning in context and to develop the knowledge, skills, and attitudes identified in the NETS-S.
Model Digital-Age Work and Learning	Teachers exhibit knowledge, skills, and work processes representative of an innovative professional in a global and digital society.
Promote and Model Digital Citizenship and Responsibility	Teachers understand local and global societal issues and responsibilities in an evolving digital culture and exhibit legal and ethical behavior in their professional practices.
Engage in Professional Growth and Leadership	Teachers continuously improve their professional practice, model lifelong learning, and exhibit leadership in their school and professional community by promoting and demonstrating the effective use of digital tools and resources.

individual students, and teaching one on one and in small groups. How much time the teacher can spend on such activities will depend on the extent of the instructional role assigned to technology and media. Indeed, under certain circumstances, the entire instructional task can be left to technology and media. In fact, media are often "packaged" for this purpose—objectives are listed, guidance in achieving objectives is given, materials are assembled, and self-evaluation guidelines are provided. This is not to say, of course, that instructional technology can or should replace the teacher, but rather that technology and media can help teachers become creative managers of the learning experience instead of mere dispensers of information.

THE DIGITAL STUDENT

Digital students learn in classrooms where the technology is a seamless component of learning that expands the educational environment beyond the classroom walls. Devices and digital connections extend the existing capabilities of learners in many directions.

Interactive Tools. The digital student uses mobile wireless devices in a variety of ways in and out of the school setting by taking technology where it is needed. For example, students on the reading rug find Internet resources on wireless laptop computers. Students bring personal data assistants (PDAs), handheld computers, or "netbooks," smaller and lighter computers, to the library to take notes from archived community newspaper articles. Student pairs use a

Carefully designed technology can make independent learning more effective.

Shutterstock

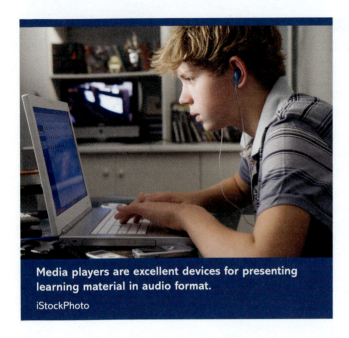

Media players are excellent devices for presenting learning material in audio format.

iStockPhoto

digital camera to capture examples of symmetry found on the school campus. Elementary students with digital probes record the pH of six soil types used to grow radish plants. A high school student with a reading access barrier listens to an MP3, or compressed audio file, of Michael Chabon's "Inventing Sherlock Holmes," a homework reading assignment for the class (www.assistivemedia.org). These wireless devices extend and embellish the learning experience beyond anything nondigital methods can produce.

Interacting with Others. Never before have students been so connected with each other as they are in today's wireless digital environments. Phones, PDAs, and laptops are used to send voice, text, and animated messages; to listen to music, news, and sports; and to watch the latest music videos and movie previews. Students communicate with their digital devices by voice commands, by handwritten notes, or by using an onscreen or mini-keyboard. Documents with digitally embedded comments and edits are instantaneously exchanged between students and their teachers, among students, and with experts. Student learning communities extend around the globe through web-based interactive communication tools and social media sites such as **blogs** (publicly accessible personal journals), **wikis** (web information that can be edited by any registered user), and **podcasts** (Internet distributed multimedia file formatted for direct download to mobile devices). For example, students create a blog on global warming in which they regularly exchange commentary and related hyperlinks with students located around the world. Middle school students use wikis to interact with college students who respond to their writing activities, while a high school American literature class uploads podcasts of interviews with authors to the class website.

These tools are becoming increasingly popular, as seen in a 2010 Nielsen Company report showing a one-year 82 percent increase in the time spent on social media sites. Wikipedia is similarly popular, with over three million entries available in over 200 languages as of July 2010 (http://en.wikipedia.org/wiki/Main_Page). As with digital teachers, the digital students of today embrace and use technology to explore, inquire, and advance their personal learning, as well as contribute to the knowledge of others.

NETS FOR STUDENTS

The National Educational Technology Standards for Students (NETS-S) provide six critical skills students need to achieve success in school and in future careers (ISTE, 2007). Notice in Table 1.4 that the NETS-S closely align with 21st century knowledge and skills. Also interesting is the placement of Technology Operations and Concepts as the last or sixth standard, a shift from the original arrangement that listed it as the first standard (ISTE, 1998). It is important that as a teacher you are familiar with the NETS-S and build your technology skills to match what is expected of your students. Throughout the text we provide multiple examples of how the NETS-S are integrated into ASSURE lesson plans.

TODAY'S LITERACIES

Classroom experiences must provide multiple opportunities for gaining new knowledge and skills that are encompassed in a critical set of literacies. This text prepares you to embed eight key areas of literacy that students need to improve learning and achieve successful careers.

GENERAL LITERACY

Teachers need an understanding of **general literacy,** or the ability of a student to comprehend or decode information and to use, transform, and create new information. As you follow the ASSURE model to develop lesson plans, always include opportunities for students to build general literacy knowledge and skills.

TEXT LITERACY

If current growth patterns continue, the "digital universe" of information is predicted to double in size every 18 months

Table 1.4 National Educational Technology Standards for Students (NETS-S)

Standard	Description
Creativity and Innovation	Students demonstrate creative thinking, construct knowledge, and develop innovative products and processes using technology.
Communication and Collaboration	Students use digital media and environments to communicate and work collaboratively, including at a distance, to support individual learning and contribute to the learning of others.
Research and Information Fluency	Students apply digital tools to gather, evaluate, and use information.
Critical Thinking, Problem Solving, and Decision Making	Students use critical-thinking skills to plan and conduct research, manage projects, solve problems, and make informed decisions using appropriate digital tools and resources.
Digital Citizenship	Students understand human, cultural, and societal issues related to technology and practice legal and ethical behavior.
Technology Operations and Concepts	Students demonstrate a sound understanding of technology concepts, systems, and operations.

(Farmer, 2009). Students will need **text literacy** skills to use text-based resources as a means to gather, interpret, and communicate information.

COMPUTER LITERACY

Computer literacy, as defined in this text, encompasses the knowledge and skills teachers need to select and use technology to enhance learning opportunities for their students. This includes knowing how to operate systems and how to recognize and find solutions to hardware and software problems.

DISTANCE LEARNING LITERACY

Distance learning literacy comprises three main components that are applicable when teachers and students are separated by time or distance: designing and facilitating learning experiences, modeling and promoting learning and responsibility, and engaging in lifelong learning.

CYBERLEARNING LITERACY

Cyberlearning involves the use of a variety of technology tools to connect students with people and resources beyond the boundaries of a normal classroom setting. To maximize their learning in this environment, students need **cyberlearning**

literacy, or the knowledge and skills to be successful in the use of these tools.

VISUAL LITERACY

Textbooks, workbooks, digital media, newspapers, books, and magazines are filled with visual images. In order for students to learn from visual media included in your instruction, they will need **visual literacy** skills, or the learned ability to interpret and create visual messages accurately.

AUDIO LITERACY

Audio has always been an important aspect of teaching, and lecturing or verbally presenting information to students is still a key role of teachers. Students need **audio literacy** skills to understand the role of hearing and listening in learning. In addition, as technology becomes increasingly influential in classrooms, they must also have the skills to create audio.

VIDEO LITERACY

With its increasing accessibility in digital formats such as DVD and downloadable files, video is being integrated into teaching and learning activities with greater frequency. To learn effectively from video, students will need **video literacy skills** to understand and evaluate video messages and to create video that appropriately achieves the intended outcomes.

MEDIA LITERACY

As will be demonstrated throughout this text, a wide variety of media is available to integrate into your instruction. Your media-enhanced instruction will need to support students' **media literacy** knowledge and skills. In other words, your students must to be able to interpret and produce a wide variety of media, including text, audio, visuals, and video, which are often combined to form multimedia.

THE CLASSROOM CONTINUUM: TRADITIONAL TO DIGITAL

The trend for today's teachers is a shift from traditional teaching methods and tools to digital approaches that better meet the needs of 21st century students. However, the transition from traditional to digital classroom environments varies greatly from teacher to teacher and school to school. Prensky (2006) describes teachers in this variable process of technology adoption and adaptation as moving, whether slowly or quickly, through a four-phase process: (1) dabbling, (2) doing old things in old ways, (3) doing old things in new ways, and (4) doing new things in new ways (p. 43) (see Figure 1.4).

The process begins with Phase 1—"dabbling" with technology by randomly adding technology tools to a few

A 21st century classroom representing Phase 4: doing new things in new ways.

Bob Daemmrich/PhotoEdit

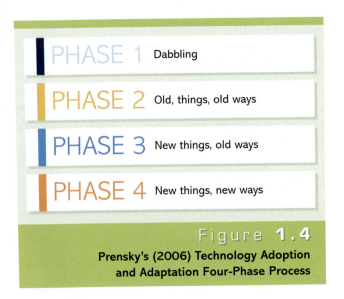

PHASE 1 Dabbling

PHASE 2 Old, things, old ways

PHASE 3 New things, old ways

PHASE 4 New things, new ways

Figure **1.4**

Prensky's (2006) Technology Adoption and Adaptation Four-Phase Process

classrooms or the library. In Phase 2, technology is used to do "old things in old ways," as when teachers display lecture notes in PowerPoint rather than using overhead transparencies. It is not until Phase 3, "doing old things in new ways," that technology begins to shows its promise, as, for example, when a teacher uses a virtual 3D model to demonstrate the structure of a compound rather than drawing it on a chalk board or students use word processing and clip art rather than notebook paper and hand-drawn images to create a short story. Finally, Phase 4, "doing new things in new ways," fully utilizes the power of technology and media, but it requires providing our students "future-oriented content [to] develop their skills in programming, knowledge filtering, using their connectivity . . . with cutting edge, powerful, miniaturized, customizable, one-to-one technology" (p. 45).

Many of today's classrooms have achieved Phase 4 by adopting and adapting their environments with digital tools that support and enhance digital teacher and student capabilities. For example, technology extends environments beyond the classroom walls by connecting students with other students, outside experts, and parents. Teacher websites provide access to homework calendars, assignment details, online resources, and often offer parents access to real-time reports of student progress.

Within these phases three primary types of instruction are used: face-to-face instruction, distance learning, and blended learning. We have all experienced face-to-face instruction at school, at home, and during extracurricular activities. When done well, it is an excellent method of teaching that is prevalent in PK–12 schools. Distance learning occurs when the teacher and students are not in the same physical location during instruction. In 2008–2009, nearly 60 percent of states (29 of 50) offered students options for taking middle or high school online virtual classes (Hightower, 2009). Other schools are offering courses that combine face-to-face instruction with distance learning to create blended instruction, allowing students to see teacher demonstrations and work with other students during hands-on activities, such as labs, drama and musical arts performances, or building 3D models. Different types of instruction are discussed in more detail in Chapter 4, Achieving 21st Century Learning Environments.

THE CHANGING ROLE OF MEDIA CENTERS

Many school libraries have been merged into what are now called **media centers,** which offer traditional library reading resources but now also include a variety of information technology assets. Most media centers are equipped with multiple Internet-connected computers, often with subscriptions to PK–12 online resources such as libraries of digital books, reference materials, and educational software. The media centers also provide teachers with a variety of classroom support materials ranging from lab kits to subject-specific software and videos. The role of the media specialist is continually expanding to require increasing expertise in accessing the array of digital resources as well as understanding basic computer technology to assist students using the equipment in the center.

COPYRIGHT CONCERNS: THE COPYRIGHT LAW

To protect the financial interests of the creators, producers, and distributors of original works of information and art,

nations adopt copyright laws. **Copyright** refers to the legal rights to an original work. These laws set the conditions under which anyone may copy, in whole or part, original works transmittable in any medium. Without copyright laws, writers, artists, and media producers would not receive the compensation they deserve for their creations. The flow of creative work would be reduced to a trickle, and we would all be the losers.

Technology, especially the Internet, has made it much easier to copy from a variety of digital materials—text, visuals, audio, and video. All material on the Internet is copyrighted unless stated otherwise. In 1998 the Conference on Fair Use issued a report (www.uspto.gov/web/offices/dcom/olia/confu/confurep.pdf) that, despite not being a legal document, provides a consensus view (until tested in a court of law) on use of copyrighted material.

You have a legal and ethical responsibility to serve as a role model for your students; therefore, use all materials in a professional and ethical manner. We also recommend teaching relevant aspects of copyright laws to your students, even very young students. If you are unsure what to do, ask for your school's copyright guidelines. Librarians and media/technology specialists at your school may be able to help you interpret the national guidelines. Ignorance of the law is no excuse!

Please note that the copyright information in this book is *not* legal advice. It is based on what the authors have read in the literature and online. For more information on copyright, refer to the Print Resources at the end of this chapter and websites on MyEducationKit.

EDUCATORS AND THE COPYRIGHT LAW

What happens if an educator knowingly and deliberately violates the copyright law? The Copyright Act of 1976 contains both criminal and civil sanctions. Possible fines for copyright infringement are from $750 to $30,000 per infringement. If it can be proven that the law was broken by willful intent, the find may be raised to $150,000. Willful infringement for private or commercial gain carries a possible fine of $250,000 and up to 5 years in prison. Copyright violation is a serious crime.

FAIR USE

Fair use provides an important copyright exception for teachers and students. Small portions of copyrighted works may be used in teaching, if properly cited and noted that they are copyrighted and by whom. Although there are no absolute guidelines for determining what constitutes fair use in an educational setting, the law sets forth four basic criteria for determining the principle of fair use:

- *Purpose and character of the use, including whether such use is for nonprofit educational purposes rather than of a commercial nature.* Using a copyrighted work for an educational objective is more likely to be considered fair use than using it for commercial gain or entertainment.

- *Nature of the copyrighted work.* If the work is for a general readership, such as a magazine or periodical not specifically designed for education, it would tend to support fair use in the classroom. Works of an entertainment nature, such as movies or music, are less likely to be considered fair use. If the work itself is educational in nature, this would tend not to support a judgment of fair use because of potential impact on sales.

- *Amount and substantiality of the portion used in relation to the copyrighted work as a whole.* Using a smaller amount of the total work is more likely to be considered fair use than using a larger amount.

- *Effect of the use on the potential market for or value of the copyrighted work.* Use that negatively affects potential sales of the original work weighs against fair use.

Until the courts decide otherwise, teachers and media professionals can use the fair use criteria to decide when to copy materials that would otherwise be protected. For example, if the school media center subscribes to a journal or magazine to which you refer students and you make digital slides of several graphics to help students understand an article, this would be fair use based on the following criteria:

- The nature of the work is general, and its audience (and market) is not predominantly the educational community.
- The character of use is nonprofit.
- The amount copied is minimal.
- There is no intent to replace the original, only to make it more useful to students in conjunction with the copyrighted words.

SEEKING PERMISSION TO USE COPYRIGHTED MATERIALS

Aside from staying within the guidelines that limit but recognize our legal right to free use of copyrighted materials, what else can we do to ensure students have access to these materials? We can, obviously, seek permission from copyright owners and, if requested, pay a fee for their use. Certain requests will ordinarily be granted without payment of fee—transcripts for the blind, for example, or material to be

tried out once in an experimental program. Permission is not needed for use of materials in the public domain—materials on which copyright protection has run out or materials produced by federal government employees in the course of their regular work.

In seeking permission to use copyrighted materials, it is generally best to contact the distributor or publisher of the material rather than its creator. Whether or not the creator is the holder of the copyright, the distributor or publisher generally handles permission requests and sets fees. If the address of the producer is not given on the material, you can usually find it on the Internet.

When seeking permission:

- Be as specific as possible. For printed materials, give the page numbers and exact amount of print material you wish to copy. If possible, send along a photocopy of the material. Describe nonprint material fully. State how you intend to use the material, where you intend to use it, and the number of copies you wish to make.

- Remember that fees for reproduction of copyrighted materials are sometimes negotiable. If the fee is beyond your budget, do not hesitate to ask whether it can be lowered.

- If for any reason you decide not to use the requested material, make this fact known to the publisher or producer. Without this formal notice it is likely to be assumed that you have in fact used it as requested and you may be charged a fee you do not in fact owe.

- Keep copies of *all* your correspondence and records of all other contacts that you make relevant to seeking permission to use copyrighted instructional materials.

- Another solution is to obtain "royalty free" collections of media. Many vendors now sell CDs that contain collections of images and sounds that can be used in presentations or other products without payment of royalties. Be sure to read the fine print. What "royalty free" means varies from one collection to the next. In one case, there may be almost no restrictions on the use of the materials; in another, you may not be allowed to use the materials in any kind of electronic product.

TERM OF PROTECTION

The term, or duration, of copyrights was changed by the Sonny Bono Copyright Term Extension Act of 1998. For an individual author, the copyright term continues for 70 years after his or her death. If a work is made for hire (i.e., by an employee or by someone commissioned to do the work), the term is 100 years from the year of creation or 75 years from the date of first publication or distribution, whichever comes first. Works copyrighted prior to January 1, 1978, are protected for 28 years and then may have their copyright renewed. The renewal protects them for a term of 75 years after their original copyright date.

CHANGING MATERIAL'S FORMAT

Even though you (or your school) have the capability to convert analog materials to a digital format, it is usually a violation of copyright laws and guidelines. The originators of copyrighted material are granted the sole right to make derivatives of their original work. For example, it is illegal to purchase an analog VHS video and convert it to a digital format. Likewise you cannot convert copyrighted printed materials into a digital format.

Converting copyrighted materials from one media format to another is also prohibited. Copyright law protects the format in which ideas are expressed (Becker, 2003). Teachers cannot make audio recordings of library books or textbooks for student use. One exception in the law permits the audio recording of books for use by students who are legally blind.

STUDENTS WITH DISABILITIES

For PK–12 students with disabilities, the National Instructional Materials Accessibility Standard (NIMAS) guides the production and electronic distribution of digital versions of textbooks and other instructional materials so they can be more easily converted to accessible formats, including Braille and text-to-speech.

Additional guidelines include the concept of universal design for learning (UDL), which was created to expand learning opportunities for all individuals, especially those with disabil-

ities (Center for Applied Special Technology [CAST], 2009). The UDL framework consists of three primary principles:

- *Multiple means of representation,* to give diverse learners options for acquiring information and knowledge
- *Multiple means of action and expression,* to provide learners options for demonstrating what they know
- *Multiple means of engagement,* to tap into learners' interests, offer appropriate challenges, and increase motivation (CAST, 2009)

Summary

We began this chapter with the foundations that will be important in your study of technology and media as they affect learning. The chapter then discussed the roles of technology and media in learning from both the teacher's perspective and the student's perspective. Key literacies needed to achieve effective learning were introduced as well as the variety of learning settings now available based on technological tools.

To check your comprehension of the content covered in Chapter 1, go to the Book Resources section in the **MyEducationKit** for your book and complete the Study Plan for Chapter 1. Here you will be able to take a chapter quiz, receive feedback on your answers, and then access resources that will enhance your understanding of the chapter content.

Continuing My Professional Development

Demonstrating Professional Knowledge

1. What are the key components of the framework for 21st century learning?
2. How would you describe the status of the technology gap in today's PK–12 schools?
3. What are the differences between technology and media?
4. What are the six basic categories of media and the key features of each?
5. In what ways are teacher and student use of technology and media different?
6. What are the primary features of the eight types of literacy needed by today's students?
7. How would you describe the three types of instruction (face-to-face, distance, and blended) as they relate to the classroom continuum?
8. What are the key concerns regarding copyright law for educational uses?

Demonstrating Professional Skills

1. Prepare a 10-minute presentation on your reaction to the framework for 21st century learning. (ISTE NETS-T 5.C)
2. Analyze an instructional situation (either real or hypothetical) and identify the literacy skills being reinforced in the lesson. (ISTE NETS-T 2.C)
3. Prepare a concept map that depicts the benefits and concerns of the three types of instruction (face to face, distance, or blended) presented in this chapter. (ISTE NETS-T 5.C)
4. Create a copyright job aid that will assist you in following copyright laws for educational uses. (ISTE NETS-T 5.C)

Building My Professional Portfolio

- *Enhancing My Portfolio*. Select a technology integration lesson from from the Web. After citing the source of the lesson, analyze it according to topics discussed in this chapter. Specifically, take note how or if the lesson addresses the following: (1) use of technology and media, (2) types of media used, (3) types of literacy skills required, (4) type(s) of instruction, (5) teacher use of technology, (6) student use of technology, and (7) areas where copyright laws will need to be followed. Reflect on this lesson analysis, providing strengths, weaknesses, and recommendations for using technology and media to enhance student learning. (ISTE NETS-T 5.C)
- *Reflecting on My Learning*. Reflect on the eight literacy skills as compared to the knowledge and skills required for your own PK–12 educational experiences. What are the primary differences? What do you see as the greatest benefits and as your most difficult challenges in ensuring that your students build 21st century knowledge and skills? (ISTE NETS-T 2.B)

SUGGESTED RESOURCES

Print Resources on Technology Integration

Ashburn, E., & Floden, R. (2006). *Meaningful learning using technology: What educators need to know and do*. New York: Teachers College Press.

Brooks-Young, S. J. (2009). *Making technology standards work for you* (2nd ed.). Washington, DC: International Society for Technology in Education.

Brown, J. M. (2002). Enhancing on-line learning for individuals with disabilities. *New Directions for Teaching and Learning, 91*, 61–68.

Burke, J. J. (2006). *Library technology companion: A basic guide for library staff* (2nd ed.). New York: Neal-Schuman.

Clyde, W., & Delohery, A. (2005). *Using technology in teaching*. New Haven, CT: Yale University Press.

Cummins, J., Brown, K., & Sayers, D. (2006). *Literacy, technology, and diversity: Teaching for success in changing times*. Boston: Allyn & Bacon.

Lamb, A. (2006). *Building treehouses for learning: Technology in today's classroom* (4th ed.). Emporia, KS: Vision to Action.

Male, M. (2002). *Technology for inclusion: Meeting the special needs of all students* (4th ed.). Boston: Allyn & Bacon.

Scherer, M. J. (2003). *Connecting to learn: Educational and assistive technology for people with disabilities*. Washington, DC: American Psychological Association.

Print Resources on Copyright

Becker, G. H. (2003). *Copyright: A guide to information and resources* (3rd ed.). Lake Mary, FL: Gary H. Becker (P.O. Box 951870, Lake Mary, FL 32795-1870).

Bielfefeld, A., & Cheeseman, L. (2006). *Technology and copyright law: A guidebook for the library, research, and teaching professions* (2nd ed.). New York: Neal-Schuman.

Bottertbush, H. R. (1996). *Copyright in the age of new technology*. Bloomington, IN: Phi Delta Kappa Educational Foundation.

Web Links

To easily access these web links from your browser, go to the MyEducationKit for your text, then go to Chapter 1 and click on the web links.

Association for Educational Communications and Technology (AECT) Copyright Committee Blog

http://aect.motime.com

This blog disseminates Committee presentations, news, and announcements.

Edutopia

www.edutopia.org

Sponsored by the George Lucas Foundation, Edutopia provides teachers current and archived access to special reports, blogs, and videos.

eSchool News

www.eschoolnews.com

This website offers a convenient way to keep up to date electronically with what is going on in schools.

Fair Use Guidelines for Educational Multimedia

www.utsystem.edu/ogc/intellectualproperty/ ccmcguid.htm

The Conference on Fair Use (CONFU) developed these guidelines to help educators determine what constitutes fair use of multimedia projects.

Gary Becker's Copyright Information Site

www.beckercopyright.com

This site provides copyright law information and resources for librarians and educators.

Internet Law Library

www.lawguru.com/ilawlib/?id=325

This site provides links to legal resources for intellectual property and copyright law.

Technology, Education, and Copyright Harmonization (TEACH) Act (2002)

www.ala.org/ala/issuesadvocacy/copyright/teachact/ highlightsS487.pdf

The American Library Association has summarized the TEACH Act, which expands the circumstances under which copyrighted works can be used for educational purposes.

U.S. Copyright Office Home Page

www.copyright.gov

This site provides key publications, links to copyright law, copyright records, Congressional testimony, and the latest regulations.

CHAPTER TWO

Understanding
21st Century Learners

This chapter addresses ISTE NETS-T 2, 4, and 5.

1. Describe the characteristics of the 21st century learner.

2. Discuss the learning theories described in this chapter.

3. List principles of effective instruction for the 21st century learner.

4. Discuss the principles of effective technology and media utilization.

5. Discuss the concept of text literacy.

6. Compare and contrast the advantages and limitations of integrating text into learning.

Goal

Understand the characteristics of the 21st century learner.

INTRODUCTION

Learning is the development of new knowledge, skills, or attitudes as an individual interacts with information and the environment. Learning doesn't happen by magic. Rather, teachers must make important decisions to ensure learning, especially when integrating technology and media into a lesson. In this chapter we will look at the learner in more detail and at principles of effective instruction with technology and media that can aid the educational process for 21st century learners.

Learners in the 21st century need to be better educated to assume the challenges of continually evolving knowledge and skill requirements for the future (Partnership for 21st Century Skills, n.d.). What students are learning today needs to prepare them for an uncertain tomorrow, and lifelong learning is a cornerstone to guiding students toward understanding how to approach the shifting knowledge and skills of their future. By creating seamless access to the global community and opening new avenues for addressing how and what to learn, technology and media have become an essential interface for learners as they move forward in their education.

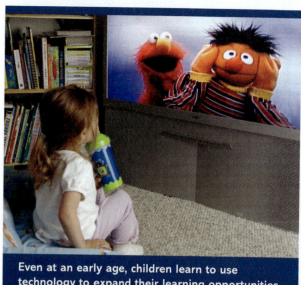

Even at an early age, children learn to use technology to expand their learning opportunities.
Jonathan Nourok/PhotoEdit

Students are entering the classroom with greater understanding of worldwide issues. Many come into school speaking more than one language, and it is predicted that by 2025 nearly half of all classrooms will have students who do not speak English as their first language (Partnership for 21st Century Skills, n.d.). In addition to greater exposure to multicultural influences, students also have greater fluency with technology and media. Even before today's children enter school, many have experience with television as a learning tool. Many also understand how computers can be used for learning and for communicating. Another medium for communication and interactivity, the cell phone, has become the great equalizer for all students regardless of their social and ethnic backgrounds.

The resources available to students today offer them many opportunities for learning.
Shutterstock

CHARACTERISTICS OF 21ST CENTURY LEARNERS

Donovan and Bransford (2005) suggest that teachers need to understand the characteristics of their students in order to prepare quality learning experiences for them. They state that 21st century learners enter classrooms

Teachers can help guide the 21st century learner in exploring new information.

Ron Nickel/Newscom

engaged in active, hands-on learning experiences. They wish to be empowered to explore their ideas in their own ways, expecting the teacher to serve as a coach or facilitator, not as the person delivering the information.

Furthermore, the learners we encounter in our classrooms need to develop their own competency in inquiry. Because knowledge grows at an exponential rate, it is impossible for an individual to keep a reservoir of requisite information "at hand." Therefore, it is critical for teachers to help students develop inquiry approaches for gathering content facts while also assisting them in constructing conceptual frameworks within which to address the content, with the goal of facilitating their understanding and application of that knowledge.

However, 21st century learners do not learn content in isolation. These students engage in multitasking and view information in a broad and networked format. These learners expect to work on interdisciplinary projects that challenge their reading and inquiry skills as they work on problems requiring knowledge and skills in overlapping content areas such as mathematics, social studies, science, and health. Each student enters this type of learning experience with the understanding that there are specific outcomes and expectations, but the avenue to reach those outcomes may be different for each individual (see Taking a Look at Technology Integration: New Tech High).

with preconceived notions of how the world works. They do not necessarily connect classroom knowledge with their ideas, but when engaged in active learning experiences will draw on their ideas to explore and test them to advance their knowledge. The learners of the 21st century expect to be

TAKING A LOOK
AT TECHNOLOGY INTEGRATION

New Tech High

Started in California, the New Tech Network is a national initiative to develop innovative high schools. It is an outgrowth of the philosophy that empowering students through an alternative instructional approach will help them to become creators, leaders, and tomorrow's productive citizens. New Tech Network advocates learning environments that provide student-centered settings where

- Problem-based learning engages learners
- Students and teachers have ownership of their learning experiences
- Technology is integrated throughout the entire learning experiences

The goal is to provide students with an integrated curriculum that focuses on critical thinking, collaboration, and problem solving as vehicles to learning. And they have the data to demonstrate that their ideas are working, with graduation rates that are significantly higher than the national averages. Also, more of the graduates from New Tech high schools pursue careers in mathematics, science, and engineering than their regular high school peers.

Shutterstock

The learners of the 21st century also demonstrate a strong desire to learn from multiple formats beyond books, using multiple sources gathered via technology resources such as video, audio, and online sources. And they share that information with others through nonstructured means such as blogs or online journals. They also rely on their social networks for ways to enhance their learning experiences. Technology is already a seamless part of their personal lives with their connection to mobile technologies such as the cell phone. Integrating social media tools such as texting or Facebook into learning experiences moves the teacher and learners closer together in a 21st century learning community.

Multitasking within multiple formats requires 21st century learners to take control of their learning outcomes. **Metacognition** is the term used to describe this ability to oversee one's personal learning and to understand how to regulate oneself in the learning process. Guiding students to assume responsibility for learning requires teachers to not only develop experiences that allow students to explore their knowledge-gathering capacities, but also to monitor their rate (efficiency) and level of learning (effectiveness). Students need to be aware of their levels of learning to ensure that they approach the learning task efficiently while effectively engaging in deep understanding of the knowledge and skills they seek. This self-monitoring of one's own learning helps ensure achievement of successful inquiry and enables the learner to apply the skills in similar learning situations. It is the teacher's role to guide the learner to self-regulation of learning.

Motivation, the desire to see a task to completion, is a critical metacognitive skill for all students to learn. It is an internal state that defines what people *will* do rather than what they *can* do (Keller, 1987). The 21st century learner needs the ability to not only engage in metacognitive skills for self-monitoring, but to be motivated to use all types of experiences and opportunities to expand knowledge and skills.

A helpful approach to understanding student motivation is Keller's ARCS model. Keller describes four essential aspects of motivation that teachers can address when designing lessons:

- *Attention.* Develop lessons that your students perceive as interesting and worthy of their consideration.
- *Relevance.* Ensure that the instruction is meaningful and meets students' learning needs and goals.
- *Confidence.* Design lessons that build student expectations to succeed based on their own efforts.
- *Satisfaction.* Address intrinsic and extrinsic rewards students receive from the instruction.

MULTIPLE INTELLIGENCES

It is important for teachers to be aware of the multiple types of student intelligences when planning lessons. The concept of **multiple intelligences** was developed by Gardner (2006), who was dissatisfied with the concept of IQ and its unitary view of intelligence. Noting that not everyone has the same abilities nor do they learn in the same way, he identified nine aspects of intelligence:

- Verbal/linguistic (language)
- Logical/mathematical (scientific/quantitative)
- Visual/spatial (imagining objects in space/navigating)
- Musical/rhythmic (listening/movement)
- Bodily/kinesthetic (dancing/athletics)
- Interpersonal (understanding other people)
- Intrapersonal (understanding oneself)
- Naturalist (relating to one's surroundings)
- Existentialist (ability to reflect)

Gardner's theory implies that effective teachers need to consider the different learning abilities of their students, recognizing that students vary widely in terms of strengths and weaknesses in each of these areas. The best way to do this is by designing lessons that actively address the range of learning abilities, considering students' perceptual preferences and strengths, information processing habits, motivational factors, and physiological traits that influence their ability to learn. Your 21st century learners come into your classroom with abilities in varying states of development. Your responsibility is to determine how best to address their learning needs while also attending to their individual approaches to acquiring knowledge and skills.

Most lessons can include a variety of technology and media that address the wide range of student abilities. For example, your lessons can include writing activities for students with verbal/linguistic strengths, use of graphics for visual/special abilities, or out-of-seat activities for students who prefer bodily/kinesthetic learning.

PERCEPTUAL PREFERENCES AND STRENGTHS

Your students will vary as to which sensory gateways (visual, auditory, tactile, and kinesthetic) they prefer using and which they are especially adept at using. Interestingly, research has shown that most students do not have a preference or strength for auditory reception, yet direct instruction is still the most prevalent instructional practice in PK–12 classrooms (Ross, Smith, Alberg, & Lowther, 2004). Research has shown that slower learners tend to prefer hands-on, active engagement involving tactile or kinesthetic experiences.

However, dependence on the tactile and kinesthetic modalities decreases with maturity (Ross et al., 2004).

INFORMATION PROCESSING HABITS

As a teacher, you will find differences in the ways that your students learn or process information. These **information processing** habits, or "mind styles," are used to group learners according to concrete versus abstract and random versus sequential styles (Butler, 1986). The grouping yields four categories:

- *Concrete sequential* learners prefer direct, hands-on experiences presented in a logical order. They learn best with workbooks, computer-based instruction, demonstrations, and structured laboratory exercises.
- *Concrete random* learners lean toward a trial-and-error approach, quickly reaching conclusions from exploratory experiences. They prefer strategies such as games, simulations, independent study projects, and discovery learning.
- *Abstract sequential* learners decode verbal and symbolic messages adeptly, especially when presented in logical sequence. Reading and listening to presentations are preferred strategies.
- *Abstract random* learners are distinguished by their capacity to draw meaning from human-mediated presentations; they respond to the tone and style of the speaker as well as the message. They do well with group discussion, lectures with question-and-answer periods, and mediated experiences involving the use of media, such as an interactive DVD on complex topics such as world poverty.

PHYSIOLOGICAL FACTORS

Factors related to gender differences, health, and environmental conditions also influence learning. Boys and girls tend to respond differently to various school experiences. For example, boys tend to be more competitive and aggressive than girls and consequently respond better to competitive games, whereas girls often prefer learning activities that involve student engagement in discussions and sharing of ideas. And of course it is important to keep Maslow's hierarchy of needs (Maslow & Lowery, 1998) in mind when analyzing learner needs. If students' basic needs such as hunger, temperature, noise, lighting, and time of day are not addressed, they will be less able to mentally engage in meaningful learning activities. You will find that your students have different preferences and tolerances regarding these factors.

LEARNING STYLE MEASUREMENTS

More than a decade ago, Dunn and Dunn (1992) developed a set of standardized instruments to measure the learning styles and environmental preferences of learners. They are still among the best-known and most widely used instruments in school applications. Teachers who have prescribed individual learning programs based on such analyses feel that they have practical value in improving academic achievement, attitude, and discipline. (See Free and Inexpensive: Learning Styles Measurements at the end of the chapter.)

The intent in using information about a student's learning style is to adapt instruction to better meet the individual needs of learners. Luckily, common patterns are found in student learning styles. This allows you to provide general adaptations for multiple students with the same or similar learning styles. Examples of class adaptations include providing reading spaces with rugs and comfortable chairs or arranging learning stations with subdued lighting that are somewhat private and quiet. To help students who have difficulty learning in complete silence, some teachers allow students to quietly listen to music on their MP3 players.

The ASSURE model (see Chapter 3) can help guide you in making good decisions about addressing your students' learning needs, offering useful strategies and resources in that process. You will find that there are multiple strategies and an array of technologies and media that can help your students in their learning endeavors.

Classrooms that provide areas with comfortable seating are better able to meet the varied learning styles of students.

Anthony Magnacca/Merrill

LEARNING THEORIES

How teachers view the role of technology and media in the classroom depends very much on their beliefs about how people learn. Over the past half-century there have been several dominant theories of learning. Each has implications for instruction in general and for the use of technology and media in particular. We briefly survey each of the major perspectives on learning and discuss their implications. Driscoll (2005) discusses learning theories and their impact on teaching decisions in greater detail.

BEHAVIORIST PERSPECTIVE

In the 1950s, B. F. Skinner, a psychologist at Harvard University and a proponent of **behaviorism,** conducted scientific studies of observable behavior. He was interested in voluntary behavior, such as learning new skills, rather than reflexive behavior, as illustrated by Pavlov's famous salivating dog. He demonstrated that reinforcing, or rewarding desired responses, could shape the behavior patterns of an organism. Skinner based his learning theory, known as reinforcement theory, on a series of experiments with pigeons. He reasoned that the same procedures could be used with humans. The result was the foundation for computer-assisted instruction. Unlike earlier learning research, Skinner's work was very logical and precise, leading directly to improved instruction and learning.

Behaviorists refuse to speculate on what goes on internally when learning takes place. They rely solely on observable behaviors. As a result, they are more comfortable explaining relatively simple learning tasks. Because of this posture, behaviorism has limited applications in teaching higher-level skills. For example, behaviorists are reluctant to make inferences about how learners process information. Although most would argue that in the 21st century, behavioral concepts are not necessarily applicable to the types of learners you are encountering in your classrooms, you may determine that some basic knowledge or skills require a behaviorist approach to instruction.

COGNITIVIST PERSPECTIVE

In the latter half of the twentieth century, cognitivists made new contributions to learning theory by creating models of how learners receive, process, and manipulate information. **Cognitivism,** based on the work of Swiss psychologist Jean Piaget (1977), explores the mental processes individuals use in responding to their environment—that is, how people think, solve problems, and make decisions. For example,

Learning is sometimes done best by the individual student working alone.

Richard B. Levine/Newscom

behaviorists simply state that practice strengthens the response to a stimulus. Cognitivists, on the other hand, create a mental model of short-term and long-term memory. New information is stored in short-term memory, where it is rehearsed until ready to be stored in long-term memory. If the information is not rehearsed, it fades from short-term memory. Learners then combine the information and skills in long-term memory to develop cognitive strategies, or skills for dealing with complex tasks.

Cognitivists have a broader perception of learning than that held by behaviorists. Students are less dependent on the guiding hand of the teacher and rely more on their own cognitive strategies in using available learning resources. Many would suggest that the cognitivist approach to instruction is a good compromise between required benchmarks, those standards against which students are tested, and a more metacognitive approach to teaching the 21st century learner.

CONSTRUCTIVIST PERSPECTIVE

Constructivism is a movement that extends beyond the ideas of cognitivism, considering the engagement of students in meaningful experiences as the essence of experiential learning. Shifting from passive transfer of information to active problem solving and discovery, constructivists emphasize that learners create their own interpretations of the world of information. They argue that students situate the learning experience within their own experience and that the goal of instruction is not to teach information but to create conditions in which students can interpret information for their own understanding. The role of instruction is to provide students with ways to assemble knowledge rather than to dispense facts. Constructivists believe that learning occurs most effectively when students are engaged in authentic tasks that relate to meaningful contexts (i.e., learning by doing). The ultimate measure of learning is therefore the ability of the student to use knowledge to facilitate thinking in real life, an approach that fits with the learning abilities 21st century learners need for an uncertain future, in which they must solve problems that not only capitalize on their existing knowledge but also require them to seek additional information or skills in finding effective solutions.

SOCIAL PSYCHOLOGY PERSPECTIVE

Social psychology is another well-established approach to the study of instruction and learning. Social psychologists look at how the social organization of the classroom affects learning. What is the group structure of the classroom—independent study, small groups, or the class as a whole? What is the authority structure—how much control do

Together a pair of students can collaborate on their learning.

Bob Daemmrich/PhotoEdit

students have over their activities? And what is the reward structure—is cooperation rather than competition fostered?

Researchers such as Robert Slavin (1990) have taken the position that cooperative learning is both more effective and more socially beneficial than competitive and individualistic learning. Slavin developed a set of cooperative learning techniques embodying the principles of small-group collaboration, learner-controlled instruction, and rewards based on group achievement. We discuss these techniques more fully in Chapter 4.

The 21st century learner enters your classroom with many skills developed from technology-based social networking. The ideas fostered in the social psychology perspective address such interdependent collaborative abilities that 21st century learners need to use as part of their learning.

Teachers need to develop an eclectic attitude toward the various schools of learning psychology. We are not obliged to swear allegiance to a particular learning theory. We use what works. If we find that a particular learning situation is suited to a behaviorist approach, then we should use behaviorist techniques. Conversely, if the situation seems to call for cognitivist or constructivist strategies, those are what we should use. When dealing with the 21st century learner in your classroom, consider which learning theory best applies to the particular type of learning task at hand.

INFORMATION AND INSTRUCTION

As educators, it is important to distinguish between information and instruction. **Information** is knowledge, facts, news, comments, and content. Information can be presented in a memo, in the classroom, in a textbook, or on the Web. Often the presentation, whether it is live, printed, or on the Internet, is general in content and its purpose is to give an overview of ideas or subject matter—to generate interest, to provide background information, or to give procedural details.

Learners should not be expected to be responsible for the retention or use of information they have only seen or heard. The information provided by a job aid, like a phone book, is not meant to be memorized. It is assumed that you will look up the information when needed. With computers, it has become possible to give ever more rapid and detailed information in specific situations, to the point that the computer could be said to be helping or "coaching" the individual. Although with frequent use of a job aid or a

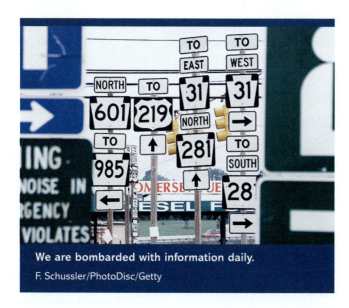

We are bombarded with information daily.

F. Schussler/PhotoDisc/Getty

computer help system, a person might gradually internalize the information from the help system, remembering more and more of the information provided, the learning is not an intentional part of the system, whose aim is only to provide just-in-time assistance or information. **Instruction,** on the other hand, refers to any intentional effort to stimulate learning by the deliberate arrangement of experiences to help learners achieve a desirable change in capability. Instruction is meant to lead to learning. Active engagement with the information—questioning it, discussing it, applying it to practice situations—is the critical component of instruction. Meaningful understanding, retention, and application require instructional activities, including practice with feedback. Instruction, therefore, has as its goal a lasting change in capability of the learner. This is a crucial point in distinguishing instruction from just providing information.

Instruction is the arrangement of information and the environment to facilitate learning. By *environment* we mean not only where instruction takes place but also the strategies, technology, and media needed to convey information and guide study. The learner or the instructor may do this. Gagné (1985) describes instruction as a set of events external to the learner designed to support the internal process of learning.

Preparing the instructional environment is a critical role for teachers. As a teacher responsible for creating learning opportunities for your students, you will need to help them work within learning communities. By using collaborative learning tools such as classroom blogs, wikis, social networking resources, and learning management systems, you can help your 21st century learners move through the various levels of learning appropriate to their goals and expected outcomes.

Principles of Effective Instruction

As a classroom teacher your role is to establish learning environments that foster the defined outcomes for your learners. At times those outcomes may be based on specific state or national learning standards; at other times they may be based on negotiated outcomes with your individual learners. Whichever direction you take, you need to think continually about how to engage your students in the learning process.

As educators continually seeking ways to improve our practice, it is important to consider how to engage learners in their learning. Because one common feature across all classroom settings is the variety of learning levels and needs among students, it is also critical to determine the best ways to meet the needs of all our learners. Teachers need to become skilled at differentiating instruction to ensure that all learners are challenged adequately and appropriately in their learning.

In addressing these concerns, teachers needs to consider how to use "best" or research-based classroom practice in ways to engage learners. The following principles of effective instruction have evolved from a variety of sources.

• *Assess prior knowledge.* Before you can properly provide instruction, you should gather relevant information about each student's knowledge and skill level. You need to know what knowledge your students already have learned. To learn from most materials and activities, students must

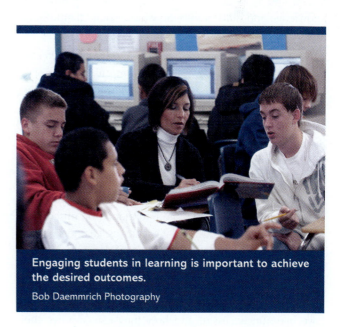

Engaging students in learning is important to achieve the desired outcomes.

Bob Daemmrich Photography

possess prerequisite knowledge and skills (Newby, Stepich, Lehman, & Russell, 2010).

- *Consider individual differences.* Learners vary in terms of personality, general aptitude, knowledge of a subject, and many other factors. Be aware of the multiple learning needs of your students—for example, whether a language other than English is spoken in a child's home. You need to consider the technology and media experiences your students have had and what resources are essential to help your students learn. Effective instruction allows individuals to progress at different rates, cover different materials, and even participate in different activities (Cooper & Varma, 1997).

- *State objectives.* For you and your students to know where instruction is going and what is to be accomplished, the goals must be specified. Learning objectives must match expected outcomes or standards (Mager, 1997).

- *Develop metacognitive skills.* The skills of selective monitoring, evaluating, and adjusting their approaches enhance students' learning and help to make them lifelong learners. Learners need assistance in understanding how they learn and what resources help in that process (Nelson, 1992).

- *Provide social interaction.* Teachers and peers serving as tutors or group members can provide a number of pedagogical as well as social supports. Learners gain experience and expertise when collaborating with others in and beyond the classroom (Jonassen, Howland, Marra, & Crismond, 2008).

- *Incorporate realistic contexts.* Learners are most likely to remember and to apply authentic knowledge presented in a real-world context. Rote learning leads to "inert knowledge"; that is, learners know something but cannot apply it to real life. Students benefit from understanding how their knowledge and skills fit into the world around them (Bransford, Brown, & Cocking, 2000).

- *Engage students in relevant practice.* The most effective learning experiences are those requiring learners to practice skills that build toward the desired outcome. Learner participation increases the probability of learning. Practice, especially in varying contexts, improves retention rate and the ability to apply the new knowledge, skill, or attitude. Practice promotes deeper, longer lasting learning (Morrison & Lowther, 2010).

- *Offer frequent, timely, and constructive feedback.* Student learning requires accurate information on misconceptions, misunderstandings, and weaknesses. Learners need to know if their thinking is on track. Feedback may come from a teacher, a tutor, electronic messages from a computer, the scoring system of a game, or oneself. In addition to knowing that responses are incorrect, students need to know why they have been unsuccessful and how they can improve their performance. Further, knowing details about their correct responses in terms of how and why they are accurate helps students understand more about what they have learned (Black & William, 1998).

Many of these principles are incorporated within the AS-SURE model described in Chapter 3.

PRINCIPLES OF EFFECTIVE TECHNOLOGY UTILIZATION

Teachers are expected to be competent in the use of technology in their teaching (Bowes, D'Onofrio, & Marker, 2006). This is especially true when working with 21st century learners and addressing the skills outlined for them, for which

Teachers are models for how to use technology for learning.
Shutterstock

teachers not only need to use technology effectively in their teaching but also need to guide students in using those tools to enhance their learning. The advent of newer technologies requires critical decisions related to the best tools to integrate into teaching. We will be addressing many of these newer technology resources throughout the remaining chapters of this textbook.

The **National Education Technology Standards for Students (NETS-S),** noted in the following list, specifically outline expectations for student use of technology to guide their learning (International Society for Technology in Education [ISTE], 2007).

- Creativity and Innovation
- Communication and Collaboration
- Research and Information Fluency
- Critical Thinking, Problem Solving, and Decision Making
- Digital Citizenship
- Technology Operations and Concepts

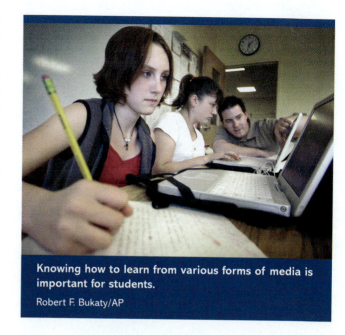

Knowing how to learn from various forms of media is important for students.

Robert F. Bukaty/AP

Many of these standards address the essential elements for success in acquiring 21st century knowledge and skills. As a teacher you will be expected to enhance students' abilities to engage in the use of technology to support their learning and address these six areas of competency, also known as **technology literacy** skills.

You can combine knowledge and skills related to content areas and information literacy skills by using technology in ways that help students learn information and communicate knowledge. For example, in a science lesson on weather, you can present a problem to your students that will require them to search websites for data or information, use communication tools to collaborate with outside experts, generate solutions to the problem collaboratively, and present their ideas to classmates using creative resources. By approaching your instruction in that manner, you have addressed many of the standards by which your students will be measured and will have given them guided practice in developing their knowledge and skills.

the content, and how to create new media messages (Stansbury, 2009).

Text, television, video, and a host of other media sources that will be covered within this textbook are all valid and vital sources of information. Your role is to guide your students to use these media as sources for their learning in ways that are wise, safe, and productive. For example, students need to learn to find multiple sources to verify facts they may have heard on the television news. They need to learn to be critical users of these resources to ensure that they are well informed and their conclusions are accurate. As mentioned earlier, the ISTE NETS-S address many of the skills learners need to be successful consumers of the media resources surrounding them.

Furthermore, your teaching approach should provide students with opportunities to explore how to use these media resources to communicate their knowledge. Later in this textbook you will see examples of how teachers guide their students to use a variety of media to express their knowledge and skills.

PRINCIPLES OF EFFECTIVE MEDIA UTILIZATION

We are continually learning from multiple sources of media that provide us with information and challenge our thinking. As users of these sources we need **media literacy** skills to know how to access them, how to understand and analyze

PRINCIPLES OF EFFECTIVE TEXT UTILIZATION

Text is everywhere in students' learning experiences. Text materials include textbooks, fiction and nonfiction books, newspapers, booklets, computer screens, magazines, study

Learning from text is a part of classroom experiences.

David R. Frazier/DanitaDelimont.com/Newscom

ADVANTAGES

- *Availability.* Text-based materials are readily available on a variety of topics and in many different formats.
- *Flexibility.* Text is adaptable to many purposes and may be used in any well-lit environment.
- *Portability.* Texts are easily carried from place to place and do not require any equipment or power supply.
- *User friendly.* Properly designed text materials are easy to use, requiring no special effort to "navigate" through them.
- *Economical.* Text-based materials are relatively inexpensive to produce or purchase and can be reused. In fact, some may be obtained at little cost or for free.

LIMITATIONS

- *Reading level.* The major limitation of text materials is the reading level needed for comprehension. Some students are nonreaders. Others lack adequate literacy skills for text materials above their reading level. Still others lack the prerequisite knowledge to comprehend the vocabulary and terminology.
- *Memorization.* Some teachers require students to memorize many facts and definitions, which diminishes text materials to mere memorization aids.
- *Vocabulary.* Some textbooks introduce a large number of vocabulary terms and concepts in a short amount of space, placing a heavy cognitive burden on students, which may be overwhelming for some.
- *One-way presentation.* Because most text materials are not interactive, they tend to be used in a passive way, often without comprehension.
- *Curriculum determination.* Sometimes textbooks dictate the curriculum rather than supporting it. Textbooks are often written to accommodate the curriculum guidelines of particular states or provinces. Consequently, the preferences of these authorities disproportionately influence textbook content and its treatment.
- *Cursory appraisal.* Selection committees might not examine textbooks carefully. Sometimes textbooks are chosen by the "five-minute thumb test"—whatever catches the reviewer's eye while thumbing through the textbook.

guides, manuals, and worksheets, as well as word-processed documents prepared by students and teachers. Textbooks have long been the foundation of classroom instruction. The other forms of technology and media discussed in this textbook are frequently used in conjunction with and as supplements to text-based materials. The 21st century learner encounters text as part of daily interactions with technology and media (see Technology for Diverse Learners: Text Readers and Digital Books). The ability to use text as a means to gather information or to communicate is known as **text literacy.** The two aspects to becoming literate in the use of text as part of the learning process are reading and writing. Reading is the ability to look at text and gather knowledge from the message. Writing is the ability to generate text through tools such as pencils, pens, or computers to communicate. Both skills develop over time and the technology and media you use as a teacher can help address their development.

INTEGRATION

The most common application of text materials is presenting information. Students are given reading assignments and

TECHNOLOGY
for Diverse Learners

Text Readers and Digital Books

Students who are poor readers because of learning disabilities or because English is a second language find reading to be slow, inaccurate, and boring. They frequently have to reread passages, struggle to decode unfamiliar words, and suffer from fatigue and stress. On the other hand, gifted learners often find the text materials in the classroom too simple or boring to challenge them.

There are many resources for helping these and other students access information in suitable text formats within the classroom. Audio or digital books allow instant access to any page, chapter, or subheading with the touch of a button. To listen, students need either a portable media player equipped to play the books or a multimedia computer with a CD drive and specialized software. The Kindle, an electronic book device, provides a text-based means to manipulate reading materials.

Students with visual impairments or severe learning disabilities have access to thousands of digital books available for download or on CD from Recording for the Blind and Dyslexic (www.rfbd.org). A collection of over 6,000 digitally recorded educational titles, including popular young adult fiction books, have been added to the nonprofit organization's collection of 91,000 accessible textbooks.

An additional adaptive technology resource for students with limited sight is the Kurzweil Reader (www.kurzweiledu .com), a text-to-speech device that provides a multimedia approach by enhancing printed or electronic text with additional visual and audible cues. It can "read" text to the student who cannot manage that independently. It can even read webpages and email.

held accountable for the material during class discussions and on tests. Teacher-made handouts can also complement a teacher's presentation, or students may use them to study independently. Students can use text materials to augment either teacher-presented information or other forms of media. Students frequently refer to supplementary printed materials (such as books and magazines from the media center) to locate information on a specific topic not covered in their textbook.

Teachers need to understand the best ways to use text to facilitate learning. Designing good text-based materials involves a few basic elements:

- *Font choice.* Remember to select a clear font that helps learners to read the information. Select only one or two fonts; it is not necessary to use many different typefaces in a single document. Keeping it simple and clean is best when selecting fonts for your text materials.

- *Background and patterns.* When putting text on a page, website, or PowerPoint presentation, use backgrounds that are not busy with distracting images. Don't scrimp on the page margins or use of space. It is better to use double spacing and wide margins, making it easy for learners of all ability levels to read.

- *Arrangement.* Use space and text styles, like bold and italics, to help your learners find the information quickly and easily. By using headings and changes in text styles,

Information can be learned from materials other than textbooks.

Davis Barber/PhotoEdit

The school media center serves to meet student learning needs

Bob Daemmrich/PhotoEdit

You should also carefully review and be prepared to revise your phrasing of certain critical text such as instructions to help ensure that all your students will understand the message correctly.

Text-based materials are used in all subject areas and with students of all ages once they learn to read. The media center provides a variety of text materials on countless topics and in almost every conceivable format. Guidelines and examples are found in When to Use Text-Based Materials and Using Text Materials in the Classroom.

EVALUATION

As a teacher you will want to consider all the types of text-based materials your students will be encountering in your classroom as well as their individual reading abilities. You'll want to be sure that they are able to read and comprehend the messages that they encounter. Address your students' literacy levels by assessing their reading ability and putting them into appropriate learning groups to develop reading and literacy skills. Address materials by taking the time to evaluate all reading materials in your classroom. For example, textbooks are often prepared at a general grade-specific reading level without regard to the actual reading levels of individual children in your classrooms. You will also want to be sure that your students can read other content area text and resources as well. You will find the Selection Rubric: Text Materials at the end of this chapter helpful when you review text-based materials in your classroom.

you guide your learners through the material to help them garner the most important information. This is especially useful when you have challenged readers in your classroom.

- *Check and revise.* Always be sure to proofread your materials. Spell-checker software helps but is not perfect. You might mean to type the word "then" but only manage to type "hen." Your spell-checker will accept this as correct, when the meaning is clearly impacted by the misuse of the word.

W H E N to U S E Text-Based Materials

Use when student learning will be enhanced by ...

Guidelines	Examples
. . . reading text information for which they will be held accountable	High school students read an assigned article from an online source.
. . . supplementing teacher-presented material	Students use library books, encyclopedias, or newspapers to add to their knowledge of a topic.
. . . using handouts that guide them through learning activities	Students use a step-by-step guide to write a book report.
. . . implementing an **SQ3R** method (see Using Text Materials in the Classroom, p. 31)	Students **S**urvey, ask **Q**uestions, **R**ead, **R**ecite, and **R**eview printed information about the Bill of Rights.

USING
Text Materials
in the Classroom

- Get learners actively involved with the materials. One technique is to have students use the "SQ3R" method: Survey, Question, Read, Recite, and Review. The Survey stage requires students to skim through the text material and read the overview and/or summary. In the Question step, they write a list of questions to answer while reading. For the Read stage, students are encouraged to look for the organization of the material, put brackets around the main ideas, underline supporting details, and answer the questions written in the previous step. Recite requires them to test themselves while reading and to put the content into their own words. Finally, Review suggests that the students look over the material immediately after reading it, the next day, a week later, and so on (Robinson, 1946).

- Direct student reading with objectives or questions, and provide a worksheet if one is not included with the materials.

- Emphasize the use of visuals in text materials and teach students to study visuals in an effort to increase their comprehension of the content (see Chapter 8).

SUMMARY

In this chapter we discussed the characteristics of the 21st century learner and how teachers need to adapt to working with a variety of students. Teachers need to design instruction to meet the needs of 21st century learners. As a teacher you will want to be prepared to engage your students with technology and media to motivate them and help them to gain the types of knowledge and skills they need to be successful learners.

PEARSON
myeducationkit™

To check your comprehension of the content covered in Chapter 2, go to the **MyEducationKit** for your book and complete the Study Plan for Chapter 2. Here you will be able to take a chapter quiz, receive feedback on your answers, and then access resources that will enhance your understanding of the chapter content.

CONTINUING MY PROFESSIONAL DEVELOPMENT

Demonstrating Professional Knowledge

1. What are three characteristics of the 21st century learner?
2. Describe the similarities and differences in the learning theories discussed in this chapter.
3. What are the eight principles of effective instruction?
4. Describe the similarities and differences in the principles of effective technology and media utilization.
5. What is text literacy?
6. Describe the advantages and limitations of integrating text into learning.

Demonstrating Professional Skills

1. Prepare a 10-minute presentation on your reaction to a topic in the chapter. (ISTE NETS-T 5.C)
2. Analyze an instructional situation (either real or hypothetical) and identify the psychological perspective on learning and the technology and media used. (ISTE NETS-T 5.C)
3. Prepare a position paper on the roles of technology and media in education. (ISTE NETS-T 5.C)
4. Describe an actual use of instructional technology and/or media in an education setting based on your experiences or readings. (ISTE NETS-T 5.A)

Building My Professional Portfolio

- *Enhancing a Lesson.* Select a lesson from the Web or a classroom. Indicate how specific portions of the lesson illustrate, if present, the psychological perspectives addressed in this chapter (behaviorist, cognitivist, constructivist, and social psychology perspectives). Cite the source of the lesson. Reflect on this analysis, providing strengths, weaknesses, and recommendations for teaching this lesson to a specific group of students. (ISTE NETS-T 2.C)

- *Reflecting on a Lesson.* Reflect on the four learning theory perspectives discussed in the chapter. Give examples of technology lessons based in each from the perspective both of a teacher and a learner. (ISTE NETS-T 5.C)

SUGGESTED RESOURCES

Print

Anderson, R., Grant, M., & Speck, B. (2008). *Technology to teach literacy: A resource for K–8 teachers* (2nd ed.). Boston: Allyn & Bacon.

Callison, D. (2003). *Key words, concepts and methods for information age instruction: A guide to teaching information inquiry.* Englewood, CO: Libraries Unlimited.

Del, A., Newton, D., & Petroff, J. (2007). *Assistive technology in the classroom: Enhancing the school experiences of students with disabilities.* Upper Saddle River, NJ: Prentice Hall.

Erben, T., Ban, R., & Castanda, M. (2008). *Teaching English language learners through technology.* New York: Routledge.

Jonassen, D. H., Howland, J., Moore, J., & Marra, R. M. (2002). *Learning to solve problems with technology: A constructivist perspective* (2nd ed.). Upper Saddle River, NJ: Merrill/Prentice Hall.

O'Bannon, B., & Puckett, K. (2010). *Preparing to use technology: A practical guide to curriculum integration* (2nd ed.). Boston: Allyn & Bacon.

Roblyer, M., & Doering, A. (2010). *Integrating educational technology into teaching* (5th ed.). Boston: Allyn & Bacon.

Web Links

To easily access these web links from your browser, go to the MyEducationKit for your text, then go to Chapter 2 and click on the web links.

eSchool News

www.eschoolnews.com

This site offers a convenient way to keep up to date electronically with what is going on with technology in schools.

International Society for Technology in Education

www.iste.org

ISTE is an association focused on improving education through the use of technology in learning, teaching, and administration. ISTE members include teachers, administrators, computer coordinators, information resource managers, and educational technology specialists.

Kathy Schrock's Guide

http://school.discovery.com/schrockguide/index.html

Among the many resources for teachers is one developed by classroom teacher Kathy Schrock. This site offers classroom teachers an array of links, lesson plans, and professional development suggestions.

Partnership for 21st Century Skills

www.21stcenturyskills.org

The Partnership for 21st Century Skills works with leaders in business, education, and policy to infuse 21st century skills into education and provide tools and resources to help facilitate and drive change.

FREE & INEXPENSIVE
Learning Styles Measurements

Memletics Learning Styles Inventory

**www.learning-styles-online.com/inventory/questions
.asp?cookieset=y**

The Memletics learning styles inventory has 70 questions that assess dominant and secondary learning styles concerning the following areas: aural, visual, verbal, physical, logical, social, and solitary.

Abiator's Online Learning Styles

www.berghuis.co.nz/abiator/lsi/lsitest1.html

This assessment consists of 30 items that measure auditory, visual, and tactile learning styles.

Learning Styles Inventory for Students with Learning Disabilities

www.ldpride.net/learning_style.html

LDPride.net offers an inventory to identify the preferred learning style of students with learning disabilities. The inventory results provide educators and parents a better understanding of students' learning preferences. This information will assist in adapting learning environments to better meet the needs of individual learners.

Selection Rubric: TEXT MATERIALS

To download and complete this rubric for your own use, go to the MyEducationKit for your text, then go to Chapter 2 and click on Selection Rubrics.

Search Terms Used to Locate Resources

_____

_____

_____

Title _____

Source/Location _____

©Date _____   Cost _____   Length _____ minutes

Subject Area _____   Grade Level _____

Instructional Strategies _____

Brief Description

Format

_____ Textbook

_____ Fiction

_____ Nonfiction

_____ Computer Screen

_____ Manual

_____ Other _____

Standards/Outcomes/Objectives

Prerequisites (e.g. prior knowledge, reading ability, vocabulary level)

Strengths

Limitations

Special Features

Name _____   Date _____

Rating Area	High Quality	Medium Quality	Low Quality
Align to Standards, Outcomes, Objectives	Standards/outcomes/objectives addressed and use of text material should enhance student learning.	Standards/outcomes/objectives partially addressed and use of text may enhance student learning.	Standards/outcomes/objectives not addressed and use of text will likely not enhance student learning.
Accurate and Current Information	Information is correct and does not contain material that is out of date.	Information is correct, but does contain material that is out of date.	Information is not correct and does contain material that is out of date.
Age-Appropriate Language	Language used is age-appropriate and vocabulary is understandable.	Language used is nearly age-appropriate and some vocabulary is above/below student age.	Language used is not age-appropriate and vocabulary is clearly inappropriate for student age.
Interest Level and Engagement	Topic is presented so that students are likely to be interested and actively engaged in learning.	Topic is presented to interest students most of the time and engage most students in learning.	Topic is presented so as not to interest students and not engage them in learning.
Technical Quality	The material represents best available media.	The material represents media that are good quality, although there may be some problems using it.	The material represents media that are not well prepared and are of very poor quality.
Ease of Use (Student or Teacher)	Material follows easy to use patterns with nothing to confuse the user.	Material follows patterns that are easy to follow most of the time, with a few things to confuse the user.	Material follows no patterns and most of the time the user is very confused.
Bias Free	There is no evidence of objectionable bias or advertising.	There is little evidence of bias or advertising.	There is much evidence of bias or advertising.
User Guide and Directions	The user guide is an excellent resource to support a lesson. Directions should help teachers and students use the material.	The user guide is good resource to support a lesson. Directions may help teachers and students use the material.	The user guide is poor resource to support a lesson. Directions do not help teachers and students use the material.
Reading Level	The material is presented at an appropriate reading level so that most students can understand the information.	The material is presented at a reading level so that some students can understand the information.	The material is presented at a reading level so that few students can understand the information.
Clarity of Organization	The material is presented in such a way that most students are able to use the information.	The material is presented in such a way that some students are able to use the information.	The material is presented in such a way that few students are able to use the information.
Table of Contents/Index	The Table of Contents and Index are useful for students to access information.	The Table of Contents and Index are moderately useful to access information.	The Table of Contents and Index are not useful for students to access information.

Recommended for Classroom Use: _____ Yes _____ No

Ideas for Classroom Use:

CHAPTER THREE

Integrating
Technology and Media into
Instruction: **The ASSURE Model**

This chapter addresses ISTE NETS-T 2, 4, and 5.

1. State the three primary types of learner analysis criteria and describe the role of the criteria in the systematic planning process for learning.

2. Discuss the rationale and purposes of learning objectives.

3. Write learning objectives that include the audience, behavior, conditions, and degree of mastery.

4. Describe the procedures for selecting, modifying, and designing instructional materials, indicating when each choice is appropriate.

5. Create examples of the five basic steps in utilizing technology, media, and materials.

6. Describe and justify methods for eliciting student participation when using technology and media during instruction.

7. Compare and contrast the techniques for evaluating student achievement, technology, media, strategies, and the instruction.

Goal

Use the ASSURE model to systematically plan lessons that effectively integrate classroom use of technology and media.

The ASSURE model is designed to help teachers plan lessons that effectively integrate classroom use of technology and media. To illustrate how to use the six steps of the ASSURE model, we provide a classroom case study of each step after it is described. These steps taken together constitute a sample ASSURE lesson plan that describes the instructional planning of actual classroom teachers.

This ASSURE classroom case study describes the instructional planning used by Tiare Ahu, a high school English teacher who wants to increase student learning and communication skills through the use of electronic portfolios, often referred to as e-portfolios. Tiare feels that her ninth-grade students often lack interest in improving their writing and oral communication skills. Her students typically complete each class assignment without reflecting on past learning experiences—thus inhibiting their ability to grow and improve. She first addresses the concern by having students create paper-based portfolios of their writing. However, it proves difficult for students to revise and improve an existing paper-based assignment and equally difficult to add reflective comments without detracting from the original documents. Her solution is to use e-portfolios that allow students to easily update, modify, and add written or video reflections to their assignments. Throughout the chapter you can follow Tiare's use of the ASSURE model to design a lesson that integrates the use of electronic portfolios.

To view the **ASSURE Classroom Case Study** *Video for this chapter, go to the MyEducationKit for your text and click on the ASSURE Video under Chapter 3 to view the video of Ms. Ahu's ninth-grade English class working on their electronic portfolios.*

PEARSON

myeducationkit™

INTRODUCTION

Today's teachers have exciting opportunities to go beyond traditional practices through the use of innovative technology and media to prepare students for the 21st century. This chapter introduces you to the ASSURE model, which uses a step-by-step process to create lessons that effectively integrate the use of technology and media to improve student learning. Lessons created with the ASSURE model directly align with the National Education Technology Standards for teachers (International Society for Technology in Education [ISTE], 2008) and students (ISTE, 2007) (hereafter referred to as NETS-T and NETS-S, respectively) as well as curriculum standards from the local to the national level. In addition, the ASSURE model utilizes a standard research-based approach to lesson design that easily aligns with any school or district lesson plan template.

THE ASSURE MODEL

All effective instruction requires careful planning. Teaching with instructional technology and media is certainly no exception. This chapter examines how to plan systematically for the effective use of technology and media. We have constructed a procedural model to which we have given the acronym ASSURE—it is intended to *assure* effective instruction.

Some aspects of teaching and learning have stayed consistent over the years, such as the progressive stages or "events of instruction" that occur (Gagné, 1985). Research has shown that well-designed lessons begin with the arousal of students' interest and then move on to present new material, involve students in practice with feedback, assess their understanding, and provide relevant follow-up activities. The ASSURE model incorporates all these events of instruction.

ANALYZE LEARNERS

The ASSURE model provides you with a systematic approach for analyzing learner characteristics that impact ability to learn. The analysis information is used to plan lessons tailored to meet the needs of your students. The learner analysis examines general characteristics, specific entry competencies, and learning styles.

GENERAL CHARACTERISTICS

It is critical to understand the general characteristics that may influence student learning. These characteristics range from constant variables, such as gender and ethnicity, to those that vary on a regular basis, such as attitudes and interest.

Review student records to identify the age differences of your students and better understand behavioral patterns or ability to focus during learning activities. When planning group work, consider gender differences that may impact student attention and willingness to participate. For example, mixed-gender groups may work well in early elementary classes but inhibit student learning for some middle school students. When students represent multiple ethnic groups, select instructional materials and examples that give high priority to cultural identity and values. For example, select photos and clip art with children of the same ethnicity as your students to increase their connection to the lesson topic. Once you have this background understanding, it will be coupled with your observations of student attitudes and interest to design and implement meaningful lessons that address the unique needs of each student.

SPECIFIC ENTRY COMPETENCIES

Recent research reveals that students' prior knowledge of a particular subject influences how and what they learn more than does any psychological trait (Dick, Carey, & Carey, 2009). Therefore, a critical component of designing lessons is to identify the specific entry competencies of your students. You can do this informally (such as in-class questioning) or by more formal means (such as reviewing standardized test results or giving teacher-made tests and assessments). **Entry tests** are assessments that determine whether students possess the necessary **prerequisites,** or competencies, to benefit from instruction. For example, if you are going to teach

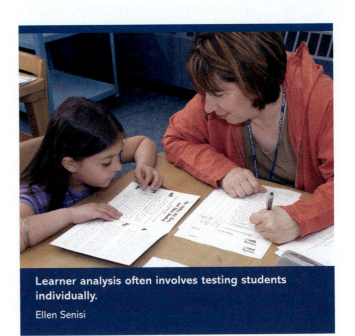

Learner analysis often involves testing students individually.

Ellen Senisi

A Model to Help ASSURE Learning

Analyze Learners

The first step in planning a lesson is to identify and analyze learner characteristics shown to be associated with learning outcomes. This information will guide your decision making during the design of your lesson. The key areas to consider during learner analysis include (1) general characteristics of learners, (2) specific entry competencies (knowledge, skills, and attitudes about the topic), and (3) learning styles.

State Standards and Objectives

The next step is to state the standards and learning objectives as specifically as possible. Begin with the curriculum and technology standards adopted by your district, as these are based on state and national student performance criteria. Well-stated objectives name the learners for whom the objective is intended, the action (behavior) to be demonstrated, the conditions under which the behavior or performance will be observed, and the degree to which the new knowledge or skill must be mastered. For this text, the condition will include the use of technology and media to support learning and to assess achievement of the standard or learning objectives.

Select Strategies, Technology, Media, and Materials

Once you have analyzed your learners and stated the standards and objectives, you have established the beginning points (students' present knowledge, skills, and attitudes) and ending points (learning objectives) of instruction. Your task now is to build a bridge between these two points by choosing appropriate instructional strategies, technology, and media, and materials to achieve the objectives.

Utilize Technology, Media, and Materials

This step involves planning your teaching role for utilizing the technology, media, and materials to help students achieve the learning objectives. To do this, follow the "5 Ps" process: Preview the technology, media, and materials; Prepare the technology, media, and materials; Prepare the environment; Prepare the learners; and Provide the learning experience.

Require Learner Participation

To be effective, instruction should require learners' active mental engagement. Provide activities that allow them to practice the new knowledge or skills and to receive feedback on their efforts before being formally assessed. Practice may involve student self-checks, computer-assisted instruction, Internet activities, or group exercises. Feedback can come from the teacher, a computer, other students, or self-evaluation.

Evaluate and Revise

After implementing a lesson, evaluate its impact on student learning. This assessment not only examines the degree to which students achieved the learning objectives, but also examines the entire instructional process and the impact of using technology and media. Wherever there are discrepancies between learning objectives and student outcomes, revise the lesson plan to address the areas of concern.

Analyze Learners

General Characteristics

Tiare Ahu is teaching the basic ninth-grade English course geared toward the average learner. The students are 14 and 15 years old. Several students have identified learning disabilities, whereas others are above-average readers and writers. Her students come from primarily moderate to low socioeconomic environments and represent an ethnic population common to an urban setting. Generally, the students are well behaved. However, they show lack of interest and apathy toward learning when activities are textbook and paper-and-pencil oriented.

Entry Competencies

The students in general are able to do the following:

- Create and save word-processed documents
- Navigate the Internet
- Create and save digital video
- Respond via written and verbal communication that ranges from below to above grade-level proficiency

Learning Styles

Tiare has found that her students appear to learn best from activities that incorporate technology and media. Using computers provides intrinsic motivation through the creation of personalized work and the careful reflection of learning. Her students vary in their preferred forms of expression: some favor inputting their thoughts as written text, others choose to capture them with digital video, and still others prefer audio recordings. Tiare has also discovered that most of her students have difficulty working in a completely silent atmosphere and therefore allows the option of listening to music on MP3 players when they work on their digital portfolios.

Visit the Chapter 3 section of MyEducationKit to view the video of Ms. Ahu's ninth-grade English class working on their electronic portfolios.

---

students to calculate the area of geometric shapes, the entry test would focus on multiplication skills to identify students who need remediation prior to the lesson. An important prerequisite skill for many lessons is reading ability. Therefore, you may want to test or arrange to have your students' reading abilities determined.

Once specific entry competencies are identified, list them in your lesson and include entry tests to identify students who need remediation prior to lesson implementation. You may also include a pretest to ensure that students have not already mastered what you plan to teach.

LEARNING STYLES

Learning style refers to the following psychological traits that determine how an individual perceives, interacts with, and responds emotionally to learning environments: multiple intelligences, perceptual preferences and strengths, information processing habits, motivation, and physiological factors.

The information you learn from analyzing the general characteristics, specific entry competencies, and learning styles of your students will guide your decision-making process as you design your ASSURE lesson (see the ASSURE case study for an example of the process).

STATE STANDARDS AND OBJECTIVES

The second step in the ASSURE model is to state the standards and learning objectives for the lesson. What new capability should learners possess at the completion of instruction? The learning objectives are derived from curriculum and technology **standards,** descriptions of expected student performance outcomes established at the school district, state, or national level. As seen in Table 3.1, curriculum and technology standards provide general descriptions of expected student performance, whereas learning objectives, typically written by the teacher or school district, are very specific. It is important to note that a **learning objective** is a statement of what each learner will achieve, not how the lesson will be taught.

IMPORTANCE OF STANDARDS AND OBJECTIVES

Basis for Strategies, Technology, and Media Selection. Why should you state standards and learning objectives? When you have clear statements of what students will know

TABLE 3.1 Going from National Curriculum and Technology Standards to Learning Objectives: PK–4 and 9–12 Examples

National Curriculum Standards	National Technology Standards	Learning Objective Aligned to National Standards
National Center for History in the Schools (NCHS) (see http://nchs.ucla.ed) **K–4 Content Standards:** *Topic 2:* The History of the Students' Own State or Region *Standard 3A:* The student understands the history of indigenous peoples who first lived in his or her state or region. **Grades 3 and 4** Therefore the student is able to compare and contrast how Native American or Hawaiian life today differs from the life of these same groups over 100 years ago.	National Educational Technology Standards for Students (NETS-S) (see www.cnets.iste.org) **Standards:** 1. **Creativity and Innovation** Students demonstrate creative thinking, construct knowledge, and develop innovative products and processes using technology. 2. **Communication and Collaboration** Students use digital media and environments to communicate and work collaboratively, including at a distance, to support individual learning and contribute to the learning of others. 6. **Technology Operations and Concepts** Students demonstrate a sound understanding of technology concepts, systems and operations **Grades PK–4** *Performance Indicator 4:* In a collaborative work group, use a variety of technologies to produce a digital presentation or product in a curriculum area. (1,2,6)	Given five different storybooks that describe the lifestyles of Southwest Native Americans over the past 100 years, the third-grade students will create a six-slide PowerPoint presentation for Parent Night that compares and contrasts the housing, diets, traditions, and work of today's Southwest Native Americans with those from 100 years earlier.
National Standards for Arts Education (NSAE) (see http://artsedge.kennedy-center.org/teach/standards.cfm) **Grades 9–12: Visual Arts** *Content Standard: 1:* Understanding and applying media, techniques, and processes *Achievement Standard:* Students conceive and create works of visual art that demonstrate an understanding of how the communication of their ideas relates to the media, techniques, and processes they use.	NETS-S (see www.cnets.iste.org) **Standards:** 1. **Creativity and Innovation** Students demonstrate creative thinking, construct knowledge, and develop innovative products and processes using technology. 2. **Communication and Collaboration** Students use digital media and environments to communicate and work collaboratively, including at a distance, to support individual learning and contribute to the learning of others. **Grades 9–12** Create and publish an online art gallery with examples and commentary that demonstrate an understanding of different historical periods, cultures, and countries. (1,2)	Given a digital camera, computer, and PhotoShop software, the tenth-grade student will (1) create a visual art product that includes at least three digital photos and two descriptive words to represent the concept of freedom, and (2) provide a written rationale that supports their choice of media, techniques, and processes to demonstrate an understanding of freedom.

and be able to do at the conclusion of the lesson, you are better able to carefully select strategies, technology, and media that will ensure learning.

Basis for Assessment. Stating standards and learning objectives also helps ensure accurate assessment of student learning. Explicitly stated student outcomes guide the creation of assessments that measure the targeted knowledge and skills and directly align with required standardized tests.

Basis for Student Learning Expectations. Your students are better able to prepare for and participate in learning activities when they know the expected outcomes. The learning objectives may be viewed as a type of contract between teacher and learner: "My responsibility as the teacher is to provide learning activities suitable for your attaining the objective. Your responsibility as the learner is to participate conscientiously in those learning activities."

THE ABCDs OF WELL-STATED LEARNING OBJECTIVES

The ABCDs of well-stated objectives provide an easy-to-follow process for writing learning objectives: Specify the Audience for whom the objective is intended, the Behavior to be demonstrated, the Conditions under which the behavior will be observed, and the Degree to which the new knowledge or skill must be mastered.

Audience. Because learning objectives focus on what learners will know and be able to do after the lesson, it is important to clearly identify the targeted learners—for example, "second-grade students." For students you will be teaching all year, you may choose the common audience identifier, "The learner will . . . ," often abbreviated as TLW. For students who have individual education plans, the objectives will be targeted to students by name.

Behavior. The heart of the objective is the verb describing the new capability that learners will have *after* instruction.

This verb is stated as an observable behavior, such as *define, categorize,* and *demonstrate.* Vague terms such as *know, understand,* and *appreciate* do not communicate observable performance. The Helpful Hundred list in Table 3.2 offers verbs that highlight performance.

Strive to solicit student behavior or performance that reflects deep understanding and real-world capability. In other words, rather than having students "select the correct answers on a test about water conservation," have them "compare and contrast two water conservation systems to identify which is most eco-friendly." Or rather than selecting names of geometric shapes on a worksheet, have students identify shapes used in the Golden Gate Bridge.

Conditions. Learning objectives should include the conditions under which the performance is to be assessed. In other words, what materials or tools will students be allowed or disallowed for use in demonstrating mastery of the objective? Thus, an objective might state, "Given a list of earthquake occurrences over the past 100 years, the student will generate a line graph to demonstrate trends over time." A language arts objective might say, "Without references, the student will write a 300-word essay on the relationship of nutrition to learning."

Degree. The final requirement of a well-stated objective is the degree of accuracy or proficiency by which minimally acceptable performance will be judged. Certainly students

| Table **3.2** The Helpful Hundred |

Suggested Performance Terms					
Add	Compute	Draw	Label	Predict	State
Alphabetize	Conduct	Estimate	Locate	Prepare	Subtract
Analyze	Construct	Evaluate	Make	Present	Suggest
Apply	Contrast	Explain	Manipulate	Produce	Swing
Arrange	Convert	Extrapolate	Match	Pronounce	Tabulate
Assemble	Correct	Finish	Measure	Read	Throw
Attend	Cut	Fit	Modify	Reconstruct	Time
Bisect	Deduce	Generate	Multiply	Reduce	Translate
Build	Defend	Graph	Name	Remove	Type
Categorize	Define	Grind	Operate	Revise	Underline
Change	Demonstrate	Hit	Order	Select	Verbalize
Choose	Derive	Hold	Organize	Sketch	Verify
Classify	Describe	Identify	Outline	Solve	Weave
Color	Design	Illustrate	Pack	Sort	Weigh
Compare	Designate	Indicate	Paint	Specify	Write
Complete	Diagram	Install	Plot	Spell	
Compose	Distinguish	Kick	Position	Square	

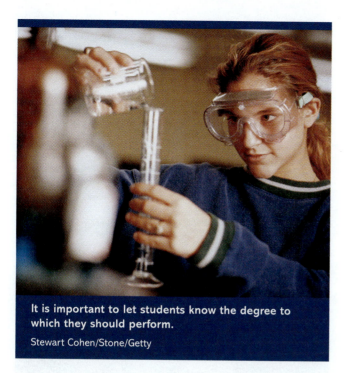

It is important to let students know the degree to which they should perform.

Stewart Cohen/Stone/Getty

can exceed the stated expectations. A high school chemistry objective may read, "Given six unknown substances and testing equipment, students will identify five of the six unknown substances." When stating the degree or criterion for assessing student products that are more comprehensive in scope, a rubric rating scale is appropriate. For example, the degree of proficiency for a PowerPoint presentation on 18th century monarchies could be stated as follows: "Achieve an overall rubric rating of 3 (on a 4-point scale where 4 = Exceeds Expectations)." Details on creating rubrics are presented in the Evaluate and Revise section of this chapter.

ABCD OBJECTIVES CHECKLIST

Use the ABCD Objectives Checklist (Figure 3.1) to assess the degree to which your objectives communicate the intent of the learning. Further guidelines for writing objectives are discussed in Gronlund's (2009) *Writing Instructional Objectives for Teaching and Assessment.*

ABCD Objectives Checklist

	Appropriately Stated	Partly Stated	Missing
Audience			
Specifies the learner(s) for whom the objective is intended	☐	☐	☐
Behavior (action verb)			
Describes the capability expected of the learner following instruction • Stated as a learner performance • Stated as observable behavior • Describes a real-world skill (versus mere test performance)	☐	☐	☐
Conditions (materials and/or environment)			
Describes the conditions under which the performance is to be demonstrated • Equipment, tools, aids, or references the learner may or may not use • Special environmental conditions in which the learner has to perform	☐	☐	☐
Degree (criterion)			
States, where applicable, the standard for acceptable performance • Time limit • Range of accuracy • Proportion of correct responses required • Qualitative standards	☐	☐	☐

Figure **3.1**
ABCD Objectives Checklist

You will find that learning objectives appearing in curriculum standards, textbooks, online lessons, and other instructional materials are written in a general format that often lacks one or more of the ABCD components. Teachers can modify such objectives to meet the specific learning needs of their students. For example a district standard may state: "The learner will be able to divide fractions." If you have students who struggle with math, you could adapt the objective by adding the following condition: "Given manipulatives, the learner will be able to divide fractions." The same objective for more advanced students would not include manipulatives.

Many curriculum standards also lack the use of technology to assist students in achieving the learning objective. Therefore, you will need to modify standards to add the appropriate NETS for students (NETS-S) (ISTE, 2007) by including technology in the Condition component of the objective, as in the following examples:

- *Given spreadsheet software and data on population growth, natural resources, and global warming,* sixth-grade science students will use a spreadsheet to estimate the impact of population growth on natural resources from at least three perspectives.
- *Given clip art and PowerPoint software,* first-grade students will construct a four-slide presentation with one student-selected clip art image per slide to demonstrate four student moods: happy, sad, angry, and bored.
- *Given access to word processing software and web-based resources on American wars,* American history high school students will generate *a word-processed table* that shows 25 similarities of and differences between World War I and World War II.
- *Given a list of randomly grouped words and Inspiration software,* seventh-grade language arts students will create a concept map that arranges the words into six parts-of-speech groups.

LEARNING OBJECTIVES AND INDIVIDUAL DIFFERENCES

It is important to adapt learning objectives to the abilities of individual learners. The stated philosophy of most schools is to help students achieve their full potential. In a physical education class with students of mixed ability, for instance, the midsemester goal might be for all students to complete a run of 100 meters, with time standards that vary to show similarity of achievement. For a few, 12 seconds might be attainable; for many others, 16 seconds; and for some, 20

When teaching learners who have disabilities, there may be as many different standards for each objective as there are individuals.

Elizabeth Crews

might be realistic. For a student with physical disabilities, it might be a major victory to move 10 meters in 1 minute.

Learning objectives are not intended to limit what students learn, but rather are intended to provide a minimum level of expected achievement. Serendipitous or incidental learning should be expected to occur (and should be encouraged) because learning takes different forms with different students. Class discussions and other kinds of student involvement in the instructional situation, therefore, should rarely be rigidly limited to a specific objective. Indeed, to foster incidental learning and provide for individual differences, it is sometimes advisable to have students specify some of their own learning objectives. (See a set of standards and learning objectives in the ASSURE case study.)

Standards

- Curriculum—National Council of Teachers of English Standard 4: Students adjust their use of spoken, written, and visual language (e.g., conventions, style, vocabulary) to communicate effectively with a variety of audiences and for different purposes.

- Technology—National Educational Technology Standards for Students 3 (Technology Productivity Tools): students use technology tools to enhance learning, increase productivity, and promote creativity.

Objectives for Lesson

1. Given the following questions, the ninth-grade English student will demonstrate the ability to express reflective thinking by answering the following questions in a written or video reflection that meets the "Final Year Reflections" criteria listed on the assignment sheet.

- "What did I learn about myself, reading, writing, learning, and overall during the past year?"
- "What do I hope to accomplish in these areas next year when I am a sophomore?"

2. Using DreamWeaver software, the ninth-grade English student will create a new page titled "Final Year Reflections" that meets the formatting criteria for being included in the electronic portfolio Reflections folder.

3. Using files of previously completed work, the ninth-grade student will be able to add the written reflection or upload a video reflection in an accessible format to the "Final Year Reflections" page in the electronic portfolio folder.

Tiare Ahu discusses the curriculum and technology standards and objectives for the ninth-grade English lesson that was videotaped for Chapter 3. Visit the Chapter 3 section of MyEducationKit to view the video of Ms. Ahu's ninth-grade English class.

SELECT STRATEGIES, TECHNOLOGY, MEDIA, AND MATERIALS

The next step in creating effective lessons that support learning through the appropriate use of technology and media is the systematic selection of instructional strategies, technology and media, and lesson materials. The following guidelines discuss the selection process.

SELECTING STRATEGIES

When identifying instructional strategies for a lesson, first consider where teacher-centered approaches should be used and where student-centered strategies might be better. The teacher strategies involve your own teaching activities, as when you present a concept by showing a video or reading a story or when you use the interactive whiteboard to demonstrate how to conjugate a verb. The student-centered strategies are those that engage students in active learning, such as discussing the pros and cons of a topic, conducting an Internet search, taking digital photos of a process, or listening to podcasts on a current topic. Most lessons include several teacher and student strategies.

Wagner (2008) suggests ways to align strategies that involve student use of cyberlearning tools with NETS-S and 21st century knowledge and skills—for example, engaging students in accessing and analyzing information through critical thinking and problem solving, collaborating and communicating with others within and beyond the classroom, and learning to be adaptable as well as creative and imaginative.

The primary consideration when selecting instructional strategies is that they result in student achievement of the standards and objectives. Also, keep students' learning styles and motivation in mind as you select strategies to better ensure meeting the diverse needs of students. Review the ARCS model to see if your strategies will gain student Attention, be Relevant to their needs, require an appropriate level of accomplishment to build their Confidence, and provide Satisfaction for what they learn.

SELECTING TECHNOLOGY AND MEDIA

Selecting appropriate technology and media can be a complex task—considering the vast array of available resources, the diversity of your learners, and the specific learning objectives to be pursued. Videos, for example, raise the issue of presentation pace, which would be less relevant for a digital presentation that supports easier navigation to key content. In examining educational games, look for relevant practice and remedial feedback. When selecting an audio storybook, look for functions such as embedded definitions and ease of returning to reread sections. To help with this process, see the Selection Rubrics for technology and media in MyEducationKit.

Selection Rubrics. The Selection Rubrics provide a systematic procedure for judging the qualities of specific technology and media. Each rubric includes a set of consistent selection criteria (as shown here) as well as criteria for the designated technology or media (e.g., computer software, audio). You need to decide which criteria are most important for your students' achieving the stated learning objectives.

SELECTION RUBRIC CRITERIA

- Alignment with standards, outcomes, and objectives
- Accurate and current information
- Age-appropriate language
- Interest level and engagement
- Technical quality
- Ease of use (for student or teacher)
- Bias free
- User guide and directions

The Selection Rubrics are templates with separate fields to enter the media title, source, and a brief description along with a predefined rating scale to assess the technology/media being reviewed. Go to MyEducationKit to access the Selection Rubrics for this text.

SELECTING, MODIFYING, OR DESIGNING MATERIALS

When you have selected your strategies and the type of technology and media needed for your lesson, you are ready to select the materials to support lesson implementation. This step involves three general options: (1) selecting available materials, (2) modifying existing materials, or (3) designing new materials.

Selecting Available Materials. The majority of instructional materials used by teachers are "off the shelf"—that is, ready made and available from school, district, or other easily accessible sources. Many of these resources are free or inexpensive. Among many offerings, how do you go about making appropriate choices from available materials?

Involving the Technology/Media Specialist. You may want to begin by meeting with your technology/media specialist

Your school technology/media specialist can help you review and select instructional resources appropriate for your lesson.

Michael Newman/PhotoEdit

and discussing your learning objectives, instructional strategies, and desired media format(s). As the specialist gains a better idea of your needs, arrangements can be made to check out the appropriate materials from your school's library/media center or other media collections (public, academic, or regional).

Joining Other Teachers. Because evaluation of materials is time-consuming and complex, it may be useful to involve other teachers, especially experienced teachers, whose years of work with media and material alternatives have involved a lot of critical analysis about education resources. Working with other teachers allows a pool of shared ideas for using materials and a collective strength that may make it easier to acquire materials from museums or organizations.

Surveying Media Resource Guides. Online or paper-based media resource guides survey and review free and inexpensive materials. For example, the Gateway to Educational Materials (GEM) database (www.thegateway.org) contains more than 40,000 education resources such as lesson plans, thematic units, and student materials. Sponsored by the National Education Association, GEM draws from some of the country's best museums, universities, and government programs, including NASA, the Smithsonian Institution in Washington, DC, the National Science Foundation, and the Exploratorium in San Francisco. You can search the GEM database by subject area, grade level, and key word. GEM requires each resource to be reviewed and meet specified standards before being added to the collection. Kathy Schrock's Guide for Educators includes links to numerous resource directories, grouped in three categories: back to school, general education, and early childhood. Also included are links to recommended print titles for technology infusion, gadgets, how-to, HTML-Internet, general teaching, Second Life, and Web 2.0 (http://school.discoveryeducation.com/schrockguide/edres.html).

Modifying Existing Materials. As you strive to meet the diverse needs of your students, you will find that "off-the-shelf" materials often need modifications to more closely align with your learning objectives. Technology provides several options for modifying existing materials.

Encouragingly, many educational resources are provided as copyright-free digital files or as paper copies. Digital materials are typically found on educational websites that provide downloadable resources. Example resources include lesson handouts, teacher PowerPoint presentations, and Excel spreadsheets formatted for easy data entry.

However, when materials are only available in PDF or paper format, modifications can be accomplished with digital scanning or creative use of a copy machine. For example, materials can be scanned and modified with editing software. Another approach is to modify a paper original and then make copies of the revised resource. For instance, if you want students to label 20 grasshopper features but have a handout based on 50, you can carefully cover the 30 unwanted features and then make copies.

A word of caution about using and modifying commercially produced materials is to be sure not to violate copyright

Scanners and photocopiers can be used to copy modified instructional materials.

David Young-Wolff/PhotoEdit

laws and restrictions. If in doubt, check with your school media specialist, administrator, or legal adviser. General copyright guidelines were discussed in Chapter 1 (p. 13).

Designing New Materials. When ready-made materials are not available or existing materials cannot be easily modified, you need to design your own lesson materials, which can range from hand printing a flip chart to using your computer to create handouts, presentations, or an online WebQuest. The remaining chapters provide guidance for developing meaningful materials involving a variety of technology and media. Remember to keep learner needs and learning objectives as the key considerations when designing your lesson materials (as in the ASSURE case study on page 48).

UTILIZE TECHNOLOGY, MEDIA, AND MATERIALS

This step involves planning your role for utilizing the technology, media, and materials. Follow the "5 Ps" process: Preview and Prepare the technology, media, and materials; Prepare the environment; Prepare the learners; and Provide the learning experience.

PREVIEW THE TECHNOLOGY, MEDIA, AND MATERIALS

During the selection process you identified technology, media, and materials that are appropriate for your learners. At this stage you need to preview the selected technology and media in relation to the learning objectives. The goal is to select the portions that directly align with your lesson. For example, if your lesson is on correct use of prepositions, preview several language arts software programs to find drill-and-practice activities that match your objectives. Then design your lesson to include just the preposition sections of the software rather than the entire sequence. Similarly, if using a video documentary, identify the segments that directly align with your lesson, remembering that a DVD allows easy navigation to targeted segments.

Although your decision may have already involved published reviews, distributor's blurbs, and colleagues' appraisals, you should *insist* on previewing the materials yourself before using them. Not only will a thorough review enable you to use resources to their full potential, it will ensure that students are not exposed to inappropriate content or language found in some computer games, videos, and online or printed periodicals.

Select Strategies

Tiare Ahu selects teacher- and student-centered strategies for the electronic portfolio lesson. Teacher-centered strategies are chosen for reviewing the overall goals of using an electronic portfolio and to introduce student guidelines for completing the final reflections. The student-centered strategies are used for students' written or video reflections of their learning that are added to electronic portfolios. Tiare addresses student motivation by using the ARCS model (Keller, 1988) to consider how electronic portfolios gain student Attention. To achieve Relevance, students reflect on their personal growth over the year and set goals for next year. Their Confidence is reinforced by the lesson's use of skills previously mastered in other electronic portfolio activities. Students gain Satisfaction through personalizing their reflections with digital media such as colors, clip art, and photos.

Select Technology and Media

This lesson involves the continued use of Blackboard course management software and DreamWeaver software to create the web-based portfolios. The lesson also calls for a digital video camera to record student reflections and the use of iMovie to edit the video reflections. The following guidelines help Tiare assess the appropriateness of her technology and media selections:

- *Alignment with standards, outcomes, and objectives.* The software provides the necessary tools for her students to meet the learning objectives.

- *Accurate and current information.* Not applicable for the chosen technology and media.
- *Age-appropriate language.* The software applications are written at a level appropriate for ninth-grade students.
- *Interest level and engagement.* The software applications provide features that enable the students to personalize their electronic portfolios.
- *Technical quality.* The software applications have superior technical quality.
- *Ease of use.* The applications require initial training and periodic review of functions for students to easily use the features.
- *Bias free.* The software applications are bias free.
- *User guide and directions.* The online help features of the software are moderately easy to use. Students most frequently ask each other, the teacher, or the technology assistant for help with technical difficulties.

Select Materials

The materials for this lesson include a teacher-produced student assignment sheet that explains the details of creating and adding the final reflections to the electronic portfolio. Ms. Ahu was not able to use available materials or modify existing materials because the assignment sheet requires details very specific to the lesson.

To view the strategies, technology, media, and materials that Tiare Ahu used in her ninth-grade English class, visit the Chapter 3 section of MyEducationKit to view the video of Ms. Ahu's ninth-grade English class.

PREPARE THE TECHNOLOGY, MEDIA, AND MATERIALS

Next, you need to prepare the technology, media, and materials that will support your instructional activities. The first step is to gather all the equipment you will need. Determine the sequence for using the materials and what you will do with each one. For example, you may want to change how an instructional game is used by preparing a new set of questions at a different level of difficulty or even on a new topic. Or if the audio portion of a video doesn't align with the needs of your students, you can turn off the sound and provide the narration yourself.

Keep a list of the materials and equipment needed for each lesson and an outline of the presentation sequence of the activities. And finally, practice using the resources before implementing the lesson.

PREPARE THE ENVIRONMENT

Wherever the learning is to take place—in the classroom, in a laboratory, at the media center—the facilities will have to be arranged for effective use of the technology, media, and materials. Some media require a darkened room, a convenient power source, and access to light switches. You should check that the equipment is in working order. Arrange the

Carefully preview multiple technology, media, and materials when planning your lesson.

Lori Whitley/Merrill

Prepare the environment by arranging the facilities to ensure proper use of technology, media, and materials.

Lori Whitley/Merrill

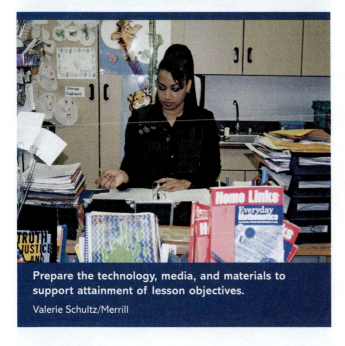

Prepare the technology, media, and materials to support attainment of lesson objectives.

Valerie Schultz/Merrill

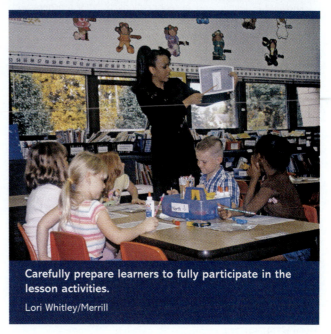

Carefully prepare learners to fully participate in the lesson activities.

Lori Whitley/Merrill

facilities so that all students can see and hear properly. Arrange the seating so students can see and hear each other when cooperative learning is included.

PREPARE THE LEARNERS

Research on learning tells us that what is learned from an activity depends highly on how learners are prepared for the lesson (Gagné, Briggs, & Wager, 1992). We know that in show business entertainers are passionate about having the audience properly warmed up. Effective instruction also requires a proper warmup, which can include one or more of the following:

- An introduction giving a broad overview of the lesson content
- A rationale telling how the content relates to real-world applications
- A motivating statement that creates a need to know the content
- Cues directing attention to specific aspects of the lesson

In most cases you will also want to inform students of the learning objectives, introduce unfamiliar vocabulary, and review prerequisite skills needed for the lesson, including any new skills needed to use technology and media.

PROVIDE THE LEARNING EXPERIENCE

Now you are ready to provide the instructional experience. A teacher-centered learning experience often involves a presentation, demonstration, drill-and-practice, or a tutorial. In using presentation as a strategy, it is important to follow the presentation skills guidelines in the accompanying box, Using Presentation Skills in the Classroom. (See the ASSURE case study on p. 52 for Tiare Ahu's approach to the Utilize Technology, Media, and Materials stage.)

USING
Presentation Skills
in the Classroom

Planning

- *Analyze your learners.* What are the needs, values, backgrounds, knowledge levels, and misconceptions of your learners with regard to the topic you will be presenting?
- *Specify the learning objectives.* What should students do? How much time do you have to present? Limit the objectives and content to the time available.
- *Specify benefits and rationale.* Why is this presentation important for your students? If you cannot answer this question, the focus should be altered to meet student needs.
- *Identify the key points.* Brainstorm the main ideas. Put them on note cards or sticky notes. Most presentations will have from five to nine main points.
- *Identify the subpoints and supporting details.* Again use note cards or stick-on notes. Try to limit yourself to five to nine subpoints for each main point.
- *Organize presentation in a logical order.* The following is an example of a simple organizing strategy.
  1. Overview: Tell them what you are going to tell them.
  2. Present: Tell them.
  3. Review: Tell them what you told them.

Rehearsing

- Use key words from your presentation rather than a script so that you are speaking and not reading.
- Mentally run through the presentation to review each idea in sequence.
- Do a standup rehearsal in the room where you will be presenting or one similar to it.
- Practice answers to questions you anticipate from learners.
- Videotape your presentation or ask a colleague to listen and provide feedback.

Setting Up

- Check room arrangements and ensure the equipment is in place and operational.

- For computer or video projection, place the screen front and center (Figure A).

A.

- Place the overhead screen or flip chart at a 45-degree angle near the corner of the room. Place the overhead screen to your right and the flip chart to the left if you are right-handed. Reverse the positions if you are left-handed (Figure B).

B.

When providing the learning experience, remember that both teacher-centered and student-centered activities may be utilized.

Lori Whitley/Merrill

- Position objects being studied front and center. Remove them when they are no longer being studied.

Presenting

Anxiety

- Nervousness and excitement are normal before and during a presentation when you are a new teacher or presenting new content.
- Proper planning and preparation should reduce your anxiety.
- Harness your nervous energy and use it positively with body movement, supporting gestures, and voice projection.
- Breathe slowly and deeply. Your cardiovascular system will slow down and ease the symptoms of anxiety.

Delivery

- Stand up when presenting to command more attention.
- Face the learners to maintain eye contact and allow them to see your facial expressions.
- When using whiteboards, complete your writing, then turn and talk (Figure C).

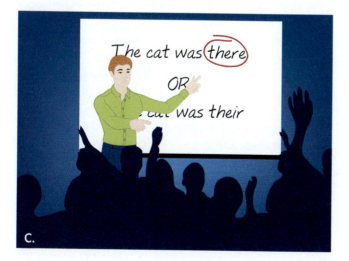

C.

- Step to the side or in front of your desk to establish more personal contact with the learners. It allows you to be seen and to seem more natural.
- Move while you speak. Teachers who stand in one spot and never gesture can easily lose student attention. Move and gesture, but don't overdo it.
- Use natural gestures. Learn to gesture in front of a class as you would if you were having an animated conversation with a friend.
- Don't put your hands in your pockets. Don't clasp your hands behind your back. Don't wring your hands nervously. Don't play with a pen or other object.

Voice

- Use a natural, conversational style. Relate to your learners in a direct and personal manner.
- Don't read your presentation. If part of your presentation is just information transfer, give the students a copy and let them read it.
- Use a comfortable pace suited to learner needs and the complexity of the content.
- Speak clearly and loud enough to be heard in the back of the room. If you are uncertain about your volume, ask students in the back if they can hear you.
- A pause (silence) after a key point is an excellent way to emphasize it. The more important the idea, the more important it is for you to pause and let the words sink in before going on to the next idea.

Eye Contact

- Maintain eye contact with your learners. Eye contact will make your presentation more like a one-on-one conversation.
- An excellent way to keep your learners' attention is to look eye to eye at each person for at least 3 seconds. Don't quickly scan the learners or look at the back wall, screen, or notes for long periods of time.

Utilize Technology, Media, and Materials

Preview the Technology, Media, and Materials

Tiare Ahu previews the site map and selection properties of DreamWeaver and how to use the digital video camera and iMovie software.

Prepare the Technology, Media, and Materials

Tiare creates a handout that explains what students should do to complete their "Final Year Reflections" in written or video formats. She also adds a "Final Year Reflection" to her sample electronic portfolio.

Prepare the Environment

The lesson will take place in the computer lab and in the video recording studio. Each computer in the computer lab needs to be checked to ensure that DreamWeaver and iMovie software are functional and that all computers can save to the server and print. The studio needs to be arranged for recording student video reflections by setting up the tripod for the digital video camera and arranging the seating in a location with an appropriate background. Tiare also needs to check that the digital media storage device has enough space to store the student video reflections.

Prepare the Learners

To prepare the students, Ms. Ahu introduces the lesson and reviews the learning objectives. Each student receives a handout about completing the "Final Year Reflection" for their electronic portfolio. In addition, the handout also includes the evaluation criteria for the reflection.

Provide the Learning Experience

Ms. Ahu guides student learning by reviewing how to add reflections to their electronic portfolios and by monitoring students as they create their written or video work.

To see how Tiare Ahu utilizes technology, media, and materials for the e-portfolio lesson, visit the Chapter 3 section of MyEducationKit to view the video of Ms. Ahu's ninth-grade English class.

REQUIRE LEARNER PARTICIPATION

As predicted by Bloom, Engelhart, Furst, Hill, and Krathwohl (1956) over 50 years ago, today's global economy will require students to have experience and **practice** applying, analyzing, synthesizing, and evaluating rather than just knowing and comprehending information. This follows constructivist views that learning is an active mental process built from relevant authentic experiences for which students receive informative **feedback,** a response that lets them know the degree to which they have achieved the objective and how to improve their performance. The NETS for Students (NETS-S) support this level of student participation through the use of a variety of technology and media (ISTE, 2007).

PRACTICE

The objectives for your lesson explicitly state what students are expected to do after instruction. Thus, it is critical to require learner participation through explicit practice with the new knowledge and skills. Four of the six NETS-S have direct applicability when planning student participation activities, in which students use a variety of technology tools for productivity, communication, research, and problem solving or decision making.

Technology as a Productivity Tool. One common way of requiring learner participation is through the use of productivity tools. For example, in early childhood experiences learning vocabulary words, word meanings can be enhanced when students use KidPix to find images representing new words and then must explain their choices. Another example involves middle school students creating PowerPoint presentations depicting trends in American folk music over the past 100 years. The activity requires summarizing key ideas from historical documents, choosing the best photos and sound clips, and sequencing content in a meaningful way. At the high school level, social studies students can use spreadsheets to examine national population trends and make growth predictions for the next 50 years.

Technology as a Communication Tool. The NETS-S consider how students can use "digital media and environments to communicate and work collaboratively, including at a distance, to support individual learning and contribute to the learning of others" (NETS-S 2) (ISTE, 2007). For example, when using projected still pictures of students living in Alaska, you can engage students in a lively discussion in which they compare themselves with the students in the photos. Students can then exchange emails with Alaskan students to gain firsthand knowledge of life in Alaska. As another example, if the outcome is to increase student awareness of their right and responsibility to express opinions, student groups could write and submit their ideas to a public opinion section of a local news website.

Technology as a Research Tool.
The Internet provides students instant access to limitless resources. Therefore, they can readily "apply digital tools to gather, evaluate, and use information" (NETS-S 3) (ISTE, 2007). As a teacher, it is critical for you to plan activities that actively engage students in processing information and reporting results that are meaningful for the assigned task. Student research should also include information from books, periodicals, and people, because multiple resources will better ensure that students do not merely cut and paste web-based information into their work. For instance, if your students are to create a concept map of events influencing the rights of women, you want to set expectations for using multiple digital and nondigital resources, paraphrasing content, and providing appropriate citations.

Technology as a Problem-Solving and Decision-Making Tool.
"Students use critical thinking skills to plan and conduct research, manage projects, solve problems, and make informed decisions using appropriate digital tools and resources" (NETS-S 4) (ISTE, 2007). Never before have students had access to such vast amounts of data and information. Students of all ages can more closely examine information than any previous generation through tools such as electronic devices (e.g., science probes and microscopes), digital audio and video equipment (e.g., cameras and whiteboards), and software in general (e.g., spreadsheets and databases). If students were addressing the question "Does the person with the most popular votes win?" they could download election results into a spreadsheet to compare electoral votes to popular vote totals. To determine whether artificial ponds are as safe for fish as natural ponds, students could gather water samples and use a variety of electronic probes to collect data to compare in a spreadsheet. Young students learning colors could solve the following problem: "Can you find a rainbow in our room?" Student pairs would use a digital camera to photograph items matching each color of the rainbow for a "Rainbows in Our Room" activity book.

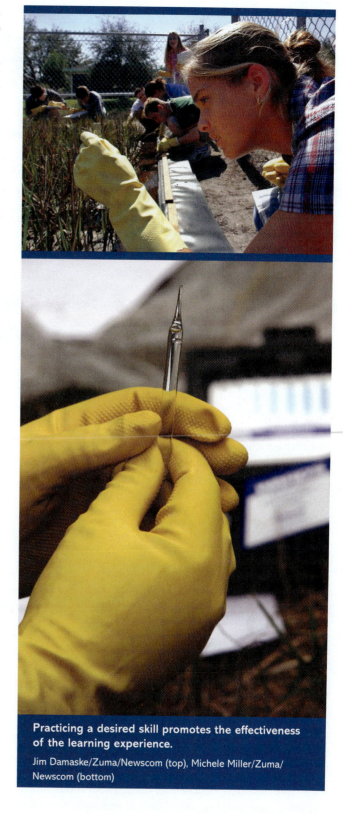

Practicing a desired skill promotes the effectiveness of the learning experience.

Jim Damaske/Zuma/Newscom (top), Michele Miller/Zuma/Newscom (bottom)

Technological tools specifically designed to engage students in problem solving include computer games and simulations. Games use competition, intrigue, and inquisitiveness as vehicles for students to gain content knowledge. An

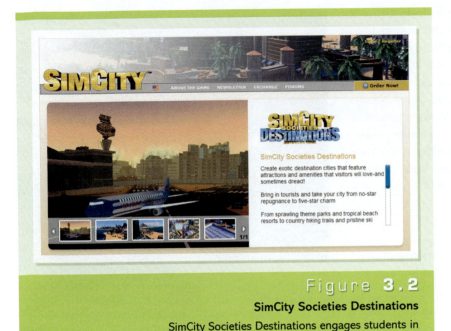

game in which students design and manage a city from the "ground up" (Figure 3.2)

Using Educational Software for Practice. In addition to NETS-S activities, educational software provides excellent resources for engaging students with diverse abilities in individualized learning activities focused toward basic knowledge and skills. The programs allow students of lower-than-average abilities to move at their own pace while providing immediate feedback and remediation. Other students can try more challenging activities after demonstrating mastery of previous skills.

Figure **3.2**

SimCity Societies Destinations

SimCity Societies Destinations engages students in problem-solving and decision-making experiences.
Source: Sim Cities Societies Destinations materials © 2010 Electronic Arts, Inc. All rights reserved. Used with permission.

Using Other Media for Practice. Discussions, short quizzes, and application exercises can provide opportunities for practice and feedback during instruction. Teacher guides and manuals often suggest techniques and activities for eliciting and reinforcing student responses. However, many of these resources do not integrate the use of technology and media. Therefore, you will need to use applicable components of the ASSURE model to decide where student use of these tools is appropriate.

excellent example is Math Blaster, award-winning software that engages students in fast-action games to learn standards-based math content. Simulations use the same features, yet allow learners great flexibility in making choices that affect outcomes in the games. SimCity is a well-known simulation

Require Learner Participation

ASSURE
Classroom
Case Study

Student Practice Activities

Students individually write responses to the reflection question, "What did I learn this year about myself; about reading, writing, and learning; and about life generally?" Students have the option of using written or video reflections.

The students use computers and DreamWeaver software as production tools to add reflection pages to their personal electronic portfolios. Students who choose to write their reflections add them directly to the page. Those choosing video meet with Ms. Ahu to record their reflections with a digital camera. The file is then transferred to students' computers for editing with iMovie before uploading to their electronic portfolios.

Feedback

Tiare Ahu uses the assignment criteria to review each student's electronic portfolio. She adds individualized comments to each student's file in the gradebook section of Blackboard for the electronic portfolio assignment.

The various levels of student participation required for Tiare Ahu's ninth-grade students to create electronic portfolios are captured on the video for this chapter. Also included are scenes showing her providing feedback to students about their work. Visit the Chapter 3 section of MyEducationKit to view the video of Ms. Ahu's ninth-grade English class.

Feedback from the teacher helps students improve their learning.
Bill Aron/PhotoEdit

FEEDBACK

In all cases, learners should receive feedback on the correctness of their response. The feedback may come from the teacher, or students may work in small groups and give one another feedback. Feedback may also be part of a self-check activity done independently or with a mentor, often using the computer. Regardless of the source, the important thing is that students receive helpful feedback (as in the ASSURE case study on p. 54).

EVALUATE AND REVISE

The final component of the ASSURE model, Evaluate and Revise, is essential to the development of quality instruction, yet this component of lesson design is often neglected. Without this step, it is often impossible to know whether instruction is successful or how to revise unsuccessful strategies. It also makes it difficult to judge the efficacy of different types of technology and media.

ASSESSING LEARNER ACHIEVEMENT

The ultimate question regarding instruction is whether students have learned what they were supposed to learn. Can they demonstrate the capabilities specified in the stated standards and objectives? The first step in answering this question was taken near the beginning of the ASSURE model, when you formulated your learning objectives, including a criterion of acceptable performance. Now you need to develop

assessment tasks that require students to demonstrate the behavior stated in the objective.

The method of assessing achievement depends on the nature of the objective. Some learning objectives call for relatively simple cognitive skills—for example, stating Ohm's law, distinguishing adjectives from adverbs, or summarizing the principles of the Declaration of Independence. Learning objectives such as these lend themselves to conventional written tests.

Other objectives may call for process-type behaviors (e.g., diagramming a sentence, solving quadratic equations, or classifying animals), the creation of products (e.g., a sculpture, a written composition, a PowerPoint presentation, or a portfolio), or an exhibit of attitudes (e.g., choosing to read during free-time activities, placing used paper in the recycle bin, or eating healthy snacks). This type of learning objective requires a more comprehensive, **authentic assessment,** such as a performance-based evaluation of a student's demonstration of learning in a natural context.

Authentic Assessment. Rising interest in authentic assessment of students is driven by commitment to a constructivist perspective. Authentic assessments require students to use processes appropriate to the content and skills being learned and to how they are used in the real world. It is the difference between learning science facts and doing what scientists do. How many people take paper-and-pencil tests as a part of their occupation? A special type of authentic assessment, the **portfolio,** made up of student-selected exemplary work representing performance over time along with student reflections on why this work represents their best effort, will be discussed next in its own subsection.

Authentic assessments can be applied to most performances or products. The most commonly used rating scales for authentic assessments include performance checklists, attitude scales, product-rating checklists, and rubrics.

When assessing basic process skills, a performance checklist can be an effective, objective way of recording student performance. Figure 3.3 shows a primary grade checklist for using an audio storybook. Notice the simple Yes or No recording system.

Although attitudes are admittedly difficult to assess, measurement tools have been devised, such as attitude scales (see the biology example in Figure 3.4). The five-point scale (Strongly Agree to Strongly Disagree) offers the opportunity to capture a range of attitudes. A number of other suggestions for attitude measurement can be found in Robert Mager's *How to Turn Learners On . . . Without Turning Them Off* (see this chapter's Suggested Resources).

For product skills, a product-rating checklist can guide your evaluation of critical subskills and make qualitative

Performance Checklist: Using an Audio Storybook

Name _____ Class _____

Indicate Yes or No with an "X" in the appropriate column.

Did the Student   Yes   No

1. Locate the assigned audio storybook? _____ _____
2. Complete the Material Checkout Form for the storybook? _____ _____
3. Select the appropriate CD player? _____ _____
4. Select the appropriate headphones? _____ _____
5. Correctly insert the storybook CD? _____ _____
6. Correctly connect the headphones? _____ _____
7. Play the CD and follow along as the storybook was read? _____ _____
8. Remove the CD and headphones when the story was finished? _____ _____
9. Return the audio storybook, CD player, and headphones to the proper location? _____ _____
10. Complete the Materials Return Form? _____ _____

Teacher Name _____ Date _____

Figure **3.3**

A Sample Performance Checklist

judgments more objective, as in the rating form in Figure 3.5 for a student-created digital concept map. This checklist provides more detailed information regarding student performance because each product component is rated from Poor to Excellent rather than with a Yes/No scale.

Used to provide a more comprehensive assessment of student performance, a **rubric** is a set of assessment criteria for appraising or judging student products or performances. A rubric typically consists of a rating scale for performance criteria based on level-of-performance descriptors. The performance criteria are the key areas of focus for the performance or product (e.g., problem presentation, supporting graphics, appropriate labels). Rating scales to measure achievement of performance criteria normally range from three to six levels designated by names and/or numbers. A 3-point scale might be shown as (1) Needs Work, (2) OK, and (3) Good. An example 4-point scale might show the following levels: (1) Beginning, (2) Developing, (3) Accomplished, and (4) Exemplary. The descriptors for the levels of performance describe the student performance or product at each level of performance. By comparing an actual student product or performance to the descriptors, a teacher can give a numerical score. An example rubric for a multimedia product is presented in Figure 3.6 (p. 59). See Free and Inexpensive: Rubrics for rubric resources.

$ FREE & INEXPENSIVE

RUBRICS

Rubistar

http://rubistar.4teachers.org/index.php

Rubistar is a free online tool designed to assist teachers in creating a variety of rubrics. The website has numerous examples of rubrics that can be accessed through key word searches. If you are new to rubrics, the site offers a rubric tutorial. When you are ready to try it out, Rubistar provides an easy-to-use template to create and print rubrics. If you complete the registration, you can save and edit rubrics online.

Kathy Schrock's Assessment and Rubric Information

http://school.discovery.com/schrockguide/assess.html#rubrics

This site provides a vast array of links to rubric resources. The links are categorized by Student Web Page Rubrics, Subject-Specific and General Rubrics, Rubric Builders, Educator Technology Skills and Rubrics, and Related Articles.

Rubrics and Evaluation Resources

www.ncsu.edu/midlink/ho.html

This site provides a collection of rubric resources that range from specific rubrics (e.g., book report rubric, multimedia project rubric, and writing assessment rubrics) to generic rubric templates.

Attitude Scale: Biology

Each of the statements below expresses a feeling toward biology. Please rate each statement on the extent to which you agree. For each, you may select (A) strongly agree, (B) agree, (C) undecided, (D) disagree, or (E) strongly disagree.

A	B	C	D	E
Strongly Agree	**Agree**	**Undecided**	**Disagree**	**Strongly Disagree**

_____ 1. Biology is very interesting to me.

_____ 2. I don't like biology, and it scares me to have to take it.

_____ 3. I am always under a terrible strain in biology class.

_____ 4. Biology is fascinating and fun.

_____ 5. Learning biology makes me feel secure.

_____ 6. Biology makes me feel uncomfortable, restless, irritable, and impatient.

_____ 7. In general, I have a good feeling toward biology.

_____ 8. When I hear the word *biology*, I have a feeling of dislike.

_____ 9. I approach biology with a feeling of hesitation.

_____ 10. I really like biology.

_____ 11. I have always enjoyed studying biology in school.

_____ 12. It makes me nervous to even think about doing a biology experiment.

_____ 13. I feel at ease in biology and like it very much.

_____ 14. I feel a definite positive response to biology; it's enjoyable.

Figure **3.4**

A Sample Attitude Scale

Portfolio Assessment. If your assessment plan involves determining the overall individual performance of each student, traditional or electronic portfolio assessments can help achieve your goal. Portfolios are used to assess tangible products that exemplify student accomplishments in terms of analysis, synthesis, and evaluation. A key component of portfolios is their requirement for student self-reflection on their own learning as demonstrated in the portfolio products. For example, students are asked to select a piece of work that demonstrates achievement of a learning objective and then to explain why they chose the piece and how it shows the target knowledge and skills. The reflections can be extended to develop metacognitive skills by asking the students to describe what they would do differently to improve their learning.

To use portfolios, begin by deciding between traditional or electronic formats. Then identify the types of artifacts that will demonstrate student achievement of the standards and objectives and select or develop an appropriate rating scale (as described previously). The rubrics should be given to students before they begin working on the products. The types of artifacts that a portfolio might contain include the following:

- Written documents such as poems, stories, or research papers
- Audio recordings of debates, panel discussions, or oral presentations
- Video recordings of skits, lab experiments, or 3D models
- Computer multimedia projects such as animated timelines, podcasts, or WebQuests

Traditional vs. Electronic Portfolios. Traditional portfolios are physical collections of student work, whereas electronic portfolios contain digital work. Traditional portfolios consist of paper documents, photos, video and audio recordings, or perhaps 3D models. The portfolios are often kept in large

Product Evaluation Checklist: Digital Concept Map

Name _____   Date _____

Rate the digital concept map on the basis of content and layout by checking the appropriate box.

Content	Poor	Fair	Good	Very Good	Excellent
• Key ideas are represented	☐	☐	☐	☐	☐
• Supporting ideas are logical	☐	☐	☐	☐	☐
• Information is accurate	☐	☐	☐	☐	☐
• Paraphrasing is appropriate	☐	☐	☐	☐	

Comments about the content:

Layout	Poor	Fair	Good	Very Good	Excellent
• Main idea shapes are appropriate	☐	☐	☐	☐	☐
• Supporting idea shapes are appropriate	☐	☐	☐	☐	☐
• Connecting lines are meaningful	☐	☐	☐	☐	☐
• Graphics support concepts	☐	☐	☐	☐	☐
• Use of colors is appropriate	☐	☐	☐	☐	☐
• Font is clear and easy to read	☐	☐	☐	☐	☐

Comments about the layout:

Overall Evaluation:

____ Poor
____ Fair
____ Good
____ Very Good
____ Excellent

Overall Comments:

Figure **3.5**

A Sample Product Evaluation Checklist

three-ring binders and storage boxes, which are moved from teacher to teacher as the student progresses through school. As can be imagined, over time the portfolios can become quite large and hard to manage and store.

Electronic portfolios (called **e-portfolios**), on the other hand, store all the student work as digital files. For example, any computer-generated products, such as spreadsheets, word-processed reports, or WebQuests, can be directly added to the portfolio. Student work created on paper, such as drawings, handwritten poems, or illustrated stories, can be converted into digital format with a scanner (see MyEducationKit Tutorials for "Skill-Builder Tutorial: Scanning"). By capturing actual student performance, digital audio and video are also important components of an electronic portfolio, including readings, skits or presentations, student-created 3D models, or lab experiments conducted by students. The digital format also allows students to add their self-reflections as text or audio narration.

Multimedia Product Rubric

Student's Name _____ Date _____

Category	4	3	2	1
Content	Covers topics in-depth with details and examples. Subject knowledge is excellent.	Includes essential knowledge about the topic. Subject knowledge appears to be good.	Includes essential information about the topic but there are 1–2 factual errors.	Content is minimal OR there are several factual errors.
Sources	Source information collected for all graphics, facts, and quotes. All documented in desired format.	Source information collected for all graphics, facts, and quotes. Most documented in desired format.	Source information collected for all graphics, facts, and quotes, but not documented in desired format.	Very little or no source information was collected.
Organization	Content is well organized, uses headings or bulleted lists to group related material.	Uses headings or bulleted lists to organize, but the overall organization of topics appears flawed.	Content is logically organized for the most part.	There was no clear or logical organizational structure, just lots of facts.
Requirements	All requirements are met and exceeded.	All requirements are met.	One requirement was not completely met.	More than one requirement was not completely met.
Originality	Product shows a large amount of original thought. Ideas are creative and inventive.	Product shows some original thought. Work shows new ideas and insights.	Uses other people's ideas (giving them credit), but there is little evidence of original thinking.	Uses other people's ideas, but does not give them credit.

Figure 3.6

A Sample Multimedia Selection Rubric

Source: Adapted from 4teachers.org's Rubistar http://rubistar.4teachers.org/index.php. Copyright 1995–2006 ALTEC, the University of Kansas. Funded by the U.S. Department of Education Regional Technology in Education Consortium, 1995–2005 to ALTEC (Advanced Learning Technologies in Education Consortia) at the University of Kansas, Center for Research on Learning.

Electronic portfolios can be created with specialized portfolio software, at online sites, or with combinations of basic software such as PowerPoint. Drawbacks for electronic portfolios include availability of equipment and time as well as questions of access and security. All students as well as the teacher need access to the tools. Moreover, creating e-portfolios is initially time-consuming because teachers and students need to learn how to scan, save, and format documents in a useful and appealing manner. However, once the process is mastered, e-portfolios take less time to maintain and obviously require less storage space than traditional portfolios. Security is a concern when deciding who will have access to the files among parents, principals, counselors, teachers, and other students. For some practical tips on using Google Docs as an open source software solution for e-portfolios (Figure 3.7), visit Dr. Barrett's "ePortfolios with GoogleApps" at http://sites.google.com/site/eportfolioapps/Home.

EVALUATING AND REVISING STRATEGIES, TECHNOLOGY, AND MEDIA

Evaluation also includes assessment of strategies, technology, and media. Were the instructional strategies effective?

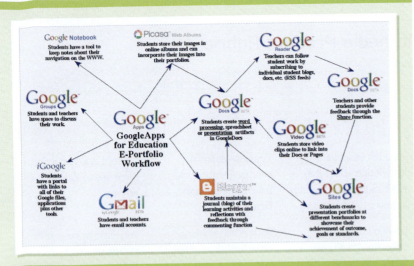

Figure **3.7**

GoogleApps

GoogleApps provides multiple tools for use with e-Portfolios.

Source: http://electronicportfolios.com/google/index.html. © 2007, Helen Barrett, Ph.D.

survey similar to Figure 3.8 can be used to collect learner comments.

You can also obtain student feedback regarding your instructional strategies and use of technology and media through discussions and interviews. For example, you may learn that students would have preferred independent study to your choice of group presentation. Or perhaps students didn't like your selection of online resources and feel they would have learned more from watching a video. Your students also may let you know, subtly or not so subtly, that your own performance left something to be desired.

Evaluation of the Teacher. A critical component of any classroom setting is the teacher, who should be evaluated along with other instructional components. Although evaluation of your teaching may evoke some apprehension, the resulting information will provide excellent feedback for addressing areas of needed improvement—and for celebrating areas of high-quality teaching. There are four basic types of teacher evaluation: self, student, peer, and administrator.

For self-evaluation, you can create an audio or video recording of your instruction that you then listen to or view at a later time while using an evaluation form such as Figure 3.9.

Could they be improved? Did the technology and media assist students in meeting the learning objectives? Were they effective in arousing student interest? Did they support meaningful student participation? A key component to the evaluation and revision of a lesson is learner input. You may solicit learner input on the effectiveness of specific media, such as a video, an activity, or on the entire lesson. A student

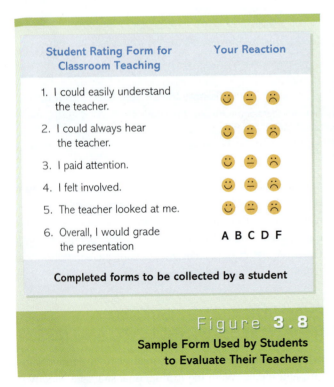

Figure **3.8**

Sample Form Used by Students to Evaluate Their Teachers

Work closely with students to obtain their reactions to specific learning activities.

Harry Cabluck/AP

Presentation Evaluation Form

Teacher _____ Evaluator _____ Date _____

SA = Strongly Agree   A = Agree   D = Disagree   SD = Strongly Disagree

1. Presenter appeared nervous.   SA   A   D   SD
    Comment ....
    ....

2. Content was delivered well.   SA   A   D   SD
    Comment ....
    ....

3. Movement enhanced presentation.   SA   A   D   SD
    Comment ....
    ....

4. Voice was natural and conversational.   SA   A   D   SD
    Comment ....
    ....

5. Vocal variety was used.   SA   A   D   SD
    Comment ....
    ....

6. Presenter could be easily heard.   SA   A   D   SD
    Comment ....
    ....

7. There were no distracting mannerisms.   SA   A   D   SD
    Comment ....
    ....

8. Eye contact was established and maintained.   SA   A   D   SD
    Comment ....
    ....

9. Natural gestures were used.   SA   A   D   SD
    Comment ....
    ....

10. Overall, presentation was well done.   SA   A   D   SD
    Comment ....
    ....

Strengths of presenter
....
....

Weaknesses of presenter
....
....

Overall comments
....
....

Figure **3.9**

Sample Instructor Evaluation Form for Self, Peer, or Administrator

Evaluate and Revise

Assessment of Learner Achievement

Tiare Ahu uses the following rating form to evaluate students' Final Year Reflections:

Reflection Rating Scale

1 = Response is minimal, primarily states facts

2 = Response is adequate, reveals moderate reflection

3 = Detailed response that demonstrates meaningful reflection

- At what level did the student write reflections for each item in question 1? "What did I learn about the following?"
  - Myself
  - Reading
  - Writing
  - Learning
  - Overall
- At what level did the student write a reflection for question 2? "What do I hope to accomplish in these areas next year when I am a sophomore?"

Technology Rating Scale

1 = Did not complete task as described

2 = Completed task as described

- Did the student use DreamWeaver software to create a new page titled "Final Year Reflections" in his or her electronic portfolio folder?
- Did the student add a written or video reflection to the "Final Year Reflections" page in their DreamWeaver electronic portfolio folder?

Evaluation of Strategies, Technology, and Media

To evaluate the strategies, technology, and media utilized, Tiare Ahu conducts debriefing activities with the students. In addition, she talks informally with students during the entire process. Ms. Ahu invites comments that address the importance of using an electronic portfolio to assess learning over time. The primary purpose of this debriefing session is to determine whether the students think creating electronic portfolios is worthwhile. In addition, they are asked to write their ideas for improving the lesson.

Revision

The students and Ms. Ahu complete a teacher-developed form for an overall evaluation of learner achievement, strategies, technology, and media. Ms. Ahu compares the student responses and overall average rating with her own perceptions. For items that appear discrepant, Tiare will address the need for revision in her choice of learning activities, technology and media selections, and evaluation materials.

Tiare Ahu shares her ideas and strategies for evaluating her ninth-grade students' electronic portfolios in the video for this chapter. Visit the Chapter 3 section of MyEducationKit to view the video of Ms. Ahu's ninth-grade English class working on their electronic portfolios.

Students, even in early grades, can provide valuable feedback through age-appropriate surveys. Students may be reluctant to "evaluate" their teacher in open-class discussions, but might share ideas in a group or submit comments anonymously.

You may ask a colleague, usually another teacher, to sit in the back of the room and observe your teaching skills. Feedback could be given in an open-ended evaluation (blank sheet of paper) or you may design a form that addresses areas for which you would like to receive feedback.

In most schools, administrators visit teachers on a scheduled sequence, often annually or semiannually. You may ask an administrator to visit more frequently on an "unofficial" basis. Many schools have a standard form that administrators use to observe teachers and provide feedback to them. You may also inform your administrator of other characteristics you would like her to observe.

Revision of Strategies, Technology, and Media. The final step of the instructional cycle is to sit back and look at your assessment and evaluation data. Examine discrepancies between your intentions and what actually happened. Did student achievement fall short on one or more of the learning objectives? How did students react to the instructional strategies, technology, and media? Are you satisfied with the value of the materials you selected?

Reflect on the lesson and each component of it. Make notes immediately following completion of the lesson, and refer to them before you implement the lesson again. If your evaluation data indicate shortcomings, now is the time to go back to the faulty part of the plan and revise it. The model works, but only if you constantly use it to upgrade the quality of your instruction (as in the ASSURE case study on p. 62).

use technology and media to support and enhance student learning. The model incorporates critical aspects of instructional planning by addressing the following questions:

- Who are your learners?
- How do your learning objectives meet the standards?
- Which strategies, technology, media, and materials will you select for your learners?
- How can you and your learners make the best use of materials?
- How will learners be involved in learning?
- How will you evaluate both the learners and your instruction?
- What revisions are needed if you implement the lesson again?

SUMMARY

This chapter introduced you to the ASSURE model and demonstrated how it can be used to plan lessons that effectively

ASSURE Lesson Template

Analyze Learners

- General Characteristics (Describe the class as a whole—age, grade, etc.)
- Entry Competencies (Describe the types of knowledge expected of the learners before instruction.)
- Learning Styles (Describe the learning style preferences of individual students.)

$\boxed{S}$tate Standards and Objectives

- List curriculum and technology standards to be achieved.
- Describe the learning objectives using the ABCD format.

$\boxed{S}$elect Strategies, Technology, Media, and Materials

- Describe the strategies, technology, media, and materials that are essential to the lesson.
- Provide rationales for selections.
- Use Selection Rubrics to evaluate the appropriateness of technology and media.

$\boxed{U}$tilize Technology, Media, and Materials

- Preview Technology, Media, and Materials (It is essential to know the technology, media, and materials prior to teaching with them.)
- Prepare Technology, Media, and Materials (Practice using the technology, media, and materials prior to the lesson.)
- Prepare the Environment (Arrange the facilities for effective use of the technology, media, and materials.)
- Prepare the Learners (Knowing what is expected of them helps ensure learner involvement in the learning.)
- Provide the Learning Experience (Provide teacher-centered and student-centered learning experiences.)

$\boxed{R}$equire Learner Participation

- Require active mental engagement by learners.
- Engage learners in practice of new knowledge or skills.
- Support learning with technology and media.
- Provide performance feedback prior to formal assessment.

$\boxed{E}$valuate and Revise

- Use traditional and authentic assessments to determine learner achievement of stated standards and objectives.
- Examine the entire instructional process and the impact of using technology and media.
- If discrepancies between learning objectives and student outcomes are identified, revise the lesson plan to address the areas of concern.

CONTINUING MY PROFESSIONAL DEVELOPMENT

Demonstrating Professional Knowledge

1. What are the primary types of criteria used to analyze learners?
2. Why are learning objectives an important aspect of lesson planning?
3. What are the four components of a well-written objective?
4. List and describe the procedures for selecting, modifying, and designing strategies, technology, and media.
5. What are the five basic steps for utilizing technology, media, and materials?
6. Describe methods of eliciting student participation when using technology and media during instruction.
7. In what ways are the techniques for evaluating student achievement, technology, media, strategies, and instruction similar and different?

Demonstrating Professional Skills

The Demonstrating Professional Skills activities in the remaining chapters are designed to address many of the International Society for Technology in Education's National Educational Technology Standards for Teachers (NETS-T) (ISTE, 2008). Items aligned to NETS-T are noted with the standard number in parentheses.

1. Write a learner analysis of your students or those you plan to teach. Describe their general characteristics, note their specific entry competencies for a topic of your choice, and discuss their learning styles. If you are not yet a teacher, you may need to do some research on students in the grade level you plan to teach.
2. Write at least five learning objectives for a lesson you might teach and assess each objective with the Objectives Checklist (Figure 3.1).
3. Select a topic you might teach that would incorporate student use of technology and develop a set of learning objectives and associated assessment instruments (including traditional and authentic assessments). (NETS-T 2.A, 2.C, & 2.D)
4. Locate a lesson, perhaps using the Internet, that does *not* provide learner practice and feedback. Design activities for the lesson that provide those elements.

Building My Professional Portfolio

An important component for continuing your professional development is the creation of a professional portfolio to demonstrate the knowledge and skills gained from this text.

- *Creating My Lesson.* Using the ASSURE model, design a lesson for a scenario from the table in Appendix A, from an example in the chapter, or use a scenario of your own design. You can do this by selecting a content area standard or topic you plan to teach. Be sure to include information about the learners, the learning objectives, and all other elements of the ASSURE model. When you have finished, reflect on the process you used and what you have learned about matching learners, content, strategies, technology, media, and materials.
- *Enhancing My Lesson.* Enhance the lesson plan you created by describing how you would meet the diverse needs of learners in your class. Specifically, describe strategies you would include for students who already possess the knowledge and skills targeted in your lesson plan. Also describe strategies, technology, and media you could integrate to assist students who have not met the lesson prerequisites or who have disabilities that impact their ability to learn. For example, how would you meet the needs of students with visual or hearing limitations, or the needs of students who are reading below or above grade level?

  Describe other types of technology and media that can be integrated into your instructional strategies for the lesson. If the lesson requires word-processed reports, you might consider having students take photos with a digital camera and make interactive presentations of their reports. Or if students use drill-and-practice software to learn multiplication facts, you could have them create their own PowerPoint electronic flashcard practice set. (NETS-T 2.A, 2.B, 2.C, 3.B, & 4.B)

- *Reflecting on My Lesson.* Reflect on the lesson you created for this chapter and on how you enhanced the lesson. Address the following in your reflections: How did use of the ASSURE model strengthen the lesson? What aspect of the ASSURE model do you consider the most critical for the lesson you created? How could your ASSURE lesson be improved? (NETS-T 4.B & 5.C)

SUGGESTED RESOURCES

Print

Arter, J., & Chappuis, J. (2006). *Creating and recognizing quality rubrics.* Portland, OR: Educational Testing Service.

Bailey, G., & Ribble, M. (2007). *Digital citizenship in schools.* Washington, DC: International Society for Technology in Education.

Bray, M., Brown, A. H., & Green, T. D. (2005). *Technology and the diverse learner: A guide to classroom practice.* Thousand Oaks, CA: Corwin.

Brooks-Young, S. J. (2009). *Making technology standards work for you* (2nd ed.). Washington, DC: International Society for Technology in Education.

Carr-Chellman, A. A. (2010). *Instructional design for teachers.* New York: Routledge.

Chapman, C., & King, R. S. (2006). *Differentiated reading and writing strategies for middle and high school classrooms: A multimedia kit for professional development.* Thousand Oaks, CA: Corwin.

Hartnell-Young, E., & Morriss, M. P. (2006). *Digital portfolios: Powerful tools for promoting professional growth and reflection.* Thousand Oaks, CA: Corwin.

Jones, S. J. (2003). *Blueprint for student success: A guide to research-based teaching practices K–12.* Thousand Oaks, CA: Corwin.

Keller, J. M. (1999). Using the ARCS motivational process in computer-based instruction and distance education. *New Directions for Teaching and Learning, 78,* 39–47.

Klein, M. S., Cook, E. W., & Richardson-Gibbs, A. M. (2001). *Strategies for including children with special needs in early childhood settings.* Florence, KY: Thomson Delmar Learning.

Mager, R. F. (2003). *How to turn learners on . . . without turning them off* (3rd ed.). Atlanta, GA: Center for Effective Performance.

O'Donoghue, J. (2006). *Technology supported learning and teaching: A staff perspective.* Hershey, PA: Information Science.

Ormrod, J. E. (2005). *Artifact case studies: Interpreting children's work and teachers' classroom strategies.* Upper Saddle River, NJ: Merrill/Prentice Hall.

Stiggins, R. J. (2005). *Student-involved classroom assessment* (4th ed.). Upper Saddle River, NJ: Merrill/Prentice Hall.

Stiggins, R. J., Arter, J., Chappuis, J., & Chappuis, S. (2004). *Classroom assessment for student learning—Doing it right, using it well.* Portland, OR: Assessment Training Institute.

Tomei, L. A. (2003). *Challenges of teaching with technology across the curriculum: Issues and solutions.* Hershey, PA: Information Science.

Walker-Tileston, D. E. (2006). *Teaching strategies for active learning: Five essentials for your teaching plan.* Thousand Oaks, CA: Corwin.

Web Links

To easily access these web links from your browser, go to the MyEducationKit for your text, then go to Chapter 3 and click on the web links.

Electronic Materials for Children and Young Adults

www.eduscapes.com

This site offers links to educational materials for a range of learners on multiple topics.

EvaluTech: Timely, Reliable, Useful, and Free Resources for Teachers

www.evalutech.sreb.org

A variety of evaluation tools for teachers are located on this site.

ISTE Wikispaces: NETS-S 2007 Implementation Wiki

http://nets-implementation.iste.wikispaces.net

This wiki hosts discussions on how to implement the 2007 NETS for Students into classroom instruction. The site provides opportunities to participate in surveys about technology integration practices and policies.

How to Do Research on the Internet

www.lib.monash.edu.au/vl/www/wwwcon.htm

This site offers detailed steps for conducting Internet-based research. It provides hints for achieving successful searches, how to evaluate the content on websites, and how to provide correct citations.

Tech & Text Teaching Techniques

www.techlearning.com/story/showArticle .jhtml?articleID=185303854

Susan Bishop offers numerous tips for using technology to teach a variety of subject areas.

Web Walkabout: Educational Resources by Subject

http://ntweb.mcps.k12.md.us/schools/travilahes/walkabout .html

This is a very useful site when looking for web-based classroom materials for a specific subject area and grade level.

Writing Educational Goals and Objectives

www.personal.psu.edu/staff/b/x/bxb11/Objectives/index.htm

Hosted by Penn State, this website provides teachers easy-to-follow guidelines for writing educational goals and objectives. The site also includes multiple examples of goals and objectives for various subject areas and grade levels.

CHAPTER FOUR

Achieving
21st Century Learning Environments

This chapter addresses ISTE NETS-T 1, 2, 3, and 5.

1. Differentiate between teacher-centered and student-centered learning strategies.

2. Compare and contrast the advantages and limitations of ten types of learning strategies.

3. Describe how to select technology and media that facilitate learning experiences.

4. Discuss the types of learning environments and settings you might encounter in PK–12 schools.

5. List the advantages and limitations of integrating free and inexpensive materials into instruction.

Goal

Understand how to select and use appropriate learning strategies, technology, media, and materials to achieve 21st century learning in different PK–12 environments.

The ASSURE Classroom Case Study for this chapter describes the instructional strategies used by teachers Lindsay Kaiser and Jena Marshall, who co-teach a fifth-grade social studies class at a school in a middle-income rural neighborhood. The students read at or above grade level and are experienced users of a variety of technology applications. Each student is equipped with a laptop with high-speed Internet access. The teachers are challenged by the students' lack of interest in U.S. history and try to address this concern by engaging students in a variety of activities about the Lewis and Clark expedition. A key activity includes designing a boat that could have been used by Lewis and Clark. The lesson begins with student pairs completing an interactive Lewis and Clark WebQuest to learn about the expedition and various "boat issues" they faced. To assist with the boat design, students conduct Internet searches to expand on information learned from the WebQuest. Students create an advertisement to sell their boat and write a letter to the president of a boat manufacturing company to seek interest in reproducing the Lewis and Clark boat. The students with the best design will receive an award.

To view the **ASSURE Classroom Case Study** *Video for this chapter, go to the MyEducationKit for your text and click on the ASSURE Video under Chapter 4 to explore how Ms. Kaiser and Ms. Marshall use strategies, technology, media, and materials to achieve 21st century learning environments.*

Throughout the chapter you will find reflection questions to relate the chapter content to the ASSURE Classroom Case Study. At the end of the chapter you will be challenged to develop your own ASSURE lesson that incorporates use of these strategies, technology, media, and materials, for a topic and grade level of your choice.

INTRODUCTION

In this chapter we explore a variety of instructional strategies and settings, such as the cooperative learning arrangement used by Ms. Kaiser and Ms. Marshall, that are foundational components of a 21st century learning environment. First we discuss important distinctions between teacher- and student-centered strategies. Next we examine 10 commonly used instructional strategies, discussing the advantages and limitations of each and offering ideas for integrating technology and media. Following that is an introduction to five learning contexts: fact-to-face, distance, blended, independent, and informal. The final section provides ideas for integrating free and inexpensive materials into instruction, their advantages and limitations, and suggestions for obtaining and evaluating them. As you will see, well-planned instructional strategies supported with appropriate technology and media not only promote student learning but also better prepare students for 21st century careers.

Figure **4.1**

21st Century Learning Environment Components

21ST CENTURY LEARNING ENVIRONMENTS

The explosion of information available in the 21st century requires teachers to create learning environments that engage this new generation of students in authentic experiences that promote increased knowledge and skills and a better understanding of the world around them. As seen in Figure 4.1, the 21st century learning environment encompasses learning strategies that are teacher-centered or student-centered; integration of technology, media, and materials to support learning; and a variety of learning contexts. We provide guidance to help you carefully plan and manage these learning environment components to ensure that students achieve the intended standards and objectives stated in the ASSURE model.

TEACHER- AND STUDENT-CENTERED STRATEGIES

This section provides information about and examples of instructional strategies proven to be successful with learners of all ages in a variety of settings. We have divided them according to **teacher-centered strategies,** those directed specifically by the teacher, and **student-centered strategies,**

those in which students are largely responsible for their own learning. In both categories, the teacher is key to the design of the instruction. What is different is the focus or orientation of the strategy.

TEACHER-CENTERED STRATEGIES

The ASSURE model, in which every letter of the acronym stands for a step in the process, helps you plan how to approach any learning situation. Once you have Analyzed the learners, Stated the standards and objectives, and Selected the different aspects of the lesson (strategies, technology, media, and materials), the next step is to Utilize strategies, technology, media, and materials. It is during the Utilize step that teacher-centered strategies are implemented. Specifically, the teachers are the "drivers" who direct the learning in very purposeful ways (see When to Use Teacher-Centered Strategies). Examples of teacher-centered strategies include presentations, demonstrations, drill-and-practice, and tutorials. It is important to ensure that teacher-centered strategies engage students in higher-order thinking and enhance learning opportunities with effective use of technology and media. For example, a teacher can demonstrate the behavior of an amoeba with a digital microscope, use an interactive whiteboard to have students collaboratively build sentences, or conduct a whole-class virtual interview with a leading scientist. Students can use "clickers" to answer teacher questions or to compete in a projected online math game that the teacher directs. See Technology for Diverse Learners to

Instructional Situation	Strategy	Potential Technology/Media
The whole class needs to learn how to conjugate verbs.	Presentation	A PowerPoint presentation that interactively shows variations of a verb by clicking on key words.
		Using Camtasia or Captivate, the teacher creates a video that includes text showing the variations of each verb and video clips of students demonstrating the action noted in the verb.
Because of safety issues, students need to observe the teacher handling chemicals for an experiment.	Demonstration	Teacher models correct use of certain types of chemicals to ensure that safety measures are addressed in the classroom setting.
		Teacher shows a YouTube video about how to safely handle the chemicals.
Students need to review and practice information learned as part of earlier instruction.	Drill-and-Practice	Teacher uses interactive whiteboard and students use "clickers" to respond to math problems.
		Drill-and-practice software is made available in a learning center for students to use during the day.
The teacher has determined from tests that several students are having difficulty with the concepts or skills associated with information taught earlier in the week.	Tutorials	Students complete free online tutorials that include practice and immediate feedback to assess learning.
		Teacher selects specific lessons on the school's integrated learning system for students to complete.
		Teacher provides links to podcasts that offer online tutorials on the topics for which students need remediation.

TECHNOLOGY for Diverse Learners

English Language Learners

Robertson (2008) offers teachers seven strategies for using technology with English language learners (ELLs) to prepare them to be 21st century learners. Although Robertson's strategies are targeted for English learners, they represent best practice that may be useful for all students, from struggling to advanced.

1. *Build vocabulary.* Introduce new technology terms based on individual needs. Use props and demonstrations to depict meanings. Check student understanding before progressing to new vocabulary.
2. *Use handouts.* Use handouts with visuals of the computer screen to assist with language barriers.
3. *Create simple assignments for beginners.* Have students work with familiar content, such as material about major cities in their countries of origin, to focus learning on the new technology skills rather than new content.
4. *Extended practice time.* Provide ELLs extra time to practice basic computer skills that may be commonplace for other students, such as using a mouse or basic commands like Save, Print, and Copy/Paste. The extra time is needed because the students have to translate software language as well as learn how to use the technology.
5. *Use pair and group work.* When English learners and native English speakers are paired to learn technology skills, the ELLs not only build English language skills but may also assist their partners to learn different ways to complete technology tasks.
6. *Establish meaningful goals.* Focus technology projects on new technology skills and on improving English literacy skills. Plainly outline the technology project criteria, such as number of slides, photos, and hyperlinks in a presentation, as well as providing clear expectations for subject area content.
7. *Teach students to consider the source.* Some English learners may come from cultures with limited access to information, creating a susceptibility to believing online information. Teachers can assist by preparing students to evaluate information for accuracy and relevance to their needs.

learn about specific instructional strategies to assist English language learners (ELL) students.

STUDENT-CENTERED STRATEGIES

Student-centered strategies occur during the Require learner participation step of the ASSURE model. With student-centered strategies, teachers serve as facilitators who offer guidance as students engage in interactive learning activities and experiences that are directed by the students. Current curriculum and technology standards emphasize the importance of engaging students in authentic, hands-on student-centered

activities. The theory base supporting student-centered strategies suggests that learning is enhanced when students are actively engaged in meaningful activities (Marzano, Pickering, & Pollock, 2001). These activities often involve student decision making to create a model, solve a problem, or win a game, individually or in a cooperative group (see When to Use Student-Centered Strategies). Examples of student-centered strategies include discussion, cooperative learning, games, simulation, discovery, and problem solving. Although students appear to "drive" their learning, teachers are responsible for planning and facilitating the arrangements that put students at the center of learning.

WHEN to USE Student-Centered Strategies

Instructional Situation	Strategy	Potential Technology/Media
Students are learning about a specific topic and the teacher has presented them with questions to answer.	Discussion	Teacher posts question to online discussion board. Teacher projects PowerPoint slide showing the discussion questions.
The teacher seeks to increase student learning by having them work cooperatively to research, share, evaluate, and synthesize new content into a group product that demonstrates their learning.	Cooperative Learning	Students meet using free online collaboration tools (NING, Google Docs, Social Bookmarking, etc.). Computer software (e.g., a database) lets students enter information about what they've learned together. Real objects can be used for the development of a final product.
Students review newly introduced content by playing games focused on topics related to the material.	Games	Students select from several teacher-provided links to online games related to the new topic. Student groups create digital Jeopardy games that they swap and play to see who can earn the highest scores.
The teacher recognizes that the students need to apply their knowledge or skills in a "real-world" situation.	Simulations	Computer software (e.g., Decisions, Decisions) guides the students through a situation to be resolved. The teacher selects a video that presents a situation and guiding questions for the students to apply their knowledge or skills to resolve the video situation. Students use the Internet to participate in an activity with other students in a virtual reality setting.
The teacher wants students to discover key concepts in order to instill deeper levels of understanding.	Discovery	Students create digital concept maps to discover relationships among new information. Students download weather data sets into a spreadsheet to discover how weather is predicted.
The teacher wants to challenge students into thinking about what they know and need to know about a topic.	Problem Solving	Students are provided with handheld computers to collect field data that will be compared with data collected from students in a different state. A forensic lab is created for students to use equipment and resources to "solve a crime" that the teacher has created for them.

PRESENTATION

In a **presentation,** a source tells, dramatizes, or otherwise disseminates information to learners. Information sources include the teacher, textbooks, Internet sites, audio, video, or other students. Presentations can be highly interactive, involving questions and comments among the teachers and learners as a whole class or in small groups. Technology can play a major role during a presentation, such as including a live Internet broadcast from the Orion Space Capsule, a podcast of an author reading her poetry, or a concept map of bird migration that students build on an interactive whiteboard. However, classroom presentations can also involve nontechnological support strategies, such as reading a book or giving a lecture.

ADVANTAGES

- *Present once.* You only have to present the information once for all the students.
- *Note-taking strategies.* Students can use a number of different note-taking strategies to capture the information presented.
- *Information sources.* Technology and media resources can serve as quality sources for the most current information.
- *Student presentations.* Students can present information they have learned to the whole class or a small group.

LIMITATIONS

- *Difficult for some students.* Not all students respond well to a presentation format to learn information; therefore, the lesson will need to include more than one way of presenting content (e.g., reading, listening, or viewing a video).

- *Potentially boring.* Without interaction, a presentation can be very boring. It is important to include ways to keep students interactive through questions and answers, check sheets to complete, or dialog.
- *Note-taking difficulty.* Students may need to learn how to take notes to benefit from a presentation. One solution is to provide a partially completed notes sheet to assist with note-taking skills.
- *Age appropriateness.* Younger students may have difficulty sitting for lengthy presentations, so it is important to adjust presentation time based on student age and attention level.

INTEGRATION

There are a number of technology and media resources that can enhance your presentation of information. For example, you can use an interactive whiteboard to seamlessly move from a video to a spreadsheet chart to notes recorded from student comments. PowerPoint slides are another very

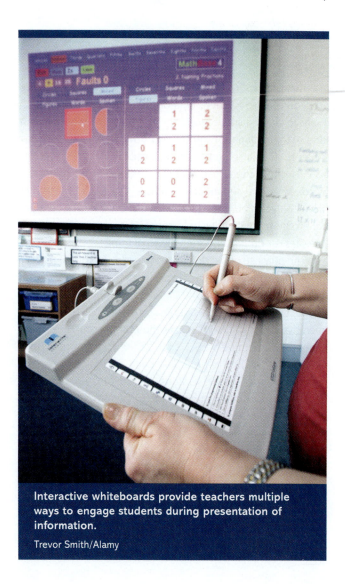

Interactive whiteboards provide teachers multiple ways to engage students during presentation of information.

Trevor Smith/Alamy

common way of presenting information that can include hyperlinks to Internet information or animated diagrams to illustrate a concept, along with summarized content and related images. Just ensure that you and your students follow copyright guidelines when adding information to presentations. Student "clickers" are technology tools that can enhance presentations by immediately displaying student responses to questions. Another way to integrate technology into a presentation is by the use of document cameras, which project printed materials and small three-dimensional objects. Examples include closely examining an old photo of a landmark, displaying a storybook as it is read, or watching the metamorphosis of a caterpillar into a butterfly.

Presentation is a core instructional strategy that has been successfully used for many generations. Today's teachers have the advantage of expanding on tried-and-true strategies by integrating technology and media to further engage students in deep-level thinking and processing to yield even higher levels of meaningful learning.

DEMONSTRATION

In a demonstration, learners view an exhibition of a skill or procedure to be learned. Demonstrations can be used with a whole class, a small group, or an individual who needs a little extra explanation on how to do a task. With younger students, teachers demonstrate basic procedures such as how to print letters, use a digital camera, or pronounce a word, whereas secondary teachers usually demonstrate more complicated processes, such as how to solve an algebra problem, read tables of historical data, create interactive websites, or understand the way something works.

The purpose of the demonstration may be for the learner to imitate a physical performance, such as using a digital wind gauge, or to adopt the attitudes exemplified by a role model, such as how to ask questions when working in cooperative groups. In some cases the point is simply to illustrate how something works, such as the effect of heat on a bimetallic strip. Just-in-time peer demonstrations often take the form of one-on-one sessions, with the experienced student showing another student how to perform a procedure, such as using the copy/paste function in a word processing program. This arrangement allows questions to be asked and answered during active learning.

ADVANTAGES

- *Seeing before doing.* Students benefit by seeing something done before having to do it themselves.

- *Task guidance.* A teacher can simultaneously guide a large group of students to complete a task.
- *Economy of supplies.* Only a limited number of supplies are necessary because not everyone will be handling all materials.
- *Safety.* As a safety feature, a demonstration allows the teacher to control the potential danger to students when using caustic materials or dangerous equipment.

LIMITATIONS

- *Not hands-on.* Students do not get direct hands-on experience unless they are following along as the teacher demonstrates steps or skills.
- *Limited view.* Every student may not have an equal view of the demonstration, thus possibly missing some aspect of the experience. A technological solution involves using a document camera to project the demonstration.
- *Nonflexible pacing.* Not all students may be able to follow the demonstration's pace of presentation. Recording the procedure on video will allow students to review the demonstration as needed.

INTEGRATION

Demonstrations can be enhanced by including technological equipment such as digital cameras. Digital video cameras can be used to record a demonstration during or before class. The recording can be viewed with the class to further examine various aspects of the demonstration or used by small groups or individuals to review the process. Students can be assigned as videographers. If more than one camera is available to record the demonstration the tapes can be merged with iMovie or MovieMaker. Creating videos is particularly effective with complex procedures or messy projects using actual objects for the demonstration.

Other types of digital equipment used during demonstrations include devices that record specific phenomena such as wind, temperature, moisture, speed, and pH, as well as magnification devices, such as digital microscopes. These devices are primarily useful in mathematics and science demonstrations in which the results are projected for whole-class or small-group viewing.

Another option involves integrating demonstrations with digital video from online sources such as YouTube. These demonstrations might include the basics of using an abacus application, how to divide integers, or how to test pond water pH. As expected, multiple examples emerge when searching for online videos, so review carefully before using them in class and remember to follow all copyright guidelines.

DRILL-AND-PRACTICE

In **drill-and-practice,** learners complete practice exercises to refresh or increase fluency in content knowledge and skills, most commonly in mathematics and language arts. Use of this strategy assumes that learners have received some instruction on the concept, principle, or procedure they are practicing. To be effective, the drill-and-practice exercises should include feedback to reinforce correct responses and to remediate errors learners might make along the way.

ADVANTAGES

- *Corrective feedback.* Students receive feedback on their responses.
- *Information chunking.* Information is presented in small chunks, allowing students to review the material in small bits.
- *Built-in practice.* Practice is built into the small chunks of information, giving immediate opportunities to try out the new knowledge in some positive way.

LIMITATIONS

- *Repetitive.* Not all students respond well to the repetitive nature of drill-and-practice. It is important to limit the time spent or number of exercises to prevent monotony.
- *Potentially boring.* Some drill-and-practice materials have too many items, which can lead to boredom. A solution is to review the content and only assign material that is relevant.
- *Nonadaptive.* If a student is making repeated errors, continued use of drill-and-practice material does not help the student learn. Keep track of student progress and use a different intervention if learning doesn't improve.

INTEGRATION

Many computer applications offer students opportunities to review information and practice their knowledge or skill while enjoying a game-like experience. Other drill-and-

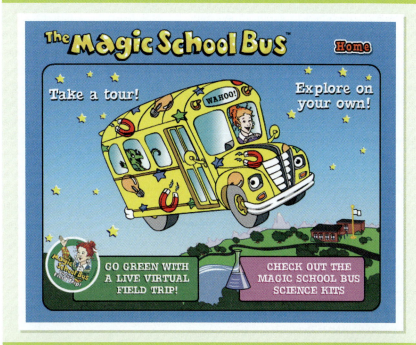

practice software titles follow more traditional approaches such as online flashcards and interactive worksheets. Digital versions of drill-and-practice are available as stand-alone software packages, like Math Blaster and Reader Rabbit, and as free interactive online programs, like the Magic School Bus series (see Figure 4.2). There are also many nondigital drill-and-practice resources with years of proven effectiveness that offer a tactile alternative to working on the computer. Most popular are items that students can use individually or in pairs, such as flashcards, word cards, and worksheets in spelling, mathematics, and language instruction.

TUTORIAL

Tutorials involve learners working with an agent—in the form of a person, computer software, or special printed materials—that presents the content, poses questions or problems, requests the learner's responses, analyzes the responses, supplies appropriate feedback, and provides practice until the learner demonstrates a predetermined level of competency. Students often work independently or one-on-one with someone as they are provided chunks of information designed to build knowledge. Students learn through practice with feedback after each small section. The difference between a tutorial and drill-and-practice is that the tutorial introduces and teaches new material, whereas the drill-and-practice focuses on content previously taught (e.g., lecture) in another type of lesson.

ADVANTAGES

- *Independent work.* Students can work independently on new material and receive feedback about their progress.
- *Self-paced.* Students can work at their own pace, repeating information if they need to review it before moving on to the next section of the material.
- *Individualization.* Computer-based tutorials respond to students' input by directing their study to new topics when content is mastered or to remediation activities when review is needed.

LIMITATIONS

- *Potentially boring.* The repetition can become boring if the tutorial follows a single pattern that lacks variation.
- *Possibly frustrating.* Students can become frustrated if they do not seem to be making progress while working on the tutorial. Care needs to be taken to assign students to tutorials that are aligned with their ability.
- *Potential lack of guidance.* The lack of a teacher's guidance can mean that a student does not move through the material effectively. To avoid this, teachers must carefully select and provide ongoing support when tutorials are used.

INTEGRATION

Tutorial arrangements include instructor-to-learner (e.g., Socratic dialog), learner-to-learner (e.g., peer-tutoring), computer-to-learner (e.g., computer-assisted tutorial software); and print-to-learner (e.g., workbook) pairings. Tutorials are often helpful for students who have difficulty working in large-group situations or who need extra assistance as they learn new material.

As a teacher providing instructor-to-learner tutoring, you can work with an individual or small group of students, guiding them carefully at their pace through the material being presented. Learner-to-learner tutoring needs oversight from the teacher to ensure the peers have clear instructions for the one-to-one sessions. Computer-to-learner tutoring is very popular in PK–12 classrooms due to the immediate,

individualized feedback such programs can provide in a patient and consistent manner. For example, **integrated learning systems (ILS),** such as SuccessMaker, NovaNet, and Plato Learning, offer computer/Internet-based instruction. A student is required to follow a **log-on** procedure, entering a specific name and password, to begin a new tutoring session or continue with a previously started session. Student progression through the tutorial is based on mastery of content. Because ILS systems can be expensive, they are typically purchased at the district rather than the school level.

Your **school media center,** a central location in the school setting, is an excellent source of tutorials. Most centers have a wide variety of tutorial formats, including computer software, audio recordings, and print that you can check out to use with students.

DISCUSSION

As a strategy, **discussion** involves the exchange of ideas and opinions among students or among students and the teacher. Available at any time during instruction in small or large groups, it is a useful way of assessing the knowledge, skills, and attitudes of a group of students before determining instructional objectives, particularly when introducing a new topic or at the beginning of the school year when the teacher is less familiar with the students. Discussion can help teachers establish the kind of rapport within the group that fosters collaborative and cooperative learning.

Discussions can be an effective way to introduce a new topic or to delve more deeply into foundational concepts. Teachers can lead discussions by introducing questions to elicit student responses or assign discussion topics to student groups. Be sure to focus questions on what you wish to have students learn. Also, use higher-level questions involving "What if . . ." and "How would . . ." statements to give students the opportunity to think about the topic or issue (Marzano, Pickering, & Pollock, 2001). When asking higher-level questions, provide ample "wait-time" for students to generate responses.

ADVANTAGES

- *Interesting.* Often more interesting for students than sitting and listening to someone tell them facts.
- *Challenging.* Can challenge students to think about the topic and apply what they already know.
- *Inclusive.* Provides opportunity for all students to speak, rather than only a few answering teacher questions.

- *Opportunity for new ideas.* Can be a way to bring in new ideas to the information presentation.

LIMITATIONS

- *Potential for limited participation.* Not all students participate, making it important for the teacher to be certain that everyone has a chance to talk.
- *Sometimes unchallenging.* Sometimes students don't learn beyond what they already know and are not challenged to extend their knowledge.
- *Difficulty level.* Some questions asked to elicit a discussion may be too difficult for students to consider based on their level of knowledge.
- *Age appropriateness.* May not be an effective strategy to use with younger students without teacher direction.

INTEGRATION

Technology-supported discussions are becoming more popular in today's classrooms as a method to extend the conversation beyond the classroom. Video-conferencing with software such as Skype allows students from two or more locations to see and hear each other during discussions. Students can also engage in online discussions that may allow others beyond the classroom to join in at certain times. Technology and media can also be used to support an in-class discussion. For example, concept-mapping software can help record key ideas and issues raised during the conversation to guide further input and archive the session.

Students in New York and the Netherlands share ideas through Skype-based discussions.

Steve Nesius/AP

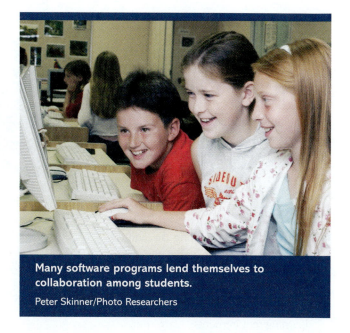

Many software programs lend themselves to collaboration among students.

Peter Skinner/Photo Researchers

COOPERATIVE LEARNING

Cooperative learning is a grouping strategy in which students work together to assist each other's learning. Research has long supported the claim that students learn from each other when they work on projects as a team (Johnson & Johnson, 1999; Slavin, 1989–1990). Two or three students at a computer terminal learn more as they work through the assigned problem together than would the students working individually.

Johnson and Johnson (1999) suggest the following conditions need to be present for successful cooperative learning groups:

- Members who view their role as part of a whole team
- Interactive engagement among the members of the group
- Both individual and group accountability
- Interpersonal and leadership skills
- The ability to reflect on personal learning and group function

You can create formal cooperative groups designed to ensure that specific learning outcomes will be accomplished (Marzano, Pickering, & Pollock, 2001). As a teacher you may wish to assign specific roles to each member of the group, such as secretary, time keeper, task director, and so on.

Cooperative learning experiences can be informal as well. Students may determine their own learning needs and work with others to enhance their learning experiences. Informal groups will need to be monitored to ensure that all students in the group benefit from the interactions.

Many educators have criticized the competitive atmosphere that dominates many classrooms and interferes with students' learning from each other. To instead allow students to gain knowledge from each other, teachers engage them in cooperative learning situations, which have the additional benefit of equipping students with the skills required for success in the 21st century world of work.

ADVANTAGES

- *Learning benefits.* Mixing the ability levels of students within a group leads to learning benefits for all.
- *Formal or informal.* Groups can be informal or formal based on the learning requirements.
- *Learning opportunity.* Long-term groups can be developed, creating multiple learning opportunities.
- *Content areas.* Cooperative learning can be used with all content areas.

LIMITATIONS

- *Size limitation.* Groups need to be kept small (three to five students) to ensure equal participation.
- *Potential overuse.* If the strategy is overused, it can lose its effectiveness. Choose cooperative learning when student learning will be enhanced from discussion and sharing ideas.
- *Group member limitation.* Grouping members of the same ability level does not enhance learning opportunities for all students. Form groups carefully to ensure that multiple levels of ability are represented.

INTEGRATION

Students can learn cooperatively not only by discussing text material and viewing media but also by producing media. For example, students can design and produce a podcast, video, or PowerPoint presentation. The teacher should be a working partner with the students in such learning situations.

If your classroom has a single computer, it is possible to establish cooperative groups to allow all students access. A team of students can easily use programs like World Hunger—Food Force (see Figure 4.3). Such software programs can accommodate cooperative grouping because of the **collaborative** or sharing nature of the experience.

You can have groups prepare presentations on topics for the rest of the class. Thus, each group becomes an expert on a portion of the total content. Preparing presentations

Figure 4.3
Food Force

World Hunger Food Force is presented by the United Nations World Food Programme (WFP) to help children learn about the fight against world hunger.
Source: www.supersmartgames.com/Big_Kids/Social_Studies/ World_Hunger-Food_Force. Reprinted by permission

requires students to achieve a higher level of mastery than can be derived from studying (see Taking a Look at Technology Integration: Westward Movement).

GAMES

Educational gaming provides a competitive environment in which learners follow prescribed rules as they strive to attain a challenging goal. Involving from one to several learners, games are highly motivating, especially for tedious and repetitive content. Games often require learners to use **problem-solving skills** in figuring out solutions or to demon-

Students take turns playing a computer game.
Valerie Schultz/Merrill

Westward Movement

Connie Courbat, a third-grade teacher, was aware of the various ability levels of her students and wanted them all to have a positive experience studying the westward movement of the 1800s. The lesson objectives were focused on helping students gain a better understanding of the impact of historical events on lifestyle choices. She introduced the topic by forming cooperative groups who used the Oregon Trail software on the one computer in her classroom to experience the adventures of a pioneer traveling the Oregon Trail. She grouped the students to ensure that all ability levels were represented within each group, thus allowing all students to benefit from the experience. Ms. Courbat was careful to establish roles for each member of the group, such as team leader, recorder, and materials manager. She moved among the groups as they worked together, helping them to address questions and ensuring that they were accomplishing the tasks. Each group gave a presentation of their travels westward, explaining their successes and failures in achieving the goal of reaching Oregon.

Corbis RF

strate mastery of specific content demanding a high degree of accuracy and efficiency.

By playing games, students begin to recognize patterns found in particular situations (Moursund, 2006). For example, young children playing a game of concentration will learn to match patterns and increase their memory recall. Older students can learn French, German, Italian, or Spanish with Leonardo's Language Bridge game, in which students are taken on a fun adventure requiring use of the new language to build virtual bridges over a variety of obstacles.

Challenging and fun to play, computer and traditional games add variety to learning experiences and offer opportunities to practice skills. Students like to play games and benefit by extending their learning experiences into challenging environments.

ADVANTAGES

- *Engaging.* Students are quickly engaged in learning through games.
- *Match to outcomes.* They can be adapted to match learning outcomes.

- *Variety of settings.* They can be used in a variety of classroom settings, from whole-class to individual activities.
- *Gain attention.* Most games are colorful, interactive, and competitive, helping to gain student attention for learning specific topics or skills.

LIMITATIONS

- *Competition concerns.* Because of the orientation to winning, games can become too competitive unless caution is used.
- *Levels of difficulty.* Less able students may find the game structure too fast or difficult. Provide alternate games to match student ability.
- *Expense.* Games such as computer games can be expensive to purchase. Often a similar game is available for free on the Web.
- *Misdirection of intention.* The learning outcomes may be lost because of the interest in winning rather than learning. Make sure to clearly state learning objectives before students use games.

INTEGRATION

The variety of games used for educational purposes includes digital or paper-based crossword puzzles, Suduko, jigsaw puzzles, and logic puzzles—sometimes called brainteasers. Puzzles can be used to practice information such as spelling words or state capitals, to build problem-solving and logic skills with Suduko puzzles, or to strengthen thinking skills with jigsaw puzzles.

One common type of instructional game involves learning about business. In PK–8 classrooms, students practice buying and selling products in a store. At middle school and high school levels, students may prepare a product, which they then market and sell to demonstrate their understanding of the world of business, as in the computer game Hot Dog Stand: The Works. The team with the highest corporate profits is the winner.

The Web offers a multitude of free games for students of all ages across core content areas from highly reputable sources. Example providers include NASA's Space Place (see Figure 4.4), Smithsonian Education, The Environmental Protection Agency's Environmental Kids Club Game Room, and PBS Kids Go! from the Public Broadcasting Service. Teachers should carefully review games prior to use to ensure that the activity supports achievement of the stated standards and objectives. Also note that students should only com-plete the game activities that are directly associated with the lesson.

SIMULATIONS

Simulation allows learners to confront a scaled-down version of a real-life situation. It permits realistic practice without the expense or risks otherwise involved. With the advent of newer technology, 3D simulations are readily available on the Web or as educational software. Simulation may also involve participant dialog and manipulation of materials and equipment.

Simulations can be used as whole-class or small-group activities, offering experiences that might not otherwise be possible in the real world. For example, students can learn about the various aspects of voting by engaging in a class election process. They can create campaign information, determine voter registration guidelines, set up voting booths, and elect a counting commission to record and report the results.

Beyond role playing, simulations can represent situations that may be too large or too complex to bring into the classroom. For example, in a science lesson about internal combustion, a teacher can use two types of simulation resources. For direct hands-on experience, she can use a small color-coded automobile engine model that students can manipulate to learn about internal combustion. Then the students can watch a 3D simulation of an engine, such as the 4-Stroke Engine Simulator, to see it in action (see Figure 4.5). By using the model engine and viewing the 3D simulation, the students are able to get the inside look they need to help them understand the concepts being presented while being protected from the hazards of operating a real engine.

Online simulations such as The Whole Frog Project (and other suggested websites in MyEducationKit) provide another type of simulated learning experience. The Whole Frog Project engages high school students in a complex study of frogs using technology such as MRI imaging to reveal digital images of internal organs they would not have access to in their classroom, allowing them to gather information about the frog's circulatory, digestive, and muscular systems.

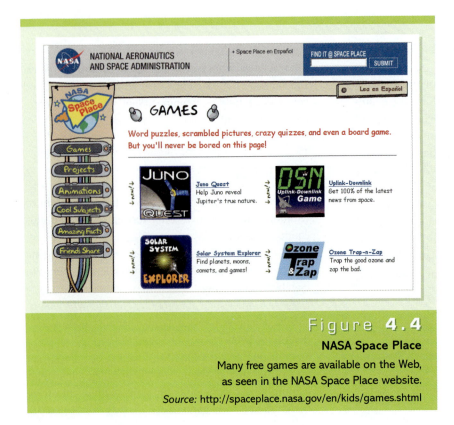

Figure 4.4

NASA Space Place

Many free games are available on the Web, as seen in the NASA Space Place website.

Source: http://spaceplace.nasa.gov/en/kids/games.shtml

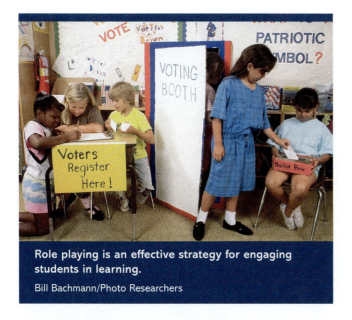

Role playing is an effective strategy for engaging students in learning.

Bill Bachmann/Photo Researchers

ADVANTAGES

- *Safety.* Provides a safe way to engage in a learning experience.
- *Recreate history.* May be the only way to engage in the situation (e.g., role-playing ancient Roman history).
- *Hands-on.* Offers opportunities for hands-on experience.
- *Variety of ability levels.* Students of all ability levels can be included in the experience.

LIMITATIONS

- *Questionable representation.* May not be truly representative of the actual event when the simulation is

an artist's rendering rather than video or photos of an event.
- *Complexity.* May become too complex or intense for the classroom setting. Review all simulations before use and only integrate relevant sections.
- *Time factor.* May require too much time to complete. Search for a model that demonstrates the concepts in a shorter time frame.

INTEGRATION

Interpersonal skills and laboratory experiments in the physical sciences are popular subjects for simulations. In some simulations learners manipulate mathematical models to determine the effect of changing certain variables, such as controlling the speed of a skier by changing the degree of incline.

Role playing is another common form of simulation. Software such as Tom Snyder's Decisions, Decisions provides roles for each member of a group, a real-life situation that needs to be resolved, and information to help members as they move along in the process. Decisions, Decisions sample topics include Ancient Empires, The Constitution, Violence in Media, and The Cold War. This software has the additional benefit of requiring only one computer in the classroom for use with a whole class.

DISCOVERY

The **discovery** strategy uses an inductive, or inquiry, approach to learning that fosters a deeper understanding of the content through the learner's involvement with it. A common approach to discovery is the "scientific method," which involves creating a hypothesis or question, trying out a possible solution, and analyzing the information learned to determine whether the approach worked. Various software applications (e.g., spreadsheets, databases, and concept-mapping applications) and digital devices (e.g., science probes and microscopes), assist students in organizing, analyzing, and reporting data and information needed to discover the answer to a question.

When using the ASSURE model or other lesson plans to design discovery lessons, ensure that the selected strategies include sufficient guidance and support when students are utilizing technology, media, and materials to solve

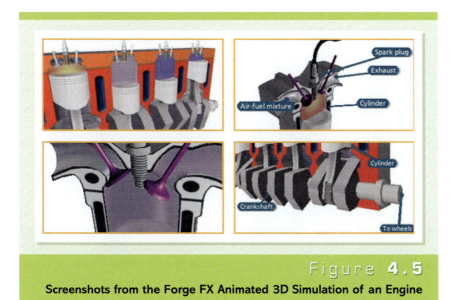

F i g u r e **4.5**

Screenshots from the Forge FX Animated 3D Simulation of an Engine
Source: Developed by ForgeFX for Pearson Prentice Hall. www.forgefx.com

LIMITATIONS

- *Time factor.* Time-consuming for design and implementation. An option is to adapt web-based discovery lessons.
- *Preparation is critical.* Requires teachers to think through all the possible issues that students might encounter. This becomes easier with practice.
- *Misunderstanding.* Can lead to misunderstandings about a content area. Make sure to debrief students after a lesson.

INTEGRATION

There are a variety of ways that instructional technology and media can help promote discovery or inquiry. For instance, students can set up a digital camera to take time-lapse photos of a plant during the day to discover that plants follow the sun or they can examine a series of GPS images of the same location on a river to discover how landscapes change over time. Students can use word processing tools to discover the reading level of well-known documents, such as the Bill of Rights and Preamble to the Constitution, or to compare excerpts from classic books to discover whether fiction is easier to read than historical biographies.

Digital video may be used for discovery teaching in the sciences by allowing the teacher to stop, enlarge, or slow down naturally occurring events to allow the development of curiosity and student questions. You will guide them by asking questions or having the students tell you what they have "discovered" or learned.

PROBLEM-BASED LEARNING

Lifelike problems can provide the starting point for learning. In the process of grappling with real-world challenges, students acquire the knowledge and skills needed for success in the 21st century. Through the use of **problem-based learning** students actively seek solutions to structured or ill-structured problems situated in the real world.

Structured problems present students with a clear sense of what might constitute an appropriate response. For example, math word problems are often structured applications of math computation skills students already possess. On the other hand, ill-structured problems can be solved in more than one way. For example, if students are asked to propose solutions to increase student participation in school recycling, multiple responses will be submitted. Because there is more than one correct way to solve the problem, tools such as rubrics will be needed to assess whether students have attained the stated objectives. See the accompanying box on the Ebola Problem

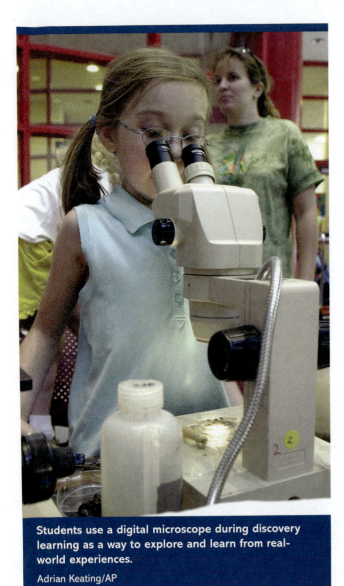

Students use a digital microscope during discovery learning as a way to explore and learn from real-world experiences.

Adrian Keating/AP

the problem. This will involve a carefully planned **scaffold** approach, building on prior knowledge as students progress through the learning experience. For instance, you will need to consider what supports will be needed if students fail to complete a step along the way as they move through the experience.

ADVANTAGES

- *Engaging.* Very engaging for students at all levels of learning.
- *Repeated steps.* Can use procedures or steps that have been taught previously.
- *Student control of learning.* Allows students the feeling of control over their own learning.

The Ebola Problem

Some high school students walked into class recently and found this memo on their desks: You are a United Nations doctor stationed in Brazzaville, Congo. When you arrived at your office this morning a message marked "Urgent" was on your desk from a tribal chieftain in a village 100 miles west of your clinic.

The message read: "Come quickly! This village has been stricken with something no one has seen before. Twenty villagers have terrible fevers, diarrhea, and have become demented. Four have already died a terrible death. The other sixteen sick people have been placed in a hut where we will keep them until you get here. Please help!"

After forming hypotheses about the possible illness and designing a data-gathering plan, students used their handheld PDAs to create an initial spreadsheet with the known data. Next, the students left their classroom and walked to a darkened room, the village hut, where they found 14 paper cutouts of people on the floor. (Yes, the discrepancy in numbers was the first problem to solve. An additional death had occurred and another person had left the hut to rejoin the general population.) On each cutout was a card that listed that person's symptoms, which were entered into the spreadsheet. With help from online medical diagnosis sites, such as virtualmedicalcentre.com, the students examined the spreadsheet information to determine what the villagers might be facing and how far the outbreak had progressed. The class reached a consensus that the village was facing an outbreak of Ebola and a case of malaria that had been mistakenly grouped with the other sick villagers. The students then developed a word-processed proposal of next steps to treat the afflicted and to prevent the outbreak from spreading.

Source: Stepien, W. J. (1999). Consortium for Problem-Based Learning, Northern Illinois University. Retrieved from http://ed.fnal.gov/trc_new/tutorial.

San Diego Union Tribune/Zuma/Newscom

for an excellent example of problem-based learning in which technology is used to reach a solution.

Jonassen, Howland, Marra and Crismond (2008) suggest that technology becomes an "intellectual partner" with students by engaging and supporting them during problem-based learning. The technology provides the environment and tools students use to access, manipulate, and display information. The processes require students to use cognitive learning strategies and critical-thinking skills.

ADVANTAGES

- *Engaging.* Students are actively engaged in real-world learning experiences.
- *Context for learning.* The relationship between knowledge and skill becomes apparent as students work toward a problem solution.
- *Levels of complexity.* Introducing additional problem issues over time can control the level of problem complexity.

LIMITATIONS

- *Difficult to create.* Creating quality problems for learning can be difficult. It can help to develop problem-based lessons with other teachers and use web resources.
- *Age appropriateness.* Age and experience levels of students may require more control by the teacher.
- *Time-consuming.* Creating and using problem solving lessons can be very time-consuming. Use the ASSURE evaluation step to refine and reuse lessons.

INTEGRATION

Many computer applications are available to support problem-based learning. Software packages like The Factory Deluxe provide specific pattern design problems that start out being relatively easy but gain complexity as students progress. Cognitive mapping software such as Inspiration provides tools to graphically represent information, with links between concepts to depict relationships needed

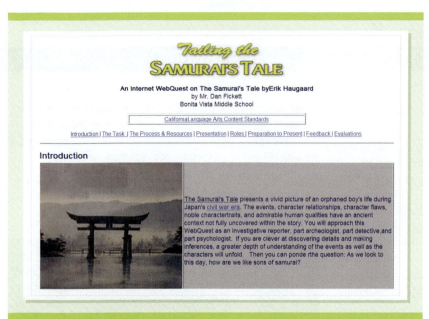

Figure **4.6**

Example of a WebQuest

This award-wining WebQuest uses The Samurai's Tale as the foundation for a problem-solving lesson.
Source: http://edtech.suhsd.k12.ca.us/inprogress/act/dfickett/japan/samuraistale.htm. Reprinted by permission of Dan Fickett.

to solve problems. Database software such as Access permits students to develop and explore data sets for answers. For example, students could create a database of U.S. presidents to provide information for the following problem statement: "What are the most common traits of U.S. presidents?"

WebQuests are structured problems that include specific steps for students to follow, identified online resources, and instructions for students to prepare a report or presentation on their solution. Numerous teacher-developed WebQuests are available on the Web, as is software for teachers who want to create their own WebQuests. Figure 4.6 presents the opening screen to The Samurai's Tale WebQuest, a problem-based lesson for high school history students.

ASSURE Case Study Reflection

Review the ASSURE Classroom Case Study and video at the beginning of the chapter. What learning strategy could Ms. Kaiser and Ms. Marshall integrate into a social studies lesson that would achieve the goal of increasing student interest in U.S. history while being exciting and fun? How could this strategy assist in achieving this goal?

LEARNING CONTEXT

There are a variety of learning strategies that address different learning contexts. The five contexts or situations most frequently encountered in PK–12 environments are (1) face-to-face classroom instruction, (2) distance learning, (3) blended instruction, (4) independent study (structured), and (5) informal study (nonstructured).

FACE-TO-FACE CLASSROOM INSTRUCTION

Although other learning contexts are gaining prominence, face-to-face instruction remains the most prevalent type of instructional setting in PK–12 schools. Because the teacher and students are in the same room, the options for learning experiences in the classroom setting, including those just covered, seem unlimited. Many of the types of technology and media you will be reading about in later chapters are easily used in the face-to-face classroom setting. For example, teachers can use student clickers to collect student opinions during lectures or use interactive whiteboards to show videos of historical events, play podcasts of mathematicians explaining how to solve a problem, or conduct live interviews with archaeologists in Egypt.

DISTANCE LEARNING

Although distance learning has been around for over 100 years, starting with correspondence study using the post office to exchange materials and assignments, recent technology innovations have made it more convenient and dynamic. Students can be in one location while other members of the class and the teacher can be at other locations. If you are invited to teach at a distance, you will need to think about the classroom as if it were divided into many little parts. When you think of it this way, you can begin to consider ways to teach in such a setting. Your students will not be in the classroom with you and may be unable to hear or see you. The instructional choices you make will depend on the technology resources available for getting materials to and from your students efficiently and effectively.

Students enjoy educational opportunities when offered via distance education.

Spencer Grant/PhotoEdit

BLENDED INSTRUCTION

As it sounds, **blended instruction** is a mix of synchronous settings (e.g., face-to-face or real-time video/television) and **asynchronous settings,** in which the teacher and students are not together at the same time. For example, high school students enrolled in a blended instruction Algebra 1 course might meet in a face-to-face classroom on Mondays and Wednesdays every other week. When not meeting in class, students use online courseware to work on assignments at times convenient for them. Students follow a schedule of due dates for uploading completed student products.

INDEPENDENT STUDY— STRUCTURED

Structured independent study is based on the idea that students can learn information and acquire skills without the teacher's direct instruction. However, you will have to prepare the independent study context, using materials you have selected or developed yourself. The Web provides unlimited access to current and archived information that extends content covered in the text. Students will be able

to work at their own pace and come to class ready to apply the knowledge.

Independent study can also occur during class through the use of learning centers. You can use a variety of technology, media, and materials, such as web resources, text, audio, video, and computer software. Or you can develop remedial materials for students who are having difficulty with the topic being taught in class.

INFORMAL STUDY— NONSTRUCTURED

Students today have many opportunities to learn from their experiences outside of the classroom. You can prepare your students to successfully engage in informal study through the application of information and communication technology (ICT) literacy skills during class activities. At the same time you can use techniques to help instil in them a love for learning and demonstrate through your own enthusiasm how to be a lifelong learner.

The nature of the study is what makes it informal. Many students seek information on the Internet and challenge themselves to learn about topics that might not be part of their in-class study. For example, student self-study may involve online discussions on how to "go green," search for information about the history of pandas after visiting the zoo, or examination of sites about earthquakes to discover why they occur. Another example of informal learning occurs when students watch television shows on the History Channel, the National Geographic Channel, or Public Broadcasting System. These experiences increase general knowledge without your directed instruction.

By selecting independent study materials, the teacher can help students achieve success.

Patrick White/Merrill

INTEGRATING FREE AND INEXPENSIVE MATERIALS

With the ever-increasing costs of instructional materials, teachers should be aware of the variety of materials they may obtain for classroom use at little or no cost. The types of free and inexpensive materials available online are almost endless. Of key importance to schools with limited technology budgets are **open source** websites that offer free productivity suites (e.g., word processing, spreadsheets, presentation software) similar to Microsoft Office and Apple iWork. Among the most popular are Google Docs and Oracle's OpenOffice.

Additionally, by connecting to websites around the world, teachers and students can acquire digital video, audio, photos, and materials. The Web also offers free collaboration tools to facilitate cooperative learning and connections with classrooms around the globe. Many teachers post lesson ideas, media, and materials for an array of subjects on the Web.

Free and inexpensive materials include all the types of media. Commonly available items include posters, games, pamphlets, brochures, reports, charts, maps, books, CDs, audio, video, multimedia kits, and real objects. The more costly items are usually sent only on a free-loan basis and must be returned to the supplier after use. In some instances, single copies of computer software, audio and video files, or DVDs will be donated to your school media center to be shared among many users.

ADVANTAGES

- *Up to date.* Free and inexpensive materials from online resources can provide current information not found in textbooks or other media.

- *In-depth treatment.* Subject-specific materials typically provide in-depth information on a topic (travel brochures).
- *Variety of uses.* Students can access open source applications outside of school. Audiovisual materials can be used for self-study or for presentation to the class. Posters, charts, and maps can be combined to create topical displays.
- *Student manipulation.* Materials that are expendable have the extra advantage of allowing learners to get actively involved with them. They can also scan printed information and visuals to import into digital products.

LIMITATIONS

- *Bias or advertising.* Many free and inexpensive materials are produced and distributed by particular organizations. These organizations, whether private corporations, nonprofit associations, or government agencies, often have a message to convey. Carefully preview materials to ensure they are appropriate for classroom use.
- *Promotion of special interests.* Some materials do not contain advertising but do promote a special interest in a less obvious way. Soliciting materials on a topic from a variety of sources can help provide different points of view.
- *Limited quantities.* With the increasing expense of producing and shipping printed materials, your supplier may limit the quantities available at one time. You may not be able to obtain a copy for every student in the class.

SOURCES FOR FREE AND INEXPENSIVE MATERIALS

There are local, state, national, and international sources for free and inexpensive materials, and many of these are now available online. Table 4.1 lists many popular sources of free educational materials.

OBTAINING FREE AND INEXPENSIVE MATERIALS

As seen in the list of sources, most classroom materials are available in a format that can easily be downloaded from the provider's website. For those resources that are not available online, you can submit your request via email, phone, fax, or mail. Some agencies may require the request to be submitted

Table 4.1 Sources of Free and Inexpensive Materials

Source	Types/Topics of Materials
Business organizations and chambers of commerce	Guest speakers and materials on entrepreneurship, investing, budgeting, and so on
Community organizations	Brochures on special interest topics (American Red Cross, the League of Women Voters, etc.)
Federal publications	Posters, charts, brochures, and books (see Figure 4.7) from the U.S. Government Printing Office (www.gpoaccess.gov) and the National Technical Information Services (www.ntis.gov)
Foreign governments	Posters, maps, travel booklets, and videos on a free-loan basis
Government agencies	Classroom materials on topics related to each service—Cooperative Extension Services (e.g., agriculture, animals, biotechnology, environment, technology); Department of Public Health (speakers, reports, brochures on health issues, public readiness for emergencies), and National Park Service (speakers, field trip planning, videos to loan, etc.)
Medical societies	Health resources such as booklets or guest speaker podcasts and information from the National Medical Association, including Tox Town audio, video, brochures, handouts, slide shows, and clip art (see Figure 4.8)
Museums	PDF copies of booklets on culture, art, how to visit a museum, lesson plans—Smithsonian, Natural History Museum, National Gallery of Art (Teaching Packets with image CDs, DVDs, videos, online interactive materials, etc.)
News broadcasters	Interview videos/audio podcasts, articles
Police and fire departments	Safety presentations and materials
Public broadcasting	Handouts, online activities, videos/audio on history, social studies, health, environment, and so on
Public libraries	Videos, prints, software, books, speakers
Utility companies	Classroom materials to teach energy conservation, going green, and safety
Weather stations	Guest speakers and materials on severe weather, the difference between climate and weather, and so on

on school letterhead and signed by your principal, such as scheduling a police officer for a guest presentation. Any student requests should include your endorsement. When ordering hard copies of materials, please ask for a preview copy before requesting multiple copies, and when possible, share the resources with other teachers. When obtaining online resources from sites with feedback options, respond with descriptions of how the materials were used along with student reactions. Be courteous, but be honest! Many suppliers attempt to improve free and inexpensive materials on the basis of user comments. When online feedback isn't possible, send a thank you note.

EVALUATING FREE AND INEXPENSIVE MATERIALS

As with any other types of material, evaluate the educational value of free and inexpensive materials critically. Some are very slick (technically well presented) but not educationally sound. Use the appropriate Selection Rubric for the type of media (web resources, videotape, etc.) you are evaluating. All the Selection Rubrics in this book have the rating criterion "Bias Free." Use it judiciously when reviewing free and inexpensive materials. To select among Selection Rubrics, view the list in MyEducationKit.

Figure 4.7

Government Printing Office

Numerous resources are available from the Government Printing Office

Source: www.gpoaccess.gov

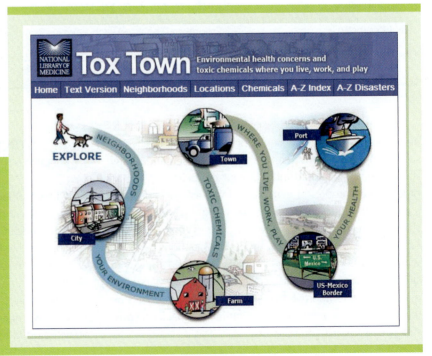

Figure 4.8

Tox Town

The National Library of Medicine's Tox Town provides an interactive experience to learn about toxic chemicals and environmental health risks as well as a suite of teacher resources (audio, video, brochures, handouts, slide shows, clip art, etc).

Source: http://toxtown.nlm .nih.gov/index.php

INTERACTIVE MULTI-TOUCH DESKS

Classrooms of the future will no longer have desks and separate laptops. Interactive multi-touch desks resemble the navigational interface used in the TV series "Star Trek." The screen serves as an individual workspace, an interactive whiteboard, and a collaboration tool for several students. Students use fingers or pens to interact with the desk and can define their own space with an icon or avatar. The desks are connected through a fully interactive classroom system, which is monitored with a teacher's console that can also be used to view student work on every screen or display example work.

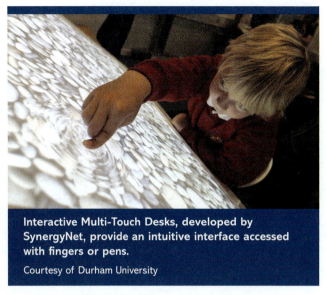

Interactive Multi-Touch Desks, developed by SynergyNet, provide an intuitive interface accessed with fingers or pens.
Courtesy of Durham University

SUMMARY

In this chapter we explored the differences between teacher-centered and student-centered instruction and discussed in detail ten commonly used instructional strategies. We included advantages and disadvantages of each and provided multiple examples for integrating the strategies into your classroom. We also emphasized how to include specific technology, media, and materials to enhance student learning. We examined five contexts for learning commonly found in PK–12 education: face-to-face classroom instruction, distance learning, blended instruction, independent study (structured), and informal study (nonstructured). The chapter ended with a discussion of the types and sources of free and expensive materials.

To check your comprehension of the content covered in Chapter 4, go to the **MyEducationKit** for your book, and complete the Study Plan for Chapter 4. Here you will be able to take a chapter quiz, receive feedback on your answers, and then access resources that will enhance your understanding of the chapter content.

ASSURE Lesson Plan

The following ASSURE Lesson Plan provides a detailed description and analysis of the lesson in the ASSURE Classroom Case Study and video at the beginning of the chapter. To review the video again, go to the MyEducationKit for your text and click on the ASSURE Video under Chapter 4. The video explores how Ms. Lindsay Kaiser and Ms. Jena Marshall implement a Lewis and Clark lesson in which fifth-grade students complete a WebQuest and design a "Lewis and Clark" boat.

Analyze Learners

General Characteristics. Ms. Kaiser and Ms. Marshall's fifth-grade students are of mixed ethnicities and from middle-income homes. They are fairly equally distributed with regard to gender and are all either 10 or 11 years old. All students are reading at or above grade level. Student behavior problems are minimal.

Entry Competencies. The fifth-grade students are, in general, able to do the following tasks required to complete the lesson activities:

- Conduct an Internet search
- Create and save word processing documents
- Create and save documents with publishing software (e.g., MS Publisher)
- Use graph paper to draw images to scale

Learning Styles. The fifth-grade students learn best when engaged in hands-on activities that are interesting and challenging. The students' level of interest and motivation increases when working as a team to win a competition. The students vary in the style with which they prefer to demonstrate their learning. For example, when creating the boat advertisement, some students prefer to write the content, whereas others choose to select and arrange photos and images to express their ideas.

State Standards and Objectives

Curriculum Standards. National Center for History in the Schools, United States Grades 5–12 Standards, Era 4 Expansion and Reform (1801–1861): Standard 1: United States territorial expansion between 1801 and 1861, and how it affected relations with external powers and Native Americans; Standard 1A: The student understands the international background and consequences of the Louisiana Purchase.

Technology Standards. National Educational Technology Standards for Students 3.B—Research and Information Fluency: Locate, organize, analyze, evaluate, synthesize, and ethically use information from a variety of sources and media.

Learning Objectives

1. Given Internet resources and drawing materials, pairs of grade 5 students will design a boat appropriate for the challenges faced by Lewis and Clark during their expedition (e.g., able to withstand rough currents while portable enough for carrying across rugged terrain).
2. Using the student-created boat design, pairs of grade 5 students will create an advertisement for their Lewis and Clark boat that clearly defines the reasons why it fulfills the requirements of suitability for the Lewis and Clark expedition.
3. Using the student-created boat design, pairs of grade 5 students will write a persuasive letter to the president of a boat manufacturing company about why their Lewis and Clark boat should be produced by the company.

Select Strategies, Technology, Media, and Materials

Select Strategies. Ms. Kaiser and Ms. Marshall select four student-centered strategies: discussion, problem solving, discovery, and cooperative learning. Examples include working in cooperative pairs to complete a WebQuest, conducting Internet searches for information on boats used by Lewis and Clark, designing the boat, creating an advertisement to sell the boat, and writing a letter to the president of a boat manufacturing company.

Select Technology and Media. This lesson involves student use of Internet-connected computers, the Lewis and Clark WebQuest, an Internet browser to locate information about boats, publishing software to create the advertisement, library resources, and word processing tools to write the letters. Students might also need access to a scanner to copy paper-based photos for their advertisements.

- *Align to standards, outcomes, objectives.* The WebQuest, Internet and library resources, and production software (publishing and word processing) provide the necessary tools for students to meet the learning objectives.
- *Accurate and current information.* Students will access multiple resources of Lewis and Clark information, which will allow the students to crosscheck content accuracy. Current information may be used for new ideas on building handmade boats with tools available at the time.
- *Age-appropriate language.* The WebQuest is written at an appropriate level for fifth-grade students. The teacher may need to assist with interpretation of some web-based resources.
- *Interest level and engagement.* The combined use of the WebQuest, the boat design, and advertisement competition will keep student interest and engagement at a high level.
- *Technical quality.* The WebQuest and production software used by the students are of high technical quality.
- *Ease of use.* The WebQuest is designed for fifth-grade students. Students can easily use word processing software; however, the publishing application may require initial training and support.
- *Bias free.* The WebQuest and production software are bias free.
- *User guide and directions.* The online help features of the WebQuest and production software are fairly easy for fifth-grade students to use. However, students most frequently will ask each other, Ms. Kaiser, or Ms. Marshall for assistance with technical difficulties.

Select Materials. Ms. Kaiser and Ms. Marshall selected the WebQuest on Lewis and Clark because it provides information needed for students to achieve the learning objectives. They met with the media specialist to create a special collection of relevant resources and preselected example websites that provide grade-appropriate Lewis and Clark information.

Utilize Technology, Media, and Materials

Preview the Technology, Media, and Materials. Ms. Kaiser and Ms. Marshall preview the WebQuest and an online bookmarking site to list relevant Internet resources.

Prepare the Technology, Media, and Materials. Ms. Kaiser and Ms. Marshall prepare the lesson instructions and rubrics for the boat design, letter, and advertisement. They add the WebQuest link and Internet resources links to Lewis and Clark information on the class webpage.

Prepare the Environment. Ms. Kaiser and Ms. Marshall check the classroom laptops to ensure the Internet connections are functional and that the publisher software is loaded on all machines. They retrieve the library cart with Lewis and Clark material and set out all instruction sheets and rubrics for the lesson.

Prepare the Learners. Ms. Kaiser and Ms. Marshall provide a brief overview of U.S. history studied up to the 1800s to provide a context for learning about the Lewis and Clark expedition. They also ask students to share personal boating experiences and projects in which they designed or built a model.

Provide the Learning Experience. Ms. Kaiser and Ms. Marshall begin the class by presenting a brief introduction to Lewis and Clark and the historical background of the time. They then present the boat competition challenge and explain how the lesson activities are structured.

Require Learner Participation

Student Practice Activities. The students in Ms. Kaiser and Ms. Marshall's class use computers, the Internet, and word processing and publishing software to complete their work assignments. Each student individually completes the Lewis and Clark WebQuest. Students then join their partners and conduct research using the Internet and resources from the library cart. The goal is to locate additional information about the Lewis and Clark boats and boat construction. This research allows students to crosscheck information learned in the WebQuest. The students use the information to design their boat, create the advertisement, and write their letter. All the activities provide opportunities for the students to engage in practice and relearning of Lewis and Clark information.

Feedback. Ms. Kaiser and Ms. Marshall provide ongoing feedback to students as they conduct Internet and library information searches, draft beginning boat designs, and write the first drafts of their letters to the boat manufacturer. Student use the rubrics (see next section) for these three products to check progress and focus of the work.

Evaluate and Revise

Assessment of Learner Achievement. Ms. Kaiser and Ms. Marshall use the rubrics to assess each team's final boat design, advertisement, and letter. The rubrics assess demonstration of content knowledge, as seen in the students' advertisements and letters and in their technology skills. Ms. Kaiser and Ms. Marshall assess these skills by evaluating the final student advertisements and letters according to the assignment criteria.

Evaluation of Strategies, Technology, and Media. Ms. Kaiser and Ms. Marshall evaluate the strategies, technology, and media. Evaluation of the lesson strategies involves reviewing the students' final products to determine the degree to which students have met the learning objectives. They also engage in continuous communication with the students to learn what is working and identify areas of needed improvement. Ms. Kaiser and Ms. Marshall regularly communicate with the school's technology support staff regarding technology upkeep and problems.

Revision. Ms. Kaiser and Ms. Marshall review the information collected from evaluation of the lesson strategies, technology, and media. The evaluation shows that the Lewis and Clark WebQuest was an excellent source of information to guide the remaining boat design activities. However, students struggled with writing the persuasive letter. Ms. Kaiser and Ms. Marshall revised the lesson to include a review and practice for writing persuasive letters.

CONTINUING MY PROFESSIONAL DEVELOPMENT

Demonstrating Professional Knowledge

1. Differentiate between teacher-centered and student-centered learning strategies.
2. Compare and contrast the advantages and limitations of ten types of learning strategies.
3. Describe how to select technology and media that facilitates learning experiences.
4. Discuss the types of learning environments and settings you might encounter in PK–12 schools.
5. List the advantages and limitations of integrating free and inexpensive materials into instruction.

Demonstrating Professional Skills

1. Develop a table that lists the ten types of instructional strategies in the first column. In the second column write a brief description of how you could use each strategy in an ASSURE lesson. (ISTE NETS-T 2.A & 2.B)
2. Using the table developed for Item 1, add a third column to the table that describes how technology can be used to support each of the ten learning experiences. (ISTE NETS-T 2.A & 2.B)
3. Design an ASSURE lesson for one of the learning contexts and settings. (ISTE NETS-T 2.A & 2.B)
4. Using the district or state curriculum guide from the grade level and subject area that you teach or plan to teach, create an annotated list of free and inexpensive resources you could integrate into your teaching and describe how you could use the resources. (ISTE NETS-T 5.C)

Building My Professional Portfolio

- *Creating My Lesson.* Using the ASSURE model, design a lesson for one of the case studies presented in the Case Study Chart in Appendix A or use a scenario of your own design. Incorporate into your lesson one or more of the instructional strategies and technology and media ideas described in this chapter. Choose a learning context appropriate for your lesson. Carefully describe the audience, the objectives, and all other elements of the ASSURE model. Be certain to match your intended outcomes to state or national curriculum and technology standards for your content area.

- *Enhancing My Lesson.* Using the lesson you created in the previous activity, consider how to meet the needs of students with varying abilities. What adaptations are needed to keep advanced learners actively engaged

while helping students who struggle with reading? What changes are needed to ensure that students transfer knowledge and skills to other learning situations? You might look for free and inexpensive resources to enhance the lesson. How can you integrate additional use of technology and media into the lesson?

- *Reflecting on My Lesson.* Reflect on the process you have used in the design of your lesson and your efforts at enhancing that lesson to meet student needs within your class. How did information from this chapter about instructional strategies, learning contexts, and free and inexpensive materials influence your lesson designing decisions? In what ways did the technology and media you selected for your lesson enhance the learning opportunities for your students?

Suggested Resources

Print

Conklin, W. (2007). *Instructional strategies for diverse learners.* Huntington Beach, CA: Teacher Created Materials.

Elementary teachers guide to free curriculum materials (67th ed.). (2010). Randolph, WI: Educators Progress Service.

Herr, N. (2008). *The sourcebook for teaching science, grades 6–12: Strategies, activities, and instructional resources.* San Francisco: Jossey-Bass/Wiley.

Hoffner, H. (2007). *The elementary teacher's digital toolbox.* Upper Saddle River, NJ: Merrill/Prentice Hall.

Lengel, J. G., & Lengel, K. M. (2006). *Integrating technology: A practical guide.* Boston: Allyn & Bacon.

Middle school teachers guide to free curriculum materials (12th ed.). (2010). Randolph, WI: Educators Progress Service.

Nash, R. (2009). *The active classroom: Practical strategies for involving students in the learning process.* Thousand Oaks, CA: Corwin.

SchifferDanoff, V. (2008). *Easy ways to reach & teach English language learners: Strategies, lessons, and tips for success with ELLs in the mainstream classroom.* New York: Scholastic.

Secondary teachers guide to free curriculum materials (119th ed.). (2010). Randolph, WI: Educators Progress Service.

Web Links

To easily access these web links from your browser, go to the MyEducationKit for your text, then go to Chapter 4 and click on the web links.

The Federal Reserve Board

www.federalreserve.gov/kids

This website is designed to inform students aged 11 to 14 about the role of the Federal Reserve Board, why it was created, and its primary responsibilities. The site includes a built-in assessment.

Leon M. Lederman Science Education Teacher Resource Center

http://ed.fnal.gov/home/educators.shtml

The U.S. Department of Energy collaborated with Fermi National Accelerator Laboratory to develop a teacher resource center. Teachers can explore a variety of mathematics and science materials developed to enhance PK–12 education.

Resources to Help ELL Students

www.mcsk12.net/SCHOOLS/peabody.es/ell.htm

This page, created by Judie Haynes, provides suggested strategies for using online activities and games to assist ELL students to increase their understanding of English and improve their language skills each time they visit a site.

The Whole Frog Project

http://froggy.lbl.gov

The U.S. Department of Commerce collaborated with a variety of publicly supported science labs across the United States to prepare instructional materials for teachers and students in science areas such as astronomy, biology, earth science, and environmental control.

Selection Rubric:
SIMULATIONS AND GAMES

 To download and complete this rubric for your own use, go to the MyEducationKit for your text, then go to Chapter 4 and click on Selection Rubrics.

Search Terms Used to Locate Resources

_____

_____

_____

Title _____

Source/Location _____

©Date _____ Cost _____

Subject Area _____ Grade Level _____

Learning experiences _____

Primary Format

_____ Simulation

_____ Game

Primary User(s)

_____ Student

_____ Teacher

Brief Description

Standards/Outcomes/Objectives

Prerequisites (e.g., prior knowledge, reading ability, vocabulary level)

Strengths

Limitations

Special Features

Name _____ Date _____

Rating Area	High Quality	Medium Quality	Low Quality
Alignment with Standards, Outcomes, and Objectives	Standards/outcomes/ objectives addressed and use of simulation or game should enhance student learning.	Standards/outcomes/ objectives partially addressed and use of simulation or game may enhance student learning.	Standards/outcomes/objectives not addressed and use of simulation or game will likely not enhance student learning.
Accurate and Current Information	Information is correct and does not contain material that is out of date.	Information is correct, but does contain material that is out of date.	Information is not correct and does contain material that is out of date.
Age-Appropriate Language	Language used is age appropriate and vocabulary is understandable.	Language used is nearly age appropriate and some vocabulary is above/below student age.	Language used is not age appropriate and vocabulary is clearly inappropriate for student age.
Interest Level and Engagement	Topic is presented so that students are likely to be interested and actively engaged in learning.	Topic is presented to interest students most of the time and engage most students in learning.	Topic is presented so as not to interest students and not engage them in learning.
Technical Quality	The material represents the best technology and media.	The material represents technology and media that are good quality, although they may not be best available.	The material represents technology and media that are not well prepared and are of very poor quality.
Ease of Use (Student or Teacher)	Material follows easy-to-use patterns with nothing to confuse the user.	Material follows patterns that are easy to follow most of the time, with a few things to confuse the user.	Material follows no patterns and most of the time the user is very confused.
Bias Free	There is no evidence of objectionable bias or advertising.	There is little evidence of bias or advertising.	There is much evidence of bias or advertising.
User Guide and Directions	The user guide is an excellent resource to support a lesson. Directions should help teachers and students use the material.	The user guide is good resource to support a lesson. Directions may help teachers and students use the material.	The user guide is poor resource to support a lesson. Directions do not help teachers and students use the material.
Practice of Relevant Skills	Much valuable practice of skills to be learned.	Some practice of skills to be learned.	Little or no practice of skills to be learned.
Game: Winning Depends on Player Actions	The actions of players determine their success in the game.	Success in the game is determined by both player actions and chance.	Winning or losing the game is determined by chance.
Simulation: Realistic, Accurate Depiction of Reality	The simulation is an accurate representation of actual situations.	There is some relationship between the simulation and actual situations.	There is little or no correlation between the simulation and the actual situations.
Clear Descriptions for Debriefing	The debriefing directions are clearly stated and easy for users to understand.	The debriefing directions are confusing for users at some points.	The debriefing directions are poorly stated and difficult for users to understand.

Recommended for Classroom Use: _____ Yes _____ No

Ideas for Classroom Use:

Engaging
Learners with Computers

Goal

Select and integrate computer resources into instruction to promote student learning.

The Chapter 5 ASSURE Classroom Case Study describes the instructional planning of Kerry Bird, an elementary teacher for nearly 30 years and one of the first in his school to embrace new technology. Kerry, who views the advent of computers as one of the biggest changes in education during his career, is currently teaching fourth grade, where he strives to integrate a variety of computer projects into instruction. He has found that student motivation and learning increase during active hands-on engagement with computers. As one of his projects, he is considering how to upgrade his presentation of the water cycle, a concept his students have struggled with. He currently teaches this process by having students create water cycle posters. He would like his students to use computers to demonstrate their understanding of the water cycle, but is not sure of the best approach.

To view the **ASSURE Classroom Case Study** *Video for this chapter, go to the MyEducationKit for your text and click on the ASSURE Video under Chapter 5 to explore how Mr. Bird decides on strategies to teach the water cycle and then chooses technology, media, and materials to achieve 21st century learning environments.*

Throughout the chapter you will find reflection questions to relate the chapter content to the ASSURE Classroom Case Study. At the end of the chapter you will be challenged to develop your own ASSURE lesson that incorporates use of these strategies, technology, media, and materials, for a topic and grade level of your choice.

INTRODUCTION

Computers have become one of the key instructional technologies in education, especially in light of what we know about the 21st century learner. The computer plays multiple roles within the curriculum, ranging from tutor to student creativity resource. Teachers can use the computer as an aid to collect student performance data as well as to manage classroom activities. To make informed choices on computer use, you need to be familiar with the various computer applications—word processing, graphics, and presentation software; games and simulations; tutorials; and teacher resources. It is extremely important to develop critical skills for appraising instructional software because there are so many available programs. The hardware, too, becomes much less intimidating when you know some of the basic technology. Whether you teach with a single computer in the classroom or a room full of them, you can learn to make optimal use of the computer to support student learning. This chapter focuses on the types of computer resources available for the classroom, as well as how to go about selecting software to support student learning. To help understand how computers operate, there is information on the components of the computer, as well as classroom setup options to optimize computer use.

USING COMPUTERS IN THE CLASSROOM

COMPUTER LITERACY

Computer literacy can be explained as the ability to use computers and technology efficiently (Wikipedia, 2009). It has also been described as skill in applying computer software to achieve desired outcomes, such as using a word processing program to write, edit, and complete a document. Computer literacy also includes knowing the components of the computer and how they operate. Part of this definition is the ability to recognize a problem and even troubleshoot the computer system if necessary.

When the International Society for Technology in Education (ISTE) first developed standards for students, they started their list of knowledge and skills with the ability to operate the equipment. In 2007, ISTE reordered the list for students and changed the importance of computer operations and concepts from the first skill to the last (ISTE, 2009). Although determining that it was still important for students to know about and be able to operate the computer efficiently, ISTE decided that knowing how to use tools to support learning was more important than being able to label the parts of a computer or select and use applications.

ISTE also developed a set of standards for teachers that parallel those for the students. The teacher standards also do not place much emphasis on the operations of the tools but rather emphasize the ability to create learning opportunities for students with computers and technology. Teachers are expected to model appropriate use of the resources and to guide students as part of their learning experiences. The decisions teachers make about applying computer resources to support learning are considered to be more important than knowledge of basic operations. This definition of computer literacy as skill in using computers to support learning will be our focus in this chapter.

STRATEGIES AND APPROACHES

Educating 21st century students has shifted from providing information to opening doors for them to explore topics and create meaningful learning experiences for themselves. Computer technology has been incorporated as a central feature of this process. The implication is that educators are moving away from the idea of school as a place to get knowledge to the view that *school is a place to learn how to learn*. The challenge for you as a teacher is to provide opportunities for all students to use technology in meaningful ways to accomplish learning tasks. This may mean selecting specific software for individual students—for example, to practice

As a tool, the computer can be useful to students in their learning.
Modern Curriculum Press/Pearson

TAKING A LOOK
AT TECHNOLOGY INTEGRATION

Testing the Waters

A school in Ann Arbor, Michigan, was being bothered by an odor from a stream in a small park next to its property. A trio of science teachers decided to integrate their classes and present students with the problem of the smelly stream. They introduced the scientific inquiry model and provided an array of technologies that could help students analyze and hypothesize. Groups worked together to investigate the source of the problem and initiated community action to alleviate it. Reorganizing the science classes and integrating technologies to successfully solve real problems demonstrated to the administration that problem-based learning is a constructive and beneficial way for students to learn.

Source: Adapted from a lesson developed by the Hi-Ce Research Group, University of Michigan, http://sitemaker.umich.edu/hice/home.

Anthony Magnacca/Merrill

math skills or to search online databases. Or it may mean changing your entire approach to a lesson. Student projects such as working on an ecology report are not new within the school curriculum, but the approach certainly can be.

You should be a model user of computer software for your students. Students will quickly notice if the teacher makes illegal copies of programs and doesn't follow copyright guidelines. Remember, actions speak louder than words (see Copyright Concerns: Computer Software). Check with your technology coordinator, library media specialist, or principal for the specific guidelines followed by your school.

Students can interact directly with the computer as part of their instructional activities in a variety of ways, from working with material presented by the computer in a controlled sequence, such as a drill-and-practice program, to a student-initiated creative activity, such as a desktop-published book of student poems. The computer can help both the teacher and students in maintaining information about their learning and in guiding instruction. That is, the computer can organize and store easily retrievable information about each student and about relevant instructional materials. Learners may take tests on the computer or input information into personal **e-portfolios** (see Chapter 3 for further discussion of e-portfolios). Computer programs can also diagnose the learning needs of students and prescribe optimal sequences of instruction for each student.

Traditionally, computers were used to reinforce classroom instruction. Software was designed to provide direct instruction or practice for students, often programmed to

branch to other segments of the lesson based on student responses. Many of these designs are still in use today. Based on the constructivist view of learning, current instructional strategies try to engage students in ways that allow them to develop, or construct, their own mental structure in a particular area of study. To engage students in this type of learning, the environment must provide them with materials that allow them to explore. Early research by Papert serves as

Students can produce their own written materials with minimal time and little computer expertise.

© Corbis RF

Copyright Concerns

Computer Software

Congress amended the Copyright Act to clear up questions of fair use of copyrighted computer programs. The changes defined the term *computer program* for copyright purposes and set forth rules on permissible and nonpermissible use of copyrighted computer software. According to the amended law, you are permitted to do the following with a single copy of a program:

- Make one backup or archival copy of the program.
- Use a "locksmith" program to bypass the copy-prevention code on the original to make the archival copy.
- Install one copy of the program onto a computer hard drive.
- Adapt a computer program from one language to another if the program is not available in the desired language.
- Add features to a copyrighted program to make better use of the program.
- Adapt a copyrighted program to meet local needs.

Without the copyright owner's permission, you are prohibited from doing the following:

- Make multiple copies of a copyrighted program.
- Make additional copies from an archival or backup copy.
- Make copies of copyrighted programs to be sold, leased, loaned, transmitted, or given away.
- Sell a locally produced adaptation of a copyrighted program.
- Make multiple copies of an adaptation of a copyrighted program even for use within a school or school district.
- Put a single copy of a program onto a network without permission or a special site license.
- Duplicate the printed copyrighted software documentation unless allowed by the copyright-holding software company.

For general information on copyright, see the copyright section on pages 13 through 15 of Chapter 1. Suggested resources (print and web links) on copyright appear at the end of Chapter 1.

the foundation for digital "microworlds," environments that permit students to freely experiment, test, and invent (Papert, 1993a,b). These environments reinforce 21st century skills by allowing students to focus on a problem area and create solutions that are meaningful to them.

Jonassen, Howland, Moore, and Marra (2003) have expanded the idea that computers can engage and support students in their learning. They have suggested that students learn from the computer environment because it encourages students to use cognitive learning strategies and critical-

Students of all ages can manage CD-ROM discs to support their learning.

Nicola Sutton/PhotoDisc/Getty

Laptop computers have changed the way people use computers. Combined with wireless technology, they have made computing truly portable.

Maria B. Vonada/Merrill

Students can enjoy books on CD-ROM.
David Young-Wolff/PhotoEdit

learning environments and to assist students in constructing their own mental models.

ADVANTAGES

- *Learner participation.* The R of the ASSURE model is achieved with computer materials because they require learners to engage in activities. These materials help to maintain students' attention.
- *Individualization.* Computer resources allow students to manage the rate and sequence of their learning, giving them more control over outcomes. High-speed personalized responses to learner actions yield immediate feedback and reinforcement.
- *Special needs.* Computer resources are effective with special learners, gifted and at-risk students, and students with diverse physical or demographic backgrounds. Their special needs can be accommodated to ensure that instruction proceeds at an appropriate pace.
- *Monitoring.* The record-keeping ability of the computer makes instruction more individualized; teachers can prepare individual lessons for all students and monitor their progress.

thinking skills. Students control how and when the computer provides them with the information they need. Part of the teacher's responsibility is to choose from among the many computer software packages available to create such

TECHNOLOGY for Diverse Learners

Computer Software

Computer applications can help with a variety of learning needs. The following examples demonstrate ways that learners can use computers to help with specific learning problems.

Students can work on improving their problem-solving abilities with The Factory Deluxe (www.Sunburst.com), software that highlights different strategies for problem solving, such as working backward, analyzing a process, and determining a sequence. Learners are given a square on the computer and four types of machines to shape it as they work through a series of levels that build their knowledge of geometric attributes in order to prepare a product. The "rotator" machine can be programmed to rotate the square from 30 to 180 degrees. The "puncher" machine can punch square or triangular holes in the square. The "striper" machine paints thin, medium, or thick stripes of various colors. And the "cutter" cuts off and discards parts that are not needed. Learners must apply problem-solving strategies in order to successfully manufacture a product with the machines.

For students with visual impairments who need to use computer software, email, or the Internet, adaptive software programs called screen readers use speech synthesizers to

read aloud the text and names of icons. Learners can navigate using the keyboard, hitting the tab button to move from icon to icon. Nontext items, such as graphics and photos, are labeled with alternative textual descriptions, called **alt-tags,** which allow learners with visual impairments to hear descriptions of these items. These software programs are available on both PC and Mac operating systems in a section of the operating software called "universal access."

Students with advanced learning skills can be challenged to put on their thinking caps and create interesting solutions by completing complex puzzles. Puzzles are an interactive way to engage students in finding alternative ways to examine an issue or problem. For example, using inquiry and imagination, students link their knowledge of facts to the resolution of the puzzles presented in the Jewel Quest game (www.iWin.com). Students are given clues along the way to help them find the golden path. And in the process students learn some information about archeology. Jewel Quest is only one of many types of puzzle-based games available to challenge students.

- *Information management.* Computer resources can cover a growing knowledge base associated with the information explosion. They can manage all types of information—text, graphic, audio, and video. More information is easily accessible by teachers and students.
- *Multisensory experiences.* Computer resources provide diverse learning experiences. These can employ a variety of instructional strategies that use audio, visual, and tactile approaches at the level of basic instruction, remediation, or enrichment.

LIMITATIONS

- *Copyright.* The ease with which software and other digital information can be duplicated without permission has inhibited some commercial publishers and private entrepreneurs from producing and marketing high-quality instructional software (see Copyright Concerns: Computer Software, p. 100).
- *High expectations.* Users, both learners and teachers, may have unrealistic expectations for computers. Many view computers as magical and expect learning to happen with little or no effort, but in reality (and as with all other learning resources) users derive benefits proportional to their investments.
- *Complex.* More advanced programs may be difficult to use, especially for student production, because they require the ability to use complex skills.
- *Lack of structure.* Students whose learning style requires more structured guidance may become frustrated. Students may also make poor decisions about how much information to explore.

INTEGRATION

The ultimate value of computers in education depends on how fully and seamlessly computers are integrated into the curriculum. The computer in the classroom is not an additional "thing" that teachers must include, but rather is integral to the support and extension of learning for all students (ISTE, 2009). Teachers need a framework for using computer technology that covers a variety of learning styles and accommodates varied teaching strategies. Most important, results need to be measurable to align with a clear set of standards and objectives—the second step in the ASSURE model. In classrooms where computer technology is integrated successfully, students use it with the same ease with which they use books, maps, pencils, and pens. In computer-rich classrooms students and teachers engage in problem solving,

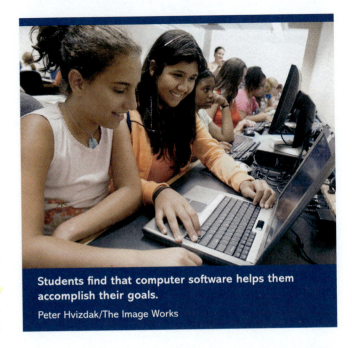

Students find that computer software helps them accomplish their goals.
Peter Hvizdak/The Image Works

cultivate creativity, collaborate globally, and discover the value of lifelong learning.

With increasing ease of use, computers are becoming more natural tools to use in problem-solving and cooperative learning strategies. Software is now available to provide students with experiences in working together to solve complex problems. Often students incorporate several different types of applications to explore a problem situation. For example, when assigned to prepare a report on ecology, a group of students might use computer databases to search for information resources to include in their report. They might send email messages to people in different locations requesting information. They might use database and spreadsheet programs to store and sort their information.

Some computer software can be valuable for tasks that must be shown rather than simply told. Printed materials and lecture cannot adequately present some instruction alone. Learners who want to interact with the instruction may need to find an appropriate software choice. Many newer versions of software now come with interactive media demonstrations. For example, The Ellis Island Experience is an interactive documentary with a wealth of information about the role this primary immigration station played in U.S. history from 1892 to 1954. Designed for middle school and high school students, the software lets them explore five modules filled with images, audio, and video to learn more about the experiences of immigrants as they entered the United States. An artifact viewer resource lets students look at images, memorabilia, and documents in detail.

TYPES OF COMPUTER RESOURCES

The computer provides virtually instantaneous response to student input, has extensive capacity to store and manipulate information, and is unmatched in its ability to serve many students simultaneously. The computer's role in instruction is to serve as a resource for rich learning experiences, giving students the power to influence the depth and direction of their learning. It has the ability to control and integrate a variety of media—still and motion pictures, graphics, and sounds, as well as text-based information. The computer can also record, analyze, and react to student responses typed on a keyboard, selected with a mouse, or activated by voice. As students begin to work with information, they find the computer resources available to them help make the process easier and more fun. Students can use the technology to gather information and to prepare materials that demonstrate their knowledge and understanding of that information.

Besides providing information, computers are also tools for creativity and communication. Because computers also allow collaborations with others around the world via social media resources, students often strive to achieve their "best" writing or productions because they can go beyond the teacher and classroom with their audiences.

Computers have become pervasive in education. Most learners have access to and are influenced by computer-based instruction.

Anthony Magnacca/PhotoEdit

Computers are used widely for word processing and desktop publishing. Most students have access to word processing programs to produce papers and assignments. Some students create multimedia projects, integrating graphics, sound, and motion for presentations to their classmates or

WHEN to USE Computers

Use when student learning will be enhanced by . . .

Guidelines	Examples
Practicing what they have just studied in class	Students who need extra help with a skill or task can play a drill-and-practice game to practice skills or reinforce their understanding.
Learning independently	A computer can be part of a kindergarten classroom learning center. Young students can complete learning tasks by using a tutorial type of activity-based software to advance their knowledge.
Creating learning opportunities for gifted students	Gifted students can be challenged to expand or enhance their learning by using more complex software programs or by extending classroom activities with challenging problems.
Working collaboratively with other students	Students can work together to navigate through instructional materials to help each other understand the information.
Reaching a student who is having difficulty in learning	Students can use the material in personally meaningful ways, navigating through the material as appropriate to their style of learning.
Challenging students to present information in a new way	Students can create their own materials to share their knowledge with others in the class or school.

other groups. Presentation software, which incorporates the computer with a digital projector, allows students to share and discuss their work.

INFORMATION

Today's students need to learn to manage information—to retrieve, sort, organize, and evaluate. For inquiry and research, students can use a **database,** a collection of related information organized for quick access to specific items. Whereas a telephone book is a printed database, computer databases are electronic file cabinets filled with information that is easily accessible in many different ways (e.g., a computer phonebook that can show telephone numbers by name or after-school activity). A database is a versatile and easy-to-learn computer tool (Figure 5.1).

Classroom Databases. Databases can be created by students. For example, students can design information sheets and questionnaires, collect data, input relevant facts, and then retrieve data in a variety of ways. The facts selected might include student information, book reports, or sample math problems. Having constructed databases as part of their research, students are better able to engage in higher-level thinking skills as they analyze and interpret the data.

Commercial Databases. Commercial databases are produced for purchase on CD-ROMs or via an Internet connection. For example, Fifty States, a database available both on disc and the Web, contains information for all the states in the United States, including data about population, the capital, geography, and economic data, as well as the state bird, flower, and tree. Larger databases are available online and may contain medical information, environmental statistics, historical data, census figures, and the like. Your school media specialist can help identify commercial databases suitable for particular areas of inquiry.

COMMUNICATION

Email Messages (Text Messages). Today's students are familiar with sending email to friends or text messages using computer instant messaging or cell phones. This type of message format is quick and easy to use. In the classroom you may wish to engage students with email messages as a means for connecting with classmates or students from a distant location (e-pals). As text messaging has taken hold of the cell phone communication industry, you may want to take some time to teach your students when to use appropriate abbreviations and when to use full-text for their messages.

Oral and Visual Messages. Communication in your class is not limited to text-based messages. You can encourage students to incorporate audio files they create with voice rather than text to enhance their communication with others. Students are very creative and can use images captured on their cell phones or digital cameras to enhance their messages or substitute for words when possible.

WORD PROCESSING AND DESKTOP PUBLISHING

Using concept-mapping programs such as Inspiration or PicoMap, which is designed for a handheld device, students can gather their ideas into concept maps (Figure 5.2). They can then begin to work those ideas into connected text from outlines generated by the concept-mapping programs. These outlines are imported into a word processing program, which makes it easy for students to edit their work. The word processor makes it possible for students to work with their ideas and to quickly make changes as they explore various ways to present them. Spelling and grammar checking are available to assist students in identifying and correcting errors in draft versions of their papers. A thesaurus helps them find the right

Record

Record entry ▶ ABC DEF

File (on disk)

Storage (disk)

Figure 5.1
Database Organization
A database is used to organize information so the user can easily sort, rank, calculate, and store it.

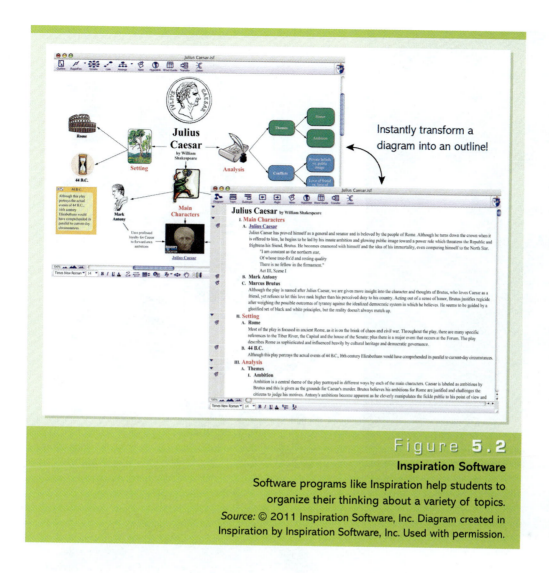

Instantly transform a diagram into an outline!

Figure 5.2

Inspiration Software

Software programs like Inspiration help students to organize their thinking about a variety of topics.

Source: © 2011 Inspiration Software, Inc. Diagram created in Inspiration by Inspiration Software, Inc. Used with permission.

word for a specific situation. Editing, a process children are not prone to enjoy, suddenly becomes easier. Students are more willing to make changes when editing is simplified.

Students enjoy putting their ideas onto paper. They especially enjoy seeing their work in finished copy. Desktop publishing allows students to design layouts that are creative and enjoyable to read. Using a desktop publishing program, students can add graphics to their pages. They can see how the pages will look before they print or publish them to the Web. Students of all ages like to produce their writings in formal documents, such as small books and newsletters. Class newsletters are also very popular, as students work together to produce a document they are proud to share with family and friends.

CREATIVITY

Graphics. Drawing and creating graphics is a fun activity for students. Computer software such as KidPix Delux can make drawing even more pleasurable. This software allows a variety of engaging effects with special tools such as a "rubber stamp" that makes noise as it marks on the screen or a "drippy" paintbrush for drawing lines that have paint drips across the screen. Another tool is one that allows users to use an eraser to clear an image on the screen to find a hidden picture behind it. Computer technology thus changes the dynamics of art for children. As students gain skill with drawing software, they can learn more complex drawing and drafting programs. High school students can use computer-aided design (CAD) and graphics programs to prepare complex visuals. Many of the skills associated with these types of software are easy for students to learn. As another example, an art program such as Photo Deluxe allows students to develop complex projects with an array of tools ranging from basic drawing tools for lines and shapes to advanced tools for editing and redesigning. They may create their own pictures or begin with commercially designed clip art available from many suppliers

Working collaboratively, students can produce school newsletters and yearbooks with desktop publishing programs.

Michael Newman/PhotoEdit

Figure **5.3**

Examples of Clip Art

Clip art can add an important visual element to student work.

(Figure 5.3). A simple picture can be developed into a very artistic piece with only a few keystrokes.

Students can use graphics software programs to manipulate digital photos they have taken to make the images more appropriate for a particular purpose. For example, students can take a photo, crop it, and then use it as a **link,** a way to connect sections of a file, or within their PowerPoint slides. They can add images to their word-processed documents as well.

Audio Resources. Many types of audio resources are available for learners to create exciting representations of their learning. For example, students can add narration to a presentation, create an audio podcast that discusses opinions on global warming, or enhance a digital story with sound effects (a closing door, footsteps, a cat purring). Students who enjoy music or have musical talent can create interesting vocal and instrumental music with such programs as GarageBand. Their musical files can be incorporated into their PowerPoint files.

PRESENTATION SOFTWARE

Presentation software has become a very popular format for teachers and students alike. With the computer connected to a digital projector, it is possible to create colorful and animated slides. Many students enjoy preparing presentations for their classmates using programs such as PowerPoint and Apple's Keynote. The software can also be used to create additional media materials, such as electronic portfolios or digital storybooks, allowing students to demonstrate their knowledge or to challenge other learners. Supervise carefully though; individuals sometimes spend more time deciding the color scheme, the transitions, or the font style than they do actually preparing the content of the presentation.

GRAPHING CALCULATORS AND SPREADSHEETS

Most computers include calculators as one of the basic tools built into the operating system, with newer computers offering graphing calculators as an option. Learners can use them to solve complex mathematical calculations, as a traditional calculator is used, but with increased power and speed. Students can also learn to use a spreadsheet program to prepare sets of data collected as part of a project (Figure 5.4). The computer can facilitate data gathering when connected to laboratory equipment. The collected data are downloaded to a spreadsheet program for data analysis and to prepare tables or graphic displays of the results.

GAMES AND SIMULATIONS

Games and simulations are instructional tools that support students in learning knowledge and skills and involve the use of problem-solving strategies and techniques. Games and simulations incorporate many good learning principles, such as interactivity, challenge, problem solving, systems thinking, distributed knowledge, and performance related to competency (Gee, 2005). In short, games and simulations provide learners with multiple opportunities to practice solving structured or ill-structured problems, engaging students in complex, higher-order thinking. Students are asked to analyze a task, determine the conditions to address that task, identify cues, and engage in self-monitoring and evaluation. Problems can be introduced to students as a way to have them practice skills in practical applications. Providing students with rich and varied problems challenges them to integrate knowledge and skills into their learning strategies

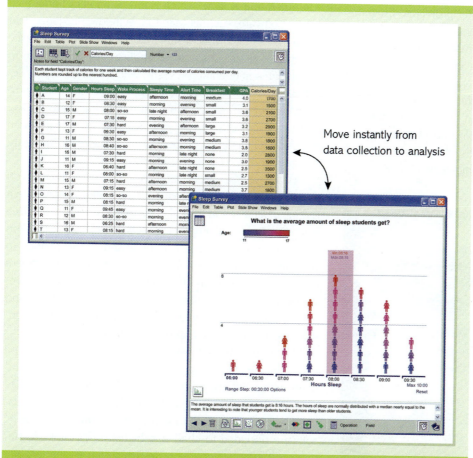

Move instantly from data collection to analysis

Figure 5.4

Example of a Spreadsheet

A spreadsheet is a page of rows and columns that displays text, numeric, and formula entries. Students can use a spreadsheet to record, average, and manipulate science data.

while engaged in a meaningful activity within a virtual world (Shaffer, Shaffer, Squire, & Gee, 2005).

COMPUTER-ASSISTED INSTRUCTION

Students benefit from practice on basic skills or knowledge. **Computer-assisted instruction (CAI)** helps students learn specific knowledge and skills. The computer serves as an easy-to-use device to reinforce classroom instruction. The variety of instructional software across all content areas is vast. Types of software range from basic drill-and-practice and tutorials to more extended and complex learning problems. For students who need review or practice, drill-and-practice programs can challenge students to remember the specific steps needed to complete a task. For example, Math Blaster Plus assists students in learning math facts (addition, subtraction, multiplication, and division) through drill-and-practice using an arcade game format, giving students the opportunity to practice what they have learned.

Software is capable of providing students with complex tasks that engage them in real-world problems. Programs such as National Inspirer ask students to engage in activities related to geography, helping them learn how geography plays an important part in the economy of any state in the United States. International versions of Inspirer cover Europe, Africa, and Asia. Video technologies can easily be incorporated, focusing attention on tangible examples of geographic occurrences and how they impact the economy. Word processing, graphics, and a host of computer software help students organize and communicate their ideas.

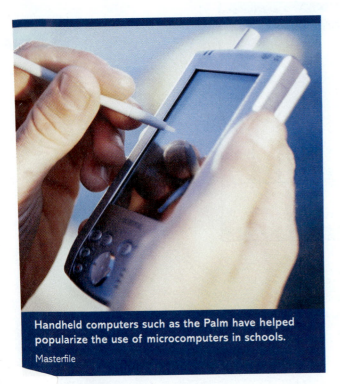

Handheld computers such as the Palm have helped popularize the use of microcomputers in schools.

Masterfile

COMPUTER-MANAGED INSTRUCTION

Use computer resources to assist you in the process of facilitating student learning. For example, you can use a mobile device, such as a Palm handheld, cell phone, or tablet computer, to collect information on how students are completing tasks. Or you can use the computer at the end of the day to assist you in preparing instructional materials such as handouts or presentations.

SOFTWARE SELECTION

There are several factors associated with selecting software (see Selection Rubric: Computer Software, pp. 122–123). It is very important to examine the software within the context of learning outcomes. Other factors that should be considered include how the software stimulates creativity, fosters collaboration, and provides feedback. You should also consider your **operating system,** which is the computer's underlying system software, such as Mac OS, Windows, or Unix, that functions as the computer's interface with the user. Specific software programs, also called **applications,** are written to run on different operating systems, which determine precisely how the user, computer, and application interact to produce the desired results. You must ensure that software you select is designed to run on your available operating system and that it will function properly with your specific hardware configuration (see Computer Hardware, p. 110).

When you are evaluating instructional software, you should consider how information is presented to be certain it is done in a clear and logical manner to ensure learning (see Selection Rubric: Computer Software, pp. 122–123). You need to examine the intent of the lesson and its relation to your intended outcomes, the curriculum, and the pertinent achievement standards. The information needs to be presented in a manner designed to maintain student interest and involvement in the learning tasks. Additional aspects to consider are accuracy, age appropriateness, and ease of use.

It is important that instructional software follows sound educational techniques and principles and also provides students with **feedback** on their efforts. In a drill-and-practice program, it is important that students have frequent informative feedback in order to improve their skills. When using software designed to challenge higher-order thinking, students will need feedback to determine the quality of their choices. If your goal is to provide students with collaborative learning opportunities, many programs are designed so that groups of students can work together to achieve the intended outcomes. Several of these types of programs are designed with the one-computer classroom in mind (see Media Sample: Computer Software).

Computer Software

Inspiration/Kidspiration

Inspiration Software, Inc.
(www.inspiration.com)

Concept-processing program. Inspiration is a software package that facilitates brainstorming, concept mapping, and planning. It creates visual diagrams of the ideas generated by an individual or a group. Use this program to create overviews, presentation visuals, and flow charts. Kidspiration is designed to help younger students develop similar skills. Once their thoughts have been visualized, both Inspiration and Kidspiration easily convert the concept map into a word processing outline.

JumpStart Math for Kindergarteners

Knowledge Adventure
(www.knowledgeadventure.com)

Tutorial program. JumpStart Math for Kindergarteners is one of a series of JumpStart software products for younger students. Using a game format, eight fundamental kindergarten math concepts based on National Council of Teachers of Mathematics standards are introduced. The goal is to help students learn critical math skills while they participate in planning activities for Guthry the Giant's surprise birthday party. In addition to making math fun for the students, a tracking and reporting system is built into the program for teachers to monitor progress and to adjust difficulty levels for individual students.

Zoombinis Mountain Rescue

K12 Software (www.k12software.com)

Problem-solving program. The lively and endearing Zoombinis jump into an exciting adventure to rescue fellow Zoombinis trapped in a mountain cave. Students help the creatures solve the logic problems they encounter along the way. The program encourages students to practice their math skills while challenging them to use logic to solve problems. An added feature is that the puzzles that must be solved are never the same, so students are always finding new adventures to follow.

Decisions, Decisions

Tom Snyder Productions
(www.tomsnyder.com)

Simulation program. Decisions, Decisions is a series of role-playing software packages designed specifically to generate informed discussion and decision making in the classroom using only one computer. The program has a mode for whole-

Mary Kate Denny/Stone/Getty

class discussion with the teacher leading the entire group, as in a traditional classroom. In addition, it offers a small-group option for managing a cooperative learning environment. Up to six small groups of students can move through the simulation, each independently directed by the computer. Titles include Substance Abuse, Violence in Media, Immigration, The Environment, and Town Government.

Magic School Bus Lands on Mars

Microsoft (www.microsoft.com)

Science discovery program. This is another in the Magic School Bus series of interactive software programs in which students must interact with the characters and the action onscreen to seek answers to questions. In this program, students learn about Mars and space exploration while they play games, drive a Mars rover around the planet, and participate in some science experiments.

Neighborhood MapMachine

Tom Snyder Productions
(www.tomsnyder.com)

Social studies program. Neighborhood MapMachine is a hands-on program in which students create and navigate community maps. While engaged in generating their maps, students learn concepts related to location, scale, distance, and compass navigation. Students can add pictures, movies, and website links to customize their community maps. In addition, students can use their writing and mathematics skills as they share the maps with others.

Sometimes software has special effects or features that may be essential for effective learning. Often, however, special effects are only window dressing that add no value to the learning. In fact, they may interfere with learning. Color, graphics, animation, and sound should be a part of quality software only if they contribute to student learning. Text should be presented in a consistent manner, using size, color, and location to reduce the cognitive burden of deciphering meaning. Keystroking and mousing techniques should be intuitive for students. The manner in which students interact with software needs to be transparent, allowing them to focus on content.

ASSURE Case Study Reflection

Review the ASSURE Classroom Case Study and video at the beginning of the chapter. What software would be appropriate for Kerry Bird's fourth-grade students to create a product that will demonstrate knowledge of the water cycle? What would be a good way for students to share materials with each other?

COMPUTER HARDWARE

Regardless of type of computer or complexity of the system, computers have a number of standard components. The physical equipment that makes up the computer is referred to as the **hardware.** A computer's specific combination of hardware components is called its *configuration*. The basic hardware components are diagrammed in Figure 5.5.

Input devices transmit information to the computer; output devices display the information to the user. The most commonly used input device is the keyboard. Others include the mouse, trackball, joystick, graphics tablet, and even voice. Both students and teachers can use graphics tablets to incorporate drawings into their programs. Science laboratory monitoring devices such as temperature probes can also be connected directly to a computer with the proper interface device.

Monitors are the standard output device. Another output device, allowing large-group viewing, is the digital projector. Connected to the computer, the digital projector can be used as part of class instruction, such as in a PowerPoint display or to show slides outlining steps for students to follow when using specific software in a computer lab.

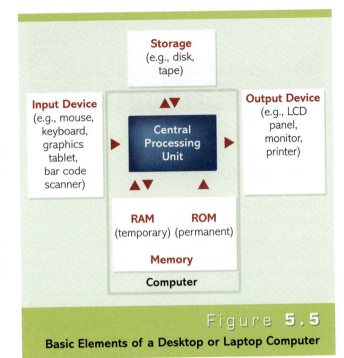

Figure **5.5**

Basic Elements of a Desktop or Laptop Computer

Computers also commonly provide output in the form of print (text or visuals), commonly called "hardcopy." Available in a range of prices and quality, printers are often combined with scanners and photocopiers, some with fax capabilities, as "all-in-one" devices.

The **central processing unit (CPU)** is the core element, or "brain," that carries out all the calculations and controls the total system. In a personal computer the CPU is one (or more) small chips (microprocessors) inside the machine.

The computer's **memory** stores information for manipulation by the CPU. The memory contains what is termed the

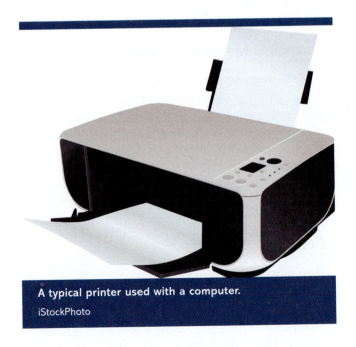

A typical printer used with a computer.
iStockPhoto

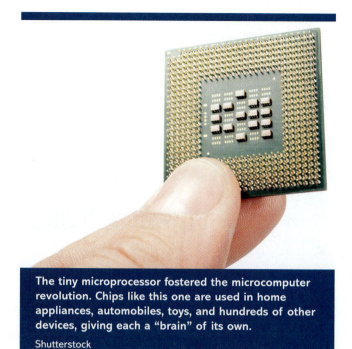

The tiny microprocessor fostered the microcomputer revolution. Chips like this one are used in home appliances, automobiles, toys, and hundreds of other devices, giving each a "brain" of its own.

Shutterstock

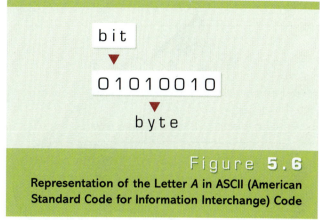

Figure 5.6

Representation of the Letter *A* in ASCII (American Standard Code for Information Interchange) Code

control function—that is, the programs written to tell the CPU what to do and in what order. In computers, control instructions and sets of data are stored in two types of memory:

- **Read-only memory (ROM).** The control instructions that have been "wired" permanently into the computer's memory make up the ROM, which the computer needs constantly, to read programming language and perform internal monitoring functions.

- **Random access memory (RAM).** The more flexible part of the memory makes up the RAM. The particular program or set of data being manipulated by the user is temporarily stored in RAM, only to be erased or transferred to storage after use to make way for the next program.

A computer's memory size is usually described in terms of how many bytes it can store at one time. A **byte** is the number of bits required to represent and store one character (letter or number) of text. A **bit** is a single unit of data, coded in binary form as either 0 (off) or 1 (on). A byte is usually made up of 8 bits of various combinations of 0s and 1s (Figure 5.6) A **kilobyte (KB)** refers to approximately 1,000 bytes (1,024 to be exact), a **megabyte (MB** or "meg") indicates 1,000 KB or approximately a million bytes, and a **gigabyte (GB** or "gig") is equal to 1,000 MB or approximately one billion bytes. Megabytes are the units used to measure the RAM storage capacity of a computer. Thus, if a computer can process 1,024,000 bytes, it is said to have 1 "meg" of memory capacity. We now talk about RAM storage in terms of **terabytes (TB),** which is a million megabytes or a trillion bytes. These more powerful

machines capable of processing more bytes simultaneously thus have more computing capacity.

A computer's memory is one of its limiting factors. You need to be sure that the computer has enough memory to run the software you will be using. If you plan to use more than one application at a time, it is recommended you have a minimum of 1 GB. Although one megabyte of memory can hold approximately 2,000 single-spaced pages of text, many graphics and animations require several megabytes to display properly. The computer's operating system, application programs, and data files are usually stored on the computer hard drive, which is inside the computer. The hard drive provides a "permanent" place within the computer for these types of programs and documents to reside. But a hard drive is vulnerable and can "crash," so it is often best to keep backups of programs and data files separately from the CPU. Recordable CD-ROMs are a common way to store programs, and recordable DVDs are also available on most machines. Storage capacity (measured in MB or GB) has expanded to keep pace with the rapidly growing memory demands of today's software and the ever-increasing size of graphics- and animation-laden data files.

High-capacity removable media devices serve as the portable storage format of choice. Usually called **removable-storage devices,** they are small, portable, and used primarily for backing up and archiving data files. **USB (universal serial bus)** is a hardware interface technology that allows the user to connect a device without having to restart the computer. A USB minidrive, sometimes called a **flash drive** (or *jump drive*), is a form of removable storage device that lets you store files in a portable unit, whose capacity can range from a few megabytes to a gigabyte or more. Some minidrives have removable flash memory cards, allowing the user to increase the memory capacity of the minidrive by changing the memory chip. This same memory chip might also fit into a digital camera or a handheld device, thus making the interchange of visual and text information very flexible. The

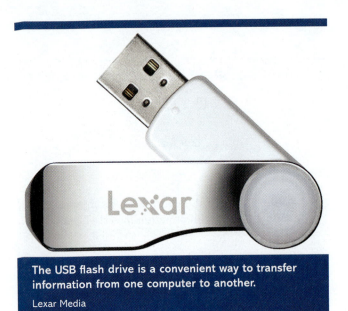

The USB flash drive is a convenient way to transfer information from one computer to another.

Lexar Media

USB minidrive does not require any special wiring and can fit into your pocket. One additional feature is its suitability for either Windows or Mac computers, permitting users to switch between platforms with ease.

Removable-storage devices have many uses, including the following:

- Archiving old files that you don't use anymore but may want to access someday
- Storing unusually large files, such as graphic images that you need infrequently
- Exchanging large files with someone
- Moving your files from one computer to another, perhaps from your desktop to your laptop computer or from your home computer to a classroom computer
- Keeping certain files separate from files on your hard disk (e.g., old test files)

CD-ROM discs can digitally store and reproduce music, verbal narration, text, or graphics. A CD-ROM can hold approximately 250,000 pages of text. An entire encyclopedia can be stored on a single CD-ROM with room to spare. A computer can find and list all page references to any topic in that encyclopedia within seconds.

Nearly all computers now have built in CD-ROM read/write drives, allowing the computer not only to read what is on a CD-ROM but also to copy data to a blank CD-R (recordable CD). Most computers are now available with DVD-R (recordable DVD) devices to play and record DVD media. DVD devices are capable of reading both DVD and CD-ROM discs. A single-layer DVD can store up to 4.7 gigabytes of data at a cost of less than a penny per megabyte

of storage. Newer high-definition (HD) DVDs can store up to 60 GB. Its vast storage capacity makes the DVD an extremely attractive medium for reference materials, multiple media applications, simulations and games, virtual reality experiences, and complex problem-solving exercises. See Table 1.1 (p. 2) for a comparison of CDs and DVDs.

ASSURE Case Study Reflection

Review the ASSURE Classroom Case Study and video at the beginning of the chapter. What hardware will be needed for students to create, save, and present their final water cycle products? What storage system would be appropriate for Kerry Bird's fourth-grade students to save the files they have created?

COMPUTER ACCESS

We have seen a trend in schools toward the multiple-computer classroom, in particular toward the use of laptop carts. In earlier days when schools had a limited number of computers, they often assembled them in a computer laboratory. As more computers became available, single computers were assigned to individual classrooms. Teachers soon discovered how to successfully use multiple computers in their classrooms. Some schools therefore dismantled the laboratories, distributing the computers to individual classrooms and increasing the number of classrooms with multiple computers.

ONE-COMPUTER CLASSROOM

In some schools access to computers is still limited. Often there is just a single computer lab where a teacher can take a whole class of students to work on computers as part of a lesson (See Taking a Look at Technology Integration: Classroom Use of a Single Computer with a Large Group). However, increased interest by many teachers in incorporating computers into lessons limits the availability of the computer lab. One solution has been to place a computer in each classroom that teacher and students can use throughout the day.

It is possible for a teacher to use a single computer in creative ways with a whole class of students. Although some

TAKING A LOOK
AT TECHNOLOGY INTEGRATION

Classroom Use of a Single Computer with a Large Group

A high school economics teacher uses a single computer with a class of 24 students, coupling the computer with a data projector that allows all students to see what is on the monitor. The teacher uses prepared computer graphics instead of overhead transparencies for key points and illustrative graphs. She can advance from one visual to the next as needed and also reveal key words from the presentation with the touch of a key.

The biggest advantage of the computer in a large-group instructional situation is its usefulness in presenting "what if" results. For example, while presenting the concepts of supply and demand, students can discuss the effect of an increase in availability of a product on its cost. Following the discussion the teacher can project the results. When the teacher puts student-suggested values into the computer, the class sees the results immediately. Economics comes alive in the classroom when years of data can be manipulated within minutes for all to see.

Ellen Senisi

software is geared for use by single students in work on specific tasks, other software is designed for group activities. For example, with the series Decisions, Decisions, groups of students interact with the computer to get specific information before they can proceed with their group activity. The students do not need to work on the computer during the entire lesson. While one group interacts with the computer, the remaining groups are working at their desks.

The one-computer classroom allows several formats for use of the equipment:

- *Large group.* With a digital projector you can demonstrate to a whole class how to use a particular software program or how to manage a particular set of data.

- *Small group.* A small group of students can work together on the computer. Each group has a turn using the software to gather or present data and then returns to their seats, allowing the next group to have their turn.

- *Learning center.* Individual students or small groups can go to a learning center anchored by the computer. By integrating a particular specific software program, you create an interactive learning center on that subject.

- *Personal assistant.* The computer can assist you with maintaining grades, communicating with parents, and preparing instructional materials.

MULTIPLE-COMPUTER CLASSROOM

Many classrooms have several computers available. This can be helpful when groups of students need to use the same software simultaneously (Figures 5.7 through 5.9). Student groups of two or three can share one computer. The teacher may also have a projection device to display information for all students on one screen.

LAPTOP CART CLASSROOM

A popular variation of the multiple-computer classroom is the mobile computer cart. Many schools provide a laptop cart as

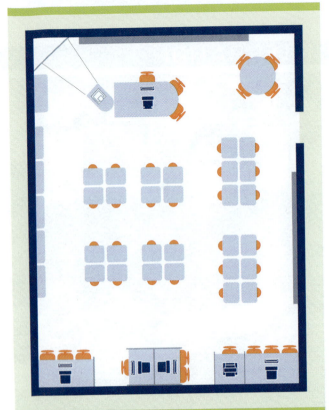

Figure **5.7**

**Elementary Classroom with Four Computers
Used for Individual and Small-Group Study**

Source: Plan developed by Interactive
Learning Systems, Inc., Cincinnati, OH.

walls of the computer lab with the monitors facing the center of the room (see Figure 5.10), allowing you to quickly see what each student is doing and respond to student questions individually. In some networks the teacher can control and monitor what is shown on each student computer.

There are advantages to using a computer lab. A group of students can be taught the same lesson simultaneously, which might be more efficient for the teacher. Also, software can be located in one place conveniently. Supervision and security are often easier when all the computers are located in a single room. Labs are often structured to facilitate ease of use by putting all the computers on one network, sharing software stored on a central server. This allows connected computers to be placed throughout the school building so students can connect to the network from the computer lab, their classrooms, or the media center.

The foremost limitation with the computer lab is access. If there are no other computers available to students outside the lab, then students will have to wait until the lab is not scheduled to use the facilities. If one class is scheduled to use the lab, the other classes will have to wait. Also, because

a way to offer multiple computers for the classroom without the major expense of installing permanent computers. The cart allows teachers access to a set of laptop computers when needed. Teachers share the cart and benefit from computers in classroom settings, rather than having to leave the classroom to go to a computer laboratory. Additionally, the carts take advantage of wireless technology, thus providing access to the Internet or to software available on the central school server.

COMPUTER LABORATORY

When a teacher wants each individual student to be working on a computer during a lesson, it is necessary for the whole class to have access to computers simultaneously. Schools often place 20 to 25 networked computers together in a single room shared by all. The computer laboratory or "lab" is appropriate if you want students to be working independently or in small groups on different programs and different activities. To monitor student activity and keep them on task, as well as preventing students from viewing inappropriate or irrelevant material, the computers can be placed around the

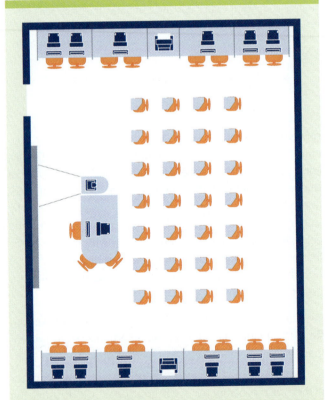

Figure **5.8**

**High School Classroom with 12 Computers
and 2 Printers Used Individually**

Source: Plan developed by Interactive
Learning Systems, Inc., Cincinnati, OH.

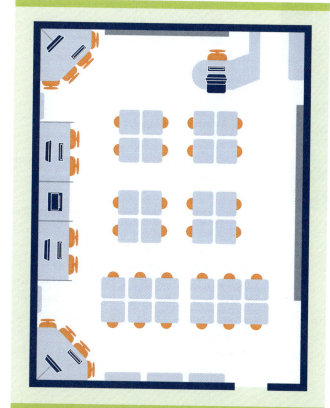

Figure 5.9
Middle School Classroom with Chairs Arranged at Computers for Collaborative Learning
Source: Plan developed by Interactive Learning Systems, Inc., Cincinnati, OH.

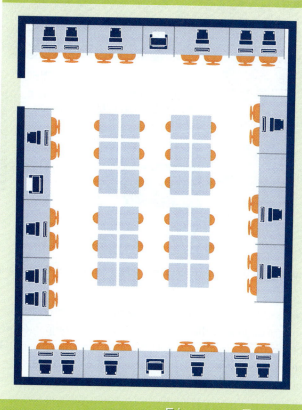

Figure 5.10
Computer Lab
Computers around the wall in a laboratory allow one teacher to monitor all student activity.

of scheduling problems, some classes may not have access to the lab at all. Creative use of school-wide networks can ease some of the congestion problems so that classroom and laptop cart computers can be connected to the resources. Thus, if the lab is not available, students can use the classroom computer or laptops from the cart to do what they needed to do in the lab.

ASSURE Case Study Reflection

PEARSON
myeducationkit™

Review the ASSURE Classroom Case Study and video at the beginning of the chapter. What type of computer access would be appropriate for Kerry Bird's fourth-grade students as they work on their product? Describe the advantages and limitations of each of his choices.

on the **HORIZON**

DIGITAL FABRICATOR
A Printer for Real Objects

3D printers or rapid prototyping machines, also known as "fabbers" (short for fabricators), are a relatively new form of computer output device that can build 3D objects by carefully depositing materials drop by drop, layer by layer. Using a geometric blueprint from a CAD program and the proper type of fast-setting liquid, you can create complex objects that would normally take special tools and skills when using conventional manufacturing techniques. A fabber can allow you to explore new designs, email physical objects to other fabber owners, and most importantly—set your ideas free.

Source: www.dimensionprinting.com. Image courtesy of Stratasys, Inc.

Traditional 3D printers are room-sized and cost thousands of dollars. As the technology improves, companies are able to make smaller printers, such as the Dimension 3D printer shown here, for school, home, or small business use. The Fab@Home digital fabricator printer is even smaller—the size of a desktop printer—and is comparable in cost to a home computer system. It uses common materials to create the three-dimensional objects. Silicon calk, fast-drying liquid resin, and even Cheez Whiz work well in the fabricator. The one thing the printer cannot print is paper! If you can imagine it, you can build it on your fabricator.

These printers are appearing in schools around the world where students are learning to use CAD programs. Now students can design their ideas with the CAD program and then

actually print or "fab" them on the spot. They can hold the object and view it from all directions, permitting 21st century learners to move literally into new dimensions of learning.

Summary

Computers are by far the most common and important instructional technology device used in education. Students can use them for active, hands-on learning experiences. The teacher can use the computer to help in collecting information about student progress in the classroom and for preparing and presenting instructional materials. Whether you have one or a few computers in your classroom, you can effectively integrate them into student learning. Many schools have computer labs; however, the trend is to make laptop carts available so that any classroom can be converted into a lab setting.

PEARSON myeducationkit™

To check your comprehension of the content covered in Chapter 5, go to the **MyEducationKit** for your book and complete the Study Plan for Chapter 5. Here you will be able to take a chapter quiz, receive feedback on your answers, and then access resources that will enhance your understanding of the chapter content.

ASSURE Lesson Plan

PEARSON myeducationkit™

The following ASSURE Lesson Plan provides a detailed description and analysis of the lesson in the ASSURE Classroom Case Study and video at the beginning of the chapter. To review the video again, go to the MyEducationKit for your text and click on the ASSURE Video under Chapter 5. The video explores how Mr. Kerry Bird implements a lesson in which fourth-grade students complete a PowerPoint project to demonstrate their knowledge of the water cycle.

Analyze Learners

General Characteristics. The students in Kerry Bird's fourth-grade class are of mixed ethnicities and from low- to middle-income homes. They are fairly equally distributed by gender and all are 9 or 10 years old. The majority of the students are reading at grade level, with four reading above grade level and three struggling with reading. Generally, the students are well behaved, but tend to become restless when required to complete traditional seatwork.

Entry Competencies. The students are, in general, able to do the following:

- Create and save PowerPoint presentations
- Locate and download digital files from the server
- Insert graphics into presentations
- Enter and edit presentation text

Learning Styles. Kerry's fourth-grade students learn best when engaged in hands-on activities. Their level of motivation increases when using computers because they can personalize their work. Some students prefer to express their creativity through written narratives or drawn images, whereas some choose to create or find existing images to express their ideas. Students' learning styles also vary in their preference for working independently or with other students.

State Standards and Objectives

Curriculum Standards. National Science Education Standards—Content Standard D: As a result of their activities in grades K–4, all students should develop an understanding of changes in earth and sky.

Technology Standards. National Educational Technology Standards for Students 3—Technology Productivity Tools: Students use technology tools to enhance learning, increase productivity, and promote creativity.

Learning Objectives

1. The students will illustrate and accurately label the four stages of the water cycle in a hand-drawn storyboard.
2. The students will create a PowerPoint presentation meeting the following criteria: contains five slides, with first slide as title slide; each slide includes a graphic, text, and sound; transitions are used between each slide; the presentation uses a design template that supports the water cycle theme. The PowerPoint presentation illustrates and provides an accurate text explanation of each of the four phases of the water cycle.
3. The students will verbally describe each of the four phases during their PowerPoint presentations of the water cycle.

Select Strategies, Technology, Media, and Materials

Select Strategies. Kerry Bird selects teacher- and student-centered strategies. The teacher-centered strategies involve a review of the water cycle process by the use of a wall poster and a student question-and-answer session. Kerry also guides students through the beginning stages of producing their water cycle storyboards to ensure they understand the process. The student-centered strategies occur in three stages. First, students complete their water cycle storyboards by writing descriptions of each phase and sketching images to illustrate the concepts. Next, students go to the computer lab to create PowerPoint presentations of the water cycle. The final strategy involves how students present their water cycle projects.

Select Technology and Media. This lesson involves student use of computers and PowerPoint software to create water cycle presentations. Kerry uses the computer lab for the lesson because each student is required to create an individual PowerPoint presentation. The lab also has a digital projector and screen for the student presentations. Students download digital photos of local areas and insert audio files of weather sounds and music to their PowerPoint presentations. Kerry uses the following guidelines to assess the appropriateness of his technology and media selections:

- *Alignment with standards, outcomes, and objectives.* PowerPoint provides the necessary tools for students to meet the learning objectives.
- *Accurate and current information.* Not applicable for the chosen technology and media.
- *Age-appropriate language.* PowerPoint is written at a somewhat advanced level for fourth-grade students; however, the icons assist with understanding.
- *Interest level and engagement.* PowerPoint provides features, such as inserting graphics and sound and personalizing backgrounds and color, that increase student interest level and engagement.
- *Technical quality.* PowerPoint has superior technical quality.
- *Ease of use.* Use of PowerPoint requires initial training and support when using some features, such as inserting graphics from a server or the Web.
- *Bias free.* PowerPoint is bias free.
- *User guide and directions.* The online help features of PowerPoint are difficult for fourth-grade students to use. Students most frequently ask each other or the teacher for assistance with technical difficulties.

Select Materials. The materials for this lesson include a color poster of the water cycle, a teacher-created storyboard, and blank drawing paper for students to produce storyboards of the water cycle. The water poster is commercially produced and was purchased with school funds.

Utilize Technology, Media, and Materials

Preview the Technology, Media, and Materials. Kerry previews the PowerPoint software to ensure it has the features needed for the lesson. He previews the water cycle poster to ensure it has content that matches the lesson standards and objectives. He also previews the digital photos saved on the school server to ensure that images accurately reflect water cycle stages.

Prepare the Technology, Media, and Materials. Kerry prepares two sets of materials for the lesson. The first is a hand-drawn storyboard of the water cycle that will serve as a model for the student products. The second is a PowerPoint presentation of the water cycle that not only serves as a model for the students, but also ensures that the planned activities are workable. In other words, students will be able to access and download files from the server, students will be able to insert and listen to audio files, and the presentations will be viewable with the digital projector.

Prepare the Environment. The lesson takes place in the classroom and the computer lab. Computers in the lab should be checked to ensure that PowerPoint software is functional and that all computers have access and can save to the school server. The projector needs to be tested to ensure that it projects clear images, is properly connected to the appropriate computer, and displays PowerPoint presentations with full functionality.

Prepare the Learners. To prepare the students, Kerry introduces the lesson and reviews the learning objectives. When in the computer lab, he reviews the basics of using PowerPoint software, downloading files from the server and operating the digital projector.

Provide the Learning Experience. The learning experience occurs in the classroom and the computer lab. It involves both teacher-centered and student-centered activities and the use of computers to produce and present student-created PowerPoint presentations of the water cycle.

R equire Learner Participation

Large-Group Activities. Kerry introduces the lesson, reviews the learning objectives, and asks students questions about the water cycle as he completes the first two stages of a "class-size" storyboard. Kerry uses the questions to check for student understanding of previously learned content.

Independent Student Activities. Following the large-group activity, the students individually complete their water cycle storyboards. Taking the storyboards to the computer lab, the students use computers and PowerPoint software to create water cycle presentations. Students produce the basic five-slide presentation and add text to each slide as it is written on their storyboards. They then review images saved on the server and select one or more for each water cycle stage. When the text and images are in place, students can add audio, change the backgrounds and color schemes, and add transitions between slides. For the final activity, students present their water cycle PowerPoint products to the class.

E valuate and Revise

Assessment of Learner Achievement. Kerry assesses learner achievement in two ways. He first assesses demonstration of content knowledge from the information in students' PowerPoint displays and in their oral narrations during the presentations. The second part of his assessment considers the technology skills shown, which Kerry assesses by evaluating the final student presentations according to the assignment criteria stated in the learning objectives: five slides, the first of which is the title slide; each slide containing a graphic, text, and sound; transitions used between each slide; presentation based on a design template that supports the water cycle theme.

Evaluation of Strategies, Technology, and Media. Kerry evaluates the water cycle lesson strategies, technology, and media by continually checking with students during lesson implementation and by also conducting a whole-class discussion of the process at the conclusion of the lesson. His goal is to determine student impressions of this use of technology and to solicit their ideas for improving the process. Also, because Kerry keeps notes for each lesson, he can review past water cycle lessons and compare the current lesson to identify strengths and weaknesses.

Revision. The evaluation reveals that the students really enjoyed creating the PowerPoint presentations but were uncomfortable presenting them to the class, primarily due to feeling unprepared and from lack of student interest in their presentation. Kerry revises the lesson by providing instruction on how to give an oral presentation. He also introduces the use of a peer evaluation form that includes student ideas about what an "excellent" presentation would include.

CONTINUING MY PROFESSIONAL DEVELOPMENT

Demonstrating Professional Knowledge

1. What are techniques for integrating computers resources in the curriculum?
2. Describe five types of software that can be used in the classroom.
3. Discuss the advantages and limitations of using computer resources in learning.
4. Discuss the differences among a one-computer classroom, a multiple-computer classroom, laptop carts, and computer laboratories in terms of setups and uses.
5. Describe an appropriate instructional situation for using computer resources to support student learning. Include the setting, topic, audience, objectives, content of the materials, and rationale for using this media format.

Demonstrating Professional Skills

1. Create a list of topics you would include if you were to conduct a one-day computer implementation workshop for teachers in your content area. (ISTE NETS-T 5.D)
2. Describe how you can use a computer resource as a learning tool within your content area. (ISTE NETS-T 2.A & 2.B)
3. Select at least five computer programs suitable for your content area. Critique each program using the Selection Rubric: Computer Software found in this chapter. (ISTE NETS-T 2.A)
4. Select a topic or standard that can be used in a classroom setting of your choice. Describe three ways to use computer software to address the diverse learning needs of students and three ways to develop students' higher-order thinking skills and creativity. (ISTE NETS-T 2.A, 2.B, & 2.C)

Building My Professional Portfolio

- *Creating My Lesson.* Using the ASSURE model, design a lesson for one of the case studies presented in the Case Study Chart in Appendix A or use a scenario of your own design. Use one of the instructional strategies described in Chapter 4 and information from this chapter related to incorporating computers into your instructional setting. Be sure to include information about the audience, the objectives, and all other elements of the ASSURE model. Be certain to match your intended outcomes to state or national learning standards for your content area. (ISTE NETS-T 2.A)

- *Enhancing My Lesson.* Using the lesson you have just designed, consider your audience again. Assume that some of your students have special needs, such as physical or learning impediments. Also assume that several students are identified as gifted. How will you adapt or change your lesson design to ensure that these students are recognized and supported to allow them to succeed in your lesson? (ISTE NETS-T 4.B)

- *Reflecting on My Lesson.* Reflect on the process you have used in the design of your lesson and your efforts at enhancing that lesson to meet student needs within your class. What have you learned about matching audience, content, instructional strategy, and materials? What could you have done to develop your students' higher-order thinking or creativity skills?

In what ways did the materials you selected for your lesson enhance the learning opportunities for your students? (ISTE NETS-T 5.C)

SUGGESTED RESOURCES

Print

Cook, A., & Hussey, S. (2007). *Assistive technologies: Principles and practice* (3rd ed.). St. Louis, MO: Mosby.

Counts, E. L. (2003). *Multimedia design and production for students and teachers.* Boston: Allyn & Bacon.

Gura, M. (2005). *Recapturing technology for education: Keeping tomorrow in today's classrooms.* Latham, MD: Scarecrow Education.

Ivers, K. S., & Barron, A. E. (2005). *Multimedia projects in education: Designing, producing, and assessing* (3rd ed.). Westport, CT: Libraries Unlimited.

O'Bannon, B., & Puckett, K. (2010). *Preparing to use technology: A practical guide to curriculum integration* (2nd ed.). Boston: Allyn & Bacon.

Roblyer, M., & Doering, A. (2010). *Integrating educational technology into teaching* (5th ed.). Boston: Allyn & Bacon.

Web Links

To easily access these web links from your browser, go to the MyEducationKit for your text, then go to Chapter 5 and click on the web links.

Awesome Library

www.awesomelibrary.org

This website provides links to resources for technology use in the classroom at all levels and for helping schools with technology decisions.

Classroom Connect

http://corporate.classroom.com

Classroom Connect provides resources and guides for professional development and technology integration to help classroom teachers and school districts.

Education World

www.education-world.com

Lesson plans, school resources, and new technology ideas are all included in Education World's site.

InTime

www.intime.uni.edu

InTime provides many different video examples of teachers using and describing technology in their teaching.

Kathy Schrock's Guide

http://school.discovery.com/schrockguide

Among the many resources for teachers is one developed by classroom teacher Kathy Schrock. This site offers classroom teachers an array of links, lesson plans, and professional development suggestions.

Selection Rubric: COMPUTER SOFTWARE

To download and complete this rubric for your own use, go to the MyEducationKit for your text, then go to Chapter 5 and click on Selection Rubrics.

Search Terms Used to Locate Resources

_____

_____

_____

Title _____

Hardware Required _____

Source/Location _____

© Date _____   Cost _____   Length _____ minutes   Primary User(s):

Subject Area _____   Grade Level _____   _____ Student

Instructional Strategies _____   _____ Teacher

Brief Description

Standards/Outcomes/Objectives

Prerequisites (e.g., prior knowledge, reading ability, vocabulary level)

Strengths

Limitations

Special Features

Name _____   Date _____

Rating Area	High Quality	Medium Quality	Low Quality
Alignment with Standards, Outcomes, and Objectives	Standards/outcomes/objectives addressed and use of software should enhance student learning.	Standards/outcomes/objectives partially addressed and use of software may enhance student learning.	Standards/outcomes/objectives not addressed and use of software will likely not enhance student learning.
Accurate and Current Information	Information is correct and does not contain material that is out of date.	Information is correct, but does contain material that is out of date.	Information is not correct and does contain material that is out of date.
Age-Appropriate Language	Language used is age appropriate and vocabulary is understandable.	Language used is nearly age appropriate and some vocabulary is above/below student age.	Language used is not age appropriate and vocabulary is clearly inappropriate for student age.
Interest Level and Engagement	Topic is presented so that students are likely to be interested and actively engaged in learning.	Topic is presented to interest students most of the time and engage most students in learning.	Topic is presented so as not to interest students and not engage them in learning.
Technical Quality	The material represents best available media.	The material represents media that are good quality, although there may be some problems using them.	The material represents media that are not well prepared and are of very poor quality.
Ease of Use (Student or Teacher)	Material follows easy-to-use patterns with nothing to confuse the user.	Material follows patterns that are easy to follow most of the time, with a few things to confuse the user.	Material follows no patterns and most of the time the user is very confused.
Bias Free	There is no evidence of objectionable bias or advertising.	There is little evidence of bias or advertising.	There is much evidence of bias or advertising.
User Guide and Directions	The user guide is an excellent resource to support a lesson. Directions should help teachers and students use the material.	The user guide is good resource to support a lesson. Directions may help teachers and students use the material.	The user guide is poor resource to support a lesson. Directions do not help teachers and students use the material.
Stimulates Creativity	Most students can use the software to create original pieces that represent learning.	Some students can use the software to start original pieces that begin to show their learning.	Most students cannot use the software to create original pieces that represent their learning.
Fosters Collaboration	Students are able to work in collaborative groups when using the software with little problem.	Students are able to work in collaborative groups when using the software most of the time.	Students are not able to work in collaborative groups when using the software.
Practice and Feedback	Software provides students with skill or knowledge practice and information that helps them complete their learning tasks.	Software provides students with some skill or knowledge practice and information that sometimes helps them complete their learning tasks.	Software does not provide students with skill or knowledge practice, nor information that helps them with their learning tasks.

Recommended for Classroom Use: _____ Yes _____ No

Ideas for Classroom Use:

CHAPTER SIX

Connecting
Learners Using Web 2.0 Tools

This chapter addresses ISTE NETS-S 1, 3, and 4.

1. Define cyberlearning and provide an example of a classroom application.

2. Describe cyberlearning literacy and discuss how it may be used in action.

3. Identify three Web 2.0 resources and demonstrate an example of how they might assist learning.

4. Explain why social networking issues are important for the classroom.

5. Identify four social–ethical issues and why they are important in working with students.

Goal

Understand the use of Web 2.0 resources to facilitate learning.

Vicki Davis is a high school technology teacher who incorporates Web 2.0 tools into her teaching. The Chapter 6 ASSURE Classroom Case Study describes the planning process she uses to create a lesson. Her primary goals are to engage her students to organize their thoughts, to communicate clearly, and to plan for the implementation of their project.

To view the ASSURE Classroom Case Study Video for this chapter, go to the MyEducationKit for your text and click on the ASSURE Video under Chapter 6 to watch how Ms. Davis decides on strategies to lead students through their discussion and sharing of ideas and then chooses technology, media, and materials to achieve 21st century learning environments.

Throughout the chapter you will find reflection questions to relate the chapter content to the ASSURE Classroom Case Study. At the end of the chapter you will be challenged to develop your own ASSURE lesson that incorporates use of these strategies, technology, media, and materials for a topic and grade level of your choice.

INTRODUCTION

Schools of the 21st century are changing. No longer are they limited to the existing structure or resources of the building. It is possible to reach beyond the school and the scheduled formal setting to create learning situations with global reach to engage the 21st century learner. **Cyberlearning** is the use of Web 2.0 networked computing and communication technologies to support learning. By dynamically integrating the Internet into instruction, cyberlearning is transforming learning opportunities while requiring new perspectives on teaching.

With Web 2.0 resources students can connect to share ideas, engage in inquiry, and search for additional information. Sometimes called **learning communities,** collaboration among students and teachers expands educational possibilities through electronic connectedness. Wagner's (2008) suggestions for improving learning opportunities outline many types of strategies that can effectively integrate web-based tools (see Chapter 4 for more details on instructional strategies).

Wagner's ideas that learners need to be engaged in experiences that frame their thinking is supported by the types of collaborative Web 2.0 resources available. Students can now engage in critical thinking and problem solving through collaborating and communicating with others and by using curiosity and imagination to explore new ideas. The **Web 2.0 tools** described in this chapter, online resources available to anyone wishing to use them, target those skills and provide students with many types of learning opportunities beyond simple information access.

CYBERLEARNING LITERACY

The ability to connect with technology tools beyond normal classroom settings depends on **cyberlearning literacy,** which is the knowledge and skills needed for successful use of Web 2.0 tools. Because students enhance their knowledge and skills by using these tools, teachers need to develop strategies for integrating cyberlearning literacy using Web 2.0 tools to provide students with learning opportunities to expand knowledge and skills and to be successful 21st century learners.

Instructional settings include formal, or organized, learning experiences for which teachers are responsible. On the other hand, **informal learning** gives students opportunities to learn from experiences outside of the classroom setting. For example, students can **surf,** or explore, websites on the Internet and find information that may be important for their formal classroom study. Because you do not assign

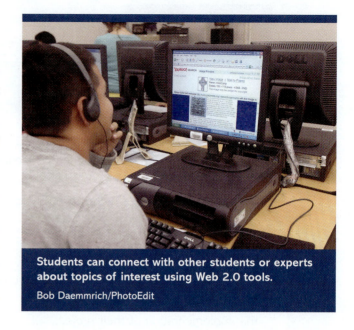

Students can connect with other students or experts about topics of interest using Web 2.0 tools.
Bob Daemmrich/PhotoEdit

this activity, this exploration becomes an informal learning experience. For instance, when students study a region of the country in social studies they can access the Internet to find a website describing the region or email someone living in that area.

Even students lacking an Internet connection at home may have access to Internet-connected computers in school media centers and libraries. And the majority of students have access to mobile technology resources through their cell phones (Johnson, Levine, & Smith, 2009). As the cell phone becomes more ubiquitous, even students from families with limited income generally have a cell phone available to them. Students learn how to seek information informally and will challenge themselves to learn about topics that might not be part of their in-class study because they find value in that type of experience.

ASSURE Case Study Reflection

PEARSON
myeducationkit™

Review the ASSURE Classroom Case Study and video at the beginning of the chapter. Consider the use of Web 2.0 Tools in helping students to organize their thoughts and communicate their ideas. How does Ms. Davis support learning through the discussion and her guidance in expressing ideas clearly? In what way is she using Web 2.0 tools to facilitate students' learning experiences?

WEB 2.0 TOOLS

Online resources that enhance student learning include audio and video, collaboration websites, mobile broadband tools, and data mashups. These types of Web 2.0 tools are organized to encourage author access and design rather than information presented in a designated framework that has been determined by someone else—for example, a website that only provides information with no opportunity for student input (Solomon & Schrum, 2007). Web 2.0 tools give learners different ways to access information and share their knowledge. As their teacher, you can integrate these resources into your lessons to ensure students are able to communicate and share their knowledge and understanding with others.

Most of the resources available as Web 2.0 tools are the products of the **open source** concept, meaning that software is unrestricted and free for anyone's use (Pfaffman, 2007). Open source resources are designed to foster collaboration and allow access to tools that make work easier. As a teacher, you need to determine when it is appropriate to use these types of tools in your lessons. There may be times when you determine that using Web 2.0 resources may not facilitate the types of learning experiences you want for your students.

Open source Web 2.0 resources include programs such as word processing, database, and image software that are freely available to educators for use in classrooms. However, because the software is free and thus not purchased and licensed, you have little control over the quality and stability of the software. You could plan to use a particular application, only to find that it is no longer available or is now only usable if you pay a fee.

One new direction for open source tools is called **cloud computing,** in which applications are available through networked computers to distribute greater access to processing power and applications. Cloud-based resources can be free or very low cost and include substantial capabilities for sharing files and information with others across the Web. The software and files are not stored on individual desktop or laptop computers but rather are stored in the cloud, or network of computers supporting the software application you have used.

One of the most familiar types of clouds to use in your classroom is a *wordle,* a visual created out of words. The wordle is a fun activity for students to practice vocabulary

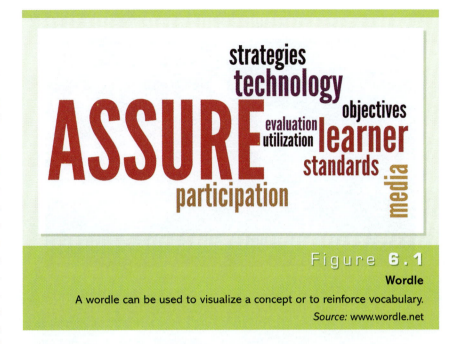

Figure **6.1**
Wordle
A wordle can be used to visualize a concept or to reinforce vocabulary.
Source: www.wordle.net

or concepts or to produce visuals that help them to see the relationships among words (Figure 6.1). Students can create their own wordles to express their ideas or, as their teacher, you can help them see the relationships among ideas through the visual you prepare in advance or as part of a group brainstorming activity. A fun site for students is Guess-the-Wordle (http://projectsbyjen.com/GTW), which features daily wordle puzzles that become more complex through the week.

ONLINE AUDIO AND VIDEO

Audio has been available as digital content on CDs for many years. More recently, digital audio files can be accessed from the Internet and **downloaded,** or copied to your computer or digital mobile device, such as a cell phone or MP3 player. For example, a **podcast** is an audio file that can be downloaded to a personal listening device such as an iPod or cell phone. Podcasts can also be **streamed,** meaning that the audio file itself stays only on the network server but is available for listening on an audio device. A number of education-oriented sites provide podcasts for teachers and students to use for enhancing learning experiences. Check out sites such as NASA (Figure 6.2), NPR, or Grammar Girls for potential podcast resources you might wish to use in your teaching.

At first, audio downloads were available only in the form of music that could be added to a personal database of audio. Music downloads are still offered as single songs or collections of music through a number of online resources such as iTunes or Amazon. More recently, educators have used downloadable audio materials to enhance student learning opportunities. For instance, you can create

broadcasts relating to events or concepts they are studying in class.

Podcasts can also be recorded in video formats. A **vidcast** allows students to see, as well as hear, the information being presented. Although video files are larger than those containing only audio, the visual element may be very important to the message. Vidcasts provide students with demonstrations that can help them with independent work outside of the classroom setting. For example, students might watch a vidcast before class demonstrating how to complete a science lab procedure, how to solve a math problem, or how to create a concept map showing the sequence of a story (see Taking A Look at Technology Integration: Insects). Then they arrive ready to engage in the actual task, making efficient and effective use of their instructional time and able to take advantage of your individual guidance.

Among the Web 2.0 tools that have become a common feature of many online resources are VoiceThread and Animoto for audio and YouTube and TeacherTube for video. These are warehouses of both academic and nonacademic audio and video material. The New Media Consortium refers to much of the video available in such sites as "grassroots video," which means they are produced on the spot with available technologies such as a cell phone to capture a few seconds of video (Johnson,

Figure 6.2

Educational Podcasts

There are many educational podcasts that can be used to enhance student learning.

Source: www.nasa.gov/multimedia/podcasting/index.html

recordings of class lectures to provide as podcasts that students can access to review material as a study guide. Or the podcast could be a prerecorded lecture for required listening prior to class, so that actual class time is focused on activity-based types of learning experiences rather than listening to lectures. Podcasts can also be used to access past news programs, famous speeches, or other related information resources, so that learners can listen to actual

TAKING A LOOK
AT TECHNOLOGY INTEGRATION

Insects

When Ms. Paszotta's kindergartners were starting their study of insects, she wanted to capitalize on the school's philosophy of integrating arts and technology into their learning experiences. And, when talking with Ms. Mullins, a fourth-grade teacher, she learned that the fourth-graders were studying insects as well. The two teachers collaborated on their lessons and decided on the culminating activity in which students worked together to create a vidcast about what they learned.

The kindergarteners selected an insect to study. They worked with a fourth-grade partner to investigate the insect and

to prepare a short presentation about what they learned together. The kindergarteners drew masks of their selected insects and their fourth-grade partner worked with them to prepare an introduction about the insect for their video.

Student pairs worked to create short videos about their insects, which they saved as vidcasts. With the aid of the technology teacher, they uploaded their vidcasts to the school's website and shared their resources with other elementary children throughout the district.

logs, are a set of personal commentaries about a specific topic. You can create your own blog using a site such as Blogger.com or you can participate in a blog developed by a group of teachers who wish to share ideas and resources, such as TeacherLingo (Figure 6.4). **Wikis** are web-based resources that let users engage in collaborative writing and editing. A group of teachers or students can work together on a paper or project, providing immediate feedback for ideas as they are entered in the document. Both of these collaboration tools provide learners with the chance to share information with others.

Blogs. Blogs, which can contain text, visuals, and links to websites, allow learners to share information with each other and with the teacher. Because, in addition to being a personal reflection or commentary about a topic, a blog can also be a dialog with a group of people all interested in the same topic or issue, you can participate with colleagues globally (Figure 6.5). The structure of a blog is arranged so that the most recent posting is first, allowing easy access to the most recent comments. Any reader who wishes, however, can scan easily through the blog postings to see earlier entries.

Levine, & Smith, 2009). For schools where access to such tools as YouTube is not permitted, TeacherTube is a possible alternative. TeacherTube is a resource that contains teacher-developed videos, lesson plans, and a variety of classroom resources for a wide range of content areas across all grade levels.

Students can create their own audio and video digital files with easy-to-use tools (Figure 6.3). For example, to create an audio podcast, students need a computer with recording software, a microphone, and access to the Internet. They can work independently or in collaborative teams to generate their own podcasts based on topics they are studying to share with others in the class or around the world. Students might also work with a teacher to use a digital video camera to create a learning vidcast for younger students. With these simple tools, anyone can be creative and generate learning materials to share.

COLLABORATION WEBSITES

Collaboration websites are resources that provide ways for users to interact with other users for education purposes, most commonly in the form of blogs and wikis. **Blogs,** short for *web*

bob sprankle
www.bobsprankle.com

| Home |
| Bit by Bit Blog |
| Seedlings @ Ning |
| Podcasts |
| Publications |
| Interviews/Mentions |
| Presentations Online |
| Workshop Links |
| Résumé |
| Wells Elementary School |
| Room 208 Site |
| The Bobby Bucket Show |

Welcome!

My name is Bob Sprankle. I'm a Technology Integrator for grades K-4 in Wells, Maine. Please check out the links on the left to learn more about me and the work I've been doing. Please join in the conversation on my blog, "Bit by Bit."

Bob Sprankle 2010 • bob[at]bobsprankle[dot]com Thursday, August 05, 2010 •

Figure **6.5**

Teachers' Websites

It can be very interesting to read about other teachers' successful use of technology in the classroom.
Source: http://bobsprankle.com/bobsprankle/index.html. Reprinted by permission.

not need to be in the same location, but can work together while one student is at home and the other is in a nearby library. Wiki spaces, such as Google Docs, are often free to educators, making them even more useful for teachers to provide guidance for students as they write collaboratively with others.

Social Networking. Another type of collaboration web-based resource, social networking sites are open to anyone who wishes to create a page about themselves and share that information with others. Familiar social networking sites include Twitter, MySpace, and Facebook. These sites allow the individual to post text, images, video, and favorite webpage links. They also offer ways for users to join others interested in similar topics or issues through community groups. Groups can be open to anyone with similar interests or can be set up as "closed" groups that require an invitation before an individual can join. Because they are shared across the Internet, information on these sites is available to anyone around the world.

Social networking sites are different from wikis because the amount of text is limited to only a few words, encouraging brief communications when exchanging information.

Content experts such as scientists often write blogs, giving students a chance to be informed about a topic with the most up-to-date information. However, although content may be current, it may not necessarily be accurate. Teachers must guide students in their search for credible sources, as many blogs may be highly subjective in nature, written by individuals as a way to express their ideas to an audience. When teaching students writing skills, a blog is a great way to offer them an audience to comment on their ideas or their writing. You may wish to start with a class blog, giving your students a chance to learn how to use good writing skills successfully in the blog environment before you engage them in public blogs.

Wikis. A wiki is a webpage that permits users to interact with a document that others have written or edited. Wikis allow users to write new information or edit the information that is posted on a collaborative site. Content can change whenever a user interacts with the page. Wikipedia, a collaborative encyclopedia, is a well-known type of wiki (Figure 6.6). The content on Wikipedia can be updated or changed by users to keep it current, unlike a large printed encyclopedia that is updated only every 10 years.

Wikis are a good tool for students working on collaborative writing projects. Students can access a Wiki using any computer and any web browser. Additionally, students do

As a teacher, your role is to guide your students as they work interactively in social media settings.
Shutterstock

Figure **6.6**

Wikipedia

Similar to an encyclopedia, Wikipedia provides a
current source about a vast array of topics.

Source: www.wikipedia.org

Figure **6.7**

Schools United Networking

As a teacher, you can create your own class social networking site.

Source: www.theschoolsunited.com/community. Reprinted by permission.

For instance, Twitter, an online communication network for sharing current, up-to-the-minute status reports in very brief messages, limits posts, or "tweets," to 140 characters. In response to the concept of quick notes, such as instant messages, tweets, and other social networking resources, users have created a type of shorthand to communicate their ideas without wasting letters. For example, a user would type the letter *u* for the word *you,* the numeral 2 for the word *to,* or BRB for "be right back." You need to help your students know when it is appropriate to use the shortcuts and when they need to practice good writing skills.

Many schools restrict access to social networking sites within the building setting, which may mean that even if you create an educational application, you may not be able to use it with your students in the school. However, the 21st century student has become very comfortable with these kinds of resources, and it is important to consider how they might be useful in educational settings. Many students already have their own MySpace or Facebook pages, using them only for social interactions. You may have your own page as well, although you may wish to consider the type of information and photos you place on your pages as they can potentially be viewed by parents, administrators, and school board members. You may want to create educational uses for these types of resources to capitalize on the popularity of their use. Some education sites are starting to mirror social networking resources but are restricted to classroom use only (Figure 6.7) as a means of better ensuring a safe environment for students.

Data Mashups. Websites that bring together content from a variety of resources, **data mashups** create sites that are new and different from the original sources. For example, online news media sites combine text, video, audio, and real-time information updated about

Use when student learning will be enhanced by . . .

Guidelines	Examples
reading and writing about shared learning experiences	Middle school students post information on a classroom blog site.
practicing English as a second language	High school English learners listen to podcasts to help them with their classroom studies.
sharing information with classmates and others	Elementary students post their digital stories on Bookr to share both their visual and written stories with others.
exchanging information about a carbon-footprint class project	Middle school students post video captured on their cell phones to a classroom blog site and write about what they have seen.

every 15 minutes. This combination of information gives teachers and students very current data to use in reports or as part of classroom activities.

Students can take advantage of mashup sites to learn more about geography or mapping skills. They can use a mashup site that combines mapping and satellite information to identify specific locations in cities around the world. The assignment might be to locate particular types of buildings or specific monuments using a site like Google Maps, in which students can easily pinpoint specific places, get directions, or view the maps to identify the location's proximity to surrounding areas.

MOBILE BROADBAND

Although not a new technology, mobile phones today offer expanded tools and applications. Cell phones can now take photos and short video, access the Internet for email and web surfing, and provide calendars and other personal management tools.

Cell phones have been dubbed the great equalizer (Paine, 2009). Today, the majority of school-age children have cell phones and learn their applications with little trouble. Although phones for younger children, often purchased for child safety reasons, may only be able to call a parent's cell phone, many older students have phones with greater access to online resources.

As educators, we need to begin thinking of ways to apply these extended cell phone capabilities as learning tools. Examples include field-based learning experiences where students can take photos of events or phenomena, such as demonstrating the carbon footprints they find within their community. Students can then upload the images to a classroom website and write a blog entry about their observations. Experts on the topic of carbon footprinting can provide additional information or guide approaches to the topic. The

classroom can be moved outside the school building and beyond the limits of the school day.

ASSURE Case Study Reflection

Review the ASSURE Classroom Case Study and video at the beginning of the chapter. Identify the types of Web 2.0 Tools that Vicki Davis has incorporated into her lesson. How have the students used these tools to support their learning?

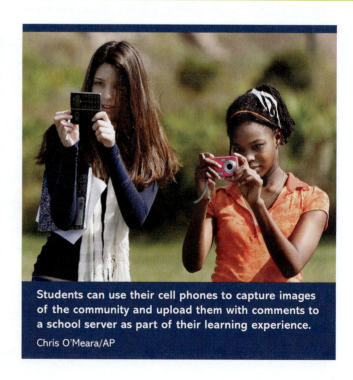

Students can use their cell phones to capture images of the community and upload them with comments to a school server as part of their learning experience.

Chris O'Meara/AP

Social–Ethical Issues

Whenever working with students on the Internet, you need to consider two important social–ethical issues: security and student interactions.

SECURITY

Students need to understand they are not to give out personal information such as their last names, cell or home phone numbers, addresses, or other information. On occasion there have been incidents where students have been contacted or even harmed by unscrupulous individuals. Your role as teacher is to encourage students to give their school's address for correspondence if they need to provide such information. Also, as an educator, you must have parental permission to let children post their photos and written work, such as essays, poems, and artistic creations, on the Web. You can learn more about online security issues through the Center for Education and Research in Information Assurance and Security (CERIAS) (www.cerias.purdue.edu).

STUDENT INTERACTIONS

When students are working in cybersettings, they need to engage in positive and appropriate interactions with others. As their teacher, you will need to guide your students in using appropriate behavior with others. It is important for you to help your students understand how to use clear and situation-specific language in their communications. For example, if the students are exchanging text messages, they will find abbreviations or word shortcuts to be effective, while in an email to an adult or an organization, they will want to use complete sentences.

One issue that has become serious and will need the teacher's monitoring and intervention is that of cyber-bullying. Cyberbullying can be annoying or even dangerous if not handled properly. The Cyberbullying Research Center (www.cyberbullying.us) offers information and research about the problem and suggestions for dealing with the issue at hand. Also, they provide examples of actual incidents and contact information for seeking assistance. The blog provides a means for professionals to discuss the examples provided and other cyberbullying issues.

ASSURE Case Study Reflection

Review the ASSURE Classroom Case Study and video at the beginning of the chapter. View how Vicki Davis ensures that her students use technology appropriately. How has she guided students to remember to exhibit appropriate online behavior?

As their teacher, it is important that you give guidance to students when they are using websites.
Christopher Barth/AP

Using Web 2.0 Tools in the Classroom

ADVANTAGES

- *Portable.* Information can be accessed and used anywhere on personal devices such as iPods and cell phones.
- *Easy to produce.* The new types of technologies simplify the process of preparing materials such as podcasts or online videos.
- *Authentic audience.* When developing literacy and communication skills, interactive tools such as blogs and wikis offer opportunities to reach readers beyond the classroom who can provide valuable feedback.
- *Connectedness.* Communication among students is facilitated, encouraging collaboration.
- *Social awareness.* Students become more sensitive to others through social networking sites where they have access to information about each other.

- *Free.* Many Web 2.0 tools are available for educational uses at no charge.

LIMITATIONS

- *Require sophisticated hardware.* Some interactive Web 2.0 Tools require hardware capabilities not available on less expensive models.
- *Quality of messages.* Because they are easy to produce and free, many types of Web 2.0 postings are of poor quality and not well prepared.
- *Credibility.* Just because it appears on the Web does not make it an authentic or authoritative source. Web 2.0 tools make it very easy to post information that may be inaccurate.
- *Safety issues.* Because of the open nature of the resources, it is essential that users understand the need for caution and concern when sharing personal information.

INTEGRATION

In the classroom there are a number of ways that Web 2.0 tools can support learning. Your role is to find the best means of optimizing the learning opportunities of your students us-ing these types of resources (See Selection Rubric: Web 2.0 Tools).

Lisa Zawilinski (2009) describes how one teacher organized a blog for her fifth-grade students to support their reading activities. After giving her students prompts about books they were reading, encouraging them to reflect on the stories and in turn demonstrate their reading comprehension, students began to ask if they could post some of their original work, such as poems or reactions to books they were independently reading. The teacher recognized an opportunity for expanding students' use of the blog format, allowing her to guide them in their exploration of literature.

Data mashups are another way to support students' learning. For example, if you are working on estimation in math, you can have your students estimate the walking distance between home and school. Once they have guessed the distance, they can link to Gmaps Pedometer to get the actual measured distance (Branzburg, 2009). For a geography or science class, you can link to a site that provides information about the location and scale of any earthquake worldwide for the past seven days (http://earthquakes.tafoni.net). You can guide students to compare that data with geology information they have on global fault lines and plate tectonics.

TECHNOLOGY for Diverse Learners

Web 2.0 Tools in the Classroom

Students may have difficulty expressing themselves in class due to limited language skills from a learning disability or because their first language is not English. They frequently tend to be quiet or not participate in class or group discussions. And gifted learners may want more challenges for their own learning. There are many resources for helping all students access information to increase their learning.

Audio podcasts allow students to hear the teacher's instruction after class so that they can review the information, follow directions that might have been presented, or prepare for a test about the material covered in class. Video podcasts provide visual information, along with the audio, to help students follow along using multiple modes of learning. These tools may help learners who benefit from seeing visual depictions of concepts or strategies to be applied. It is also helpful for students who may need to review a process more than once to gain the full benefit of the demonstration.

When writing is a challenge for students, a wiki can be a way to let them improve their skills in sharing information with classmates or other audiences. The wiki allows everyone to offer and exchange ideas. It also allows others to provide ideas about how to express those ideas in writing, thus influencing writing skills.

Challenging students with a wide range of skills and abilities is often difficult. By using collaborative social networking tools, such as the MIT New Literacies Project, gifted students can share their work with other students around the world. These types of exchanges provide students with opportunities to express themselves and to learn from others.

Social networking is a way for students to connect with others engaged in social studies inquiry. As part of a unit related to study about your state, you might have your students collect information using online resources. You can have them post their bookmarks of sites visited to Delicious (http://delicious.com) to share links with others in the class. Access to student folders with their bookmarks can be limited to members of the class. Or if you know another teacher whose students are also studying the state, you could arrange for them to exchange links to extend their study. The exchange offers students opportunities to gather additional information and learn more about the content while seeing examples of how to find additional resources. And to expand the idea of working collaboratively, you can create a wiki in which students collaborate on a report that can be shared with other students, parents, or the school board.

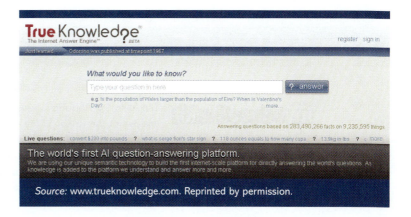

Source: www.trueknowledge.com. Reprinted by permission.

and successful in a wide range of Internet activities such as searching and sharing your knowledge with others. Your computer could also learn to connect dates, places, and people and use that information to keep your calendar, places of interest, and contacts list up-to-date without your having to do it yourself. Semantic-aware applications are making it easier to find and connect information, making learning and discovering new information much easier for everyone who has access to the Internet.

YOUR SMART WEB BROWSER
Semantic-Aware Applications

Using a current search engine like Google, you type in a key word and may get a large number of hits. Semantic-aware applications actually work with your computer to help it "understand" what you want to know and guide the search for an answer that addresses the question you've posed. Rather than searching on a group of key words, the computer makes connections based on working with your input to focus on what you wish to know. In this totally new way to engage in Internet searches, your computer recognizes the meaning of the word or question you've provided, even using images instead of words for some of the information pulled from various sites, and will gather the information you seek quickly. It makes browsing through multiple pages a thing of the past.

Semantic technology is making it much easier to pose questions and locate answers, saving you valuable time. Your computer understands more about you and tries to make the work of searching easier, helping you be more efficient

SUMMARY

Cyberlearning opportunities continue to expand. More resources are available to students and teachers to enhance and extend classroom activities through Web 2.0 tools. Teachers are no longer limited to the materials they have in their classrooms or in the school media center but rather can access resources from around the world. Teachers can provide students with experiences that help them use the Internet as a source of information, a tool of collaboration, and a place to test their creativity. Students can reach out to other students and experts for exchanges of ideas. Cyberlearning has opened classrooms to a wealth of information around the world through the Internet!

PEARSON
myeducationkit™

To check your comprehension of the content covered in Chapter 6, go to the **MyEducationKit** for your book and complete the Study Plan for Chapter 6. Here you will be able to take a chapter quiz, receive feedback on your answers, and then access resources that will enhance your understanding of the chapter content.

ASSURE Lesson Plan

The following ASSURE Lesson Plan provides a detailed description and analysis of the lesson in the ASSURE Classroom Case Study and video at the beginning of the chapter. To review the video again, go to the MyEducationKit for your text and click on the ASSURE Video under Chapter 6. The video explores how Ms. Davis collaborates with her ninth-grade students to create lessons for seventh-graders in a virtual world.

Analyze Learners

General Characteristics. The students in Vicki Davis's high school class are primarily rural students with a variety of interests in technology. They are fairly equally distributed with regard to gender and range in age from 13 to 15 years old. Student reading ability is at or above grade level although there are several students with diagnosed learning disabilities in the class. Student behavior problems are minimal.

Entry Competencies. The students are, in general, able to do the following:

- Demonstrate competency in keyboarding, document editing, and general computer skills.
- Prepare written materials such as narratives for the lessons they are going to teach to the seventh-grade students and wiki and blog entries for the class.
- Use Web 2.0 software to participate in blogs and wikis and to develop and interact in virtual world settings (primarily using OpenSim) with their own avatars.

Learning Styles. Ms. Davis's students learn best when engaged in activities that are relevant and include lively discussions of meaningful topics. Her students vary in comfort level when speaking with the seventh-graders, but are very comfortable in the virtual world created for their class to help the younger students learn about "digital citizenship" and Internet safety. Ms. Davis guides her students through their use of technology, building on their prior experiences and skills. When working in groups, her style of coaching facilitates their teamwork abilities.

State Standards and Objectives

Curriculum Standards. The following Georgia Common Core Standards for Technology and Career Education are addressed in this lesson: (2) Communicate thoughts, ideas, information, and messages using technology: Students collaborate using blogs, wikis, and preparation of instruction for younger students; (5) Organize ideas and communicate in a concise and courteous manner: Students convey their ideas within group discussions and in presentations; and (8) Modify a plan of action to achieve outcomes: Students arrange their presentations to ensure that the seventh-graders are able to learn the important elements of digital citizenship and Internet safety.

Technology Standards. National Educational Technology Standards for Students 1—Creativity and Innovation: Students use Web 2.0 tools to demonstrate creative thinking, construct knowledge, and develop innovative products and processes; 4—Critical Thinking, Problem Solving, and Decision Making: Students use technology to plan and conduct research, manage projects, solve problems, and make decisions; and 5—Digital Citizenship Students understand human, cultural, and societal issues related to technology and practice legal and ethical behavior.

Learning Objectives

1. Develop virtual worlds that engage students in scenarios in which they apply digital citizenship and safety guidelines.
2. Select appropriate technology tools to accomplish team objectives,
3. Participate in authentic research and use appropriate attribution for ideas.
4. Communicate strategies for using Web 2.0 tools to solve problems.
5. Write avatar scripts that demonstrate knowledge of digital citizenship and safety.

Select Strategies, Technology, Media, and Materials

Select Strategies. Vicki Davis selects teacher- and student-centered strategies to plan the lesson for seventh-graders. The teacher-centered strategies involve engaging the students in discussion through questions and feedback that lead to additional ideas. The student-centered strategies consist of students initiating design ideas for the lessons they plan to develop for the seventh-graders and utilizing Web 2.0 tools to share information and create interesting learning experiences.

Select Technology and Media. This lesson involves students' work with computers and Web 2.0 software to post their ideas to a wiki and blog. They also use software to develop a virtual world environment that will serve the younger students' learning needs. Ms. Davis applies the following guidelines to assess the appropriateness of her technology and media selections:

- *Alignment with standards, outcomes, and objectives*. The Web 2.0 tools provide the necessary support for Vicki Davis's students to meet the learning objectives.
- *Accurate and current information*. Students use both text-based and Internet resources to conduct their research on digital citizenship and safety.
- *Age-appropriate language*. Ms. Davis's students consider how to instruct the seventh-graders about virtual worlds and digital citizenship and safety in language that will help them understand the concepts in the lessons they design.
- *Interest level and engagement*. The ninth-grade students are excited about sharing their knowledge of digital citizenship and safety with the seventh-graders through their virtual world environment. They are very engaged with developing their lessons to help the

younger students gain skills in navigating virtual worlds and learning about digital citizenship and safety.

- *Technical quality.* The technical quality of the Web 2.0 tools allow the students to engage in a variety of online interactions and to facilitate their communications beyond the school day and setting.
- *Ease of use.* The Web 2.0 tools are fairly easy for high school students to understand, especially as they are using them regularly in their learning.
- *Bias free.* Web 2.0 software is bias free.
- *User guide and directions.* The online help features of some Web 2.0 tools are moderately easy for students to use. Students most frequently ask each other or use the help option within the software for assistance with technical difficulties.

Select Materials. Vicki Davis provides her students with a number of types of Web 2.0 tools to use for their interactions, research, and design ideas.

Utilize Technology, Media, and Materials

Preview the Technology, Media, and Materials. Vicki Davis previews the Web 2.0 software to ensure that it has the features needed for her students to be successful. She previews selected technology resources to ensure students can use them in the school setting as well as making certain the tools will meet their needs.

Prepare the Technology, Media, and Materials. Ms. Davis prepares starter questions for the group discussion following the presentation they completed for the seventh-graders.

Prepare the Environment. Vicki Davis tests the lab computers and ensures that the software needed is accessible from each computer. She also tests the capability of the technology to connect the lab classroom to the nearby school media center.

Prepare the Learners. Students in Ms. Davis' class have been involved in group discussions previously and learner preparation therefore primarily focuses on the topics to be covered during the live lesson and follow-up discussion.

Provide the Learning Experience. The learning experience occurs in three formats: live presentation to a group of seventh-grade students, interactions within the discussion following the presentation, and their online discussions on the blog and wiki for this project.

Require Learner Participation

Student Practice Activities. The students in Vicki Davis's class use computers, the virtual world they created, and Web 2.0 software to prepare for and participate in the presentation to the seventh-grade students. Her students use information from their observations and discussion to generate ideas to improve their next presentation and to develop a series of lessons about virtual worlds and digital citizenship and safety. During the discussion, students practice and test their knowledge and skills by asking and answering student-created questions. They post their ideas to the class blog for further exploration and discussion beyond the class period. Furthermore, they work collaboratively on the class wiki in the planning and design of their instruction for seventh-graders on digital citizenship and Internet safety.

Feedback. Vicki Davis provides continuous feedback as students participate in their discussion and guides them in their decisions on the best ways to interact with the seventh-grade students. She encourages them to provide feedback to each other through their online discussions.

Evaluate and Revise

Assessment of Learner Achievement. Ms. Davis reviews the discussion notes posted to the wiki. She examines the materials that are prepared for the school blog and looks at the materials her students have developed for their next seventh-grade lesson. She also reviews recordings of the video that the students have located to see whether it is appropriate for the seventh-graders. Ms. Davis uses rubrics to assess both student ability to apply technology for creativity and their communication skills by evaluating student comments and their posted notes and comments. She also uses a rubric to assess the accuracy of the digital citizenship and student safety information included in the virtual world scripts prepared by the ninth-graders.

Evaluation of Strategies, Technology, and Media. Ms. Davis evaluates the effectiveness of the lesson strategies, talking about the process with the students in her class. Evaluation of the technology and media involves examining the functionality of the Web 2.0 software and the virtual world environment created by her students.

Revision. The evaluation results revealed that student interactions could benefit from assigning students to work in design pairs to increase interactions and information exchange. Further-more, teacher notes and edits of student work on the wiki provided improved documentation of the lesson. Another revision that emerged from the evaluation results was to limit teacher-directed questions to encourage more student-to-student discussion.

CONTINUING MY PROFESSIONAL DEVELOPMENT

Demonstrating Professional Knowledge

1. Define cyberlearning and provide an example of a classroom application.
2. Describe cyberlearning literacy and discuss how it may be used in the classroom.
3. Identify three Web 2.0 resources and demonstrate an example of how they might assist learning.
4. Explain why social networking issues are important for the classroom.
5. Identify four social–ethical issues and why they are important in working with students.

Demonstrating Professional Skills

1. Prepare a 10-minute presentation on how you might use one of the Web 2.0 tools in your teaching. (ISTE NETS-T 5.A)
2. Locate resources online that provide guidance for ensuring student safety when working with Web 2.0 tools. (ISTE NETS-T 4.C)

3. Locate and critique a lesson plan that describes an actual use of Web 2.0 tools. (ISTE NETS-T 5.C)

Building My Professional Portfolio

- *Creating My Lesson.* Using the ASSURE model, design a lesson for one of the case studies presented in the list in Appendix A or use a scenario of your own design. Incorporate into your lesson a Web 2.0 tool that will facilitate student learning. Carefully describe the audience, the objectives, and all the other elements of the ASSURE model. Be certain to match your intended outcomes to state or national curriculum and technology standards for your content area.
- *Enhancing My Lesson.* Using the lesson you created in the previous activity, consider how to meet the needs of students with varying abilities. What adaptations are needed to keep advanced learners actively engaged while helping students who struggle with reading?

What changes are needed to ensure students transfer the knowledge and skills to other learning situations? You might look for additional Web 2.0 resources to enhance the lesson. How can you integrate additional use of technology and media into the lesson?

- *Reflecting on My Lesson.* Reflect on the process you have used in the design of your lesson and your efforts at enhancing that lesson to meet student needs within your class. How did information from this chapter about Web 2.0 tools influence your lesson design decisions? In what ways did the technology and media you selected for your lesson enhance the learning opportunities for your students?

SUGGESTED RESOURCES

Print

Kidd, T., & Chen, I. (2009). *Wired for learning: An educator's guide to Web 2.0.* Charlotte, NC: Information Age.

Jenkins, H. (2009). *Confronting the challenges of participatory culture: Media education for the 21st century.* Boston: MIT.

Lanclos, P. (2008). *Weaving Web 2.0 tools into the classroom.* Eugene, OR: Visions Technology in Education.

Richardson, W. (2009). *Blogs, wikis, podcasts, and other powerful web tools for classrooms* (2nd ed.). Thousand Oaks, CA: Corwin.

Vossen, G., & Hagemann, S. (2007). *Unleashing Web 2.0: From concepts to creativity.* Burlington, MA: Morgan Kaufmann Publishers.

Web Links

To easily access these web links from your browser, go to MyEducationKit for your text, then go to Chapter 6 and click on the web links.

Educause Learning Initiative

www.educause.edu/eli

The Educause Learning Initiative provides information about new directions in technology and how it might be used to

facilitate learning. Each spring the organization publishes the Horizon Report, which provides insights into short-, middle-, and long-range technology trends.

eSchool News

www.eschoolnews.com

This site offers a convenient way to keep up-to-date electronically with what is going on with technology in schools.

International Society for Technology in Education

www.iste.org

ISTE is an association focused on improving education through the use of technology in learning, teaching, and administration. ISTE members include teachers, administrators, computer coordinators, information resource managers, and educational technology specialists.

Project New Media Literacies

http://newmedialiteracies.org

The MIT New Media Literacies project explores ways to help young people understand the social skills and cultural competencies they need to become participants in a global world.

Web 2.0: Cool Tools for Schools

http://cooltoolsforschools.wikispaces.com

This site offers many types of Web 2.0 tools that teachers have used in their classrooms. Organized by category, such as presentation tools, and by content areas like math and reading, a number of resources are suggested for classroom use.

Selection Rubric: WEB 2.0 TOOLS

To download and complete this rubric for your own use, go to the MyEducationKit for your text, then go to Chapter 6 and click on Selection Rubrics.

Search Terms Used to Locate Resources

_____

_____

_____

Title _____

Source/Location _____

Date _____ Cost _____

Subject Area _____ Grade Level _____

Instructional Strategies _____

Format

_____ podcast

_____ vidcast

_____ blog

_____ wiki

_____ other _____

Brief Description

Standards/Outcomes/Objectives

Prerequisites (e.g., prior knowledge, reading ability, vocabulary level)

Strengths

Limitations

Special Features

Name _____ Date _____

Rating Area	High Quality	Medium Quality	Low Quality
Alignment with Standards, Outcomes, and Objectives	Standards/outcomes/objectives addressed and use of web tools should enhance student learning.	Standards/outcomes/objectives partially addressed and use of web tools may enhance student learning.	Standards/outcomes/objectives not addressed and use of web tools will likely not enhance student learning.
Accurate and Current Information	Information is correct and does not contain material that is out of date.	Information is correct, but does contain material that is out of date.	Information is not correct and does contain material that is out of date.
Age-Appropriate Language	Language used is age appropriate and vocabulary is understandable.	Language used is nearly age appropriate and some vocabulary is above/below student age.	Language used is not age appropriate and vocabulary is clearly inappropriate for student age.
Interest Level and Engagement	Topic is presented so that students are likely to be interested and actively engaged in learning.	Topic is presented to interest students most of the time and engage most students in learning.	Topic is presented so as not to interest students and not engage them in learning.
Technical Quality	The material represents the best available media.	The material represents media that are good quality, although there may be some problems using it.	The material represents media that are not well prepared and are of very poor quality.
Ease of Use (Student or Teacher)	Material follows easy-to-use patterns with nothing to confuse the user.	Material follows patterns that are easy to follow most of the time, with a few things to confuse the user.	Material follows no patterns and most of the time the user is very confused.
Bias Free	There is no evidence of objectionable bias or advertising.	There is little evidence of bias or advertising.	There is much evidence of bias or advertising.
User Guide and Directions	The user guide is an excellent resource to support a lesson. Directions should help teachers and students use the material.	The user guide is a good resource to support a lesson. Directions may help teachers and students use the material.	The user guide is a poor resource to support a lesson. Directions do not help teachers and students use the material.
Reading Level	Most students can use the web tools to create original pieces that represent learning.	Some students can use the web tools to start original pieces that begin to show their learning.	Most students cannot use the web tools to create original pieces that represent their learning.
Fosters Collaboration	The material is presented at an appropriate level so that most students can share information.	The material is presented at a level so that some students can share information.	The material is presented at a level so that few students can share information.
Clarity of Organization	The material is presented in such a way that most students are able to use the information.	The material is presented in such a way that some students are able to use the information.	The material is presented in such a way that few students are able to use the information.

Recommended for Classroom Use: _____ **Yes** _____ **No**

Ideas for Classroom Use:

CHAPTER SEVEN

Connecting
Learners at a Distance

This chapter addresses ISTE NETS-T 1, 2, and 3.

1. Define distance learning.

2. State a rationale for the educational use of distance learning at the elementary, middle-level, and secondary education levels.

3. Explain how audio and television systems facilitate distance learning.

4. Compare and contrast online and distance learning.

5. Describe the characteristics of local area networks (LANs), wide area networks (WANs), intranets, and wireless networks.

6. Discuss five Internet netiquette guidelines for users.

7. Select an example of a copyright concern and explain why it is an important issue.

Goal

Describe distance education and how it can facilitate student learning.

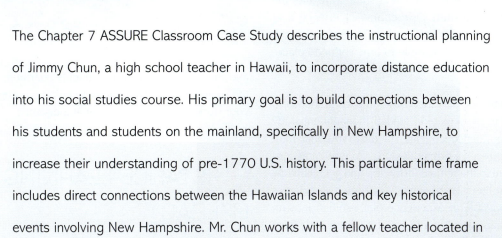

The Chapter 7 ASSURE Classroom Case Study describes the instructional planning of Jimmy Chun, a high school teacher in Hawaii, to incorporate distance education into his social studies course. His primary goal is to build connections between his students and students on the mainland, specifically in New Hampshire, to increase their understanding of pre-1770 U.S. history. This particular time frame includes direct connections between the Hawaiian Islands and key historical events involving New Hampshire. Mr. Chun works with a fellow teacher located in a New Hampshire high school. Together they develop a lesson in which students exchange historical as well as current information from their states.

To view the **ASSURE Classroom Case Study** *Video for this chapter, go to the MyEducationKit for your text and click on the ASSURE Video under Chapter 7 to explore how Mr. Chun works with another teacher to apply strategies for teaching at a distance and uses technology, media, and materials to achieve 21st century learning environments.*

Throughout the chapter you will find reflection questions to relate the chapter content to the ASSURE Classroom Case Study. At the end of the chapter you will be challenged to develop your own ASSURE lesson that incorporates use of these strategies, technology, media, and materials, for a topic and grade level of your choice.

NTRODUCTION

One of the greatest advantages offered by modern electronic technology is the ability to instruct without the teacher's direct presence in the classroom. That is, we can both **time-shift** instruction—experience it at some time after the live lesson—and **place-shift** instruction—experience it at some place away from the live teacher. The book was the first invention that made it possible to time-shift and place-shift instruction, a use that continues to the present day (Figure 7.1).

For more than a century, people in all parts of the world have been able to participate in guided independent study through correspondence courses via the traditional mail system. Learners receive printed lessons, do written assignments, send them to the remote instructor, and get feedback. However, the proliferation of newer electronic technologies now makes it possible to experience place-shifted instruction with a stunning array of additional auditory and visual stimuli far more rapidly and with a much richer range of interaction, not only with the instructor but also with other learners. This chapter introduces the foundation of distance learning concepts and provides general information about delivering instruction at a distance.

As a teacher, you need to be aware of the variety of options discussed in this chapter for both instruction at a distance, a broad concept incorporating an array of technologies, and online learning, which relies on computer-based resources. You need to be able to select the best technology

Students can use online resources to interact with other students and teachers throughout the district, across the country, and around the world.

Shutterstock

| Synchronous (Same time–different location) | Blended (Mix of time and location) | Asynchronous (Different time–different location) |

Figure 7.1
Types of Distance Education

and media to support your students' learning. You can use the suggestions in this chapter to help you prepare to guide your students who are learning at a distance.

DISTANCE LEARNING LITERACY

Distance learning has become the popular term to describe learning via telecommunications. The term **telecommunications** embraces a variety of technology and media configurations, including audio, video, and computer-based resources. What they all have in common is implied in the Greek root word *tele,* which means "at a distance" or "far off"; that is, they are systems for communicating over a distance. As we explore the broad topic of distance learning we will focus on both the more traditional forms of audio and video at a distance as well as online learning, which is a popular form of distance learning. Desmond Keegan (1980) identified key elements of a formal definition of distance education, which have not changed with the advent of newer technologies for delivery:

- Physical separation of learners from the teacher
- Organized instructional program
- Telecommunications technology
- Two-way communication

The emphasis on student learning, whether in a teacher-led or student-centered environment, is as important in a distance education setting as it is in a traditional classroom. The instructional strategies described in Chapter 4 apply to the same degree in distance settings as they do in the regular classroom. Regardless of the technology used, from live teacher to computer conferencing, an instructional telecommunication system must perform certain functions to be effective:

- *Information presentation.* A standard element for any lesson is presentation of information, involving not only

Videoconferencing systems can be designed so that the teacher can select the image to be shown to all the students with a single mouse click.

iStockPhoto

- Printed materials (e.g., textbooks, supplementary readings, worksheets)
- Audiovisual materials (e.g., CDs, DVDs, online resources)
- Computer databases (e.g., for online searches)
- Kits (e.g. for laboratory experiments or to examine specimens of real objects)
- Library materials (e.g., original source documents)

It is necessary to think about the instructional setting in a new light. The classroom is now a *series* of "rooms" connected electronically. The teacher's role may shift to that of facilitator of the learning rather than directly leading the class. The teacher must also keep a watchful eye on the class to be sure no one is falling behind.

With the latest technological advances, students can become more engaged in learning through interactions, yet it remains the teacher's responsibility to organize the instructional experience to encourage interactivity (Simonson, Smaldino, Albright, & Zvacek, 2006). Students for their part need to know how to use the distance education technology to communicate with the teacher and with each other using proper communication etiquette.

As we look at these elements of distance education we begin to see that all the ISTE NETS standards for teachers relate to the type of knowledge and skill teachers need to bring to learning experiences within a distance learning setting. Using the NETS-T standards we are prepared to define the literacy of distance learning with the following descriptors:

- Designing and facilitating learning experiences
- Modeling and promoting learning and responsibility
- Engaging in lifelong learning

teacher-led methods but also procedures within student-centered approaches. Common examples include the following:

- Teacher presentation and demonstration
- Student presentation or small-group work
- Printed text and illustrations (e.g., textbooks, handouts, correspondence, study materials)
- Live or recorded voice, music, and other sounds
- Full-motion images (video, CD, DVD)

• *Practice with feedback.* We know that the most learning takes place when learners are participating actively—mentally processing the material. Teachers induce activity in various ways, such as the following:

- Question-and-answer activities (carried out during or after the lesson)
- Discussion activities (during the class or as homework)
- Testing
- Structured group activities (e.g. role playing or games)
- Group projects
- Peer tutoring

• *Access to learning resources.* Lessons and courses are usually structured with the assumption that learners will spend time outside class working individually or in small groups with the material, doing homework, projects, papers, and the like. External learning resources include the following forms:

Teachers can use technology to help them monitor the class when teaching.

Corbis RF

The quality of the televised images has improved with technology development so that learning at a distance is similar to being in the classroom.

Joe Don Buckner/AP

you can read more about in Chapter 1. In this chapter, we present issues of copyright as they relate to distance education.

AUDIO TECHNOLOGY

Audio has a rich history of facilitating instruction at a distance. Radio was one of the first technologies used to deliver education remotely. Although not used much today in the United States, there are still instructional applications of radio in some international settings, often in rural areas where Internet connections are very limited resources.

The key to successful use of audio in instruction is to consider what resources are available to students at various locations and to be aware that sometimes audio may be sufficient to convey the learning experience. To use audio as a viable option for delivery of information, resources such as cassettes and CDs can be mailed to students for individual use or a conference call can be established among members of a class as means for two-way communication.

An **audio teleconference**—a live, interactive conversation using telephone lines, satellites, or the Internet—connects people at different locations. One issue associated with relying only on audio transmissions is the lack of visual information. However, audio can be supplemented by providing visual information such as handouts or a PowerPoint presentation sent by fax (facsimile) or email or with a course management tool such as Blackboard or Moodle.

D ISTANCE LEARNING

There are three primary types of distance learning resources used to support student learning: audio, video, and online, which we will describe briefly for you. When using any of these methods, you should consider copyright issues, which

VIDEO TECHNOLOGY

There are three major types of video technologies: streamed video, television, and CD/DVD.

Streamed Video. Delivered via the Internet to computers, **streamed video** can be viewed on individual computers or

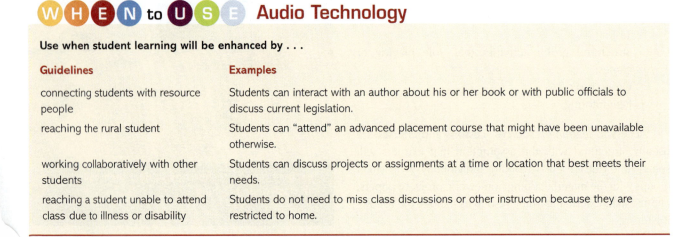

W H E N to U S E Audio Technology

Use when student learning will be enhanced by . . .

Guidelines	Examples
connecting students with resource people	Students can interact with an author about his or her book or with public officials to discuss current legislation.
reaching the rural student	Students can "attend" an advanced placement course that might have been unavailable otherwise.
working collaboratively with other students	Students can discuss projects or assignments at a time or location that best meets their needs.
reaching a student unable to attend class due to illness or disability	Students do not need to miss class discussions or other instruction because they are restricted to home.

Figure 7.2

Learn 360

Streamed video can be used in nearly every content area.

Source: www.learn360.com. Reprinted by permission.

only those portions of the video that are critical to their learning. United Streaming through Discovery Education and Learn360 are both sources for hundreds of titles in all content areas and grade levels (Figure 7.2).

Television. Television technologies offer many different types of instructional opportunities for learners. Students can engage in independent learning by viewing programs on such channels as Discovery or the History Channel. More formally, learners can be enrolled in a televised course that is required for credit or graduation from a program of study.

We use the term *one-way television* to refer to television delivery systems that transmit programs to students without an interactive connection to the teacher. However, virtually all television delivery can be converted into a *two-way television* communication system by using a device for sending audio feedback to the presenter. The talkback capability can be added by means of a telephone for calling the originating classroom (Figure 7.3). In other interactive settings with two-way communication of both audio and video, interaction is achieved by equipping both the sending and receiving sites with camera(s) and microphone(s) (Figure 7.4). A school may operate its own video teleconference facilities or lease them as needed for particular occasions. In such cases, television simulates the regular classroom setting by allowing interactions between students and teacher. Note that some interactive television systems use **compressed**

through a digital projector connected to a computer for the whole class to watch. The prerecorded video is transmitted to the computer in packets or small segments to make the downloading of the video easier and less of a memory drain for classroom computers. Video titles are available in nearly every content area for prekindergarten through grade 12, usually through a subscription obtained by the school district, thus making it possible for all teachers and students to access videos at any time. In addition, many streamed video titles also include instructional suggestions, handout masters, and other supplementary materials. To add flexibility, teachers can decide in advance to use only sections of a video, thus customizing the experience to ensure that students will view

W H E N to U S E One-Way Television Technology

Use when student learning will be enhanced by . . .

Guidelines	Examples
reinforcing classroom instruction	Younger students can watch a program at home with parents that will help reinforce a specific lesson from the classroom.
expanding the textbook material	Some textbooks have limited information on a topic that might be expanded by viewing a documentary.
supplemental information	Students can become better informed on a topic of interest while viewing an instructional or informative television program.
keeping current	Students can watch the evening news or other types of news programs to gather up-to-date information for classroom discussions.

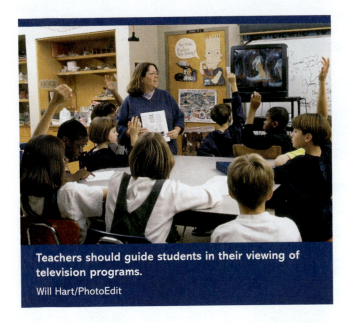

Teachers should guide students in their viewing of television programs.

Will Hart/PhotoEdit

video, which removes redundant video information, for distribution. Although the video information appears "jerky," it is much less expensive to deliver than full-motion video. Compressed video is also used for computer desktop video.

CD/DVD. Video can be stored on CD and DVD discs that can be purchased by individual schools or borrowed from a consortium collection for a period of time. Video can also be rented from a local video store or ordered online through a video rental company. A word of caution is advised regarding restrictions for the viewing of rented video (see Copyright Concerns for Video, Chapter 10). Video on CD or DVD can be viewed on individual computers or displayed for the whole class to view with a digital projector. A DVD can also be viewed on a DVD player connected to a television or monitor for whole-class viewing.

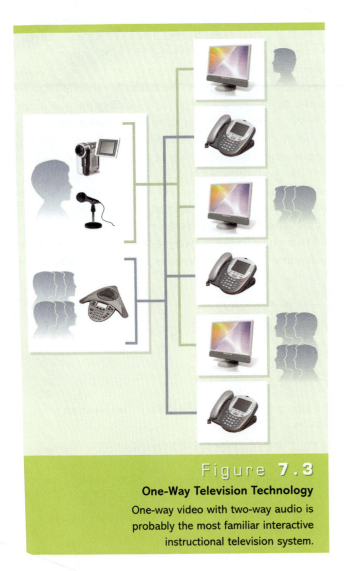

Figure **7.3**

One-Way Television Technology

One-way video with two-way audio is probably the most familiar interactive instructional television system.

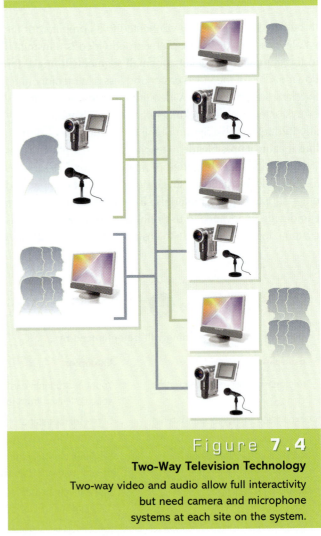

Figure **7.4**

Two-Way Television Technology

Two-way video and audio allow full interactivity but need camera and microphone systems at each site on the system.

Use when student learning will be enhanced by . . .

Guidelines	Examples
extending classroom instruction	A group of students from across the state or around the world can be added to classroom discussions to extend learning experiences.
expanding the textbook material	A guest speaker can be part of the class presentations on a topic.
reaching the rural student	Students who have limited access to courses needed to expand their knowledge or to prepare them for college can take a course from a distant school location.
supplemental information	A teacher from another school can add to the instructional experiences of a whole class.

Copyright Concerns

Distance Learning

In 2002, Congress revised the distance learning aspects of the copyright law by passing the TEACH Act. It extended fair use into the digital world and acknowledged that the boundaries of teaching space extend beyond the walls of a classroom. The act allows greater liberty to teachers in their use of materials in an online environment, permitting the display and performance of nearly all types of materials (visuals, sculpture, art, music, video, etc.) meeting the following conditions:

- The transmission is an integral part of a systematic, ongoing instructional activity mediated by an instructor.
- The transmission is directly related to and of material assistance in the teaching of content.
- The transmission is solely for and limited to students officially enrolled in the course.
- The teacher informs students that materials used may be subject to copyright protection.
- The institution employs measures to prevent retention of the materials in accessible form by the students for longer than the duration of the course.
- The institution employs measures that limit the transmission of the material to students enrolled in the course and precludes unauthorized student retention and/or redistribution to the extent technologically feasible.
- In order to facilitate digital transmissions, the TEACH Act permits scanning of some materials, but only if the material is not already available in digital form.

Certain specific restrictions are spelled out for use of copyrighted material in distance education:

- There is a time limit on use, comparable to the time the materials would be used in a face-to-face class. One may not continue to use the copyrighted materials beyond the duration of the semester the course is offered nor may the materials be used another semester without prior permission.
- Teachers may *not* transmit textbooks, printed materials, or other media (including CDs and DVDs), which are typically purchased or acquired by students.
- Off-air recordings may *not* be altered from their original content. They may *not* be combined or merged (physically or electronically) to constitute teaching anthologies or compilations.

For more information, visit the Technology, Education, and Copyright Harmonization (TEACH) Act (2002) website at www.ala.org/washoff/teach.html.

For general information on copyright, see the copyright section on pages 13 through 15 in Chapter 1. Suggested resources (print and web links) on copyright appear at the end of Chapter 1.

ONLINE TECHNOLOGY

Online learning (also called **electronic learning,** or **e-learning**) is instruction delivered electronically using computer-based media. The materials are often accessed through a network, including websites, the Internet, and intranets. However, e-learning involves not just accessing information (e.g., locating webpages) but also assisting learners with specific outcomes (e.g., meeting objectives). In addition to delivering instruction via e-learning, the teacher can monitor performance and report learner progress.

The uses of online learning in education are increasing. Students no longer need to rely only on textbooks but now have access to educational materials located far beyond the walls of the school building. You and your students can obtain information housed in many distant, physically inaccessible libraries around the world! Resources once beyond the dreams of all but the most affluent are readily available to everyone.

Students and teachers can enhance classroom learning by accessing information from an array of sources (databases, libraries, special interest groups) and by communicating via computer with other students or with experts in a particular field of study and exchanging data. Activities such as the Monarch Butterfly Journey North conducted by the Annenberg Foundation and the GeoBee Challenge of the National Geographic Society make it possible for students and teachers alike to reap the benefits of connecting into a national network of students, teachers, and scientists to investigate a variety of topics (Figure 7.5).

Teachers and their students can also access electronic documents to enrich their study. Students can actively participate because online learning provides an interactive learning environment. Students can hyperlink digital information to their papers and projects, making them "living" documents connected to other segments of their work or to additional documents or visual resources.

Because computers have the ability to deliver information in any medium (including text, video, and audio recordings of voice and music), the computer has become a boundless library. Students are able to communicate instantly with text, picture, voice, data, and two-way audio/video, and the resulting interactions are changing the roles of both students and teachers. Teachers can now be separated geographically from their students, and students can learn from other students in classrooms all over the world.

Often e-learning is combined with live face-to-face instruction and called **blended instruction,** or **hybrid instruction.** In the following sections we will explore learning using various technologies for instruction, as well as the issues associated with their use.

TEACHING AT A DISTANCE

When teaching at a distance, many issues need to be considered. Teachers have learned that it involves more than simply taking an existing lesson and "doing it" using audio, television, or the computer. There are many aspects that need to be adjusted or changed. A teacher needs to organize and sequence content as it relates to outcomes, know what resources are available, what experiences students have had with the system being used, and what they need to do to ensure quality learning experiences (Dabbagh & Bannan-Ritland, 2005).

One element often overlooked in distance learning is the access students have to resource materials. If a teacher wishes students to engage in research or working together in a problem-solving or collaborative activity, it is critical that the students have access to related materials, for example, books in the media center or Internet resources. A teacher may need to change particular types of hands-on activities or make special arrangements for materials to be sent to the classroom site. Students at a distance location should not be at a learning disadvantage because of limited resources. The teacher, often working closely with the school library media specialist, is responsible for ensuring that all students have equal access to the materials essential for learning. Although the World Wide Web has eased this concern a bit, there are still some courses in which resources for students are not readily available on the Web or copyright issues do not allow using the Web to provide those resources. Your school library media specialist should be aware of the copyright issues and able to help you provide access to materials (see Copyright Concerns: Distance Learning, p. 151).

Figure 7.5

Monarch Butterfly Journey North

Online learning projects such as this enhance classroom learning by providing access to data, videos, maps, and other resources.

Source: www.learner.org/jnorth/monarch. Reprinted by permission of Journey North.

Online Learning

Frequently, unauthorized copies of copyrighted works are posted on a website without the knowledge of the copyright owner. Recently the authors found the ASSURE model on five websites without attribution to its source. The casual observer would assume it was developed by the organization on whose website it was found. Instead, each of the cases involved a serious violation of copyright law!

Observe the following guidelines for online use of copyrighted materials:

- Contrary to popular opinion, *all* material on the Internet is copyrighted unless stated otherwise. It is copyrighted even if it does *not* display the copyright symbol.
- Email is considered an original work, fixed in a tangible medium of expression, that is covered by copyright. It can legally be read, but *not* legally forwarded or copied for instructional purposes, except under fair use. You can make one copy for your personal use.
- It is recommended that you *not* forward any email without permission, in consideration of both copyright and the Privacy Act. However, you may quote excerpts and report the "gist" of the message. For example, if a teacher has sent you an original poem, which is automatically copyrighted, and you forward it to a friend, then you have definitely violated *both* copyright law and the Privacy Act (adapted from Becker, 2003).
- Downloading an article from a newspaper's website, making copies, and distributing them to your students prior to a class discussion on the topic is permissible following the current photocopying guidelines, which permit making multiple copies for classroom use. The exception would be individually bylined, copyrighted articles, or articles from a source specifically designed for the educational market (e.g., *Scholastic Magazine*). Such articles *cannot* be copied legally for class distribution (adapted from Becker, 2003).
- You cannot post students' essays, poems, or other works on the school website unless you have permission of the students and their parents or guardians.
- Always link to the home page rather than a location within the website. In general, linking to another website is not viewed as a copyright infringement. However, it does offer the potential of becoming a copyright issue. If the link takes the user to the body of an author's work, and the initial website does not inform users they are being taken to another site, this may falsely give the impression that one is still on a page within the original website being viewed, thereby not giving credit to the linked site (Becker, 2003).
- Downloading and/or file sharing of video, audio, and other works is considered copyright infringement unless authorized by the copyright law or the owner of the work.
- Educators should treat copyrighted materials from the Internet the same way they do print formats. Because the copyright law is still muddled, the best guideline is to always obtain permission. It is usually not that difficult. When in doubt, ask!

For more information on copyright, see the copyright section on pages 13 through 15 in Chapter 1. Suggested resources (print and web links) on copyright appear at the end of Chapter 1.

WHEN to USE Online Learning Technology

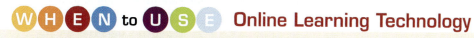

Use when student learning will be enhanced by . . .

Guidelines	Examples
practicing and receiving immediate feedback on what they have just studied in class	Students who need extra help can practice a skill or task by using an instructional module that includes a self-check with feedback.
learning independently	Students can search for information related to assignments on a classroom computer connected to the Internet.
enhancing learning opportunities for gifted students	Gifted students can be challenged to expand or enhance their learning by using more complex search techniques on the Internet.
working collaboratively with other students	Students in two locations or the same classroom can work together to navigate through a WebQuest that directs them to a particular area of study.
challenging students to investigate information in a new way	Students can participate in an online investigation of a topic with other students or scientists across the world.

Review the ASSURE Classroom Case Study and video at the beginning of the chapter. Explain how distance learning technology is helping students to learn history. How does Mr. Chun support learning through the use of information presentation, practice with feedback, and access to learning resources?

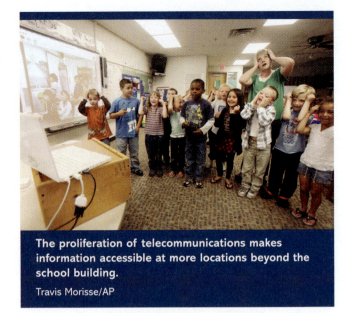

The proliferation of telecommunications makes information accessible at more locations beyond the school building.
Travis Morisse/AP

STRATEGIES AND APPROACHES

The emphasis on student learning, whether in a teacher-led or student-centered environment, is as important in a distance education setting as it is in a traditional classroom. The instructional strategies described in Chapter 4 apply in distance settings, just as they do in the regular class setting. Regardless of the audio, video, or computer-based technology used or whether the lesson takes place in actual time by computer conferencing or through time-delayed interactions, an instructional telecommunication system must perform certain functions to be effective:

• *Information presentation.* A standard element in any lesson is the presentation of some sort of information, involving not only teacher-led methods but also procedures within student-centered approaches. Common examples include the following:

- Teacher presentation and demonstration
- Student presentation or small-group work
- Text and illustrations to support presentation (e.g., digital or print images, handouts, correspondence study materials)
- Live or recorded voice, music, and other sounds
- Full-motion images (video, CD, DVD)

• *Practice with feedback.* We know that most learning occurs when learners are participating actively—mentally processing the material. Teachers induce activity in various ways, such as the following:

- Question-and-answer activities (carried out during or after the instruction)
- Discussion activities
- Testing
- Structured group activities (e.g., role playing or games)
- Group projects
- Peer tutoring

• *Access to learning resources.* Lessons and courses are usually structured with the assumption that learners will spend time outside of class working individually or in small groups with the material, doing homework, projects, papers, and the like. The external learning resources may take the following forms:

- Printed materials for additional reading (e.g., library or textbooks, supplementary readings, worksheets)
- Audiovisual materials (e.g., audio- or videocassettes, multimedia systems, CD, DVD)
- Computer databases (e.g., for online searches)
- Kits (e.g., for laboratory experiments or to examine specimens of real objects)
- Library materials (e.g., original source documents)

As in a regular classroom, various technology, media, and materials can be employed in a distance learning setting (Figure 7.6). Each of the various telecommunication systems

Audio	Video	Text
Audio teleconference	Television	Bulletin board posting
Podcasting	Vidcasting	Correspondence (email/mail)
Audio recordings (tape or digital)	Online video	Blog/Wiki

Figure **7.6**

Examples of Media Used in Distance Education

used in distance learning has strengths and limitations. The characteristics of the systems are discussed at greater length in the following sections of this chapter.

CRITICAL ISSUES

There are many important issues associated with electronic learning, especially when using the Internet. They include security, monitoring student use, acceptable use policies, and netiquette.

Security. Students should be instructed not to give out information such as their phone numbers, addresses, or other personal information over the Internet. Students have been contacted and even harmed by unscrupulous individuals. It may be wise for students to give their school's address for correspondence if they need to provide such information. Also, as a teacher, you must have parental permission to post children's photos and written work, such as essays, poems, and artistic creations, on the Web.

The Center for Education and Research in Information Assurance and Security (CERIAS) focuses on multidisciplinary research and education about information security. The organization is concerned with supporting educators on issues of privacy, ethics, and management of information. Exploring issues such as confidentiality of student records, privacy of information, and protection of students while they work online are important considerations. This organization provides guidelines for educators to establish policies within their schools to protect students, teachers, and the school community (contact them at www.cerias.purdue.edu).

Monitoring Student Use. Teachers and parents must monitor students' Internet use to ensure that their behavior is appropriate and to discourage them from exploring inappropriate material either deliberately or accidentally. The amount and level of monitoring is often based on the age of the students—younger students *may* need more monitoring than older students. Your final decisions about monitoring should be made in conjunction with parents and school administrators. Also, if a student encounters information or visuals that are inappropriate, that student should feel comfortable letting you know about it. Software can assist with monitoring student access to information. For example, Snapture software allows the teacher to prevent students from going to sites that are "off limits." The software makes it possible for the teacher to "copy" the site and save it on the local computer hard drive. In this case, students simulate visiting the Web but are not actually connected.

Close supervision is essential. There is no organization or agency controlling activity on some computer networks. It is important for teachers to work with parents to understand their responsibilities regarding student access to information

outside the school setting. Control is in the hands of individuals; consequently, students may access questionable materials. Schools and libraries are required to have an Internet filtering system installed on their networks. Software such as NetNanny or Content Barrier is available for home use to prohibit access to topics specified by a parent.

Acceptable Use Policy. Agreements among students, parents/guardians, and the school administration outlining what is considered proper use of the Internet by all parties involved, **acceptable use policies (AUPs)** have been developed by most schools. Check to see if your school has such a policy.

The policy usually includes a statement that the school will do what it can to control access to inappropriate information, that students will accept responsibility for not accessing such information, and that parents understand the possibility that children may access such information in spite of the school's efforts. All parties sign the document agreeing that they have read and will abide by the policy. Most states' departments of education have generated resources to assist educators in developing AUPs for their schools. For additional information on this topic, go to the Web Resources at the end of this chapter.

Netiquette. There are informal rules for appropriate behavior on the Internet. If the Internet is the information superhighway, these are the "rules of the road." Referred to as netiquette, they apply to email, texting, and to other interactions on the Web:

- Keep your message short and simple. Try to limit your message to one screen. Think before you write. Make it brief, descriptive, and to the point.
- Identify yourself as the sender somewhere in the communication, including your name and school address. Not all Internet addresses clearly identify the sender.
- Double check the address or URL before sending a message.
- When replying to a message, include the pertinent portions of the original message.
- Don't write anything you would not want somebody other than the receiver to read. Email can be intercepted or forwarded.
- Check spelling, grammar, and punctuation. Use lowercase letters except for proper names and beginnings of sentences. When texting, use common conventions where appropriate.
- Be sensitive to others. Treat other people with respect and courtesy, especially in reference to social, cultural, and ethnic differences.
- Don't use sarcasm. It often falls flat and doesn't come across as you intended.

- Be careful with humor. It is a two-edged sword. The reader doesn't have the benefit of your facial expression, body language, or tone of voice. You can use **emoticons** or "email body language" such as ;) for a wink or :(for a frown, but this type of humor doesn't communicate as well as being there.
- Cooperate and share. Consider yourself a guest on the system just as if you were a guest in someone's home. Make an effort to share pertinent information. In exchange for help and information you receive, be willing to answer questions and to share your resources.
- Carefully consider copyright. Just because something can be copied electronically doesn't mean it should be distributed without permission. Unless stated otherwise, *all material* on the Internet is copyrighted (see Copyright Concerns in this chapter and in Chapter 1).
- Be alert for obscenity. Laws governing obscenity apply to messages on the Internet. Moreover, even material that is not deemed legally obscene may still be inappropriate for school-age children.

ASSURE Case Study Reflection

Review the ASSURE Classroom Case Study and video at the beginning of the chapter. Identify the use of distance learning technology in helping students to learn history. How has Mr. Chun ensured student safety and appropriate interactions when his students are interacting with others? What considerations did he need to make regarding permissions?

USING DISTANCE LEARNING IN THE CLASSROOM

ADVANTAGES

- *Variety of media*. Distance learning is a versatile means of delivering information to learners around the world with a variety of media, including text, audio, graphics, animation, video, and downloadable software.

- *Up-to-date information*. Until recently, students were limited to the resources in their school buildings. Now, however, with the ability to connect to resources in the community and around the world, students can access current information.
- *Idea exchange*. Students can engage in "conversation" with experts in specific fields of study. Special speakers who can augment a class discussion or provide access to an area of study help students advance their learning.
- *Convenient communication*. Students in various locations can share ideas. They can "speak" to each other at different times and respond at their own convenience, based on the electronic record of their exchanges.
- *Interactive*. All participants get the same message—and the same interactivity in talking to the instructor or the other learners.
- *Extra/Advanced resources*. Distance learning expands the opportunities for smaller schools as well as for individuals participating in home schooling. Students who need additional challenge in their study or have moved beyond what is available in their school can access extra coursework that allows them to continue to advance in their learning.
- *Remediation/Course recovery*. Distance learning expands the opportunities for students who are in need of supplementary instruction. Students who have fallen behind due to illness or other factors can enroll in distance education courses to continue their education.

LIMITATIONS

- *Inappropriate material*. One concern is that some of the topics, especially on the Internet, are *not* appropriate for students. For example, tobacco and alcohol ads appear on the Internet along with games and music kids enjoy. Students can find their way, innocently enough, into topics that are inappropriate or into unsafe environments.
- *Copyright*. Because information is so readily accessible, it is easy for an individual to quickly download a file and illegally appropriate it. Thus, students may turn in a paper or project that is "cut and pasted" and *not* their own work.
- *Finding information*. It is estimated that several thousand new websites are added to the Internet every day. Because this growth makes finding information more difficult, teachers need to work with the school media specialist to help students learn effective search strategies. To assist in information retrieval, several commercial companies and universities provide search engines that follow web links to return results matching your query.

- *Support.* Without good technical support and thoughtful management, distance learning can be frustrating for the learner and the teacher. The teacher may have designed quality instruction, but if the technology is not working properly, the learner will find it difficult to access the information. It would be beneficial to have technical support as part of the delivery options for students at a distance.
- *Lack of quality control.* Students need to be critical thinkers and readers who know how to evaluate information. Everything posted on the Internet is *not* "fact." Anybody can post anything on the Web, including unsubstantiated, erroneous, or untruthful information.
- *Cost.* It is expensive to establish a quality distance learning program. For the learner, many of the costs for Internet access are not apparent. To be effective a program requires a large-capacity computer connected to the Internet for a file server. The design of the instruction requires not only the instructor's knowledge of content, but also the hardware and software for delivery and the technical support that is necessary to ensure success.
- *Intimidation.* Lack of experience with this type of communication technology may make some learners less willing to participate.
- *Limited experience using the systems.* Many teachers and students are unfamiliar with interactive learning systems.

INTEGRATION

Distance learning options continue to expand, from whole courses or programs to enhanced classroom activities, as well as a host of information about topics of interest.

Virtual public schools. A growing number of virtual public schools (VPS) using the Internet for delivery of instruction offer courses or whole programs of study (Wood, 2005). The VPS are typically offered as state-level initiatives in which students can access courses that might not be available to them at their local schools or take advanced placement classes from other high schools or from colleges and universities anywhere in the world. It is possible to obtain a high school or college diploma without ever setting foot in a classroom. Many software applications (e.g., WebCT, Blackboard) provide both ease of access to the instruction and resources for the instructor and students for successful study online.

The following issues need to be addressed by anyone wishing to venture into this area of academic study:

- Credentials of the institution offering the degree
- Quality and rigor of the courses
- Costs associated with online courses, such as equipment requirements, online charges, and tuition

Connecting with Email. Text communication between individuals through electronic mail (email) can be integrated into lessons and used by students to gather information from and ask questions of individuals beyond the school walls (e.g., other students and experts). For example, during a unit on weather, students can gather weather data (temperatures, rainfall, and wind direction) from students in other geographic areas. They can also request weather maps from the local TV meteorologist, which can be sent as attachments to email, or use the NOAA website for recent satellite photos (Figure 7.7). Experts from the National Weather Service can be contacted for the answers to specific questions. Of course, as the teacher, you should always make any necessary arrangements in advance.

Students can also use email to gather information for individual projects. For example, middle school students investigating careers can contact individuals in those professions for answers to student-generated questions. The products of the students' investigation can be "job reports," to be shared with the class either as an oral presentation or a written document.

One growing use of electronic learning at the PK–12 level promotes writing skills by connecting students with "electronic pen pals" or "key pals." For example, one teacher connected her elementary students with students in a language arts methods class at a university across the city (see Taking a Look at Technology Integration: Key Pals). The students exchanged email in which the university students helped the younger ones with their writing. Both groups benefited from this experience. The younger students learned ways to improve their writing, and the college students

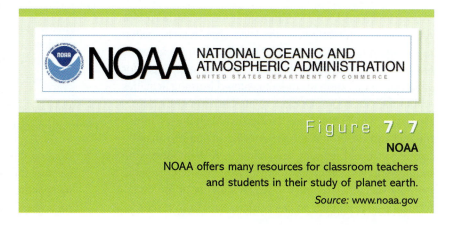

Figure **7.7**
NOAA
NOAA offers many resources for classroom teachers and students in their study of planet earth.
Source: www.noaa.gov

Key Pals

Rick Traw, a professor at the University of Northern Iowa, wanted to extend the experiences of his elementary education students in language arts applications. Because of scheduling difficulties, it was impossible to arrange a visit for his students to work on writing skills with students in a nearby urban elementary school. With the aid of the Internet, however, it was possible for the elementary students to send their stories to their university "key-pals" for review. The children had an exciting new audience for their writing, and the university students had an opportunity to learn about working with emerging writers firsthand. Traw and the classroom teacher provided guidance to the college students in techniques for assisting the young children with their writing.

Stockdisc

learned about working with children. This is an example of how mentors can be linked with students to help them learn about a variety of topics.

Systems have also been set up that allow students from different countries, even those speaking different languages, to learn about each other's cultures through computer-mediated communications. To address any language barriers, the computer can be set up to provide language translations.

Students can participate in projects conducted with classes in other locations, allowing students to plan and produce projects collaboratively. Examples include sharing local history with students in other geographic locations and collaborating with students in different classes to solve complex mathematical problems.

Integrating WebQuests. Although students can access a rich array of information on the Web, their searches often use random or low-level thinking skills. With **WebQuests** teachers can help students access the Web effectively for gathering information in student-centered learning activities within the classroom (Dodge, 1999). Developed by Bernie Dodge at San Diego State University, WebQuests infuse Internet resources into the school's curriculum to make a hybrid, or mixed learning environment. A WebQuest is an inquiry-oriented simulation activity designed with specific learning outcomes in mind in which some or all of the information that students interact with comes from resources

on the Internet. Students follow a series of steps to gather information meaningful to the task.

1. *Introduction.* A scenario points to key issues or concepts to prepare the students to ask questions.
2. *Task.* Students identify issues or problems and form questions for the WebQuest.
3. *Process.* In groups, students assume roles and begin to identify the procedures they will follow to gather information to answer their questions.
4. *Sources.* Resources are identified by the teacher and students to investigate in their WebQuest. This is one area where the teacher helps to provide the links to websites and to ensure students have access to other support materials.
5. *Conclusion.* This is the end of the WebQuest, but it invites students to continue to investigate issues or problems. WebQuests often end with an evaluation of the process students used along with benchmarks for achievement.

WebQuests can be applied to many types of lessons and information sources:

- Monitoring current events for social studies
- Science activities such as tracking weather and studying space probes to other planets (e.g., NASA at www.nasa.gov)

- Databases of information and links for expository writing assignments
- Mathematics puzzles, which require logical thinking
- Discussion groups with online exchange of ideas and information
- Job banks and resumé services for practice in job-seeking activities

Connecting with Computer Conferencing. Sometimes called desktop video conferencing, computer conferencing is real-time (synchronous) person-to-person or group conferencing on the Internet in which two or more computers are connected together for textual, visual, audio, and graphical information exchange. With special software and a video camera, you can experience audio and full-color video "chats" on the computer. Multiple individuals can participate in the "live" discussion. A group can interactively share documents and information and have access to such features as a whiteboard and chat windows.

Connecting with Parents. Communications with parents can be enhanced if they have Internet access. General information can be sent to all parents or specific information or questions can be addressed to an individual student's parents or guardians. Class webpages can inform parents of homework assignments, parent meetings, or materials needed for a special project. For those parents without Internet access,

teachers will need to employ written correspondence or the telephone.

Connecting with Other Teachers. Teachers can also use email to share ideas with other teachers. Lesson plans can be sent as attachments or placed on the school's or district's server. Questions can be asked of an individual teacher or a group of teachers (e.g., all physics teachers in a state). Another means for electronic sharing of ideas is a blog, which stands for "web log" and looks a lot like an online discussion board (discussed in more detail in Chapter 6). Blogs written by experts can provide teachers and students with access to information. Teachers can also assist students in developing personal blogs to enhance their ability to exchange ideas. One word of caution when beginning this type of electronic community: As stated throughout this book, the teacher needs to prepare students regarding their online safety, advising them not to reveal personal information in any communication.

Connecting with Communities. A number of cities have created websites that involve a broad cross section of the community, including schools, businesses, local government, and social agencies. This is another example of how the artificial wall between the classroom and the world beyond is dissolving, making it possible for students and teachers to access information and people from every imaginable source (see Taking a Look at Technology Integration: GLOBE).

TAKING A LOOK
AT TECHNOLOGY INTEGRATION

GLOBE: Networking Students, Teachers, and Scientists

The GLOBE program (www.globe.gov) is a program that uses technology to promote scientific inquiry and environmentalism. To participate, students send scientific data they collect over the Internet to the GLOBE network. In return, the class receives information about the data they sent, as well as how that data fits into the larger global picture. Students from over 100 countries participate in GLOBE projects. Professionals from many disciplines participate and use collected GLOBE data to advance scientific knowledge of environmental issues. For example, scientists use the valuable student-collected data to research global changes. Students benefit as well, learning about data collection, scientific protocols, and databases, in addition to opportunities to chat with scientists and other experts worldwide.

Bill Aron/PhotoEdit

Also, many museums and zoos are creating online "tours" of their exhibits. Your students can visit the Guggenheim and view the collections while learning more about the artists. They can visit the Natural History Museum or the Smithsonian National Zoological Park and participate in activities designed to help them learn. In addition, an increasing number of online journals and magazines are being published, either as supplements to existing print versions or as entirely new efforts. Moreover, most major publishers have put their catalogs on the Web, making it easy to locate and order books, software, and other products. Many publishers are willing to make their actual products available online, usually as trial packages that "dissolve" within a certain period of time—usually 30 days. However, the continuing prevalence of illegal copying and distribution of materials makes some publishers wary of complete and unlimited access to software and files.

ASSURE Case Study Reflection

Review the ASSURE Classroom Case Study and video at the beginning of the chapter. Identify the use of distance learning technology in helping students to learn history. What other types of distance learning resources might Mr. Chun use to support learning for his students?

Intranet Connections. School districts or schools often purchase or develop instructional modules that can be sent over an **intranet** (a way of distributing information within a school or district discussed later in this chapter). This method of delivery is used to provide students with remediation or enhance learning opportunities with the latest version of materials. Updating these materials is relatively easy because the core set of digital material can be electronically modified and made immediately available, whereas in the past revisions often required shipping printed materials or computer disks to schools. Electronic learning provides flexibility to students as well because they may study materials at any time and at any location. Students can also take tests over the intranet. Once the answers are in the database, they are scored and the results made available immediately to students and the teacher. Online learning is very useful when learners are geographically dispersed and instruction is updated frequently.

NETWORKS

It is common knowledge that computers can be used to connect students to people and resources outside of the classroom. Once you connect computers in ways that enable people to communicate and share information, you have a **network.** Networks connect schools, homes, libraries, organizations, and businesses so that students, families, and professionals can access or share information and instruction instantly in several ways.

TYPES OF NETWORKS

LAN. The simplest of all networks is a local area network (LAN), which connects computers within a limited area, normally a classroom, building, or laboratory. These networks connect individual computers to one another to permit exchange of files and other resources (Figure 7.8).

A LAN relies on a centralized computer called a **file server** that "serves" all the other computers connected to it. A computer lab is often itself a LAN because all the computers in the lab are connected to a single file server, usually tucked away in a closet or other out-of-the-way space. Whole buildings can also be connected to a local area network, usually with a single computer, generally located in the office or media center, serving as the school's file server. Through a

With a LAN a teacher can provide common instruction for all students in a lab.
Getty RF

TECHNOLOGY
for Diverse Learners

Distance Learning Resources

Students in our classrooms have a variety of learning needs. The following examples show ways that your learners can use distance learning resources to help them with their learning.

For students who have visual disabilities or difficulty reading information on a webpage, various design guidelines can be helpful. When including graphics or images, text descriptions can be a resource. For example, along with the image of a feline, add the word *cat* nearby. Avoid using complex tables with many columns. Computer text readers read across one entire line at a time instead of reading each column separately. On hyperlinks, use meaningful terms rather than a graphic or "click here" link that tells nothing about the link. Additional information is available at the World Wide Web Consortium (W3C) Accessibility Initiative (www.w3.org). Bobby (www.cast.org/bobby) is a site that will analyze webpages for accessibility to people with disabilities.

Young students who would like to learn more about using the Internet safely can join WoogiWorld (www.woogiworld.com). Through games and activities students are guided through protocols that advise them about being safe when engaging in pursuits on the Internet. Each child must have parental permission to use the site before they are allowed full access to all the resources. Parents are given information about their child's user name, password, and types of activities available.

Students who wish to advance their knowledge and be challenged in their thinking can use the Internet in a variety of ways. JingProject.com provides students with an easy way to capture visuals and integrate them into their work. In addition, with Jing, students can create simple "how-to" videos that might be helpful in learning new tasks or sharing ideas with others.

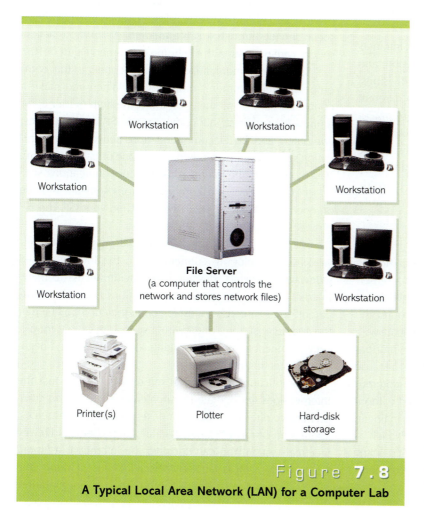

File Server
(a computer that controls the network and stores network files)

Workstation
Workstation
Workstation
Workstation
Workstation
Workstation
Printer(s)
Plotter
Hard-disk storage

Figure 7.8
A Typical Local Area Network (LAN) for a Computer Lab

LAN, all of the classrooms in a school can have access to the school's collection of software. Many schools also allow teachers and students to save their computer work in personalized folders on the server, which is very useful when multiple students use one computer. It also allows teachers access to their materials, such as a PowerPoint presentation, while in the computer lab.

Within a school, LANs can also reduce a technology coordinator's workload, which might otherwise include installing programs, inventorying software, and other such tasks. Coordinators can then spend more time working with teachers and students rather than with machines and software. For example, the media center can store its catalog of materials on the file server, giving teachers and students easy access to the information available on a certain topic.

WAN. Networks that extend beyond the walls of a room or building are called **wide area networks (WANs).** A campus or districtwide network connecting all buildings via a cable or fiber system is one such example. In this arrangement, the buildings are linked to a centralized computer that serves as the host for all the software used in common. Even though a WAN can connect computers over a wide geographic area (across a city, state, or even a country), it is most often used for smaller configurations, such as connecting the buildings within a school system.

As the name implies, a **wireless network** connects computers without wire. Instead it relies on radio frequency, microwave, or infrared technology that depends on a base station for connection to the network. Such networks use transmitters placed inside the room, throughout the building, or across a campus area and operate in the same manner as hardwired networks. Some cities have installed wireless networks in their downtown areas. Wireless networks omit the need for cabling, which can be costly to install, particularly in older buildings. Computers are no longer bound to workstations. Laptops may be used anywhere within the room, building, or campus area and still have access to the Internet.

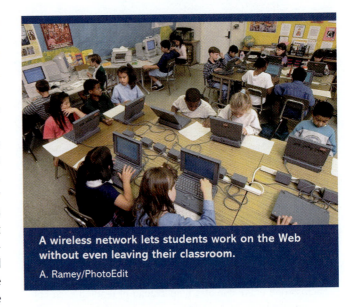

A wireless network lets students work on the Web without even leaving their classroom.
A. Ramey/PhotoEdit

Intranet. A special type of network called an **intranet** is used internally by a school or organization. It is a proprietary or closed network that connects multiple sites across the state, within the country, or around the world. Systems connected to an intranet are private and accessible only by individuals within a given school or organization.

Intranets provide internal networks for schools. Intranets are a way of increasing communication, collaboration, and information dissemination within schools where divisions, departments, and workgroups might each use a different **computer platform** (hardware and operating system), or where users work in geographically distant locations. Even though an intranet may be connected to a larger network (the Internet, for example), a software package called a **firewall** prevents external users from accessing the internal network, while allowing internal users to access external networks (Figure 7.9).

Internet. The **Internet** is a worldwide system for linking smaller computer networks together. It is a network of networks with a frequently changing collection of millions of computer networks serving billions of people around the world. Any individual on the Internet can communicate with anyone else on the Internet. Users can access any information, regardless of the type of computer they have, because of standard protocols that allow all computers to communicate with each other. Most information is shared without charge except for whatever access fee is required to maintain an account with an **Internet service provider (ISP)** such as Comcast or any of the many local or community ISPs. Many schools provide Internet accounts to teachers and students at no charge.

Both telephone companies and television cable companies provide high-speed access to the Internet. **Integrated services digital network (ISDN)** lines provide speeds up to five times that of regular phone lines. A **digital subscriber line (DSL)** provides even faster access—up to 30 times that of a standard phone line. TV cable companies also offer high-speed service through a **cable modem.** All of these access services are popular with the home consumer (Figure 7.10).

Special communication software connects the computer to a telecommunication service. When you make a connection to the Internet, you enlist the help of four communication services: your computer, the ISP, the server (host computer), and the telecommunications network (communication software and a modem and phone or cable modem). Your computer (the *client*) runs the communications software. Your modem and communications software provide an open path between your computer and your ISP. The ISP provides you a link to the Internet.

Many educational and commercial organizations networks are developing connections to the Internet called **gateways** or **portals,** designed to provide access to many Internet services. The maze of connections is largely "transparent" to the user. Users just *log on* to their computer (enter the computer system, often with a special password for privacy), connect to their networking service or ISP, and begin to exchange information.

Complicating information retrieval is the fact that the Internet does *not* operate hierarchically. There are no comprehensive directory trees or indexes for Internet resources. There is no Library of Congress cataloging scheme or Dewey Decimal system. You can consider the Internet as a library where every shelf is labeled "Miscellaneous." Finding one interesting service or item of information is no guarantee

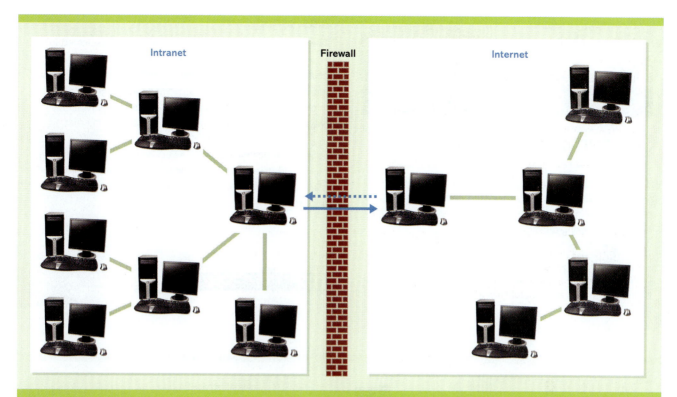

Intranet **Firewall** **Internet**

Figure **7.9**

Firewalls

A firewall protects an internal network (intranet) from external users but allows internal users to access external networks (Internet).

that you're on the right track to others. In fact, most of the Internet's resources are in little cul-de-sacs on the network, not linked in any predictable way to other, similar resources. To find information on the Internet you must use **search engines,** programs that identify websites containing user-entered keywords or phrases (see Media Samples: Search Engines for Kids).

Connecting to the WWW

Computer (client) Modem ISP Server (host)

Figure **7.10**

Internet Service Providers

You can connect to the World Wide Web from your home or classroom through an Internet service provider (ISP).

THE WORLD WIDE WEB

The **World Wide Web (the Web)** is a network of networks that allows you to access, view, and maintain documents that can include text, data, sound, and video (Figure 7.11). It is *not* separate from the Internet. Instead it rides on top of it, in the same way that an application such as PowerPoint runs on top of an operating system such as Windows.

The Web is a series of communications protocols between client and server. These protocols enable access to documents stored on computers throughout the Internet while allowing links to other documents on other computers. The Web protocol **hypertext transfer protocol (HTTP)** ensures compatibility before transferring information contained in documents called **webpages.** Each individual collection of pages is called a **website,** which users access by entering its address or **uniform resource locator (URL)** into a browser (see the list of websites at the end of this chapter). The URL incorporates the name of the host computer (server), the domain, the directory on the server, and the title of the webpage (actual filename)

Search Engines for Kids

askkids.com

This is a student version of Ask.com that uses age-appropriate content, filtering, and search terms to help kids narrow their searches by asking questions.

kidsclick.org

Librarians created this site to help students conduct searches. Main topic menus and helpful links make it a kid-friendly search engine.

kids.yahoo.com

The student version of Yahoo! includes sites preselected for young people ages 7 to 12 that present information in a colorful, interactive way. Teachers have been asked to review identified sites, and there is a parent page designed to share information about Internet safety and offer suggestions for ways to help children gain value from using the Internet.

To research this media, pick a selection rubric to evaluate the media and determine which one would work with your lesson plans. See the Web Resources Selection Rubric at the end of this chapter.

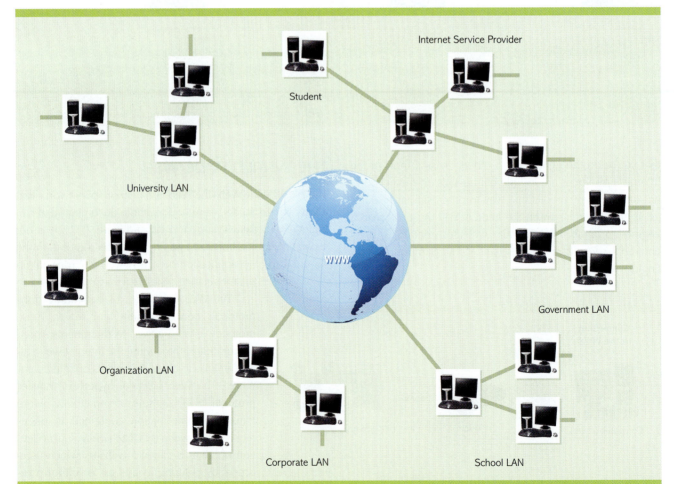

Figure **7.11**

The World Wide Web

The Internet is a collection of computer networks. A student, for example, might access the Internet from her home computer or through a school computer lab.

http://eduscapes.com/tap/index.htm

format / protocol | domain name | directory on server | actual filename

Figure 7.12
Sample Web Address or Uniform Resource Locator (URL)

Students can add a 3D view to an image in a book by taking an photograph and using AR software so the image "pops out" of the page.

Courtesy of Metaio, Inc.

(Figure 7.12). Navigation within and among webpages relies on hypertext links that, when selected, move users to another location on the same page, another website on the same host computer, or to a different computer on the Web.

To use the Web for online learning, webpages have to be designed and written, and a host computer must be available to house them. Universities and large companies are usually directly connected to the Internet and run the necessary Web hosting (server) software. A popular resource in online distance learning, the **Course Management Tool (CMT),** is software designed to make it easier for the teacher to use the resources that are part of the system, such as the Discussion Board, Test options, and Grade Book. When using a CMT program such as Blackboard or Moodle, the teacher can concentrate on the instruction and not have to be concerned with computer programming issues.

Evaluating Web Resources. There are so many resources available for students and learners on the Web that it can be difficult to determine which are the best to support learning. A selection rubric has been provided at the end of this chapter to guide you in identifying websites that will benefit your professional development or support your students' learning. You can even ask students to use the rubric to evaluate sites they find while exploring new resources for their learning experiences (See Selection Rubric: Web Resources on pages 172–173).

media, live action—with the real world to enhance the information we perceive with our senses. With the advent of wireless mobile devices such as smart phones, AR can now combine real-world data with virtual data. Using the GPS capability of a smart phone and AR software, the user can capture an image and "augment" or enhance knowledge about that image with additional information from the Internet superimposed onto it. For example, while on a field trip to a nearby city, students can photograph a building and then obtain information from the Internet about it while they view the image. Rather than just being devices for interacting socially, their smart phones become learning tools that can easily bring them information when it is most useful. By also adding 3D views to images they take with their mobile phones, images "pop out" of the page, giving students new "views" of real-world objects.

on the HORIZON

AUGMENTED REALITY
Engineering Tool Entices Education

Augmented reality (AR) has been available for some time in engineering systems to blend virtual data—documents,

Summary

Learning at a distance is not new. Both audio and television resources have been used for many years in distance teaching settings. As the technologies have advanced, these capabilities have been incorporated into more learning opportunities for students. One major advantage of access to a variety of technology assets is that teachers can augment student study and bring additional resources into the classroom. The blending of the regular classroom and distance learning resources has made it possible for students of all ability levels to enjoy an enhanced educational experience.

Distance learning opportunities continue to expand and extend classroom activities. Teachers are no longer limited to the materials in their classrooms or in the school media center. They can access resources from around the world. They can provide their students with experiences such as WebQuests that help them learn to use the Internet as a source of information. Students can reach out to other students and to experts for exchanges of ideas. The Internet has opened classrooms to a wealth of information around the world!

PEARSON **myeducationkit**™

To check your comprehension of the content covered in Chapter 7, go to the **MyEducationKit** for your book and complete the Study Plan for Chapter 7. Here you will be able to take a chapter quiz, receive feedback on your answers, and then access resources that will enhance your understanding of the chapter content.

ASSURE Lesson Plan

The following ASSURE Lesson Plan provides a detailed description and analysis of the lesson in the ASSURE Classroom Case Study and video at the beginning of the chapter. To review the video again, go to the MyEducationKit for your text and click on the ASSURE Video under Chapter 7. The video explores how Mr. Chun creates a high school social studies lesson in collaboration with another teacher in New Hampshire.

Analyze Learners

General Characteristics. The students in Jimmy Chun's high school class are primarily Hawaiian and from low- to middle-income homes. They are fairly equally distributed with regard to gender and range in age from 15 to 17 years old. Student reading ability is at or above grade level. Student behavior problems are minimal.

Entry Competencies. The students are, in general, able to do the following:

- Conduct online research
- Use Blackboard software to participate in discussion boards and exchange digital documents

Learning Styles. Mr. Chun's students learn best when engaged in activities that are relevant and include lively discussions of meaningful topics. His students vary in comfort level with speaking to students in the distance education (New Hampshire) class. Some students prefer live audio to using the text-based discussion boards.

State Standards and Objectives

Curriculum Standards. National Council for the Social Studies, III. People, Places, and Environments: Social studies programs should include experiences that provide for the study of people, places, and environments, so that the learner can (i) describe and assess ways that historical events have been influenced by, and have influenced, physical and human geographic factors in local, regional, national, and global settings.

Technology Standards. National Educational Technology Standards for Students 4—Technology communications tools: Students use telecommunications to collaborate, publish, and interact with peers, experts, and other audiences; and 5—Technology research tools: Students use technology to locate, evaluate, and collect information from a variety of sources.

Learning Objectives

1. Using content from conducting Internet and library research of pre-1770 U.S. history regarding Hawaiian and New Hampshire culture, religion, government, economy, and social structure, the students will write questions and give written responses during an online discussion.
2. Using the questions and information gained during discussion board dialog, the students will ask New Hampshire students questions regarding their pre-1770 society with respect to culture, religion, government, economy, and social structure.
3. Using the information gained during discussion board dialog and personal knowledge, the students will answer questions posed by the New Hampshire students regarding Hawaiian pre-1770 society with respect to culture, religion, government, economy, and social structure.

Select Strategies, Technology, Media, and Materials

Select Strategies. Jimmy Chun selects teacher- and student-centered strategies for the pre-1770 U.S. history lesson. The teacher-centered strategies involve providing a detailed description of the lesson objectives and how students should prepare for the video teleconference with the New Hampshire students. Mr. Chun also provides feedback to students as they complete their work. The student-centered strategies consist of students' Internet research on the pre-1770 history of their states, posting their questions on the discussion board, and participating in the two-way audio/video distance education teleconference with the New Hampshire students.

Select Technology and Media. This lesson involves student use of computers, distance education equipment, and Blackboard software to post to the discussion board and exchange documents. Mr. Chun applies the following guidelines to assess the appropriateness of his technology and media selections:

- *Alignment with standards, outcomes, and objectives*. The Internet sites, Blackboard software, and distance education video teleconference provide the necessary support for Jimmy Chun's students to meet the learning objectives.
- *Accurate and current information*. Students use both text-based and Internet resources to conduct their research on pre-1770 U.S. history.
- *Age-appropriate language*. Mr. Chun has his students access websites that are appropriate for high school students. When needed, he provides assistance for student use of Blackboard.
- *Interest level and engagement*. The Hawaiian and New Hampshire students are very excited to "meet" and discuss important pre-1770 U.S. history and current topics of interest to them on the discussion boards and during the live two-way audio/video sessions.

- *Technical quality*. The technical quality of the two-way audio/video interactions is consistent with current standards in that the video is slightly delayed. Discussion board interactions and Internet searches have consistently high technical quality due to high-speed access at both schools.
- *Ease of use*. Blackboard requires initial training and support but is fairly easy for high school students to use after basic skills training.
- *Bias free*. Students find multiple references for their research to better ensure the content is bias free. Blackboard software is bias free.
- *User guide and directions*. The online help features of Blackboard are moderately easy for students to use. Students most frequently ask each other or Mr. Chun for assistance with technical difficulties.

Select Materials. Jimmy Chun provided a list of Internet sites for students to reference when conducting online research on pre-1770 U.S. history.

tilize Technology, Media, and Materials

Preview the Technology, Media, and Materials. Jimmy Chun previews Blackboard software to ensure it has the features needed for the lesson. He previews selected resources to verify that students can find Internet and text-based information on pre-1770 U.S. history. He also previews the video teleconferencing system to make certain students will be able to see and hear each other.

Prepare the Technology, Media, and Materials. Mr. Chun prepares an assignment sheet that describes the lesson requirements and criteria that will be used to assess the final student products. He adds starter questions to the Blackboard discussion area.

Prepare the Environment. Jimmy Chun tests the Internet connections on the lab computers and ensures that Blackboard is accessible from each computer. He also tests the distance education equipment by connecting to the classroom in New Hampshire and practicing with the cameras, microphones, and lighting.

Prepare the Learners. Students in Mr. Chun's class have conducted Internet research and have participated in previous video teleconferences with the students in New Hampshire. Therefore, learner preparation primarily focuses on the topics to be covered on the discussion board and during the live session.

Provide the Learning Experience. The learning experience occurs in two distance education formats: text-based exchanges via discussion boards and live two-way audio/video interactions between the Hawaiian and New Hampshire students.

equire Learner Participation

Student Practice Activities. The students in Jimmy Chun's class use computers, the Internet, and Blackboard software to prepare for and participate in the online discussions of pre-1770 U.S. history of Hawaii and New Hampshire. The students apply information from their research and discussion board topics to generate questions to ask during the live video teleconference.

During the live session, students practice and test their knowledge by asking and answering student-created questions.

Feedback. Jimmy Chun provides continuous feedback as students conduct their research, participate in discussion boards, and interact with students from New Hampshire.

 valuate and Revise

Assessment of Learner Achievement. Mr. Chun reviews the discussion board posts of each individual student to assess knowledge of pre-1770 Hawaiian and New Hampshire society. He also reviews recordings of the video teleconference to assess student oral responses to questions asked by the New Hampshire students. Mr. Chun assesses student ability to use technology for communication and research by evaluating student Blackboard posts.

Evaluation of Strategies, Technology, and Media. Mr. Chun evaluates the effectiveness of the lesson strategies, talking about the process with the New Hampshire teacher and students and with the students in his class. Evaluation of the technology and media involves examining the functionality of the Blackboard software, the Internet browser, and the two-way audio/video distance education session.

Revision. The evaluation results revealed that student interactions could benefit from arranging students in cross-state pairs to increase interactions and information exchange. Another revision that emerged from the evaluation results was to limit teacher input during the live two-way audio/video sessions to encourage more student-to-student discussion.

CONTINUING MY PROFESSIONAL DEVELOPMENT

Demonstrating Professional Knowledge

1. What is distance learning?
2. Why use distance learning for elementary, middle-level, and secondary education?
3. How do audio and television systems facilitate distance learning?
4. Identify three differences between online learning and distance education.
5. Identify three characteristics each of LAN, WAN, intranet, and wireless networks.
6. Define Internet netiquette and list five guidelines for users.
7. Identify one copyright concern issue and explain why it is important.

Demonstrating Professional Skills

1. Interview a teacher who regularly uses audio or television for distance learning in the classroom. Prepare a brief written or recorded report addressing the objectives covered, techniques utilized, and problems encountered. An example might be elementary students using a two-way audio/video system to investigate a community issue. (ISTE NETS-T 1.B & 3.C)
2. Develop a lesson incorporating a WebQuest to engage learners. What changes did you need to make in the design of the lesson to incorporate the WebQuest? What Internet safety issues have to be confronted?

What learner skills and assessment considerations do you need to address when including a WebQuest in a lesson? (ISTE NETS-T 1.B, 2.A, 2.C, 3.D, 4.A, & 4.B)

3. Develop an Internet acceptable use policy for your school (either where you attended or where you teach). (ISTE NETS-T 4.A & 4.C)

4. Observe or participate in a class taught at a distance. Describe how the teacher and students interact with each other. Also, describe the types and uses of media within the lesson. (ISTE NETS-T 1.D & 3.C)

Building My Professional Portfolio

- *Creating My Lesson.* Using the ASSURE model, design a lesson for one of the case studies presented in the Case Study Chart in Appendix A or use a scenario of your own design. Apply one of the instructional strategies described in Chapter 4 and information from this chapter related to incorporating distance education and online learning into your instructional setting. Be sure to include information about the audience, the objectives, and all other elements of the ASSURE model. Be certain to match your intended outcomes to state or national learning standards for your content area. (ISTE NETS-T 2.A, 2.B, & 2.C)

- *Enhancing My Lesson.* Using the lesson you've designed in the previous activity, consider your audience again. Assume that some of your students have special needs, such as physical or learning impediments. Also assume that several students are identified as gifted. How will you change your lesson

design to ensure that these students are recognized and supported to allow them to succeed in your classroom? Also consider the options available to your students at a distance related to resources and technology. How might that affect your lesson design? (ISTE NETS-T 2.A, 2.B, & 2.C)

- *Reflecting on My Lesson.* Reflect on the process of designing your lesson and your efforts at enhancing that lesson to meet student needs in your class. What have you learned about matching audience, content, instructional strategy, and materials? What could you have done to better develop your students' higher-order thinking or creativity skills or to engage them more deeply in active learning at a distance? In what ways did the strategies you selected for your lesson enhance learning opportunities for your students? What considerations do you need to better address when planning another lesson for a distance setting? (ISTE NETS-T 5.C)

SUGGESTED RESOURCES

Print

Conrad, R. M., & Donaldson, J. A. (2004). *Engaging the online learner: Activities and resources for creative instruction.* San Francisco: Jossey-Bass.

Lipinski, T. A. (2005). *Copyright law and the distance education classroom: Working within the information infrastructure.* Lanham, MD: Scarecrow Press.

Moore, M. G., & Anderson, W. G. (2008). *Handbook of distance education* (2nd ed). Mahwah, NJ: Lawrence Erlbaum.

Palloff, R. M., & Pratt, K. (2007). *Building online learning communities: Effective strategies for the virtual classroom.* San Francisco: Jossey-Bass.

Shank, P. (2007). *Online learning idea book: 95 proven ways to enhance technology-based and blended learning.* San Francisco, CA: John Wiley & Sons.

Simonson, M., Smaldino, S. E., Albright, M. J., & Zvacek, S. (2011). *Teaching and learning at a distance: Foundations of distance education* (4th ed.). Upper Saddle River, NJ: Merrill/Prentice Hall.

Web Links

To easily access these web links from your browser, go to the MyEducationKit for your text, then go to Chapter 7 and click on the web links.

The Adventures of Cyberbee

www.cyberbee.com

This site is filled with helpful ideas and activities for using the Internet in education.

Classroom Connect

www.classroom.net

This valuable site for PK–12 teachers and students includes classroom links, materials for educators, addresses of other educators online, and products to bring the Internet into the classroom.

CNN Interactive

www.cnn.com

CNN is an up-to-the-minute source for world news and information about weather, sports, science, technology, show business, and health.

Public Broadcasting Service (PBS)

www.pbs.org

A nonprofit consortium of the nation's public television stations, PBS makes noncommercial television available to the public. Its website includes resources related to the quality programs and services for educators and parents.

San Diego Zoo and Wild Animal Park

www.sandiegozoo.org

This site provides a virtual tour of the San Diego Zoo and includes information about the zoo, its inhabitants, and endangered species.

Sesame Workshop

www.sesameworkshop.org

A nonprofit educational organization that creates entertaining and educational radio and television programming, the Sesame Workshop focuses on providing learning opportunities for children, while assisting teachers, day-care providers, and parents in developing quality learning experiences and curricula in a variety of media formats.

Selection Rubric: WEB RESOURCES

To download and complete this rubric for your own use, go to the MyEducationKit for your text, then go to Chapter 7 and click on Selection Rubrics.

Search Terms Used to Locate Resources

_____

_____

_____

_____

Title _____

Source/Location _____

© Date _____

Subject Area _____ Grade Level _____

Instructional Strategies _____

Hardware Required _____

Primary User(s):

_____ Student

_____ Teacher

Brief Description

Standards/Outcomes/Objectives

Prerequisites (e.g., prior knowledge, reading ability, vocabulary level)

Strengths

Limitations

Special Features

Name _____ Date _____

Rating Area	High Quality	Medium Quality	Low Quality
Alignment with Standards, Outcomes, and Objectives	Standards/outcomes/objectives addressed and use of web resource should enhance student learning.	Standards/outcomes/objectives partially addressed and use of web resource may enhance student learning.	Standards/outcomes/objectives not addressed and use of web resource will likely not enhance student learning.
Accurate and Current Information	Information is correct and does not contain material that is out of date.	Information is correct, but does contain material that is out of date.	Information is not correct and does contain material that is out of date.
Age-Appropriate Language	Language used is age appropriate and vocabulary is understandable.	Language used is nearly age appropriate and some vocabulary is above/below student age.	Language used is not age appropriate and vocabulary is clearly inappropriate for student age.
Interest Level and Engagement	Topic is presented so that students are likely to be interested and actively engaged in learning.	Topic is presented to interest students most of the time and engage most students in learning.	Topic is presented so as not to interest students and not engage them in learning.
Technical Quality	The material represents the best available technology and media.	The material represents technology and media that are good quality, although there may be some problems using it.	The material represents technology and media that are not well prepared and are of very poor quality.
Ease of Use (Student or Teacher)	Material follows easy-to-use patterns with nothing to confuse the user.	Material follows patterns that are easy to follow most of the time, with a few things to confuse the user.	Material follows no patterns and most of the time the user is very confused.
Bias Free	There is no evidence of objectionable bias or advertising.	There is little evidence of bias or advertising.	There is much evidence of bias or advertising.
User Guide and Directions	The user guide is an excellent resource to support a lesson. Directions should help teachers and students use the material.	The user guide is a good resource to support a lesson. Directions may help teachers and students use the material.	The user guide is a poor resource to support a lesson. Directions do not help teachers and students use the material.
Clear Directions	Navigation is logical and pages are well organized.	Navigation is logical for main use, but can be confusing.	Navigation is not logical and pages are not well organized.
Stimulates Creativity	Use of web resource gives students many opportunities to engage in new learning experiences.	Use of web resource gives students some opportunities to engage in new learning experiences.	Use of web resource gives students few opportunities to engage in new learning experiences.
Visual Design	The web resource is designed with appropriate use of graphics and text to ensure student understanding.	The web resource is designed with graphics and text that are of average quality.	The web resource is designed with graphics and text that are of poor quality and distract students from understanding.
Quality of Links	The web resource links facilitate navigating the material and finding additional information.	The web resource links are not easy to navigate and make it difficult to find additional information.	The web resource links make it very difficult to navigate the material and to find additional information.
Site Map	The site map is available and useful to help navigate and access information.	The site map is available and somewhat useful to help navigate and access information.	The site map is not available or not useful to help navigate and access information.

Recommended for Classroom Use: _____ Yes _____ No

CHAPTER EIGHT

Enhancing
Learning with Visuals

The chapter addresses ISTE NETS-T 2.

1. Define visual literacy in your own words and identify two general strategies that you may use to teach visual literacy.

2. Name six types of visuals and describe an example of each.

3. Describe the roles that visuals play in learning.

4. Identify four methods for viewing visuals in the classroom.

5. Describe the advantages, limitations, and integration of visuals.

6. State in your own words the goals that good visual design aims to achieve.

7. Discuss four techniques for creating visuals.

8. Discuss two methods for capturing images.

Goal

Discuss the various types and uses of visuals and the general principles for creating and using visuals to enhance student learning.

Mrs. Roman, a third-grade teacher, noted that her students' test scores indicated problems with visualizing mathematical figures. She especially noted their difficulties with mentally converting a two-dimensional picture on the test into the three-dimensional image that it represented. She spoke with Mrs. Edlund, the art teacher, to seek ways of helping her students understand visualization of ideas. Mrs. Edlund also wanted to find ways to use art to assess learning due to the school's interest in using art and technology in the learning process. She was trying to find a way to bring technology into the art classroom. Both teachers have noted that the children have difficulty thinking about their learning and expressing themselves.

*To view the **ASSURE Classroom Case Study** Video for this chapter, go to the MyEducationKit for your text and click on the ASSURE Video under Chapter 8 to explore how Mrs. Roman works with the art teacher, Mrs. Edlund, to seek ways of using art and technology to help her students understand the visualization of ideas.*

Throughout the chapter you will find reflection questions to relate the chapter content to the ASSURE Classroom Case Study. At the end of the chapter you will be challenged to develop your own ASSURE lesson that incorporates use of these strategies, technology, media, and materials, for a topic and grade level of your choice.

PEARSON

myeducationkit™

INTRODUCTION

In this chapter we will explore the selection and use of visuals for learning. Even though visuals are a commonly used classroom resource, the actual benefit to student learning is dependent on the teacher's ability to choose or create effective materials.

The design and use of visuals in instruction is an important consideration because so much learning involves visual imagery. Students must be able to visualize ideas, often using technology in the process. Most of the media discussed in this text—computer courseware, multimedia, video programs, and digital images—have a visual component.

Although teaching is saturated with images, these visuals are underused in instruction and often relegated to the motivational or decorative aspects of learning. Many students learn more readily through visual imagery, and even verbal learners need visual supports to grasp certain concepts.

VISUAL LITERACY

Visual literacy refers to the learned ability to interpret visual messages accurately and to create such messages. Visual literacy can be developed through two major approaches: helping learners to **decode,** or "read," visuals proficiently

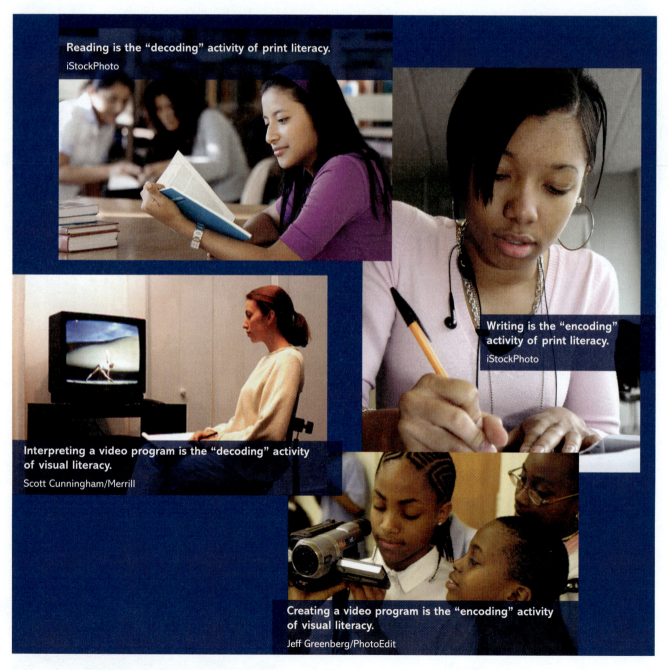

Reading is the "decoding" activity of print literacy.
iStockPhoto

Writing is the "encoding" activity of print literacy.
iStockPhoto

Interpreting a video program is the "decoding" activity of visual literacy.
Scott Cunningham/Merrill

Creating a video program is the "encoding" activity of visual literacy.
Jeff Greenberg/PhotoEdit

Visual Literacy

Visuals inundate today's students, so their ability to read, understand, create, analyze, and learn from the persuasiveness of visuals has become more important than ever. Recent research has highlighted the value of using and creating visuals as learning tools in which students exhibit their learning, share their work with a global audience, and gain the skills and competencies required to succeed in an increasingly visual world. Technology plays a critical role in visual media design, development, and production, which all utilize critical thinking and problem-solving skills that enhance students' abilities to learn. Visual literacy development has been embedded within education programs throughout the United States and in many other countries to introduce students to the concepts and skills related to interpreting visuals and communicating visually. In these programs, teachers are encouraged to think visually and to focus students' attention on the visual aspects of printed and digitally available materials, including textbooks and storybooks. With programs designed for children from preschool through high school and college and encompassing both encoding and decoding visual information in all media, visual literacy has now become well accepted as an important aspect of the curriculum at all levels of education, best developed when embedded within content areas, using activities and assessment related to local, state, or national learning standards. The International Visual Literacy Association (IVLA) is an organization established for professionals involved in visual literacy.

Programs in public schools involve students in critical viewing activities and media production projects with the aim of meeting standards in technology while achieving content standards in subject areas such as language, literacy, social studies, and science. For example, students examine materials with a focus on how elements within each medium, such as color, perspective, design, or pacing can affect the impact of visual messages. Museum websites such as the National Gallery or the Library of Congress and many others support this analysis. Teachers are encouraged to consider students' visual learning styles in selecting materials, and the importance of visuals in developing multimodal skills and assisting second language learners is emphasized. In many districts, students are engaged in learning and in using technology appropriately to create poster campaigns, design new products and advertising, examine their television viewing habits, analyze commercial messages, and digitally report the results of their research. They produce and share digital movies, create websites, and produce photo exhibits and other media to both extend their learning and share their knowledge with the global society to which they belong.

Source: Rhonda S. Robinson, Northern Illinois University

---

by practicing visual analysis skills and helping learners to **encode,** or "write," visuals to express themselves and communicate with others.

DECODING: INTERPRETING VISUALS

Seeing a visual does not automatically ensure that one will learn from it. Learners must be guided toward correct decoding of visuals. One aspect of visual literacy, then, is the skill of interpreting and creating meaning from visuals.

Many variables affect how a learner decodes a visual. Young children tend to interpret images more literally than older children. Very young children have been shown to have difficulty discriminating between realistic images and the objects they depict (DeLoache, 2005). Prior to the age of 12, children tend to interpret visuals section by section rather than as a whole. In reporting what they see in a picture, they are likely to single out specific elements within the scene. Students who are older, however, tend to summarize the whole scene and report a conclusion about the meaning of the picture.

In teaching, we must keep in mind that the act of decoding visuals may be affected by the viewer's cultural background. Different cultural groups may perceive visual materials in different ways. For example, let's say your instruction includes visuals depicting scenes typical of the home and street life of inner-city children. It is almost certain that students who live in such an area will decode these visuals differently than will students whose cultural backgrounds do not include firsthand knowledge of inner-city living. Similarly, a Native American child might interpret scenes depicting life in the Old West quite differently than an African American, Caucasian, or Mexican American child.

In selecting visuals, teachers have to make appropriate choices between the sorts of visuals that are preferred and those that are most effective. People do not necessarily learn best from the kinds of pictures they prefer. Most learners prefer colored visuals to black-and-white visuals. However, there is no significant difference in the amount of learning from either type except when color is related to the content to be learned. Most learners also prefer photographs over line drawings, even though in many situations

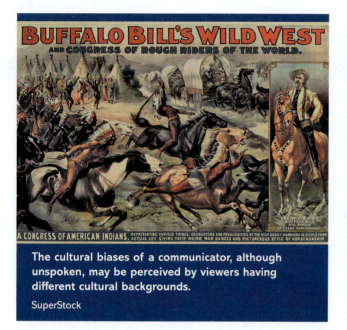

The cultural biases of a communicator, although unspoken, may be perceived by viewers having different cultural backgrounds.

SuperStock

The camcorder is a handy tool for creating visual reports.

Zunique/Newscom

line drawings may communicate better. Many learners prefer very realistic visuals to abstract representations, but teachers must strike a balance between the two to achieve their instructional purposes. Young learners prefer simple visuals and older students prefer more complex depictions, but simpler visuals are usually more effective, whatever the age group.

ENCODING: CREATING VISUALS

Another aspect of visual literacy is the ability to create visual presentations. Just as writing can spur reading, producing visuals can be a highly effective way of understanding their uses.

You should encourage students to present reports to the class by carefully selecting images from a CD or online collection, which will help them to develop their aesthetic talents. The video camcorder is a convenient tool for students to practice creating and presenting ideas and events pictorially. Students can also scan photos or drawings and insert them into a computer-generated presentation using presentation software such as PowerPoint and Keynote. Remind them to follow copyright guidelines in all these activities.

One skill nearly always included in visual education curricula is that of sequencing. Reading specialists have long known that the ability to sequence—that is, to arrange ideas in logical order—is an extremely important factor in verbal literacy, especially in the ability to communicate in writing. Students may need practice in arranging visuals into a logical sequence, which is a learned skill, like the verbal sequencing in reading and writing. For this reason, many visual education programs, especially for younger children,

emphasize activities that call for arranging visuals. The sequential nature of digital presentations such as PowerPoint assists students in acquiring this skill.

TYPES OF VISUALS USED IN THE CLASSROOM

Let's explore six types of visuals commonly found in the classroom: pictures, drawings (including sketches and diagrams), charts, graphs, posters, and cartoons.

PICTURES

Pictures are photographic (or photograph-like) representations of people, places, and things. They are readily available on the Internet and in books, magazines, and newspapers. Although pictures are two-dimensional, you can compensate for the lack of three-dimensionality by providing a group of pictures showing the same object or scene from several different angles or positions. In addition, a series of sequential still pictures can suggest motion.

You may use photographs in a variety of ways. Photographs of local architecture, for example, can illustrate a unit on architectural styles. Digital pictures taken on field trips can be valuable for classroom follow-up activities.

Students should understand that textbook pictures are not decorations but are intended to be study aids and should be used as such. Encourage students to read them just as they do the printed words. You should teach skills for decoding textbook and computer pictures and motivate learners to use them for study purposes. The quality and quantity of illustrations are, of course, important factors in textbook and media choice.

DRAWINGS

Drawings, sketches, and diagrams employ the graphic arrangement of lines to represent persons, places, things, and concepts. Drawings are readily found in textbooks and computer-based materials. You can use them in all phases of instruction, from introduction of topics through evaluation.

Teacher-made drawings can be effective aids to learning. You can sketch on a whiteboard to illustrate specific aspects of your instruction. For example, you may quickly and easily draw stick figures and arrows to show motion in an otherwise static representation.

You and your students can use such software programs as iWorks, Photoshop, and Adobe Illustrator for layout, design, and illustration. Most computer graphics software programs come with hundreds or even thousands of typefaces and clip-art images and can manipulate visuals in every imaginable way. Most word processing and presentation software comes with basic drawing tools and some enhanced tools, such as Microsoft's SmartArt.

CHARTS

Charts are visual representations of abstract relationships such as chronologies, quantities, and hierarchies. They appear frequently as tables and flowcharts. They are also presented in the form of organization charts, classification charts (e.g., the periodic table), and timelines (see Figure 8.1).

A chart should have a clear, well-defined instructional purpose. In general, it should express only one major concept or concept relationship. A well-designed chart should communicate its message primarily through the visual channel. The verbal material should supplement the visual, not the reverse. If you have a lot of information to convey, develop a series of simple charts rather than a single complex one.

GRAPHS

Graphs provide a visual representation of numerical data. They also illustrate relationships among units of data and trends over time. Data can be interpreted more quickly in graph form than in tabular form. Graphs are also more visually interesting than tables. Of the four major types of graphs—bar, pictorial, circle, and line (Figure 8.2)—the type you choose will depend largely on the complexity of the information you wish to present and the graph interpretation skills of your students.

Numerous computer software programs, typically spreadsheet software such as Microsoft Excel, make it easy to produce professional-looking graphs. Enter your data into the spreadsheet and with just a few clicks of the mouse the software creates the type of graph you wish.

POSTERS

Posters incorporate visual combinations of images, lines, color, and words. They are intended to capture and hold the viewer's attention at least long enough to communicate a brief message, usually a persuasive appeal. They must grab attention and communicate their message quickly. One drawback in using posters is that their message is quickly ignored because of familiarity. Consequently, they should not be left on display for too long.

Posters can be effective in numerous learning situations. They can stimulate interest in a new topic, announce a special event, or promote social skills. They may be employed for motivation—attracting students to a school recycling meeting or to the media center or encouraging them to read more. In industrial education courses, science laboratories, and other situations in which danger may be involved, posters can remind people of safety tips. Posters can also promote good health practices such as not using drugs and avoiding junk food or to illustrate a concept such as photosynthesis (Figure 8.3 on page 182).

You can obtain posters from a variety of sources, including commercial companies, airlines, travel agencies, government departments, and professional organizations. You can make your own posters with colored markers, computer printouts, and devices that print poster-sized pages.

CARTOONS

Cartoons are line drawings that are rough caricatures of real or fictional people, animals, and events. They appear in a variety of print media—newspapers, periodicals, textbooks—and range from comic strips intended primarily to entertain to drawings intended to make important social or political comments. Humor and satire are mainstays of the cartoonist's skill.

Cartoons are easily and quickly read and appeal to children of all ages. The best examples contain wisdom as well as wit. You can often use them to make or reinforce a point of instruction. Appreciation and interpretation, however, may depend on the experience and sophistication of the learner. Be sure the cartoons you use for instructional purposes are within the experiential and intellectual range of your students.

An additional option is for students to create cartoons with free online software, such as ToonDoo (see Figure 8.4 on page 182). The software provides an array of characters, settings, and props for students to assemble into a cartoon that depicts the assigned message. For example, students can create cartoons

Organization charts show the structure or chain of command in an organization such as a company, corporation, civic group, or government department. Usually they deal with the interrelationships of personnel or departments.

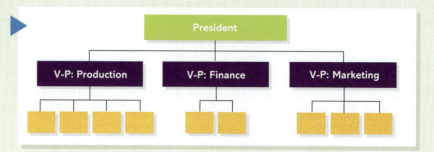

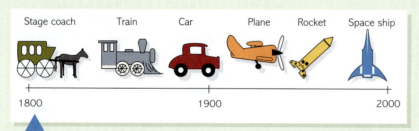

Timelines illustrate chronological relationships between events. They are most often used to show historical events in sequence or the relationships of famous people and these events. Pictures or drawings can be added to the time line to illustrate important concepts. Timelines are very helpful for summarizing a series of events.

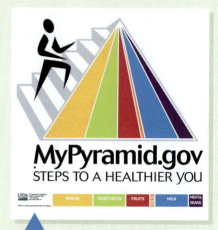

Classification charts are similar to organization charts but are used chiefly to classify or categorize objects, events, or species. A common type of classification chart is one showing the taxonomy of animals and plants according to natural characteristics. The Food Guide Pyramid uses colors to organize foods into groups and to represent the proportions of these groups in a healthy diet.

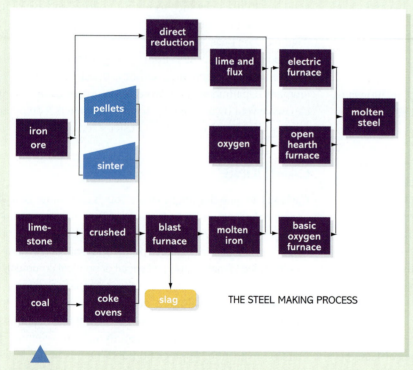

THE STEEL MAKING PROCESS

Flowcharts, or process charts, show a sequence, a procedure, or, as the name implies, the flow of a process. Flowcharts show how different activities, ingredients, or procedures are interrelated.

Import Percentages				
	Wheat	Cotton	Steel	Oil
USA	0	0	20	35
England	65	95	35	10
France	15	95	30	90
Japan	85	15	0	95
Brazil	0	0	20	70

Tabular charts, or tables, contain numerical information, or data. They are also convenient for showing time information when the data are presented in columns, as in timetables for railroads and airlines.

Figure **8.1**

Types of Charts

It is important to understand which type of chart is best for conveying information to your students.

Bar graphs are easy to read and can be used with all students. The height of the bar is the measure of the quantity being represented. The width of all bars should be the same to avoid confusion. A single bar can be divided to show parts of a whole. It is best to limit the quantities being compared to eight or less; otherwise the graph becomes cluttered and confusing. The bar graph is particularly appropriate for comparing similar items at different times or different items at the same time; for example, the height of one plant over time or the heights of several students at any given time. The bar graph shows variation in only one dimension.

Pictorial graphs are an alternate form of the bar graph in which numerical units are represented by a simple drawing. Pictorial graphs are visually interesting and appeal to a wide audience, especially young students. However, they are slightly more difficult to read than bar graphs. Since pictorial symbols are used to represent a specific quantity, partial symbols are used to depict fractional quantities. To help avoid confusion in such cases, print values below or to the right of each line of figures.

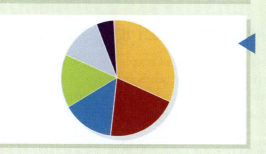

Circle (or pie) graphs are relatively easy to interpret. In this type of graph, a circle or "pie" is divided into segments, each representing a part or percentage of the whole. One typical use of the circle graph is to depict tax-dollar allocations. The combined segments of a circle graph should, of course, equal 100 percent. Areas of special interest can be highlighted by illustrating a piece of pie separately from the whole.

Line graphs are the most precise and complex of all graphs. Line graphs are based on two scales at right angles. Each point has a value on the vertical scale and a value on the horizontal scale. Lines (or curves) are drawn to connect the points. Line graphs show variations in two dimensions, or how two or more factors change over time. For example, a graph can show the relation between pressure and temperature when the volume of a gas is held constant. Because line graphs are precise, they are very useful in plotting trends. They can also help simplify a mass of complex information.

Figure **8.2**

Types of Graphs

It is important to understand which type of graph is best for conveying information to your students.

representing ideas on recycling, global warming, historical events, current events, or storylines from a book.

PURPOSES OF VISUALS

Visuals can serve a multitude of purposes in the classroom—to provide meaningful references for ideas, make abstract ideas more concrete, motivate your students, help direct attention to important concepts, repeat learning with different modalities, provide assistance in recalling prior learning, and most importantly reduce the effort required to learn.

PROVIDE A CONCRETE REFERENT FOR IDEAS

Words don't look or sound like the objects they stand for, but visuals are **iconic**—that is, they have some resemblance to what they represent (see Figure 8.5). Just like icons on a

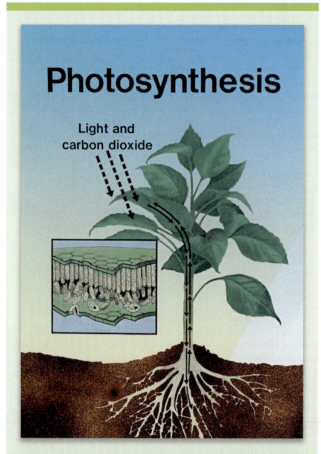

A color photograph can be a highly iconic visual, capturing much of the reality of the original referent.
Scott Cunningham/Merrill

Figure 8.3
Poster
Posters catch the eye to convey a single message.

the content being taught. For instance, a geometry teacher may bring in a bag of grocery items to teach shapes (e.g., orange = sphere, can = cylinder).

MAKE ABSTRACT IDEAS CONCRETE

Using photographs of people voting to represent freedom, a series of connected beads to show a model of DNA, or a diagram of word endings to assist beginning readers are examples of showing something "real" to illustrate abstract ideas.

MOTIVATE LEARNERS

Interest enhances motivation. Because visuals can increase interest in a lesson, they can motivate learners by attracting and holding their attention while generating engagement in the learning process. Visuals draw on learners' personal interests to make instruction relevant. For example, when teaching a history lesson, show "then" and "now" photos, such as buttons used before zippers, rotary telephones before cell phones, or butter churns before margarine tubs.

computer screen are used to represent the hard drive, your Internet browser, or the trash bin, visuals serve as an easily remembered link to the original idea. In the classroom, a teacher uses visuals to help students more easily remember

DIRECT ATTENTION

A **visual pointer** draws the learner's attention and thinking to relevant parts of a visual. Visual pointers may be color, words, arrows, icons, shading, or animation. Use these signals to focus attention to important points within complex visual content (Jeng, Chandler, & Sweller, 1997).

Figure 8.4
ToonDoo
ToonDoo software provides easy-to-use tools for students to create their own cartoons.
Source: www.toondoo.com. ToonDoo.com and the education-friendly version, ToonDooSpaces.com, are property of Zoho Corp, Inc. Reprinted by permission.

REPEAT INFORMATION

When visuals accompany spoken or written information, they present that information in a different modality, giving

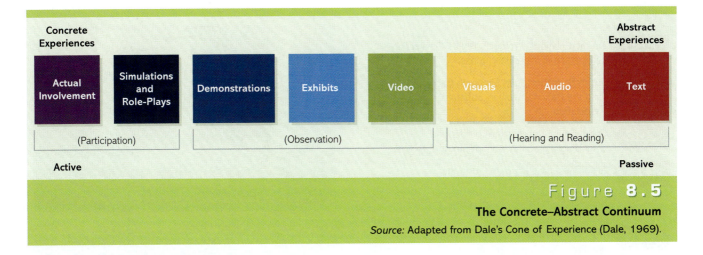

Concrete Experiences — Actual Involvement | Simulations and Role-Plays | Demonstrations | Exhibits | Video | Visuals | Audio | Text — Abstract Experiences

(Participation)   (Observation)   (Hearing and Reading)

Active   Passive

Figure 8.5

The Concrete–Abstract Continuum

Source: Adapted from Dale's Cone of Experience (Dale, 1969).

some learners a chance to comprehend visually what they might miss in verbal or text format.

RECALL PRIOR LEARNING

At the beginning of a lesson visuals can activate prior knowledge stored in long-term memory and at the end they can summarize the content from a lesson. These same visuals can be used at the beginning of the next lesson to remind the learners of what should have been learned (Figure 8.6).

REDUCE LEARNING EFFORT

Visuals can simplify information that is difficult to understand (Figure 8.7). Diagrams can make it easy to store and retrieve such information. They can also serve an organizing function by illustrating the relationships among elements, as in flowcharts or timelines. Often content can be communicated more easily and effectively visually (Mayer & Moreno, 2003). As a teacher, you want to convey your message in such a way that students expend little effort making sense out of what they are seeing, freeing them to use most of their mental effort for understanding the message itself.

CATAGORIES OF VISUALS

The visual selected for a particular situation should depend on the learning task. Visuals can be subdivided into six categories: realistic, analogical, organizational, relational, transformational, and interpretive (Clark & Lyons, 2004).

REALISTIC

Realistic visuals show the actual object under study. They can translate abstract ideas into a more realistic format (Figure 8.8), allowing instruction to move from the level of abstract

(verbal) symbols on the Concrete–Abstract Continuum (see Figure 8.5) to a more concrete (visual) level. For example, the color photograph of a covered wagon in Figure 8.9 is a realistic visual. Using natural colors can heighten the degree of realism. No representation, of course, is totally realistic. The real object or event will always have aspects that cannot be captured pictorially, even in a three-dimensional color motion picture.

Research shows that under certain circumstances, realism can actually interfere with communication and learning. Dwyer (1978) concluded that rather than being a simple yes-or-no issue, the amount of realism desired has a curvilinear relationship to learning: either too much or too little realism may affect achievement adversely (Figure 8.10, page 186).

ANALOGICAL

Analogical visuals convey a concept or topic by showing something else and implying a similarity. Teaching about electrical current by showing water flowing in a series of parallel pipes is an example of using analogic visuals. An analogy for white blood cells fighting off infection might be an army attacking a stronghold. A study by Newby, Ertmer, and Stepich (1995) showed that student learning of biological concepts benefited from the use of visual analogies. Such visuals help learners interpret new information in light of prior knowledge and thereby facilitate learning.

ORGANIZATIONAL

Organizational visuals show the qualitative relationships among various elements. Common examples include classification charts, timelines, flowcharts, and maps, discussed earlier in this chapter. These graphic organizers can show relationships among the main points or concepts in textual material. This type of visual helps communicate the organization of the content (Figure 8.11, page 186).

Figure 8.6 — History Timeline

1850	The first National Women's Rights Convention takes place in Worcester, Mass.
1869	Susan B. Anthony and Elizabeth Cady Stanton form the National Woman Suffarage Association.
1893	Colorado is the first state to adopt an amendment granting women the right to vote.
1913	Alice Paul and Lucy Burns form the Congressional Union to work toward the passage of a federal law to give women voting rights.
1920	The 19th Amendment to the Constitution, granting women the right to vote, is signed into law.
1935	Mary McLeod Bethune organizes the National Council of Negro Women to lobby against job discrimination, racism, and sexism.
1961	President John Kennedy establishes the President's Commission on the Status of Women and appoints Eleanor Roosevelt as chairwoman.
1963	Congress passes the Equal Pay Act, making it illegal for employers to pay a woman less than what a man would receive for the same job.
1964	Title VII of the Civil Rights Act bars discrimination in employment on the basis of race and sex.
1966	The National Organization for Women (NOW), the largest women's rights group in the United States, is founded by a group of feminists.
1971	*Ms. Magazine* is first published as a sample insert in *New York* magazine.
1972	Title IX bans sex discrimination in schools. As a result of Title IX, the enrollment of women in athletic programs and professional schools increases dramatically.
1996	The Supreme Court rules that the all-male Virginia Military School has to admit women in order to continue to receive public funding.
2003	The Supreme Court rules that states can be sued in federal court for violations of the Family Leave Medical Act.
2009	President Obama signs the Fair Pay Restoration Act, which allows victims of pay discrimination to file a complaint with the government against their employer.

Figure 8.6
History Timeline

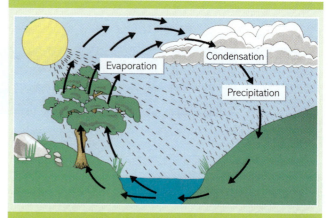

Figure 8.7
Visuals and Prior Learning
A complex process can be simplified visually and therefore made easier to understand and remember.

RELATIONAL

Relational visuals communicate quantitative relationships. Examples include bar and pie charts or line and pictorial graphs (see Types of Visuals Used in the Classroom section, page 178).

TRANSFORMATIONAL

Transformational visuals illustrate movement or change in time and space. Examples include an animated diagram showing how to perform a procedure such as tying a shoelace, a line drawing with movement indicators (Figure 8.12), or an animation of the water cycle.

ASSURE Case Study Reflection

PEARSON
myeducationkit

Review the ASSURE Classroom Case Study and video at the beginning of the chapter. Identify how the use of visuals helps students learn about visualizing three-dimensional objects. How might Mrs. Roman use visuals to assist her students in understanding how to visualize three-dimensional objects in a two-dimensional plane? What types of visuals might be most effective? How can visuals be used to facilitate learning in an art class? Would there be an advantage to using one type of visual over other choices?

Healthy
Fruit and vegetables are a good source of vitamins.

Unhealthy
Fast food tends not to have good nutritional value.

Food consumed should be well balanced.

Desserts can be a source of vitamins, but they tend to have high levels of sugar.

Figure **8.8**
Chart as Realistic Visual
Visuals carry the main message in a well-designed chart.

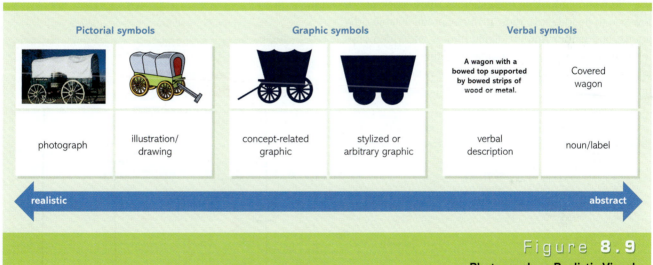

Pictorial symbols		Graphic symbols		Verbal symbols	
				A wagon with a bowed top supported by bowed strips of wood or metal.	Covered wagon
photograph	illustration/ drawing	concept-related graphic	stylized or arbitrary graphic	verbal description	noun/label

realistic ←———————————————————→ abstract

Figure **8.9**
Photograph as Realistic Visual
Photographs, illustrations, graphics, and words represent a continuum of realism for different kinds of symbols.

INTERPRETIVE

Interpretive visuals illustrate theoretical or abstract relationships. Examples include a schematic diagram of an electrical circuit, the food pyramid, or an evacuation plan (Figure 8.13). Interpretive visuals help learners build mental models of events or processes that are invisible, abstract, or both.

VIEWING VISUALS

There are many ways to view visuals in a classroom. Still images may be enlarged and displayed on a screen by sending images from a computer or document camera to a digital projector or television monitor. Display surfaces for viewing visuals include whiteboards, interactive whiteboards, bulletin boards, cloth boards, magnetic boards, and flip charts (see Using Projected Visuals in the Classroom).

PRESENTATION SOFTWARE

Presentation software provides a format for displaying computer-based visuals with a digital projector. The most widely known presentation software is PowerPoint. Students, as well as teachers, can use templates to produce

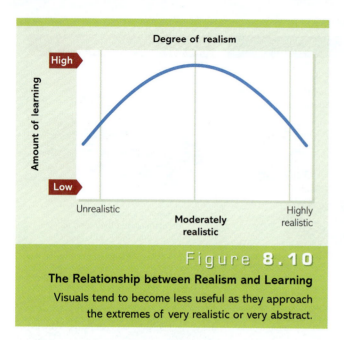

Figure **8.10**

The Relationship between Realism and Learning
Visuals tend to become less useful as they approach
the extremes of very realistic or very abstract.

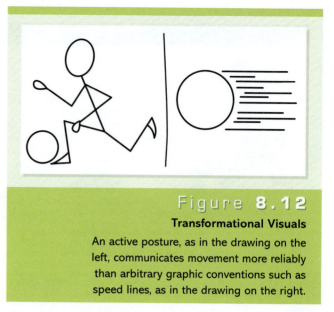

Figure **8.12**

Transformational Visuals

An active posture, as in the drawing on the
left, communicates movement more reliably
than arbitrary graphic conventions such as
speed lines, as in the drawing on the right.

very professional-looking presentations. These packages allow you to include text; draw pictures; produce tables, diagrams, and graphs; import digital photos and video clips; include audio; and create animation. Students, as well as teachers, can make digital presentations with little training on the software itself. Most software includes "Wizards," or

guides, to assist users. Templates provide a variety of designs and all the user has to do is select the template and input the content.

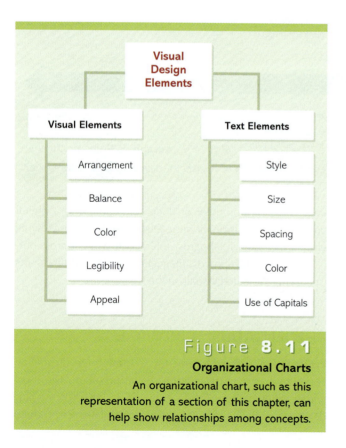

Figure **8.11**

Organizational Charts

An organizational chart, such as this
representation of a section of this chapter, can
help show relationships among concepts.

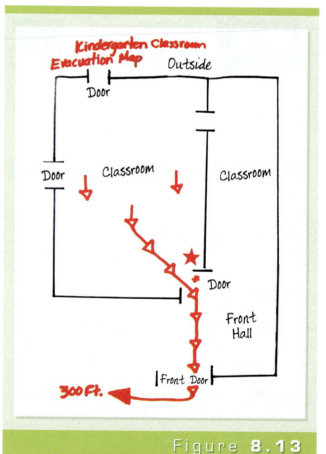

Figure **8.13**

Evacuation Plan

An evacuation plan is an example of an interpretive visual.
Source: Annie Pickert/Pearson

USING
Projected Visuals
in the Classroom

- *Use visual variety.* Mix the types of visuals, adding verbal titles to help break the presentation into segments. Use visuals that are not cluttered with illegible details.

- *Rehearse.* Plan and rehearse your narration to accompany projected visuals if it is not already recorded in an audio medium.

- *Keep it moving.* Limit your discussion of each visual. In most cases, do not show a visual for more than 20 to 30 seconds without adding to it, changing to the next visual, or using a keyboard command to change the screen to black (press "B") or to white (press "W").

- *Pause for discussion.* Get students actively involved by asking relevant questions during your presentation. Provide written or verbal cues to highlight important information contained in the visuals.

- *Summarize frequently.* Every so often, assist your audience in their efforts to "see" the big picture.

- *Set up in advance.* Position the projector so that the image fills the screen from top to bottom and from left to right. Be sure that the image is not so near the bottom of the screen that students in the back of the room cannot see the whole image.

- *Get attention.* Shift students' attention to the screen by turning on the projector; direct it back to yourself by turning it off. Don't turn on the projector again until you are ready for students to look at the screen.

- *Use notes.* Plan ways to add meaningful details to the image during projection; this infuses an element of spontaneity and helps maintain student interest and active participation. Write key words on note cards to allow you to speak naturally instead of reading from a script.

- *Test visually.* Because the presentation presumably is providing critical visual information, consider using visuals to test mastery of visual concepts. You can ask individual students to identify or describe the object or process shown.

Presentation software allows you to generate handouts for your students. From one to nine slides can be put on each sheet of paper. The software also allows you to create "Note Pages" that contain only three slides per page and include blank lines next to each slide. With this format, students take notes on the handouts, rather than frantically copying down both what is on the slides and what you say.

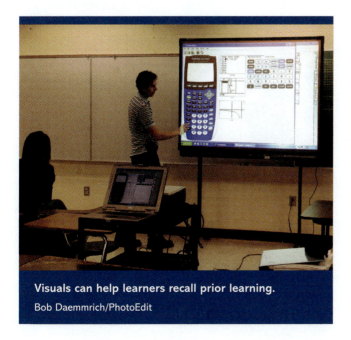

Visuals can help learners recall prior learning.
Bob Daemmrich/PhotoEdit

ASSURE Case Study Reflection

Review the ASSURE Classroom Case Study and video at the beginning of the chapter. Consider the benefits for Mrs. Roman in using PowerPoint when teaching math concepts? How can she get students to explain their ideas? How might Mrs. Edlund use PowerPoint as part of her art lessons? What can she do to have children connect what they are learning in art class with their math lessons?

DIGITAL IMAGES

Visuals can be captured and stored in a digital format by using a digital camera or a scanner (see pages 199–200). Digital storage methods include CDs, DVDs, portable storage devices, and computer hard drives. Individuals or small groups can view or project the images on a computer screen. For showing digital images to a group, you can use a large television monitor or a digital projector.

TECHNOLOGY
for Diverse Learners

Presentation Software

Teachers can use several methods to make presentations more accessible for students with visual impairments, including converting text to Braille. Another approach involves increasing the interaction between teacher and students during and immediately after the presentation. Greater verbalization and descriptions of the text and images enhances comprehension and retention by students with visual impairments—and all other students as well!

Students who are developing new mathematical concepts may find the additional visuals to be very beneficial. The ability to connect the components of a subject such as mathematics with visuals helps students make their own mental images

and thus enhances their understanding of the concepts being taught. For these students, displays such as graphs, line drawings, or charts might assist them in recalling essential information during an assessment.

Putting ideas into visual forms is a great way to challenge students who are ready to move beyond more traditional formats in demonstrating their learning. Asking students to prepare visuals in the form of drawings, charts, or graphics may allow them the flexibility to express their knowledge in unique and interesting ways.

ASSURE Case Study Reflection

PEARSON
myeducationkit™

Review the ASSURE Classroom Case Study and video at the beginning of the chapter. What kinds of images would be best for Mrs. Roman to use? What could Mrs. Edlund do with the school's digital cameras in art class?

A **document camera** is a video camera mounted on a copy stand that is pointed downward at documents, flat pictures, graphics, or small objects (such as coins). The image may be shown with a digital projector or a large-screen television monitor within the room, or it may be transmitted to distant sites via web-conferencing or telecommunications technology. Any sort of visual can be placed on the stage, and you can manipulate the material or write on paper placed on the stage.

One alternative to the copy stand version of a document camera is the computer flex camera, such as the Video Flex camera from Ken-A-Vision, which is designed for use in

Teacher or students can use document cameras to project large images of hands-on demonstrations.
Zuma/Newscom

The document camera is easy for the teacher to use to show visuals or small objects to a class.
Courtesy of AverMedia Technologies, Inc.

face-to-face classrooms as well as telecommunications. This camera can be connected to the television monitor, digital projector, or computer and used in a similar way as the document camera. The advantage to using this type of camera is that it is smaller and less expensive. A limitation is that the quality of the image may be compromised.

OVERHEAD PROJECTION

The **overhead projection** system is still widely used in classrooms because of its availability, low cost, and ease of use. The typical overhead projector is a simple device (Figure 8.14). Basically, it is a box with a large "glass" on the top surface. Light from a powerful lamp inside the box is condensed by a lens and passed through a transparency placed on the stage. A lens-and-mirror system mounted on a bracket above the box turns the light beam 90 degrees and projects the image back over the shoulder of the presenter.

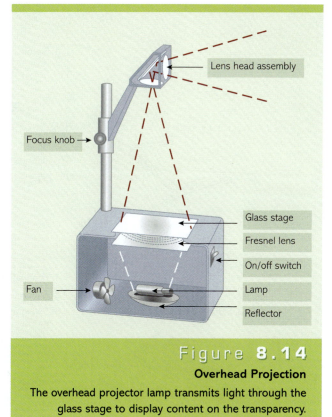

Figure 8.14

Overhead Projection

The overhead projector lamp transmits light through the glass stage to display content on the transparency.

In the instructional setting, the general term **transparency** has taken on the specific meaning of the 8-by-10-inch transparent film used with the overhead projector. You may use transparencies individually or make them into a series of images consisting of a base visual with one or more overlays. **Overlays** are sheets of transparent film, each containing additional information, that are laid over the base transparency. You may then explain complex topics step by step by

USING
Visuals
in the Classroom

- *Use large visuals that everyone can see simultaneously. Also be certain that the font size is legible. If visuals are not large enough for all to see, use one of the projection techniques described in this chapter.*

- *Use visuals that are not cluttered with illegible details.*

- *Cover irrelevant material with plain paper.*

- *Hold visuals steady when showing them to a group by resting them against a desk or table or putting them on an easel.*

- *Limit the number of visuals used in a given period of time. It is better to use a few visuals well than to overwhelm your audience with an abundance of underexplained visuals.*

- *Use just one visual at a time, except for purposes of comparison. Lay one visual flat before going on to the next.*

- *Keep your students' attention and help them learn from a visual by asking direct questions about it.*

- *Teach your students to interpret visuals.*

- *Provide written or verbal cues to highlight important information contained in the visuals.*

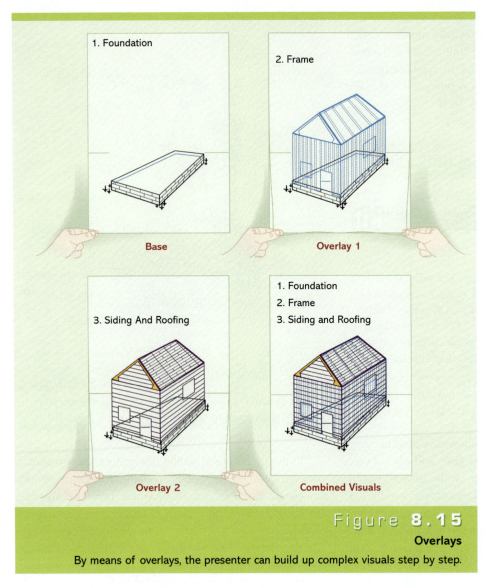

1. Foundation

Base

2. Frame

Overlay 1

1. Foundation
2. Frame
3. Siding And Roofing

Overlay 2

1. Foundation
2. Frame
3. Siding and Roofing

Combined Visuals

Figure **8.15**

Overlays

By means of overlays, the presenter can build up complex visuals step by step.

- *Ease of preparation.* You can easily prepare your own visuals and displays as described in this chapter.
- *Inexpensive.* Visuals are available at little cost. Many are free.
- *Simplification of complex ideas.* Visuals help to simplify even the most complex content and relationships. As the old adage goes, "A picture is worth a thousand words!"
- *Ease of use.* Visuals are very easy to use. Even young children can effectively use them for presentation of ideas.
- *Interactivity.* Visuals are ideal for "what if" displays of spreadsheet data or brainstorming activities using such software as Inspiration. This becomes an interactive medium when viewers' decisions or ideas are fed into the program and the outcome is displayed on the screen.
- *All students have equal view.* Properly used visuals permit everyone to have an equal opportunity to view the same material easily at the same time.

flipping a series of overlays one at a time, adding additional features to a diagram (Figure 8.15).

PRINTED VISUALS

The simplest use of visuals is in printed form in a book, on the wall, or held by the teacher. Printed visuals are easy to use because they do not require any equipment. They are relatively inexpensive; in fact, many can be obtained at no cost. They can be used in many ways at all levels of instruction and in all disciplines.

ADVANTAGES

- *Readily available.* Visuals are pervasive. They are in textbooks, computer programs, and most instructional materials.
- *Range of materials.* Visuals cover the complete range of curriculum areas and grade levels.

LIMITATIONS

- *Two-dimensional.* Visuals are two-dimensional and show only one view of an object or scene. Using multiple views or software that provides a three-dimensional perspective to images can compensate for this limitation.
- *Too much on one visual.* Some people put too many words on one visual. Limit the number of words on each.
- *Bulky hardware.* Visual displays often require a large monitor, which can be bulky, heavy, and cumbersome to move without a cart, or a digital projector, which requires a computer and a screen on which to project. You cannot use projected digital displays without a monitor or digital projector.
- *Expense.* High-quality digital cameras, scanners, and projectors are expensive to purchase. You may not be satisfied with lower-priced equipment that may lack the capability to meet your instructional needs.

INTEGRATION

Every teacher can integrate visuals effectively to promote learning. Visuals are useful in a wide variety of instructional situations. Applications may be found in all curriculum areas at all grade levels, as in the following examples:

- *Art.* Illustrate the use of color to evoke emotions; demonstrate what happens when two colors are combined; show examples of art from various periods.
- *Consumer and family science.* Group viewing of sewing patterns, textiles, and recipes; individual study of various furniture styles and layouts; guidelines for healthy eating.
- *Drama.* Put a floor plan on the base transparency and add overlays to show acting circles and how areas are lit; examples of different facial expressions; a variety of stage layouts for the same production.
- *Foreign language.* Students examine images and texts related to their study of German; the teacher assigns small groups of students to study different Spanish-speaking countries. Each small group works collaboratively to prepare a presentation, with drawings and charts, to share with the class. They use pictures to help present their information.
- *Health.* Study the need for a healthy diet to support growing bodies. For example, some posters and other visual materials were obtained by one teacher from local sources. The students put together a display of visuals showing various foods, along with additional visual materials to explain the significance of the foods that were selected.
- *Language arts.* Demonstrate examples of plagiarism; use elementary-level books with colorful visuals accompanying the story to motivate young readers; show a study

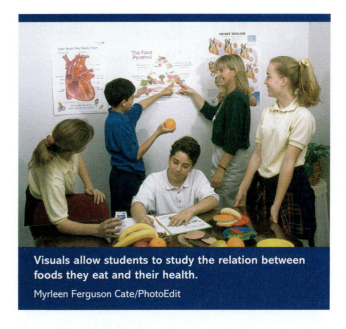

Visuals allow students to study the relation between foods they eat and their health.
Myrleen Ferguson Cate/PhotoEdit

print illustrating a rural scene and ask each student to write a short story related to the visual.

- *Library skills.* Show a floor plan of the layout of the school media center as part of library orientation; illustrate the various sections of a card from the card catalog; show examples of bibliographic citations.
- *Mathematics.* Display a graph showing the algebraic relationship between the values of x and y in an equation; demonstrate how to measure the distance between any two points on a map using a clear plastic ruler over a transparency.
- *Music.* Show a staff with notes arranged in three-part harmony, with different colored notes for each part; provide pictures of various types of instruments for students to study.
- *Physical education.* Use still pictures of warm-up exercises to remind each student of the body positions and sequence; illustrate various basketball plays.
- *Science.* Require each student before attempting a solution to visualize a physics problem by drawing a diagram that shows the relationships among the known qualities and the unknown value; provide a CD for students to view animals of the world as they prepare to present a play for the PTA depicting endangered species; demonstrate the stages of volcanic eruptions.
- *Social studies.* Compare typical living conditions of children from various countries around the world; study battles and timelines for a war; "tour" local historical sites.
- *Vocational/technical.* Invite a guest speaker from a local manufacturing company to provide a photographic tour for students without traveling to the plant; project blueprints for group study.

Students use visuals to study a foreign language.
Jonathan Nourok/Getty

Use when student learning will be enhanced by . . .

Guidelines	Examples
simplifying complex concepts	A high school teacher uses a genetics chart to show dominant and recessive traits. Students take digital photos of each classmate and classify them into genetic groups (e.g., attached ear lobes, curly hair, eye color). Middle school students select and assemble photos into a PowerPoint presentation that represents their concept of freedom.
seeing relationships	Early childhood students study historical photos from the 1800s that show children in their homes to identify similarities and differences with their current home lives. A high school history teacher projects a spreadsheet chart showing population growth in the local community over the past 100 years. She has students predict changes over the next 100 years and then shows the predicted changes on the chart by changing the numerical values of various cells.
depicting processes	Elementary students in social studies build a model Alaskan igloo while using a disposable camera to create a photo journal of the building process. An ESL elementary teacher projects an interactive bilingual (English/Spanish) chart showing the life of a seed.
stimulating interest	When introducing Shakespeare to middle school students, the teacher begins the lesson by using study prints showing different scenes of a Shakespearean play to stimulate interest in the topic. When studying cultural backgrounds, each elementary student uses the document camera to share a drawing of her or his ethnic history.
encouraging creativity	Students work in pairs to create their own political cartoons of a historical event. Middle school student pairs write original math word problems on a transparency so the problem can be solved as a whole-group activity led by the teacher.

VISUAL DESIGN GUIDELINES

Designing a visual begins with gathering or producing the individual pictorial and text elements that you expect to use. This assumes, of course, that you have already determined students' needs and interests regarding the topic and decided what objective(s) you hope to achieve through the visual you are planning. The following guidelines are applicable to computer screens, multimedia programs, printed materials, whiteboards, exhibits, overhead transparencies, PowerPoint slides, and bulletin boards.

ARRANGEMENT

First you must decide which elements to include in your visual. Then you are ready to consider its overall "look" or **arrangement.** The idea is to establish an underlying pattern—to determine how the viewer's eye will flow across your display.

If you are planning a series of visuals, such as a set of PowerPoint slides, a multipage handout, or a series of computer screens, you should be consistent in your arrangement of the elements. As viewers go through the series of visuals they begin unconsciously to form a set of rules about where information will appear in your display.

BALANCE

A psychological sense of equilibrium, or **balance,** is achieved when the "weight" of the elements in a visual is equally distributed on each side of an axis, either horizontally or vertically or both. When the design is repeated on both sides, the balance is symmetrical, or formal.

In most cases, though, for visuals that will catch the eye and serve an informational purpose you should aim to achieve an asymmetrical, or informal, balance. With asymmetrical balance there is rough equivalence of weight, but with different elements on each side (e.g., one large open

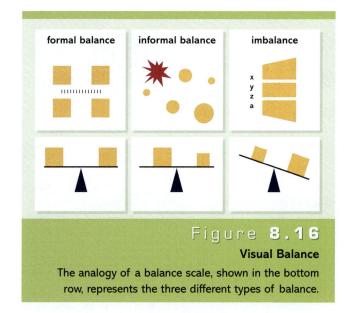

Figure **8.16**
Visual Balance
The analogy of a balance scale, shown in the bottom row, represents the three different types of balance.

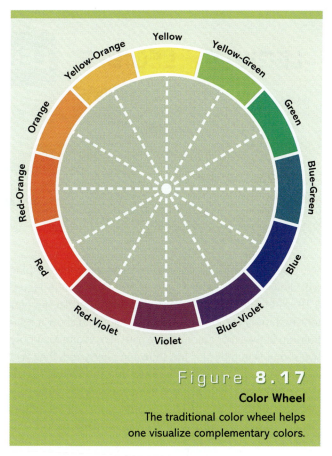

Figure **8.17**
Color Wheel
The traditional color wheel helps one visualize complementary colors.

square on one side, three small dark circles on the other). Informal balance is preferred because it is more dynamic and interesting than formal balance (Figure 8.16). In general, try to avoid imbalance—using a distinctly disproportionate weight distribution—because it tends to be jarring to the viewer.

COLOR

When choosing a color scheme for a visual, consider the harmoniousness of the colors. The color wheel is useful in helping us understand the relationships among the colors of the visible spectrum (Figure 8.17).

Any two colors that lie directly opposite each other on the color wheel are called **complementary colors**—for example, red and green or yellow and violet. Complementary colors often harmonize well in terms of an overall color scheme. However, try not to directly juxtapose two complementary colors (e.g., placing green letters on a red background). There are two reasons for this. First, if the colors are of equal value, or darkness, the letters will not have good contrast. Second, when saturated (intense) complementary colors are placed directly next to each other the eye cannot focus on both at the same time, so you get an unpleasant vibrating effect.

Colors that lie next to each other on the color wheel are called **analogous colors**—for example, blue-green, blue, and blue-violet. Analogous colors may also form pleasing combinations when used together in a visual.

When thinking about a color scheme for PowerPoint slides or a computer screen, it may be helpful to think in terms of a background color, a color for the images or text appearing against that background, and a color for highlights. Colors that work well together are shown in Table 8.1.

Different color combinations provide different contrasts. As indicated in Figure 8.18, black on yellow is the most legible combination. Obviously, a combination of dark figures on a dark background will be even less legible than the combinations shown.

Table **8.1** Effective Combinations for Background and Images for PowerPoint Slides and Computer Screens		
Background	**Foreground Images and Text**	**Highlights**
white	dark blue	red, orange
light gray	blue, green, black	red
blue	light yellow, white	yellow, red
light blue	dark blue, dark green	red-orange
light yellow	violet, brown	red

Source: Based on recommendations in Loosmore, Judy. (1994, November–December). "Color in Instructional Communication." *Performance and Instruction, 33*(10), 36–38.

Figure **8.18**

Color and Legibility

Black lettering on a yellow background (a) is the most legible; the other combinations are shown in descending order of legibility.

Colored words or images in a monochrome display will draw the eye. Notice how the "hot" arrows in Figure 8.19 stand out from the cool background. Further, a color repeated in different parts of a display tends to show a relationship between or among those parts. For example, if only two symbols in a display are shown in cherry red, they will appear to be related to each other, and the viewer's gaze will go back and forth between them. Please view these suggestions about color schemes as general guidelines, not as absolute rules, because in any situation many factors will

have an impact on whether particular colors will work well together.

Colors on a computer screen may not be the same from one computer to another. Projected colors may also be different. Colors that look good on your computer may look different when projected. It is a good idea to practice your presentation to determine whether the projected colors efficiently transmit your message.

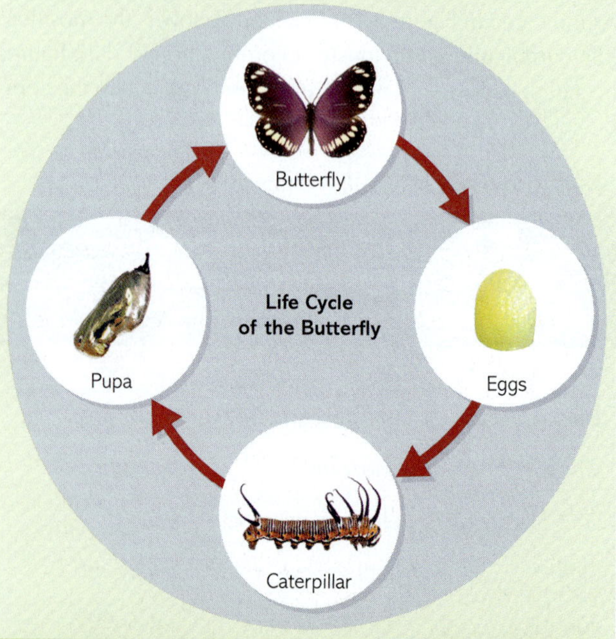

LEGIBILITY

A visual cannot do its job unless all viewers can see the words and images. It's surprising how often this simple rule is broken. Think of how many times you have heard a presenter say, "You may not be able to see what's on this, so let me describe (or read) it for you." To keep this from happening, make sure your visuals are large enough to be seen by all your audience members, even the most distant viewer. This applies to printed materials, projected visuals, and displays.

Legibility can be improved by increasing image size, type of font, and contrast among objects in a visual. Just as we discussed contrast in reference to color, contrast also applies to the total visual. Make sure the objects in your visual don't blur together. The goal of good visual design is to remove as many obstacles as possible that might impede interpretation of your message. Remember: If your students can't see it, they can't learn from it!

APPEAL

Your visual has no chance of having an effect unless it captures and holds the viewer's attention. There are several techniques to provide appeal: style, surprise, texture, and interaction.

Different audiences and different settings call for different design styles. Think about the simple, uncluttered,

Figure **8.19**

Color and Emphasis

The arrows direct the viewer's attention clockwise.

primary color "look" of a children's television show compared with the complex imagery, busy scenes, and realistic color of an adult action drama. Likewise, you would not use the same stylistic treatment for a first-grade bulletin board as you would for a presentation to show at a teachers' professional development conference. Your choice of lettering and type of pictures should be consistent with each other and with the preferences of the audience.

Most visuals are two-dimensional. However, you can add a third dimension with texture or actual materials. As a characteristic of three-dimensional objects and materials, texture can convey a clearer idea of the subject to the viewer by involving the sense of touch—for example, touching samples of different cereal grains. Or texture can simply invite involvement—for example, using cotton balls to represent clouds or passing around book jackets to entice students to read a new book.

Viewers can be asked to respond to visual displays by manipulating the included materials, perhaps to answer questions raised in the display. Students can move answer cards to math facts into the correct position. Answers to geography questions can be hidden under movable flaps. The teacher or learners can move dials on a weather display to indicate the forecast for the day or the actual weather outside the classroom. For an example of an interactive format, see Figure 8.20.

UNIVERSAL DESIGN

When designing visuals, teachers need to use the principles of universal design to assist them in making the visuals useful to as many students as possible regardless of their age, ability, or subject area. Universal design accommodates students with a variety of learning levels, including disabilities and special talents. These principles promote simple, intuitive, equitable, and flexible use of visuals. All of the ideas in this section on visual design guidelines promote universal design.

CREATING VISUALS

Planning is an important component of creating visuals. Software tools provided in Inspiration and Kidspiration are excellent for using planning techniques such as storyboarding or concept mapping. It is also helpful to understand methods such as lettering techniques or how to create simple drawings, sketches, or cartoons. Techniques for creating presentation graphics and overhead transparencies are also important tools in producing visuals.

PLANNING TOOLS

If you or your students are designing a series of visuals—such as a series of computer screens, a set of PowerPoint slides, a video sequence, or several related overhead transparencies—**storyboarding** is a handy strategy for planning. This technique, borrowed from film and video production, allows you to creatively arrange and rearrange a whole sequence of thumbnail sketches or some other simple representations of the visuals and text you plan to use. Any narration would also be included on the storyboard, along with production notes that link the visuals to the narration. After developing a series of such cards, place them in rough sequence on a flat surface or storyboard holder (Figure 8.21).

Index cards are common materials for storyboarding because they are durable, inexpensive, and available in a variety of colors and sizes. You also may use small pieces of paper. Self-sticking removable notes have become popular because they will stick to anything—cardboard, desks, walls, whiteboards, bulletin boards, and so on.

Divide the individual storyboard cards into different sections to accommodate the text or narration and the production notes (Figure 8.22). The exact format of the storyboard card should fit your needs and purposes. Design a card that facilitates your work if the existing or recommended format

Let's Catch a Noun!

A noun names a person, place, or thing.

cat

man

Take a fish from the bucket and write your noun on it.

Figure 8.20
Interaction and the Appeal of a Display

is not suitable. You can make a simple sketch, write a short description of the desired visual on the card, or use digital photographs or visuals cut from magazines.

Inspiration, although not designed for storyboarding, may be used to help you and your students organize ideas. Inspiration is a software package that facilitates brainstorming, concept mapping, and planning. It creates a visual diagram of the ideas generated by an individual or group as a way to map concepts. Use the program to create overviews, presentation visuals, and flowcharts. Inspiration enables students to easily couple images with text and move ideas around the computer screen, getting information organized. Once the group's thoughts have been visualized, Inspiration easily converts from a concept map into a word processing outline.

For younger students (PK–5), Kidspiration can promote visual thinking and learning. Designed to help younger students develop their thinking, visualizing, and concept mapping skills, Kidspiration allows even the youngest students to brainstorm ideas with words and visuals. They learn to organize and categorize information visually while exploring new ideas with thought webs and visual mapping.

LETTERING TECHNIQUES

A variety of lettering techniques can be used for visuals. The simplest is freehand lettering with felt-tip markers, which come in an array of colors and sizes. Precut letters are available in stationery and office supply stores. The letters are easy to use because most come with an adhesive backing; however, they are rather expensive. As an alternative, large letters or other shapes can be cut quickly from construction paper with scissors. Letter-cutting devices like the Ellison Prestige die cutter, in which die forms of letters are mounted into a cutter to produce copies from colored construction paper, are available in many schools or can be purchased in major hobby and scrapbook supply stores.

Figure **8.22**

Storyboard Cards

The storyboard card contains places for the visual, production notes, and the narration.

DRAWING, SKETCHING, AND CARTOONING

One often-overlooked source of visuals is *you*. You don't have to be an artist to draw. There are some basic guidelines and many how-to books that can help you communicate effectively using drawing, sketching, and cartooning. With a little practice, you may be surprised by how well you can draw. Simple drawings can enhance whiteboard presentations, class handouts, bulletin boards, and overhead transparencies.

CLIP ART

Clip art consists of prepared visual images (drawings and digital pictures) that can be inserted into a variety of digital documents and presentations. The size and placement of images can be modified to meet your needs. Recently there has been an explosion in copyright-free visuals available primarily through the Web and software collections.

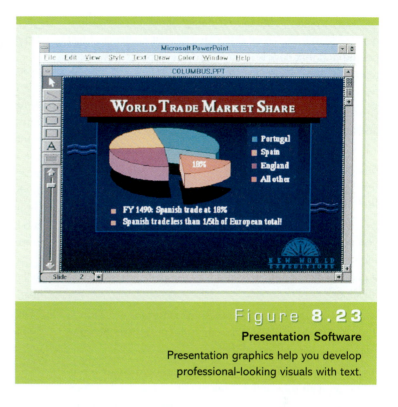

Figure **8.23**
Presentation Software
Presentation graphics help you develop professional-looking visuals with text.

DESIGNING VISUALS WITH COMPUTERS

You and your students can use drawing programs for layout and design, as well as for drawing and illustrating. Most computer graphics programs such as KidPix, iWorks, Photoshop, and Adobe Illustrator come with hundreds or even thousands of typefaces and clip-art images and can manipulate visuals in every imaginable way

The visuals created with these programs can be projected using a computer and digital projector, printed directly onto transparency film, or produced on paper and used as a master to make transparencies.

CREATING PRESENTATION GRAPHICS

With presentation graphics software, such as Microsoft's PowerPoint and Apple's Keynote, even users without specialized graphics training can create attractive graphic displays in a form suitable for professional presentation. After selecting a visual style from a menu and specifying the desired type of layout (e.g., outline, bulleted list, graph, chart, or combination), you then just type in your message where directed by the program (Figure 8.23). You can control the features wanted or let the program automatically choose legible type fonts and sizes and organize the pictures and text into a clean visual layout. Keep the following guidelines in mind when using presentation graphics software:

• *Carefully select font type, size, and color.* Choose a typeface like Arial, which is a sans serif font that does not have "hands and feet" at the ends of letters and is easy to read (see Figure 8.24). A font size of 24 point or larger ensures readability. The text color should provide adequate contrast with the background color. Use upper- and lowercase letters where appropriate.

A sans serif typeface, such as Helvetica, is well suited to projected visuals.

A serifed typeface, such as Palatino, is recommended for printed text.

serifs

Figure **8.24**
Font Types
Styles of type should be selected to suit their purpose.

- *Use a plain, light-colored background.* Busy "wallpaper" backgrounds can be distracting to your audience. Most people find that dark text on a light background is easier to read than light text on a dark background.

- *Center or left justify titles at the top of the slide.* To help your audience follow the organization of your presentation, add a descriptive title or subtitle at the top of each slide.

- *Use concise communication.* Keep the number of words on a slide to an absolute minimum. The "6 × 6 Rule" recommends no more than six words per line and no more than six lines. If you need more words, use a second slide.

- *Use a template to establish a consistent visual format.* If you want to create a presentation in which all slides show the same visual on the same background color, you can use a preformatted template or design a template to be used on all slides.

- *Use master slides to establish a consistent text format.* They allow you to place text from a specific font in the same position on every slide.

- *Minimize "bells and whistles."* You should create a presentation with substantive content rather than a lot of "pizzazz." The overuse of eye-catching features is distracting and often annoying to your audience. Don't use it just because PowerPoint has it!

- *Use appropriate graphics.* Avoid stock images that are inappropriate and irrelevant to your content. Select or create graphics that effectively communicate your message.

- *Use consistent transitions.* Transitions, the way one slide changes to the next, should be consistent throughout your presentation. Do not use random transitions and avoid "noise" (audio effects) with transitions.

- *Use simple "builds."* Build effects involve methods of introducing bulleted text or graphics within a single slide. Some build effects like "swirling" (where new text spins onto the slide) can divert your audience's attention. Watching the effect often takes longer than reading the new text.

- *Carefully use animation to support the instructional message rather than to add a dramatic element to your presentation.* For example, components of a model can be included as each is discussed, such as appending one layer at a time to the food pyramid or adding planets in order of their distance from the sun.

- *Minimize the use of sound.* Use sound only if it enhances your presentation. Screeching tires and cash register sounds quickly become distracting.

- *Use footers to identify slides.* Footers allow you to annotate the bottom of slides with your name and affiliation, the presentation topic, and date prepared or presented.

CREATING OVERHEAD TRANSPARENCIES

Despite the digital revolution, many PK–12 classrooms are still equipped with overhead projectors. Therefore we've included some helpful guidelines for creating overhead transparencies by looking closely at the processes most commonly used in the classroom. The most obvious way of quickly preparing a transparency is simply to draw directly on a transparent sheet with a marking pen. If you are doing freehand drawing and lettering, keep in mind that neatness counts, as does legibility. Your imperfections will be magnified by the size of the projection screen. Viewers can't learn from what they can't decipher!

Ordinary felt-tip pens with water-soluble ink generally will not adhere well to **acetate.** Look for a label saying "overhead projector pen," indicating it will adhere to acetate and project in color. You can erase such water-soluble ink with a damp tissue or wash the transparency completely clean and reuse it. On the other hand, virtually any permanent-ink felt-tip pen will adhere to acetate, but only those marked "overhead projector pen" are made to project in color. Most users choose permanent ink for hand-drawn transparencies prepared in advance, especially if they are going to be reused.

Many overhead projector users draw or write directly on the transparency.

David Young-Wolff/PhotoEdit

Computers have eased the task of creating overhead transparencies and similar types of visuals. With any word processing software you can prepare overhead masters incorporating visuals and text. You can print each screen directly onto transparency film specified as compatible with your printer or onto plain paper for use as a master.

CAPTURING VISUALS

Digital imaging allows users to capture, edit, display, share, and network still and video images. The technology makes the process very easy for both teachers and students. Users may send images to other digital devices, store them in computers, or share them through the Internet.

PHOTOGRAPHY

Digital cameras convert light energy to digital data, which is stored in a small digital recorder such as a removable memory card that can hold hundreds of photos. Because no film is used, there is no waiting for developing and printing, and you can immediately view images on a small monitor on the back of the camera, which allows you to see the picture before you "take" it and after it has been "captured." You can delete images you don't want and reshoot on the spot until you get exactly what you want.

You can download images to a computer for manipulation and store them on a computer hard drive, flash drive, or a photo CD. The stored digital images never degrade in quality but can be lost if the storage mechanism fails.

Digital cameras make it easy to take photos to use in computer-based programs or on a website.
Shutterstock

It is important to recognize the need for caution when digitally editing or modifying images, as there are possibilities of misrepresentation. With the advanced capabilities of computer tools, a computer user could alter an image in a way that might distort reality and present a false message to the reader or that might violate a copyright holder's rights in regard to the original image (see the copyright section in Chapter 1, pages 13–15).

Printing the digital images is quick and easy. You can use your computer to produce the images with a color printer or make copies directly from the data on the memory card with a photo printer.

Visuals

The following guidelines address use of visuals by teachers and students.

You are permitted to use:

- One illustration per book, periodical, or newspaper
- One diagram, chart, or picture from a single source
- One visual per source for presentation visuals (PowerPoint slides, overhead transparencies, etc.)

You are *not* permitted to use:

- The reproduction of copyrighted cartoon characters

For general information on copyright, see the copyright section on pages 13 through 15 in Chapter 1. Suggested resources (print and websites) on copyright appear at the end of Chapter 1.

Whether you are recording the things you see on a trip, creating a photo essay, shooting a historical subject, developing an instructional picture sequence, or simply taking pictures of family and friends, a few guidelines can make your photographs more effective.

- Include all elements that are helpful in communicating your ideas.
- Eliminate extraneous elements, such as distracting backgrounds.
- Include size indicators (e.g., a car, a person, a hand, a coin) in the picture if the size of the main object of interest is not apparent.
- Divide the picture area in thirds both vertically and horizontally. The center of interest should be near one of the intersections of the lines. This is called the "Rule of Thirds." Don't cramp the important part of the image near the edge of the picture.
- When making "how-to-do-it" pictures, take the picture from the viewpoint of the learner, not the observer.
- If a feeling of depth is important, use foreground objects (e.g., blossom-covered tree branches or moss-covered rocks) to frame the main subject.

SCANNERS

Scanners work with computers to transfer existing paper-based visual images, such as student drawings or photographs, into digitized computer graphic files. A flatbed scanner looks like the top of a photocopy machine. The user lifts the lid and places the image face down on the glass surface. Special software on a connected computer operates the scanner. As with digital photographs, students may quickly incorporate scanned images into a word processing file. They can enhance or modify them using the appropriate software. You can also easily incorporate images into your own presentations.

Scanning images is a simple task.
Shutterstock

MAKING THE CLASSROOM COME ALIVE WITH 3D IMAGES

Classrooms are coming alive with 3D images in lessons! The same technology used in movie theatres now is moving to the schools. Nothing captures the attention of students like 3D, which makes both still and moving images more compelling. The increasing use of 3D projectors in schools allows students to "walk" thorough famous architectural structures—past, present, or future. The projectors actually produce two images on the screen at the same time—one for the left eye and one for the right. The viewer wears 3D glasses that combine the two images and create an amazing 3D effect.

SUMMARY

In this chapter we discussed the importance of visuals as an important tool for learning that should be used properly by both you and your students. We began with the concept of visual literacy, and presented the critical aspects of decoding and encoding visuals. We explained how students learn best when visuals are used in instruction. We discussed the types, purposes, and categories of visuals and provided guidelines for presentation software, digital visuals, document cameras, overhead projectors, and printed visuals. We looked at advantages and limitations and techniques for integrating and utilizing visuals in the classroom. The chapter concluded by presenting guidelines that will assist you and your students in planning, creating, and capturing visuals.

PEARSON
myeducationkit™

To check your comprehension of the content covered in Chapter 8, go to the **MyEducationKit** for your book and complete the Study Plan for Chapter 8. Here you will be able to take a chapter quiz, receive feedback on your answers, and then access resources that will enhance your understanding of the chapter content.

ASSURE Lesson Plan

The following ASSURE Lesson Plan provides a detailed description and analysis of the lesson in the ASSURE Classroom Case Study and video at the beginning of the chapter. To review the video again, go to the MyEducationKit for your text and click on the ASSURE Video under Chapter 8. The video explores how Mrs. Roman, a third-grade teacher, and Mrs. Edlund, an art teacher, help students learn through the use of digital images and electronic portfolios.

Analyze Learners

General Characteristics. The audience consists of 23 third-graders who have recently completed state tests to assess their mathematics knowledge and skills. Because the school is new, they have not had many opportunities to know each other prior to this year. Some come from the same neighborhood, whereas others are from surrounding small communities. All of the students like to play at recess and enjoy movies and video games. Many of the boys are interested in sports, especially baseball. Most of the girls are interested in reading and watching television.

Entry Competencies. A number of the children have scored well on earlier tests in mathematics. A few struggle with some basic mathematics skills they have yet to master. The students have demonstrated difficulty in understanding the concepts of three-dimensional images shown on paper. As their recent test scores reflect, they have difficulty with conceptualizing how to visualize this type of image.

Learning Styles. The class members display a range of learning styles. Most of them have visual and spatial skills and good math ability. The children enjoy drawing and look forward to art classes as they find they can express their ideas with a variety of materials.

State Standards and Objectives

Curriculum Standards. National Council for Teachers of Mathematics 3—Geometry and spatial sense: Analyze characteristics and properties of two- and three-dimensional geometric objects. National Standards for Arts Education 5: Reflecting on and assessing the characteristics and merits of their work and the work of others.

Technology Standards. National Educational Technology Standards for Students 3—Technology productivity tools: Students use technology tools to enhance learning, increase productivity, and promote creativity.

Learning Objectives

1. Given art materials, the students will demonstrate their ability to build three-dimensional objects by cutting and shaping construction paper into three shapes: cylinder, cone, and box.
2. Given drawing materials, the students will draw on paper their three-dimensional objects, employing conventions learned in art class.

3. Given drawing materials, students will draw a picture of the playground, using the art conventions for showing dimension.
4. Given a digital camera and PowerPoint software, the students will create an e-portfolio of their art, reflecting on what they have learned.

Select Strategies, Technology, Media, and Materials

Select Strategies. Mrs. Roman decides to work with Mrs. Edlund, the art teacher, to find ways of enhancing her students' ability to make the connection between two-dimensional pictures and three-dimensional objects. She likes the idea of using e-portfolios as another way of demonstrating student learning, something Mrs. Edlund has been hoping to develop with her students. Together they decide to try several different approaches to instructing students. Mrs. Roman plans to combine direct instruction with some hands-on experiences using the math manipulatives that are available with the textbook.

Mrs. Edlund leads the children through a process of selecting their art for a portfolio, which because of the focus of the school on art and technology, is an electronic portfolio (e-portfolio). She demonstrates how to operate a digital camera, how to load their pictures into the computer, and how to use PowerPoint to create their e-portfolios. To help the children reflect about their art and its connections to their classroom knowledge, she guides them with thoughtful questions.

Select Technology and Media. This lesson involves student use of computers, digital cameras, Photoshop, and PowerPoint software to create electronic portfolios. Mrs. Edlund chooses to use laptop computers from the portable laptop cart. She decides on PowerPoint as the software for the e-portfolio because it is available on the laptops as well as the classroom computers. She feels that the program provides enough flexibility for children to be able to build e-portfolios without having to learn a complex program. And she knows they will be able to keep adding to their portfolios as they progress through school because PowerPoint will be available to them through high school. She uses the following guidelines to assess the appropriateness of her technology and media selections:

- *Alignment with standards, outcomes, and objectives*. The digital cameras allow students to capture their art pieces for inclusion in their portfolios. Photoshop and PowerPoint software provide the necessary tools the students need to create the portfolios as described in the learning objectives.
- *Accurate and current information*. Students are working with art that they created, so it is current. Internet information is not used, so accuracy is not of concern for this lesson.
- *Age-appropriate language*. Photoshop and PowerPoint menus are written at a level that requires initial training for third-grade students and ongoing support during use.
- *Interest level and engagement*. Use of Photoshop and PowerPoint software with self-created artwork provides students the opportunity to produce personalized electronic portfolios that demonstrate their reflections and talents in a creative fashion.
- *Technical quality*. The digital camera, Photoshop, and PowerPoint software have superior technical quality.
- *Ease of use*. After basic skills training, the third-grade students are able to effectively use the digital camera in combination with Photoshop and PowerPoint software.
- *Bias free*. Photoshop and PowerPoint are bias free.
- *User guide and directions*. The online help features of Photoshop and PowerPoint are too sophisticated for use by third-grade students. Therefore, Mrs. Edlund provides ongoing support and directions to her students.

Select Materials. Mrs. Edlund decides to have students work with clay to create three-dimensional objects. Then she shows the students how to draw their clay objects on paper, demonstrating the art conventions that show depth. She determines whether they can apply that knowledge by taking the children out to the playground to draw the area. Mrs. Edlund decides that the children are making the connections between their art and their classroom experiences. She thinks that it would be best for the children to build art portfolios as a way to demonstrate their learning and to capture points in time with their art achievement.

Utilize Technology, Media, and Materials

Preview the Technology, Media, and Materials. Mrs. Edlund previews the digital camera features and the Photoshop and PowerPoint software to ensure they have the features needed for students to create electronic portfolios of their artwork.

Prepare the Technology, Media, and Materials. Mrs. Edlund examines the digital camera to ensure it is working and reserves the laptop cart. She gathers the student artwork folders and reviews the content to check that they are complete.

Prepare the Environment. Mrs. Edlund sets up the digital camera for still shots and ensures that the digital photos download from the camera to the computer. She tests all computers to ensure that Photoshop and PowerPoint are loaded and functional. She sets out the student collections of artwork.

Prepare the Learners. Students in Mrs. Edlund's class are shown how to take digital photos of their artwork, how to use Photoshop to crop the photos, and how to process their work with PowerPoint to create the electronic portfolios.

Provide the Learning Experience. Mrs. Edlund wants to make the process easy for the third-grade students, so she focuses on having them use traditional art materials first. By letting them create their images in art class, she can guide them in their thinking about the content associated with their classroom mathematics lessons as well as mastery of art. She wants to incorporate technology into their art and feels that the idea of an e-portfolio will accomplish that end.

Require Learner Participation

Student Practice Activities. The children use various art media to demonstrate their understanding of the concepts they are acquiring in both math and art classes. They operate the digital camera, making certain their photos are of high quality to ensure capturing the essence of their art in the picture. They learn how the computer uploads their pictures, how to crop and adjust the image on screen, and how to save their pictures to the school's server. The children apply the basics of PowerPoint and then begin to explore ways to use the software for demonstrating their achievements.

Feedback. Mrs. Edlund provides ongoing guidance while the children are writing their reflections into their e-portfolios. Through this feedback, the students are able to develop an understanding of how to reflect on their ideas and begin to separate those pieces of their art that represent their current views.

Evaluate and Revise

Assessment of Learner Achievement. Mrs. Edlund and Mrs. Roman meet to look at what the children have done in their artwork. They determine that the children are able to connect their classroom mathematics study with their art. Furthermore, the e-portfolio is a way for them to demonstrate their understanding of the concepts in a meaningful way. Both Mrs. Roman and Mrs. Edlund feel that the children have learned to be more reflective in their approach to learning.

Evaluation of Strategies, Technology, and Media. Both feel that the e-portfolio experience is valuable for the children and would be a viable assessment approach in the future.

Revision. Both teachers look at the approaches to the lessons they taught and consider ways to extend their collaboration between the classroom and the art room. They also explore ways to assess learning beyond traditional testing approaches.

CONTINUING MY PROFESSIONAL DEVELOPMENT

Demonstrating Professional Knowledge

1. What is visual literacy? Identify two general strategies that you may use to teach visual literacy.
2. Name six types of visuals. What is an example of each type?
3. What roles do visuals play in learning?
4. Describe four methods for viewing visuals in the classroom.
5. What are the advantages, limitations, and integration techniques for visuals?
6. What are the goals of good visual design?
7. Discuss four techniques for creating visuals.
8. Discuss two methods for capturing images.

Demonstrating Professional Skills

1. Design a series of instructional images. Attach a description of the audience, objectives, and features that help achieve the goals of your visual design. (ISTE NETS-T 2.A)
2. Locate six visuals (both nonprojected and projected) that you believe would be useful in your own teaching and evaluate them using the Selection Rubric: Visuals. (ISTE NETS 2.C)
3. Create one graph (line, bar, circle, or pictorial) and one chart (organization, classification, timeline, tabular, or flow) for a topic you might teach. Use the Selection Rubric: Visuals as a guideline. (ISTE NETS 3.C)

Building My Professional Portfolio

- *Creating My Lesson.* Using the ASSURE model, design a lesson for a scenario from Appendix A or use a scenario of your own design. Use at least one of the instructional strategies described in Chapter 4 along with information from this chapter related to using visuals for learning. Be sure to include a description of the audience, the objectives, and all other elements of the ASSURE model. (ISTE NETS-T 2.A & 3.A)
- *Enhancing My Lesson.* Enhance the lesson you created in the previous activity by describing how you would meet the diverse needs of learners and how you would integrate different types of technology. Specifically, describe additional strategies you would include for students who already possess the knowledge and skills targeted in your lesson plan. Also describe strategies, technology, media, and materials you could integrate to assist students who have not met the lesson prerequisites. (ISTE NETS 2.D, 3.D, & 5.D)
- *Reflecting on My Lesson.* Reflect on the lesson you created and on how you enhanced the lesson. Also consider the process you used and what you have learned about matching audience, content, strategies, technology, media, and materials. What visuals were used? How can the visuals enhance the learning experiences of your students? If you were to redesign your lesson, what visuals would you select and why? (ISTE NETS 4.C & 6.B)

Print

Benjamin, A. (2005). *Differentiated instruction using technology.* Larchmont, NY: Eye on Education.

Bull, G., & Thompson, A. (2004). Establishing a framework for digital images in the school curriculum. *Learning and Leading with Technology, 31*(8), 14–17.

Carlson, G. (2004). *Digital media in the classroom.* San Francisco: CMP Books.

Evans, J. (2005). *Literacy moves on: Popular culture, new technologies, and critical literacy in the elementary classroom.* Portsmouth, NH: Heinemann.

Finkelstein, E., & Samsonov, P. (2008). *PowerPoint for Teachers: Dynamic presentations and interactive classroom projects.* San Francisco: Jossey-Bass.

Frey, N., & Fisher, D. (2008). *Teaching visual literacy: Using comic books, graphic novels, anime, cartoons, and more to develop comprehension and thinking skills.* Thousand Oaks, CA: Corwin Press.

Gangwer, T. (2009). *Visual impact, visual teaching: Using images to strengthen learning* (2nd ed.) Thousand Oaks, CA: Corwin Press.

Lidwell, W., Holden, K., & Butler, J. (2010). *Universal principles of design.* Beverly, MA: Rockport Publishers.

Lohr, L. L. (2007). *Creating graphics for learning and performance: Lessons in visual literacy* (2nd ed.). Upper Saddle River, NJ: Prentice Hall.

Luckner, J., Bowen, S., & Carter, K. (2001). Visual teaching strategies for students who are deaf or hard of hearing. *Teaching Exceptional Children, 33*(3), 38–44.

Newby, T. J., Stepich, D., Lehman, J., & Russell, J. D. (2011). *Education technology for teaching and learning* (4th ed.). Upper Saddle River, NJ: Merrill/Prentice Hall.

Stafford, T. (2010). *Teaching visual literacy in the primary classroom: Comic books, film, television, and picture narratives.* New York: Routledge.

Walling, D. R. (2005). *Visual knowing: Connecting art and ideas across the curriculum.* Thousand Oaks, CA: Corwin Press.

Woolner, P., Clark, J., Hall, E., Tiplady, L., Thomas, U., & Wall, K. (2010), Pictures are necessary but not sufficient: Using a range of visual methods to engage users about school design. *Learning Environments Research, 13*(1), 1–22.

Woolsey, K., Kim, S., & Curtis, G. (2004). *VizAbility: Learn to communicate visually.* Boston: Thomson Course Technology.

Web Links

To easily access these web links from your browser, go to the MyEducationKit for your text, then go to Chapter 8 and click on the web links.

Inspiration and Kidspiration

www.inspiration.com

Inspiration is a tool students can use to plan, research, and complete projects. With the integrated Diagram and Outline Views, they create graphic organizers and expand topics into writing. This combination encourages learning in multiple modes.

Kidspiration supports visual thinking techniques, enabling students to easily create and update graphic organizers, concept maps, idea maps, and other visuals.

Kodak

www.kodak.com

The Kodak website provides the user with information about digital cameras, printers, accessories, and more.

PowerPoint

http://office.microsoft.com/en-us/powerpoint

This site lets the user view full-featured presentations created in PowerPoint. This viewer also supports opening password-protected Microsoft PowerPoint presentations.

$ FREE & INEXPENSIVE

NASA

www.nasa.gov

Many organizations, including the government, provide free and inexpensive instructional materials. One example is NASA, which provides free informative posters showing beautiful images of planets, spacecraft, and eclipses. Informative drawings explain how an eclipse occurs. Visuals are available in printed format on CDs.

International Visual Literacy Association

www.ivla.org

The International Visual Literacy Association (IVLA) is a not-for-profit association of researchers, educators, and artists dedicated to the principles of visual literacy.

Selection Rubric: VISUALS

 To download and complete this rubric for your own use, go to the MyEducationKit for your text, then go to Chapter 8 and click on Selection Rubrics.

Search Terms Used to Locate Resources

_____

_____

_____

Title _____

Source/Location _____

© Date _____ Cost _____ Size _____ minutes

Subject Area _____ Grade Level _____

Instructional Strategies _____

Format

_____ Picture

_____ Drawing

_____ Chart

_____ Graph

_____ Poster

_____ Cartoon

Brief Description

Standards/Outcomes/Objectives

Prerequisites (e.g., prior knowledge, reading ability, vocabulary level)

Strengths

Limitations

Special Features

Name _____ Date _____

Rating Area	High Quality	Medium Quality	Low Quality
Alignment with Standards, Outcomes, and Objectives	Standards/outcomes/objectives addressed and use of visuals should enhance student learning.	Standards/outcomes/objectives partially addressed and use of visuals may enhance student learning.	Standards/outcomes/objectives not addressed and use of visuals will likely not enhance student learning.
Accurate and Current Information	Information is correct and does not contain material that is out of date.	Information is correct, but does contain material that is out of date.	Information is not correct and does contain material that is out of date.
Age-Appropriate Language	Language used is age appropriate and vocabulary is understandable.	Language used is nearly age appropriate and some vocabulary is above/below student age.	Language used is not age appropriate and vocabulary is clearly inappropriate for student age.
Interest Level and Engagement	Topic is presented so that students are likely to be interested and actively engaged in learning.	Topic is presented to interest students most of the time and engage most students in learning.	Topic is presented so as not to interest students and not engage them in learning.
Technical Quality	The material represents best available technology and media.	The material represents technology and media that are good quality, although there may be some problems using it.	The material represents technology and media that are not well prepared and are of very poor quality.
Ease of Use (Student or Teacher)	Material follows easy-to-use patterns with nothing to confuse the user.	Material follows patterns that are easy to follow most of the time, with a few things to confuse the user.	Material follows no patterns and most of the time the user is very confused.
Bias Free	There is no evidence of objectionable bias or advertising.	There is little evidence of bias or advertising.	There is much evidence of bias or advertising.
User Guide and Directions	The user guide is an excellent resource to support a lesson. Directions should help teachers and students use the material.	The user guide is a good resource to support a lesson. Directions may help teachers and students use the material.	The user guide is a poor resource to support a lesson. Directions do not help teachers and students use the material.
Legibility for Use (Size and Clarity)	The visual is presented so that most students can see and understand the information.	The visual is presented so that some students can see and understand the information.	The visual is presented so that most students cannot see and understand the information.
Simplicity (Clear, Unified Design)	The visual is well organized; students should be able to understand the information.	The visual is fairly well organized; students might be able to understand the information.	The visual is poorly organized; most students are unable to understand the information.
Appropriate Use of Color	Colors fit the nature of the subject and enhance the learning potential.	Colors marginally fit the nature of the subject and may enhance the learning potential.	Colors do not fit the nature of the subject and do not enhance the learning potential.
Communicates Clearly and Effectively	The information is presented visually in a way that will lead to learning.	The information is presented visually in a way that may lead to learning.	The information is presented visually in a way that may not lead to learning.
Visual Appeal	The visual should attract the attention of most students.	The visual may attract the attention of some students.	The visual may not attract the attention of many students.

Recommended for Classroom Use: _____ Yes _____ No

Ideas for Classroom Use:

Enhancing
Learning with Audio

This chapter addresses ISTE NETS-T 2.

1. Explain the differences between hearing and listening.

2. Identify four areas of breakdown in audio communication and specify the causes of such breakdowns.

3. Describe four techniques for improving listening skills.

4. Describe the most common types of digital and analog audio formats used for instruction. Include advantages and limitations of each type.

5. Illustrate one possible use of audio media in your teaching field. Include the subject area, audience, objective(s), role of the student, and evaluation techniques to be used.

Goal

Utilize the variety of audio materials available in the classroom. Describe the hearing–listening process and develop student listening skills.

The Chapter 9 ASSURE Classroom Case Study video describes the instructional planning used by Mr. Aina Akamu for a high school advanced speech and communications class in Hawaii. He wants to create an end-of-course student project that meets the following goals: enhance student confidence in making oral presentations that reveal personal convictions, increase student abilities to conduct research, engage students in collaborative learning, and use audio technology to help students express their creativity and ideas. Mr. Akamu selects "What it means to be Hawaiian" as the topic of this project.

*To view the **ASSURE Classroom Case Study** Video for this chapter, go to the MyEducationKit for your text and click on the ASSURE Video under Chapter 9 to explore how Mr. Akamu incorporates strategies to teach communication skills and uses technology, media, and materials to achieve 21st century learning environments.*

Throughout the chapter you will find reflection questions to relate the chapter content to the ASSURE Classroom Case Study. At the end of the chapter you will be challenged to develop your own ASSURE lesson that incorporates use of these strategies, technology, media, and materials, for a topic and grade level of your choice.

INTRODUCTION

If you were asked which learning activities consume the major portion of a student's classroom time, would you say reading, answering questions, reciting what one has learned, or taking tests? Actually, typical elementary and secondary students spend about 50 percent of their school time just listening. The importance of audio experiences in the classroom should not be underestimated. This chapter discusses various means— referred to as *audio media*—for recording and transmitting the human voice and other sounds for instructional purposes.

In this chapter we will explore audio media and how they can be used effectively in PK–12 classrooms. We will also examine the hearing–listening process and the development of listening skills. Even though delivery and recording devices have changed, the basics of using audio for teaching and learning have remained the same. From an instructional point of view, it is important to include audio regardless of its source—CD, MP3 player, a computer, the Web, or an audiocassette.

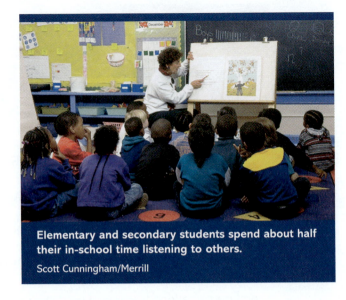

Elementary and secondary students spend about half their in-school time listening to others.

Scott Cunningham/Merrill

AUDIO LITERACY

Audio literacy is actually the merging of hearing and listening. Putting together messages that prove to be meaningful to students when they hear them is important to learning. Learning to listen is a task that requires students to practice and develop good skills so that listening becomes an effective means for learning.

HEARING AND LISTENING

Hearing and listening are *not* the same thing, although they are of course interrelated. At the risk of oversimplification, we might say that hearing is a physiological process, whereas listening is a psychological process.

Physiologically, **hearing** is a process in which sound waves entering the outer ear are transmitted to the eardrum, converted into mechanical vibrations in the middle ear, and changed in the inner ear into electrical impulses that travel to the brain.

The psychological process of **listening** begins with awareness of and attention to sounds or speech patterns (receiving), proceeds through identification and recognition of specific auditory signals (decoding), and ends in comprehension (understanding).

Hearing and listening are both communication and learning processes. As with visual communication and learning, a message is effectively composed by a sender and deciphered by a receiver to develop meaning. The quality of the prepared message is affected by the ability of the sender to articulate the message clearly and logically and in a way that addresses diverse audiences. Appropriate preparation of the message depends on the sender's skill in organizing and presenting it. For example, a teacher needs to know the vocabulary level of her students to be certain that they will be able to understand a recorded poetry reading. The efficiency of communication is also affected as the message passes from sender to receiver by the quality and efficiency of the audio medium. The understandability of the message then depends on the ability of the receiver to comprehend the message. Breakdowns in audio communications can occur at any point in the process: preparing (encoding), hearing, listening, or understanding (decoding), as illustrated in Figure 9.1. The hearing and listening process is recognized as a 21st century skill to ensure that communication informs, instructs, and motivates learners.

ASSURE Case Study Reflection

Review the ASSURE Classroom Case Study and video at the beginning of the chapter. As Mr. Akamu works with his students, how might he guide them to think about both the encoding and decoding of their messages?

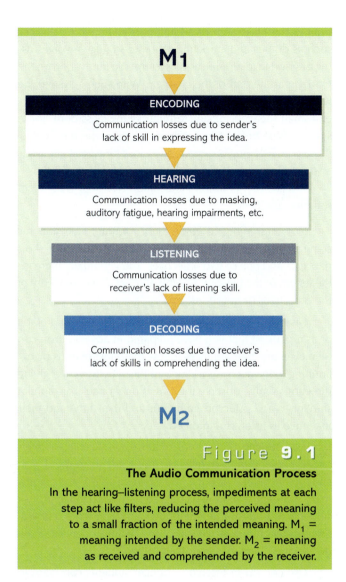

M₁

ENCODING

Communication losses due to sender's lack of skill in expressing the idea.

HEARING

Communication losses due to masking, auditory fatigue, hearing impairments, etc.

LISTENING

Communication losses due to receiver's lack of listening skill.

DECODING

Communication losses due to receiver's lack of skills in comprehending the idea.

M₂

Figure **9.1**

The Audio Communication Process

In the hearing–listening process, impediments at each step act like filters, reducing the perceived meaning to a small fraction of the intended meaning. M_1 = meaning intended by the sender. M_2 = meaning as received and comprehended by the receiver.

In addition, your conscious awareness of the noise is diminished because it is "old news" and no longer of interest. The brain has a remarkable capacity for filtering out sounds it doesn't want or need to attend to.

Third, an individual's ability to hear may be physically impaired. When students have a cold, it is possible that their ability to hear in a noisy classroom is reduced. Even a small difference in hearing acuity can cause students to have difficulty discriminating between words and phrases—thus the potential for confusion. And with the trend toward including students with significant loss of hearing acuity in regular hearing classrooms, teachers need to make special considerations for providing visual cues that ensure these students clearly understand the information.

For example, if you want a message to be heard by all the students, then use a tone and volume that ensures all students in the class can hear your message. This does not mean that you need to shout. If you want to speak to an individual student in the classroom, then it is more appropriate to move close and speak with softer volume so as to not disturb other members of the class. In addition, when you are speaking to an individual, it is important to shift your word choices to be sure the vocabulary is meaningful to that student.

If you are assigning students to prepare a presentation for the whole class, then you may wish to provide them with opportunities to practice. By practicing, students will be better able to use the appropriate intonation and volume to be certain that their classmates can clearly hear and understand the presentation. Or, you may wish to use a microphone and speaker to be sure everyone in the class can hear well.

There are a number of factors that determine whether students are able to learn from audio resources. First, the volume of the sound might be too low or too high. If too low, students may have trouble picking up the meaning with any accuracy. If too high, students may actually stop listening to the offending sounds.

Second, a sound that is sustained monotonously, such as the droning voice of a teacher, may trigger **auditory fatigue.** You have probably had the experience of hearing an annoying sound—for example, a noisy muffler on the car you are riding in. But after a while you hardly notice the sound at all. You might stop thinking about it entirely until it stops, and then you notice the cessation. This is an example of auditory fatigue, the process of gradually "tuning out" or losing consciousness of a sound source—a process that is physiological as well as psychological. That is, the neural mechanisms transmitting the sound to the brain literally become fatigued from "carrying the same load" over and over.

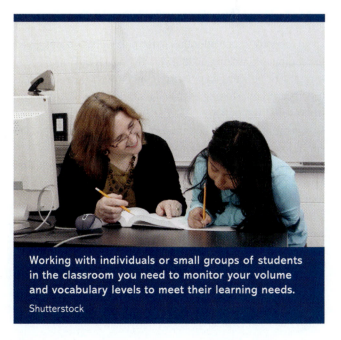

Working with individuals or small groups of students in the classroom you need to monitor your volume and vocabulary levels to meet their learning needs.

Shutterstock

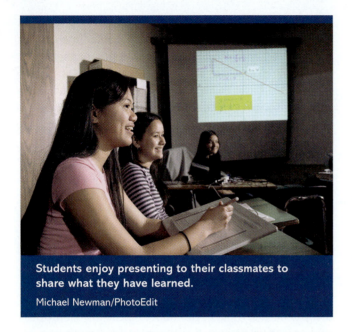

Students enjoy presenting to their classmates to share what they have learned.

Michael Newman/PhotoEdit

The message can also be affected by the learners' listening skills or lack of them. Students must be able to direct and sustain concentration on a message. They must have the skill to think ahead while receiving the message (we think faster than we hear, just as we think faster than we read or write) and use this time differential to organize and internalize the information so they can comprehend it.

Finally, communication can break down because the learner lacks the experiential background to internalize and thus comprehend the message. As their teacher, it is important to use vocabulary that is familiar and language patterns that your students understand.

DEVELOPING LISTENING SKILLS

Until recently, much attention in formal education was given to reading and writing, a little was given to speaking, and essentially none was given to listening. Now, however, educators recognize listening as a skill that, like all skills, one can improve with practice.

Hearing is the foundation of listening. Therefore, you should first determine whether all of your students hear normally. Most school systems regularly employ speech and hearing specialists to administer audiometric hearing tests that provide the data you need. Standardized tests also measure students' listening abilities. These tests are often administered by the school district, so check on the availability of listening test scores.

The classroom may not be ideal for the academic achievement of students with hearing impairments, for whom classroom noise and reverberation can cause problems. Potential solutions include relocating the student to the

front of the classroom or adding noise dampening devices such as drapes and carpeting. Another strategy involves using a sound field amplification system (see Innovation on the Horizon at the end of the chapter). With such a system the teacher wears a wireless microphone that transmits to several small speakers located throughout the classroom. These systems have been shown to help children who have colds, those with listening disorders, and those for whom English is a second language (Crandell, Smaldino, & Flexer, 2005).

You can use a number of techniques to improve student listening abilities:

• *Guide listening.* To guide their listening, give students some objectives or questions beforehand. Start with short passages and one or two objectives. Then gradually increase the length of the passage and the number and complexity of the objectives or questions.

• *Give directions.* Give students directions on audiotape or as a podcast that you have prepared in advance. You can then evaluate their ability to follow these instructions by examining worksheets or products of the activity. When giving directions orally, observe the "say it only once" rule so that students place value on both your and their time and their incentive to listen is reinforced.

• *Ask students to listen for main ideas, details, or inferences.* Keeping the age level of your students in mind, you can present an oral passage. You can read a story and ask primary students to draw a picture about what happened. Ask students to listen for the main idea and then write it down. Use this technique as well when you want students to draw details and inferences from the passage.

• *Use context in listening.* Younger students can learn to distinguish meanings in an auditory context by listening to

Listening skills are an important component of 21st century communication skills.

Will Hart/PhotoEdit

sentences with words missing and then supplying the appropriate words.

• *Analyze the structure of a presentation.* Ask students to outline an oral presentation. You can then determine how well they are able to discern the main ideas and to identify the subtopics.

• *Distinguish between relevant and irrelevant information.* After listening to an oral presentation of information, ask students to identify the main idea and then rate (from most to least relevant) all other presented ideas. A simpler technique for elementary students is to have them identify irrelevant words in sentences or irrelevant sentences in paragraphs.

AUDIO IN THE CLASSROOM

Audio adds a dimension to classroom environments that expands and deepens students' learning experiences. Imagine your students listening to Abraham Lincoln presenting his inaugural address, Einstein explaining relativity, Ernest Hemingway reading a passage from one of his novels, or Picasso interpreting one of his paintings. Also imagine a third-grade student being recorded as she reads a story for her digital portfolio and then comparing that recording with stories she recorded in first and second grade.

HOW TEACHERS CAN USE AUDIO

Teachers can prepare recordings for use in direct instruction; for example, a second-grade teacher can record directions for students to create sentences with word cards. Teacher-produced recordings can also provide skills practice, such as pronunciation of a foreign language. The possibilities are limitless—as seen in the examples below and throughout this chapter.

A teacher of ninth-grade students with learning difficulties, but average intelligence, provides instruction on how to listen to lectures, speeches, and other oral presentations. The

TECHNOLOGY for Diverse Learners

Audio

We have students in our classrooms with a variety of learning needs. The following examples demonstrate ways you can arrange to use audio resources to support learning.

The most familiar technique to assist learners with hearing impairments is closed-captioning for television and video programs. Multimedia presentations and audio materials on the Web use this feature as well. You will also find most media available today offers captioning as an option that needs to be selected. This technology is also useful for students who are learning a second language, those listening to content in a noisy environment, and readers who need additional practice.

Some students enjoy listening to stories and will often benefit from "reading along" with the audio portion of a book. Students who select books beyond their regular reading levels also benefit from audio presentation of the story. The audio book option allows students to practice vocabulary and enhance their reading experiences as part of independent reading. When working with English learners, the addition of audio cues can help them understand the text they are reading.

Students who wish to challenge their learning experiences can delve deeper into history by using audio to explore famous speeches or to enhance their experience of a particular time period. For example, students who wish to explore the speeches of Martin Luther King to develop a presentation for their classmates on his themes and timeline might listen to his speeches and incorporate audio clips into a Power-Point presentation for the class.

Anne Vega/Merrill

students practice their listening skills with CDs of recorded stories, poetry, and instructions. The teacher also uses commercially available CDs or free podcasts of speeches and narration. After the students have practiced their listening skills under teacher direction, they are evaluated using a recording they have not heard before.

A middle school teacher plays a CD for the 20 minutes she needs to set up her classroom for the school day. After a few seconds of music, the song fades as the narrator says, "What's new in classroom management techniques? Today we are going to explore together three techniques that will enhance your classroom skills . . ." The CD turns the classroom work setting into a learning environment, thereby making efficient use of the teacher's time for professional development.

An often-overlooked use of audio materials is for evaluating student attainment of lesson objectives. For example, you may prerecord test questions for class members to use individually. You may ask students to identify sounds in a recording (e.g., to name the solo instrument being played in a particular musical movement) or to identify the composer of a particular piece of music. Students in social studies classes could listen to excerpted passages from famous speeches and asked to identify the historical person who most likely made them or to identify the time period of the passages based on their content. Testing and evaluating using audio is especially appropriate when teaching and learning have also taken place in that particular mode.

HOW STUDENTS CAN USE AUDIO

A popular project in social studies classes is the recording of **oral histories,** in which students interview local citizens regarding the history of their community. All the recordings prepared during the interviews are kept in the school media center. This project serves the dual purpose of informing students and residents about local history as well as collecting and preserving information that might otherwise be lost.

Audio recordings can be used for presenting book reports, which students may record during study time in the media center or at home. The best ones are posted on the library's website and can be accessed on computers in the media center, in the classroom, or at home. These recorded reviews can be used to encourage other students to consider their options before selecting books to read.

Students can also record information gleaned from a field trip on portable devices. On returning to the classroom, students can play back the recording for discussion and review. Many museums, observatories, and other public exhibit areas now supply visitors with prerecorded messages about various items on display, which may, with

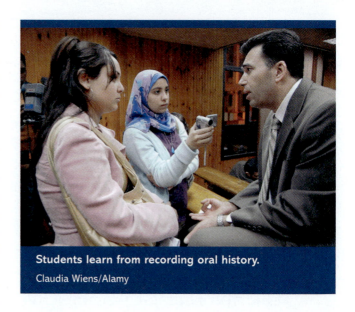

Students learn from recording oral history.
Claudia Wiens/Alamy

permission, be downloaded or rerecorded for playback in the classroom.

Students can also record themselves reciting a poem, presenting a speech, performing music, and so on. They can then listen to the recording privately or have the performance critiqued by the teacher or other students. Many small-group projects can include recorded reports for presentation to the rest of the class. These recordings can become part of each student's electronic portfolio.

A primary student at a learning center listens to a CD or audiocassette of her favorite storybook. She follows along in the book to associate letter combinations with sounds. The technique encourages reading and promotes literacy.

The elementary class performs daily physical exercises to the music and narration of a CD. The teacher hopes the experience will promote lifelong good health through daily exercise and proper diet, which he also teaches.

Students love to hear and tell stories, which can be both entertaining and informative. Storytelling is an important skill to develop in students of all ages. The goal should be teaching students to express ideas through verbal communication. Students can use Audacity open source software to prepare the recordings with special sound effects or elements of music to enhance their presentation. Students also could use an audio interview with a special "guest" as a part of their presentation.

Individual students use a keyboard connected to a computer to "compose" their own music. They can "see" the music on the screen and hear what they have composed through headphones to keep them from disturbing other students in the room. They then write stories around the music or sounds they have created.

Poet Laureate

One day a tenth-grade English teacher was listening to NPR on his way to school. That morning the show "All Things Considered" had an interview with the poet laureate of the United States, who was explaining his "favorite poem project." Essentially he traveled all over the United States randomly asking people from school teachers to welders to read and discuss their favorite poems while he recorded their responses on audiotape. He created an extensive library of people and poems. This teacher got the idea to adapt this project for his classes. The students loved it! The teacher was surprised not only by the emotional oral interpretations they submitted, but also by the depth of analysis portrayed in their short discussions of the poems, an activity in which even low-achieving students had success.

Source: Submitted by Matt Rose, Purdue University

AUDIO FORMATS

Audio comes in two primary formats: digital and analog. We will examine digital formats first. In **digital recording,** sound (whether in the form of music, speech, or sounds) is transformed into binary information—a series of 1s and 0s, the same mathematical code used in computers.

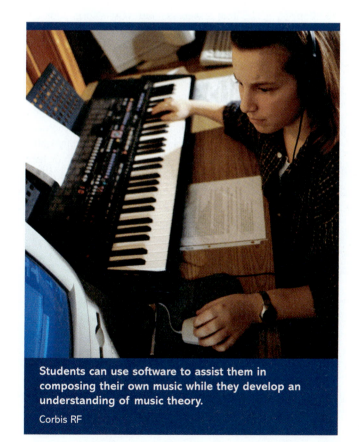

Students can use software to assist them in composing their own music while they develop an understanding of music theory.

Corbis RF

Digital audio encompasses a variety of storage formats and ways to access the files such as streaming and podcasting. Educational materials in digital audio format can be purchased on compact discs, downloaded or streamed in the MP3 format, downloaded as WAV files from the Web, or created by you or your students. Digital recordings are then played back on a variety of players.

DIGITAL AUDIO

Digital files are preserved on digital storage devices such as a CD, a computer hard drive, a flash drive, or a handheld digital recorder. The digital files are typically saved in MP3 or WAV format.

Compact Disc. Compact disc (CD) technology is a standard format in educational settings. The CD stores music or other sounds as digitized bits of information and can hold up to 80 minutes of audio information. Users of CDs can quickly locate selections on the disc and program them to play in any desired sequence. Information can be selectively retrieved by learners or programmed by the instructor. A major advantage of the CD is its resistance to damage. Stains can be washed off, and ordinary scratches do not affect playback. If a scratch does affect the quality of the audio signal, a resin is available to repair the disc.

Many computers are equipped to create or "burn" audio CDs, making it easy for teachers and students to create CD recordings. Copyright restrictions need to be checked when including prerecorded material or music (see Copyright Concerns: Music).

MP3. Audio files in the **MP3 (MPEG Audio Layer 3)** format use audio compression to shrink large audio files into smaller sizes that can quickly and easily be captured on the Internet. MP3 audio compression technology reduces upload and download time along with amount of storage space. As an "open" standard, MP3 is available to anyone with access to the Internet. The software your computer needs to use MP3 audio files is free to the user. Many audio files are also free or available for download at low cost from many subscription-based websites or at pay-as-you-go sites such as Apple Computer's iTunes Music Store.

MP3 is a way for audiophiles to enjoy their favorite pieces of music and to obtain the newest versions of a particular artist's songs. Some Internet sites let the users customize their selections so they can create unique "albums." On the downside, a word of caution related to copyright. Not all Internet sites make legal copies of music available. It is the responsibility of the user to respect the copyright laws related to audio (see Copyright Concerns: Music).

WAV. At one time the most common way to store and use audio, **WAV** files are digital versions of analog audio created by using a computer sound card and software to convert and store the file in digital format. WAV audio files can be stored on any digital storage device such as a CD, flash drive, or network drive for individual playback on a computer. Advantages of the WAV file format include the high quality of the audio files and the use of multiple channels for the sound. The limitation of WAV files is their very large size, meaning that most WAV audio clips must be short in duration. When audio files are stored as WAV format, you must first download the entire file before you can play it.

ANALOG AUDIO

Typically in the form of audiocassette tapes, analog audio is still a commonly used resource in today's classrooms for

Music

The use of music is the most highly regulated activity in the realm of copyright law. It is also heavily policed and enforced by the music industry!

Permitted copying of music includes the following:

- For academic uses other than performances, teachers and students may make copies of up to 10 percent of a musical work, provided the excerpt does not comprise a part of the whole that would constitute a performable unit such as a section, movement, or aria.
- Single copies of a recording of student performances may be made for rehearsal purposes or evaluation.
- Single copies of a recording, such as a CD or cassette, of copyrighted music may be made from a recording owned by a school or teacher for the purpose of constructing aural exercises or assessments.

The following are prohibited:

- Making an anthology, compilation, or collective work.
- Making copies of printed music scores. Additional copies must be purchased or duplication rights negotiated.
- Making an arrangement of a copyrighted musical work without permission of the copyright holder. This falls into the category of creating a derivative work.
- Performing a musical work publicly without the copyright owner's permission.

- Copying music from a website. You must also pay for the use of music you download from the Internet. The copyright owners of sound recordings have rights set forth in the Digital Performance Right in Sound Recordings Act of 1995 and the Digital Millennium Copyright Act of 1998. These laws give sound recording copyright owners rights to online performances of their recordings.

Internet transmissions may involve the reproduction and distribution of musical works and the copying of a copyrighted musical work or sound recording onto your server or hard drive (as when you load the file containing the work). Unauthorized copying constitutes exploitation of the reproduction rights. You must contact the copyright owner of the sound recording (usually the distributor) for authorization to copy the sound recording onto your server or hard drive. Some Internet sites advertise music free from copyright. You are wise to check out sites that offer music files, as it is better to ask than to be caught with illegal copies of music.

The landmark litigation between the music industry and the Napster online music sharing service in early 2000 is a prototypical example of efforts to ensure that copyright holders receive proper remuneration for all commercial transactions involving their work.

For general information on copyright, see the copyright section on pages 13 through 15 in Chapter 1. Suggested resources (print and websites) on copyright appear at the end of Chapter 1.

Students can listen to audio files using the computer.

Nivek Neslo/Taxi/Getty

reading centers, activity kits, and personalized instruction. Audiocassettes allow you and your students to record your own tapes easily and economically. When the content becomes outdated or no longer useful, you can erase the magnetic signal on the tape and reuse it. The cassette is durable, easy to use, not easily damaged, and stores easily.

Some digital recorders have built-in USB connectors to make it easy to download files to the computer.

Shutterstock

There are a few drawbacks to cassettes. For instance, longer tapes, particularly C-120s, sometimes become stuck or tangled in the recorder because of the thinness of the tape. Unless the content on the tape is unique and of considerable value it is advised to transfer the content to a digital format and discard the tape.

Quickly replacing the audiocassette recorder is the digital audio recorder. The frequency response and overall quality (fidelity) of cassette playback units are not as good as those of digital players and repairing them is often more expensive than purchasing a new higher quality digital recorder. And the digital recorder can store larger files.

ACCESSING AUDIO

You can access and listen to digital audio files in a variety of ways, including streaming audio, podcasting, Internet radio, and digital players.

STREAMING AUDIO

Audio files available as **streaming audio** are sent in packets to your computer, allowing you to listen to the first part of the file while the rest is being temporarily downloaded. Streamed MP3 is available to anyone with a computer and access to the Internet. The software your computer needs to play MP3 audio files, like Windows Media Player and iTunes, is free and typically comes installed on most computers.

PODCASTING

Podcasting (from the words *iPod* and *broadcasting*) refers to recorded audio files in MP3 format that are distributed over the Internet. These audio files can be sent automatically to "subscribers" and stored in their computers for listening at their convenience. These files need to be completely downloaded before you can listen to them. With podcasting software, students and teachers can create their own newscasts or documentaries and allow subscribers to download and listen to them on their computers or portable audio players (Figure 9.2).

Podcasts differ from traditional Internet audio in two important ways. In the past, listeners have had to either tune in to web radio on a schedule or they have had to search for and download individual files from webpages. Podcasts are much easier to download and can be listened to at any time because a copy is on the listener's computer or portable audio player. They can be automatically delivered to subscribers, so no active downloading is required. Podcasting is functionally similar to digital video recorders (DVRs), such

sound files, which are copied by connecting to a computer.

As with audiocassettes and CDs, educational applications include audio presentations, music related to courses, talking books, historical speeches, symphonies, and conversational foreign languages. You can use your portable digital audio player and a microphone to record audio files, from class lectures to poetry readings. Every curriculum comes alive when audio is part of the instruction, with endless possibilities for PK–12 education.

The portable digital audio player also opens up exciting new options for language learners. For example, students can record and rerecord reading selections and submit the electronic files to their teachers for evaluation. Students can also practice oral presentations, as well as speaking in the foreign language they're studying to assess their own speaking skills. Teachers can use them to dictate lesson plans and research notes or record to-do lists as they think of them.

Figure **9.2**

Using Podcasts to Support Student Learning

Source: www.podcastalley.com/index.php

as TiVo, that let users record and store television programs for later viewing.

Podcasting offers teachers and students remarkable opportunities for their voices to be heard in their local communities or around the world. One could think of podcasting as blogging without writing or as a way for every class to have its own radio station.

INTERNET RADIO

Internet radio refers to radio stations on the Internet that can offer a variety of programming—music, sports, science, weather, and local, national, and world news. Live and recorded programming from around the world playable on classroom computers can enhance language, social studies, science, and current events lessons.

PORTABLE DIGITAL AUDIO

A **portable digital audio player** enables users to take their audio files with them. It is also called a "portable digital music player" because most people today use them to play music. An example is the Apple iPod. Despite fitting easily into the user's hand or pocket, it can store thousands of songs or

ASSURE Case Study Reflection

Review the ASSURE Classroom Case Study and video at the beginning of the chapter. How might Mr. Aina Akamu involve his students in using different audio formats, such as MP3, audio streaming, or podcasting to demonstrate "What it means to be Hawaiian"? Describe the advantages and disadvantages for students using each format.

AUDIO RECORDER

Audiocassette and digital recorders are readily available and very easy to operate. Some students have been using them since they were small children. Even very small children enjoy recording their voices and playing them back. Another common use of audio recorders for young children is to play a prerecorded narration of a storybook as the children follow along in the book.

Cassette players/recorders are "plug-and-play." Simply insert the cassette tape and it is ready to play. Switch the cassette player on and students can listen to what is recorded on the tape. With a digital player/recorder, there are no tapes to be handled. Add a microphone and students can record their voices or other sounds.

CREATING AUDIO

Audio recording technologies allow students to dictate notes, practice foreign languages, or conduct interviews within the community. More than a music player, audio equipment is now a portable tool for dictation and sound recording, taking and hearing notes, and listening to audio books and newspapers. Creating "radio programs" with music and narration can capture students' attention and motivate their creativity in a digital world.

MUSICAL INSTRUMENT DIGITAL INTERFACE

Musical Instrument Digital Interface (MIDI) technology allows students to create music by focusing on musical ideas rather than the mechanics of playing an instrument or learning musical notation. With relatively inexpensive technology that can be plugged into most computers, MIDI and music composition software like Apple's GarageBand allow students to exercise their "musical/rhythmic" intelligence, one of Gardner's (2006) nine aspects of intelligence. MIDI technology lets students create music as easily as word processing facilitates writing. Rather than using conventional musical notation, this technology uses lines of sound on a grid whose height corresponds to pitch and whose length corresponds to duration.

DIGITAL SYNTHESIZER SOFTWARE

With digital synthesizer software, students can create original music, "radio programs," and materials for their

Students can record and edit digital audio files on a computer.

Diane Bondareff/AP

portfolios. They can produce their own audio presentations using software that gives student productions a "professional polish."

It seems everyone wants to podcast these days. Creating podcasts using digital synthesizer software puts your students in the control room of their own full-featured radio station. Software such as Mixcraft (see Figure 9.3) includes

Figure **9.3**

Mixcraft

Acoustica's Mixcraft is one example of digital synthesizer software that allows students to add and modify prerecorded music from a wide variety of instruments, music played by the students, or music from other sources, when within copyright guidelines. *Source:* www.acoustica.com/mixcraft. Reprinted by permission.

sound effects and jingles from an audio library. Students can browse and select from various stored sounds—including sounds of people, animals, and machines, which they click and drag into their podcast to sync up with the vocal track.

ASSURE Case Study Reflection

Review the ASSURE Classroom Case Study and video at the beginning of the chapter. How could Mr. Akamu's students add self-created digital music to their presentations? What guidelines would Mr. Akamu need to provide his students to ensure that creating the music was aligned to and assisted students in achieving the knowledge outcomes for the lesson?

ADVANTAGES

- *Readily available, simple to use, and portable.* Most students have been using CD players, audiocassette recorders, and MP3 devices since they were very young. These types of players are easy to operate and portable; they can even be used "in the field." Portable audio devices are ideal for home study, and many students already have their own players.
- *Inexpensive.* Once the storage devices and equipment have been purchased, there is no additional cost because the storage devices are erasable and reusable. Individual audiocassettes are inexpensive. In the case of MP3 files, many are available on the Internet for free or at low cost.
- *Reproducible.* You can duplicate audiotapes and digital files with the appropriate software and equipment. You can easily duplicate audio materials in whatever quantities you need, for use in the classroom, in the media center, and at home. Remember to observe copyright guidelines.
- *Provides verbal message to enhance learning.* Students who have limited reading ability can learn from audio media by listening and following along with visual and text material. And they can replay portions of the audio material as often as needed to understand it.
- *Offers current information.* Web-based audio is often a broadcast of live speeches, presentations, or performances.

- *Ideal for teaching second languages.* Audio resources are excellent for teaching second languages because they not only allow students to hear words pronounced by native speakers, but also enable them to record their own pronunciations for comparison.
- *Stimulating.* Audio media can provide a stimulating alternative to reading and listening to the teacher, presenting verbal messages more dramatically than text can. With a little imagination on your part, audio can be very versatile.
- *Resistant to damage.* CDs do not have tape to tangle and break. Stains can be washed off, and ordinary scratches do not affect playback. MP3 files can be stored on a computer hard drive, USB drive, or MP3 player.

LIMITATIONS

- *Copyright concerns.* Commercially produced audio can easily be duplicated, which might lead to copyright violations.
- *Doesn't monitor attention.* Some students have difficulty studying independently, so when they listen to recorded audio their attention may tend to wander. They may hear the recorded message but not listen attentively and comprehend. Unlike teachers, an audio player cannot readily detect when students are drifting away from a lecture.
- *Pacing.* Determining an appropriate pace for presenting information can be difficult if your students have a range of attention spans and experiential backgrounds.
- *Fixed sequence.* Audio media fix the sequence of a presentation even though it is possible to hear a recorded segment again or advance to an upcoming portion. It is difficult to scan audio materials as you would text materials. CDs do not share this limitation, which is why this format plays a significant role in instruction.
- *Difficulty in locating segments.* It is sometimes difficult to locate a specific segment on an audiotape. Counters on the recorders assist retrieval, but they are not very accurate. CDs give much easier accessibility to specific selections.
- *Potential for accidental erasure or deletion.* Audiotapes can be erased easily, which can be problematic. Just as they can be quickly and easily erased when no longer needed, they can be accidentally erased when they should be saved. Be sure to remove the record lockout tab of any cassette you wish to safeguard. Because they are magnetic, audiotapes must be kept away from magnets, which can cause erasure.

Review the ASSURE Classroom Case Study and video at the beginning of the chapter. How can Mr. Akamu use audio in his students' development of their presentations? What type of audio information can he prepare in advance? Can his students prepare audio for their "What it means to be Hawaiian" presentations?

INTEGRATION

The uses of audio media are limited only by the imaginations of you and your students. You can use audio media in all phases of instruction—from introduction of a topic to evaluation of student learning. Perhaps the most rapidly growing general use of audio media today is for self-paced instruction. Students with learning disabilities can go back and repeat segments of instruction as often as necessary because the playback capability is a very patient tutor. The accelerated student can skip ahead or increase the pace of instruction.

Prerecorded audio materials are available in a variety of subjects. For music classes, CDs can be used to introduce new material or to provide musical accompaniment. The sounds of various musical instruments can be presented individually or in combinations. In preschool and primary grades, tapes and CDs can be used for developing rhythm, telling stories, playing games, and acting out stories or songs. A common application of audio media is in learning centers. Sometimes these are even referred to as "listening centers" because of their use of audio-based materials.

Adding audio files is relatively easy if you have the right equipment and enough memory on the computer as audio files can be quite large unless compacted. PowerPoint even has audio files included in the software package. Using a CD or audiotape, audio files can be created using a program

Audio

LibriVox

http://librivox.org

Audiobooks from the public domain are available with titles ranging from classics to short stories and poetry. The collection is based on voluntary submissions of audio media, but the entries must all be copyright free. Over 12 languages are available, with native speakers reading familiar books.

Audio Theatre Production Kit

www.balancepublishing.com

Students can create their own audio theatre productions. The kit contains two versions of a script, one with altered vocabulary to meet the needs of below-grade readers, the second for grade-level and above-grade-level readers. In addition, there is a CD with background music and sound effects. Students, working together, record their production for later sharing. They develop technical skills while working collaboratively in a motivating way that helps them with reading and vocabulary competencies.

Joy Stories

www.joystories.com

Available in both English and Spanish, this collection of short stories has been developed to help children gain personal insight and positive self-image. Presenting issues such as diversity, determination, and disappointment, these creative stories are designed to help children view their own personal challenges in a new light.

A Kid's-Eye View of the Environment

www.mishmashmusic.com

Michael Mish based this series of songs, available on CD or as an MP3 download, on his many visits to schools in southern California to talk to children about the environment. He found them to be more aware and concerned about environmental problems than he expected. Mish took the topics that the children were most concerned about (e.g., recycling, water and air pollution, and the greenhouse effect) and put them to music. The songs are engaging, with sing-along choruses. The messages should get primary-age children talking about making this a safer, cleaner world.

Use when student learning will be enhanced by . . .

Guidelines	Examples
text being read	High school students with limited reading ability listen to a recorded reading of a Shakespeare sonnet.
listening to key political speeches	Middle school students prepare for a debate by listening to podcasts of speeches given by candidates for mayor of their city.
recording impressions	Students create a digital journal by recording monthly impressions of their most important learning experiences.
easy access to verbal examples	Students use the "Noun" menu of a Spanish-language CD to listen to new vocabulary pronounced by a Spanish speaker.
listening to an author reading her story	As a story is being projected on a screen, elementary students listen to the author reading it in a streamed recording from a children's storybook website.
hearing the sounds of nature	Intermediate-grade students use a bird website to practice identifying sounds of different birds from their local area to prepare for a nature trail field trip.
listening to an expert	Students in an art class listen to a CD recording of a successful photographer sharing tips for taking balanced photos.
listening to current events	A social studies teacher plays an Internet radio broadcast of a recent presidential address.
recording personal reading	Elementary students create a digital reading journal that contains recordings of students reading favorite stories.

such as SoundEdit. Using a microphone and SoundEdit, the teacher or student can create original audio to enhance the information presented. The process for creating a digital audio file is similar to that of creating an audiotape.

Students can study music and other content areas using prerecorded audio media.

Valerie Schultz/Merrill

ASSURE Case Study Reflection

PEARSON
myeducationkit

Review the ASSURE Classroom Case Study and video at the beginning of the chapter. How can Mr. Akamu's students use audio as a component of a multimedia project? What guidelines should he give his students to ensure the audio enhances the overall project?

INNOVATION on the HORIZON

WE CAN HEAR YOU!
Classroom Voice Amplification Systems

The 21st century classroom is moving to an audio technology system that optimizes the listening environment for all

www.lightspeed-tek.com. Reprinted by permission.

students. A lightweight wireless teacher's microphone links to a set of speakers strategically placed around the classroom. The end result is a quality listening setting that helps engage students and supports student learning and performance.

Using voice activation solutions for the amplification, the system only raises the volume level of the teacher's voice slightly above the ambient room noise. In a noisy classroom, when it is often hard to hear the teacher, her voice is amplified just a little but the end result makes it easier to listen. And there is evidence that all students benefit from the amplified sound, including those with hearing problems, students with learning disabilities, students for whom English is their second language, and even those students who have no

identified learning difficulty (Crandell, Smaldino, & Flexer, 2005).

Summary

This chapter stressed the importance of audio in teaching and learning. After discussing the hearing and listening process in some detail, including techniques for developing listening skills, we explored a variety of ways to use audio in the classroom, describing both digital and analog audio formats. Throughout the chapter we discussed many techniques for selecting various audio formats and materials, as well as techniques for producing and editing audio materials. We described audio media's distinct advantages and limitations and offered guidelines for integrating audio into instruction.

To check your comprehension of the content covered in Chapter 9, go to the **MyEducationKit** for your book and complete the Study Plan for Chapter 9. Here you will be able to take a chapter quiz, receive feedback on your answers, and then access resources that will enhance your understanding of the chapter content.

ASSURE Lesson Plan

The following ASSURE Lesson Plan provides a detailed description and analysis of the lesson in the ASSURE Classroom Case Study and video at the beginning of the chapter. To review the video again, go to the MyEducationKit for your text and click on the ASSURE Video under Chapter 9. The video explores how Mr. Akamu creates a high school communication lesson that incorporates audio.

The Chapter 9 ASSURE Classroom Case Study describes the instructional planning used by Mr. Akamu, a high school advanced speech and communications teacher, for developing an end-of-course project. Mr. Akamu wants his students to create group presentations depicting

"What it means to be Hawaiian." The presentations are to include oral speaking, a PowerPoint presentation, and an iMovie that contains interviews of native Hawaiians.

Analyze Learners

The students enrolled in Mr. Akamu's advanced speech and communications course are 16 and 17 years old. The learning ability of these students is at or above grade level. None of the students are identified as having learning disabilities. His students come from primarily moderate to low socioeconomic environments and are all Hawaiian natives. For the most part, the students are well behaved and have a high interest in work related to their culture and backgrounds.

Entry Competencies. The high school students are, in general, able to do the following:

- Create, edit, and record digital audio files
- Navigate the Internet
- Create, edit, and save digital video with iMovie
- Create PowerPoint presentations

Learning Styles. Students are fairly sophisticated and prefer to work in groups. They enjoy incorporating the use of technology and media into their coursework. Most of the students like to use audio and video because it allows them to be creative and to produce work that expresses their personal opinions. However, some of the students prefer to input their thoughts as written text and oral expressions. Most of Mr. Akamu's students learn best in a relaxed atmosphere that encourages group discussions and movement between activities.

State Standards and Objectives

Curriculum Standards. National Council of Teachers of English 7: Students conduct research on issues and interests by generating ideas and questions and by posing problems. They gather, evaluate, and synthesize data from a variety of sources (e.g., print and nonprint texts, artifacts, people) to communicate their discoveries in ways that suit their purpose and audience.

Technology Standards. National Educational Technology Standards for Students 2—Communication and Collaboration: Students use digital media to communicate and work collaboratively to support individual learning and contribute to the learning of others.

Learning Objectives

- Produce a PowerPoint presentation that reflects a basic, personal understanding about being a contemporary Hawaiian.
- Develop an interview protocol and conduct interviews with people about Hawaiian identity.
- Given equipment and software, shoot, edit, and produce a 2-minute iMovie about Hawaiian identity.

Select Strategies, Technology, Media, and Materials

Select Strategies. In considering the content of the lesson, "What it means to be Hawaiian," Mr. Akamu realizes that his students need to gather much of the information from interviews with Hawaiian natives. Therefore, one of the key strategies is for students to conduct Internet searches and brainstorm ideas about the topic. Students use this information to develop questions for their interviews. Another lesson strategy is for students to collaboratively create storyboards for their PowerPoint presentations and their iMovies. Student groups plan the final presentation by assigning the following roles: (1) furnish an oral overview, (2) present information on the PowerPoint slides, (3) provide an introduction to the iMovie, and (4) offer concluding remarks.

Select Technology and Media. This lesson involves student use of computers, digital audio recorders, digital video cameras, and PowerPoint and iMovie software. Mr. Akamu selects digital audio recorders because students need to save the interviews in a digital format that can be imported into their iMovies. The digital format is also necessary to enable editing with iMovie software. Mr. Akamu selects PowerPoint software because it provides enough flexibility for students to import interviews, music, and photographs into their presentations. He uses the following guidelines to assess the appropriateness of his technology and media selections:

- *Alignment with standards, outcomes, and objectives.* The digital audio recorders and video cameras allow students to record, transfer, and edit interviews and videos to create presentations that demonstrate achievement of the objectives.
- *Accurate and current information.* Mr. Akamu instructs his students on guidelines for collecting accurate and current information when conducting Internet research.
- *Age-appropriate language.* PowerPoint and iMovie menus are written at a level that requires initial training for high school students and ongoing support during use.
- *Interest level and engagement.* The combined use of student-created PowerPoint and iMovie presentations provides students the opportunity to express their creativity through the production of a unique oral presentation.
- *Technical quality.* The digital audio recorders, digital video cameras, and PowerPoint and iMovie software are reliable and of high quality.
- *Ease of use.* After basic skills training, the high school students are able to use the digital audio recorders, digital video cameras, and PowerPoint and iMovie software.
- *Bias free.* PowerPoint and iMovie are bias free.
- *User guide and directions.* The online help features of PowerPoint and iMovie are suitable for use by high school students, as are the user's guides for the digital recorder and camera.

Select Materials. The materials for this lesson include an overview and assignment handout and a presentation rubric created by Mr. Akamu. The overview and assignment sheet includes a description of the lesson purpose, the student objectives, presentation guidelines and format, important dates, responsibilities for group members, and the project calendar. The presentation rubric includes two ratings for each group: one for the individual student speaker and one for the group as a whole. The criteria for individual speakers include rapport, voice, fluency, body, and content. The speakers are rated on a scale from 1 to 5, with 5 being the best rating. The group evaluation is based on ten criteria of successful presentations. For example, the first criterion states, "The presentation was introduced in an engaging and appealing manner. The presenters kept my attention throughout the speaking portion of their presentation." Another says, "The information presented was credible and believable. Multiple perspectives were shared and included in the presentation." Mr. Akamu along with student peers and guest evaluators attending the presentations complete the rubric.

Utilize Technology, Media, and Materials

Preview the Technology, Media, and Materials. Mr. Akamu previews the digital audio recorder and camera features and the PowerPoint and iMovie software to ensure they have the features needed for students to create their presentations.

Prepare the Technology, Media, and Materials. Mr. Akamu checks the digital audio recorder and the camera to ensure they are working. He ensures the computer lab is reserved and makes copies of the handouts.

Prepare the Environment. He prepares the digital audio recorders and video cameras for checkout to the students. He ensures that the lab computers have PowerPoint and iMovie installed and that they are functional. He sets out the student handouts.

Prepare the Learners. Mr. Akamu shows his students how to use the digital audio recorder, digital video camera, and PowerPoint and iMovie software prior to the lesson.

Provide the Learning Experience. Mr. Akamu begins the lesson with a discussion on "What it means to be Hawaiian," to show the variety of possible responses. He talks about the differences in how the students view being Hawaiian as compared to their grandparents. He introduces the power of capturing stories with audio recording. Then Mr. Akamu presents students with the assignment for their final class project.

Require Learner Participation

Student Practice Activities. The students use the digital audio recorder and digital video camera to capture family and community member ideas about "What it means to be Hawaiian." Students work in groups to combine the audio and video into a presentation that includes a PowerPoint presentation and an iMovie. The presentation provides the group's perception of "What it means to be Hawaiian" and provides information that supports their opinions.

Feedback. Mr. Akamu designs the lesson to include feedback as a major component of the unit. Since this is an advanced speech and communications course, the audio and video presentation is the product that is assessed. Students receive feedback from each other, the teacher, and guest evaluators who attend the presentation.

Evaluate and Revise

Assessment of Learner Achievement. Mr. Akamu uses the combined rubric ratings from students, guest evaluators, and his own ratings when assessing the learning of each student. He also evaluates the final products against the criteria listed in the assignment sheet.

Evaluation of Strategies, Technology, and Media. To evaluate the strategies, technology, and media, Mr. Akamu informally interviews the guest evaluators and his students to gain insight and ideas for improving the lesson.

Revision. Suggestions for revision given to Mr. Akamu include students working individually to ensure each student develops her or his own perception of "What it means to be Hawaiian." Another is to focus the lesson on family members to gain insight into a family's Hawaiian culture. A third revision suggestion involves students in developing a "What it means to be Hawaiian" website with student-created interview podcasts, iMovies, and photographs.

CONTINUING MY PROFESSIONAL DEVELOPMENT

Demonstrating Professional Knowledge

1. Explain the differences between hearing and listening.
2. Identify four areas of breakdown in audio communication. Specify the causes of such breakdowns.
3. Describe four techniques for improving listening skills.
4. Describe the most common types of digital and analog audio media used for instruction. What are the advantages and limitations of each type?

5. Illustrate one possible use of audio media in your teaching field. Include the subject area, audience, objective(s), role of the student, and evaluation techniques to be used.

Demonstrating Professional Skills

1. Obtain commercially prepared audio materials and appraise them using the Selection Rubric: Audio Materials. (ISTE NETS-T 2.A)
2. Develop a short oral history of your school or organization by interviewing people associated with it for a long time. Edit your interviews into a five-minute presentation. (ISTE NETS-T 3.C)
3. Use an audio format to collect your thoughts and ideas about what it means to use technology in your teaching. Listen to your narration after a few entries.

What have you learned about your ideas? How does keeping your ideas on audio impact your collection of reflections? Would you consider your audio materials to be a variation of a written journal? Why or why not? (ISTE NETS-T 5.C)

Building My Professional Portfolio

- *Creating My Lesson.* Using the ASSURE model, design a lesson for a scenario from the table in Appendix A or use a scenario of your own design. Use an instructional strategy that you believe to be appropriate for your lesson.
- *Enhancing My Lesson.* Enhance the lesson you created in the previous activity by describing how you would meet the diverse needs of learners and how you would integrate different types of technology and media. Specifically, describe additional strategies you would include for students who already possess the knowledge and skills targeted in your lesson plan. Also describe strategies, technology, media, and materials you could integrate to assist students who have not met the lesson prerequisites. Describe other types of technology and media that could be integrated into the instructional strategies. For students who have

met most or all of the learning objectives for the lesson, one consideration is to have them develop a presentation about the topic of study using audio. Describe the factors they might consider in selecting appropriate audio for the presentation. What do you need to do to help them select and plan for the use of audio? (ISTE NETS 2.B, 2.C, 3.D, & 5.C)
- *Reflecting on My Lesson.* Reflect on the lesson you created and reflect on how you enhanced the lesson. Also reflect on the process you used and what you have learned about matching audience, content, strategies, technology, media, and materials. Address the following in your reflection: What audio materials were used? How can the audio enhance the learning experiences of your students? If you redesigned your lesson, what audio materials would you select and why? (ISTE NETS 5.C)

SUGGESTED RESOURCES

Print

Boyle, E. A., Rosenberg, M. S., Connelly, V. J., Washburn, S. G., Brinckerhoff, L. C., & Banerjee, M. (2003). Effects of audio texts on the acquisition of secondary-level content by students with mild disabilities. *Learning Disability Quarterly, 26*(3), 203–214.

Farkas, B. G. (2006). *Secrets of podcasting* (2nd ed.). Berkeley, CA: Peachpit Press.

Hagopian, P. (2000). Voices from Vietnam: Veterans' oral histories in the classroom. *Journal of American History, 87*(2), 593–601.

Isbell, R. T. (2002). Telling and retelling stories: Learning language and literacy. Supporting language learning. *Young Children, 57*(2), 26–30.

Jalongo, M. R. (1995). Promoting active listening in the classroom. *Childhood Education, 72*(1), n.p.

Koskinen, P. S., Blum, I. H., Bisson, S. A., Phillips, S. M., Creamer, T. S., & Baker, T. K. (1999). Shared reading, books, and audiotapes: Supporting diverse students in school and at home. *Reading Teacher, 52*(5), 430–444.

McDrury, J., & Alterio, M. (2003). *Learning through storytelling: Using reflection and experience to improve learning.* London: Kogan Page.

Petress, K. C. (1999). Listening: A vital skill. *Journal of Instructional Psychology, 26*(4), 261–262.

Roy, L. (1993). Planning an oral history project. *Journal of Youth Services in Libraries, 6*(4), 409–413.

Schmeidler, E., & Kirchner, C. (2001). Adding audio description: Does it make a difference? *Journal of Visual Impairment and Blindness, 95*(4), 197–212.

Web Links

To easily access these web links from your browser, go to the MyEducationKit for your text, then go to Chapter 9 and click on the web links.

Multimedia Seeds: Exploring Audio and Visual Collection Use

http://eduscapes.com/seeds/different.html

The site provides hints for using audio and visuals for learning. Whether you're a school media specialist working with teachers and children or a teacher working with students, there are many ways to assist your students in the effective use of audio and video media.

Podcast Alley

www.ipodder.org

This directory of links to podcast feeds contains links known as RSS–2.0 files with MP3 enclosures. It lacks descriptions, samples, and ratings for the podcasts.

Sound and Learning

http://soundlearning.publicradio.org

Sound Learning offers connections between Minnesota Public Radio programming and current academic standards, a technical guide to help you access audio files, and suggestions for effective learning strategies.

Selection Rubric: AUDIO MATERIALS

 To download and complete this rubric for your own use, go to the MyEducationKit for your text, then go to Chapter 9 and click on Selection Rubrics.

Search Terms Used to Locate Resources

_____

_____

_____

Title _____

Source/Location _____

© Date _____ Cost _____ Length _____ minutes

Subject Area _____ Grade Level _____

Instructional Strategies _____

Format

_____ Internet Audio

_____ Podcast

_____ Digital

- Compact disc
- MP3
- WAV

_____ Analog

- Audiocassete tape

Brief Description

Standards/Outcomes/Objectives

Prerequisites (e.g., prior knowledge, reading ability, vocabulary level)

Strengths

Limitations

Special Features

Name _____ Date _____

Rating Area	High Quality	Medium Quality	Low Quality
Alignment with Standards, Outcomes, and Objectives	Standards/outcomes/objectives addressed and use of audio should enhance student learning.	Standards/outcomes/objectives partially addressed and use of audio may enhance student learning.	Standards/outcomes/objectives not addressed and use of audio will likely not enhance student learning.
Accurate and Current Information	Information correct and does not contain material that is out of date.	Information correct but does contain material that is out of date.	Information is not correct and does contain material that is out of date.
Age-Appropriate Language	Language used is age appropriate and vocabulary is understandable.	Language used is nearly age appropriate and some vocabulary is above/below student age.	Language used is not age appropriate and vocabulary is clearly inappropriate for student age.
Interest Level and Engagement	Topic is presented so that students are likely to be interested and actively engaged in learning.	Topic is presented to interest students most of the time and engage most students in learning.	Topic is presented so as not to interest students and not engage them in learning.
Technical Quality	The material represents the best available technology and media.	The material represents technology and media that are good quality, although there may be some problems using it.	The material represents technology and media that are not well prepared and are of very poor quality.
Ease of Use (Student or Teacher)	Material follows easy-to-use patterns with nothing to confuse the user.	Material follows patterns that are easy to follow most of the time, with a few things to confuse the user.	Material follows no patterns and most of the time the user is very confused.
Bias Free	There is no evidence of objectionable bias or advertising.	There is little evidence of bias or advertising.	There is much evidence of bias or advertising.
User Guide and Directions	The user guide is an excellent resource to support a lesson. Directions should help teachers and students use the material.	The user guide is a good resource to support a lesson. Directions may help teachers and students use the material.	The user guide is a poor resource to support a lesson. Directions do not help teachers and students use the material.
Pacing Appropriate	The audio material is presented so most students can understand and process the information.	The audio material is presented so some students start to understand and process the information.	The audio material is presented so most students cannot understand and process the information.
Use of Cognitive Learning Aids (Overviews, Cues, Summary)	The audio material is well organized and uses cognitive learning aids.	The audio material is fairly well organized and uses some cognitive learning aids.	The audio material is not well organized and does not use cognitive learning aids.

Recommended for Classroom Use: _____ Yes _____ No

Ideas for Classroom Use:

Enhancing
Learning with Video

This chapter addresses ISTE NETS-T Standard 2.

1. Define video literacy and list the five core concepts of viewing and producing video.

2. Explain how student learning is enhanced by the application of video in each instructional domain—cognitive, affective, psychomotor, and interpersonal.

3. List and describe how the four types of educational video support student learning.

4. Describe three attributes of video and how they impact classroom instruction.

5. Compare and contrast digital versus analog video formats.

6. Outline the process for selecting and evaluating video for classroom use.

7. Describe techniques for video production by students and teachers.

Goal

Understand appropriate applications of video in the PK–12 classroom

The Chapter 10 ASSURE Classroom Case Study describes the instructional planning used by Scott James, a fifth-grade teacher in a school with students coming from low- to middle-income homes. Mr. James realizes that students learn best when lessons reflect real-world situations. He has also seen increased student motivation and interest when computers are integrated into his lessons. Scott's school recently purchased a digital video camera and iMovie software for the lab computers. To take advantage of these resources, Mr. James designs a multidisciplinary lesson on natural disasters that incorporates the use of the new digital video camera as part of building students' expository writing skills. During the lesson, student pairs create digital videos of natural disaster "news broadcasts" they have scripted. One student assumes the role of news anchor while the other is the "on the scene" news reporter.

*To view the **ASSURE Classroom Case Study Video** for this chapter, go to the MyEducationKit for your text and click on the ASSURE Video under Chapter 10 to watch how Mr. James engages students in the use of digital video. He also offers suggestions and discusses the benefits and limitations for using video to achieve 21st century learning environments.*

Throughout the chapter you will find reflection questions to relate the chapter content to the ASSURE Classroom Case Study. At the end of the chapter you will be challenged to develop your own ASSURE lesson that incorporates use of these strategies, technology, media, and materials for a topic and grade level of your choice.

PEARSON
myeducationkit™

INTRODUCTION

Today's PK–12 students are experiencing an explosion of enhanced learning through viewing and creating videos. At the click of a mouse, teachers can select from a vast array of online videos to support and enrich instructional experiences. For example, Discovery Education provides online access to more than 80,000 video clips to over one million educators and 35 million students (Discovery Education, 2010). In addition, video production equipment is rapidly becoming the next technological "wave" in PK–12 schools. A May 2010 survey of over 600 educational administrators and technology coordinators indicates that over half of the respondents "are likely" to buy video equipment during the next year with 80 percent reporting that technology plays a role in "improving how students learn" and in "helping prepare students for the workforce of the future" (Carter, 2010). In this chapter we explore the characteristics and effective uses of video in learning.

VIDEO LITERACY

"No longer is it enough to be able to read the printed word; children, youth, and adults, too, need the ability to critically interpret the powerful images of a multimedia culture" (Thoman & Jolls, 2004, p. 18). Video literacy is critical for success in the 21st century.

Any electronic media format that employs "motion pictures" to present a message can be referred to as **video.** In this text we use the term to refer to electronic storage of moving images (e.g., DVDs or computer-based and Internet video).

Video literacy encompasses the knowledge and skills needed to "consume" or meaningfully view video as well as to produce video. Five core concepts are fundamental to understanding video literacy: (1) An author constructs the message; (2) the format is unique for each message; (3) each viewer interprets the message differently; (4) points of view and values are part of each message; and (5) most messages are organized to promote a specific purpose (Jolls, 2008).

VIEWING VIDEO

Students have several options for watching educational videos, including whole-class programs with a digital projector or large-screen television monitor as well as smaller-scale viewing on computers and mobile devices such as netbooks, iPads, and iPhones. When teaching students to "critically"

view video, the process involves all levels of Bloom's taxonomy (knowledge, analysis, comprehension, application, synthesis, and evaluation). The viewing process can be guided by asking questions addressing core concepts.

1. Who created this message?
2. What creative techniques are used to attract my attention?
3. How might various people understand this message differently?
4. What values, lifestyles, and points of views are represented or omitted?
5. What is the purpose of the message? (Jolls, 2008, p. 37)

PRODUCING VIDEO

The core concepts also play an important role in helping students increase video literacy knowledge and skills to produce video. Once again, producing video requires students to engage in higher-order thinking skills in order to first plan the format that will "tell the story" and then develop, edit, and evaluate the final video to ensure the intended message is shared. Once again address core concepts with key questions to guide student production of video.

1. What am I authoring?
2. Does the message reflect understanding in format, creativity, and technology?
3. Is my message engaging and compelling for my target audience?
4. Have I clearly and consistently framed values, lifestyles, and points of view in my message?
5. Have I communicated my purpose effectively? (Jolls, 2008, p.37)

USING VIDEO IN THE CLASSROOM

According to Nugent (2005), many teachers use video to introduce a topic, to review content, to provide remediation, or to promote enrichment. Video is suitable in all instructional environments and works with whole classes, small groups, and individual students. They can take the learner almost anywhere and extend students' interests beyond the walls of the classroom. Organizations from companies to national parks provide video tours to observe phenomena as varied as assembly lines and the wonders of nature. Objects too large to bring into the classroom are studied as well as those too small to see with the naked eye. Events too dangerous to directly observe, such as an eclipse of the sun, are studied safely. Videos are available on almost any topic for every type of learner in all the domains of instruction.

VIDEO AND THE DOMAINS OF LEARNING

The multifaceted nature of videos makes them an excellent educational resource to expand student learning in the four major domains: cognitive, affective, psychomotor, and interpersonal.

Cognitive Domain. In the cognitive domain, learners can observe dramatic recreations of historical events and actual recordings of more recent events. Color, sound, and motion make personalities come to life. Video can enhance the textbook by showing processes, relationships, and techniques. Students can read books in conjunction with viewing videos. Students can read before viewing as an introduction to the topic, or you may use the video to interest students in reading about the topic.

Affective Domain. When there is an element of emotion or the desire for affective learning, video usually works well. Role models and dramatic messages on video can influence attitudes. Because of its great potential for emotional impact, video can be useful in shaping personal and social attitudes. Documentary programs have often been found to have a measurable impact on student attitudes. Documentaries made during the Great Depression, for example, bring the hardships of that era to students who have never known hard times. Cultural understanding can be developed through viewing video depicting people from all parts of the globe.

Psychomotor Domain. Video is great for showing processes involving the use of motor skills. For example, there is a short educational video called Colonial Cooper that shows how an 18th century artisan makes a barrel at Colonial Williamsburg. Demonstrations of psychomotor skills are often more easily seen through media than in real life. If you are teaching a step-by-step process with a DVD, you can show it in real time, use fast forward for an overview, stop the action for careful study, or move forward one frame at a time. Students' own performances can also be recorded to video, which enables learners to observe their efforts and receive feedback from peers, teachers, or others.

Interpersonal Domain. By viewing a video program together, a diverse group of learners can build a common base of experience as a catalyst for discussion. When students are learning interpersonal skills, such as dealing with conflict resolution or peer relationships, they observe the behavior of others on video for demonstration and analysis. Students then practice their interpersonal skills before a camera so they can observe themselves and also receive feedback from peers and teachers. Role-play vignettes can be analyzed to determine what happened and to ask learners what they would do next. Open-ended dramatizations present unresolved confrontations, leaving it to the viewers to discuss various ways of dealing with the problem.

ASSURE Case Study Reflection

PEARSON
myeducationkit™

Review the ASSURE Classroom Case Study and video at the beginning of the chapter. How does Mr. James use video to develop the cognitive, affective, psychomotor, and interpersonal skills of his fifth-grade students? Which of the four domains are reinforced during student creation and editing of the natural disaster videos? In what ways did the lesson activities reinforce learning?

TYPES OF EDUCATIONAL VIDEOS

Although there are vast numbers of commercially produced educational videos appropriate for use in PK–12 classes, most videos can be grouped into four common types: documentary, dramatization, video storytelling, and virtual field trips.

Documentary. Video is the primary medium for documenting actual or reenacted events and bringing them into the classroom. The documentary deals with fact, not fiction or fictionalized versions of fact. Documentaries attempt to depict essentially true stories about real situations and people. Many nonprofit organizations, such as the Public Broadcasting System, regularly produce significant documentaries. For example, the video *To the Ends of the Earth* allows students to "experience" the story of a perilous sea voyage based on William Golding's novel of the same name. The Civil War miniseries is a documentary of a critical period in U.S. history. Programs such as *Nova* and National Geographic specials offer outstanding documentaries in science, culture, and nature, many of which are available for viewing on the

Figure 10.1

PBS Documentaries

Public Broadcasting Service (PBS) offers a wide variety of free science and technology documentaries that are viewed from the Internet.

Source: http://video.pbs.org/program/979359664#result. Courtesy of PBS and NOVA/WGBH-TV Boston, © 1996–2010 WGBH Educational Foundation.

free Arctic Stories video series (Figure 10.2). Storytelling is also an important skill to develop in students of all ages. Video storytelling allows students to be creative while developing their writing, visual literacy, and video production skills. The goal is to teach students to express ideas through stories. In the process, students can both teach and learn from each other. See Taking a Look at Technology Integration: Bridges to Understanding for additional information on video storytelling.

Virtual Field Trips. Videos can take students to places they might not be able to go otherwise. You can visit the Amazon rainforest, the jungles of New Guinea, or the Galapagos Islands. Students can also go on a virtual tour of the Egyptian pyramids, walk on the Great Wall of China, or explore the Acropolis in Athens, Greece. Videos enhance and build on knowledge gained from reading textbooks, Internet descriptions, or listening to lectures.

Internet (Figure 10.1). Virtually all television documentaries are available for purchase.

Dramatization. Video has the power to hold your students spellbound as a drama unfolds before their eyes. Literature classics available as video, such as *Anne of Green Gables, Hamlet,* and *Moby Dick,* expand student learning opportunities as they compare and contrast the differences between the text and video. Historical fiction, such as *Shogun* and *War and Peace,* use a combination of fiction and facts to dramatize historical events. Dramatization is also an excellent venue to build positive student character and attitudes in such areas as multiculturalism, disabilities, self-esteem, and working cooperatively.

Video Storytelling. Humans are "storytelling animals." We love to hear and tell stories because they are entertaining and informative. Stories can be incorporated into instruction through videos, such as the

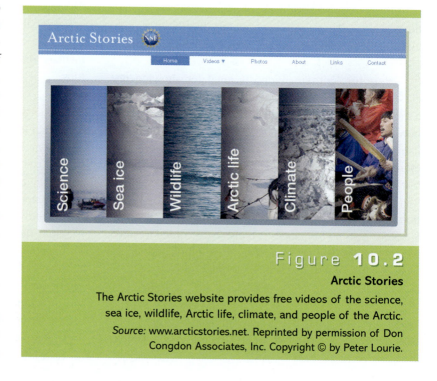

Figure 10.2

Arctic Stories

The Arctic Stories website provides free videos of the science, sea ice, wildlife, Arctic life, climate, and people of the Arctic.

Source: www.arcticstories.net. Reprinted by permission of Don Congdon Associates, Inc. Copyright © by Peter Lourie.

Bridges to Understanding

Bridges to Understanding (www.bridges2 understanding.org) is a nonprofit organization that connects middle and high school students in classrooms around the world via its interactive website. Bridges' mission is "to empower and unite youth worldwide, enhance cross-cultural understanding, and build global citizenship using digital technology and the art of storytelling." Bridges' curriculum leads small student teams in the creation and sharing of digital stories about their lives, communities, and global issues. Students also use Bridges' discussion forums to post questions and responses, learning directly about other students across the globe.

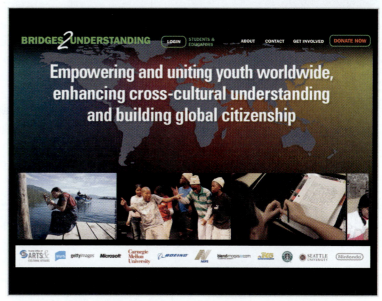

www.bridges2understanding.org. Reprinted by permission.

SPECIAL ATTRIBUTES OF VIDEO

Because most of us think of video as a medium designed to produce a realistic image of the world around us, we tend to forget that a basic attribute of video is the ability to manipulate temporal and spatial perspectives. Manipulation of time and space, use of animation, and other video conventions not only serve dramatic and creative ends but also have important implications for instruction.

MANIPULATION OF TIME

Video permits us to increase or decrease the amount of time required to observe an event. For example, it would take a very long time for students to actually witness a highway being constructed, but a carefully edited video of the different activities that go into building a highway recreates the essentials of such an event in a few minutes.

Removal of Time. Video can delete segments of time. For example, you are familiar with the type of sequence in which a scene fades out and then fades in the next day. Time has been taken out of the sequence, but we accept that the night has passed even though we did not experience it in real time.

Compression of Time. Video can compress the time it takes to observe an event. A flower can appear to open before our eyes, or stars can streak across the nighttime sky. This technique, known as **time lapse,** has important instructional uses. For example, the process of a chrysalis turning into a butterfly is too slow for easy classroom observation. However, through time-lapse videography, the butterfly can emerge from the chrysalis in a matter of minutes.

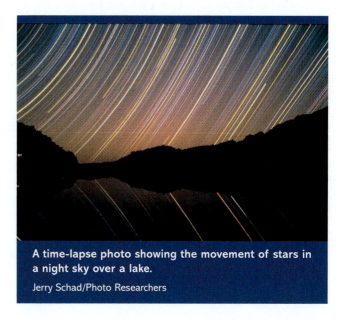

A time-lapse photo showing the movement of stars in a night sky over a lake.
Jerry Schad/Photo Researchers

In slow motion, a fast event is expanded into a longer screen time by shooting video at a high speed.

Ray Massey/Stone/Getty Images

Expansion of Time. Time can also be expanded by video through a technique called **slow motion.** Some events occur too fast to be seen by the naked eye. By photographing such events at extremely high speeds and then projecting the images at normal speed, we can observe what is happening. For example, a frog catches an insect too rapidly for the human eye to observe; high-speed videography can slow down the motion so that we can observe the process.

MANIPULATION OF SPACE

Video allows us to view phenomena in both macrocosm and microcosm—that is, at extremely close range or from a vast distance. Your students can view the earth from the space shuttle (macro view) and at the other extreme, observe cell division under a microscope (micro view). Live TV allows our students to observe two events occurring simultaneously but many miles apart on split screen. This technique is often used in news events in which one reporter is located in the station while the other is "live" on the scene, often a different country.

ANIMATION

Time and space can also be manipulated by animation. This process, which can involve several different techniques,

takes advantage of **persistence of vision** to give motion to otherwise inanimate objects. **Animation** is basically made up of a series of photographs, drawings, or computer images of small displacements of objects or images. If such an object is shown on a single frame, then moved a very short distance and reshown, moved again, reshown, and so on, the object when viewed will appear to continuously move through space.

With the continuing evolution of computer software that can manipulate visual images, we are experiencing a rediscovery of the art of animation through video. Computer-generated animation sequences are being used more and more in instructional video programs to depict complex or rapid processes in simplified form.

VIDEO CONVENTIONS

Video devices and techniques to manipulate time and space employ what are for most of us readily accepted conventions. We understand that the athlete whose jump is stopped in midair is not actually frozen in space, that the flashback is not an actual reversal of our normal time continuum, that the light bulb does not really disintegrate slowly enough for us to see that it implodes rather than explodes. Teachers, however, must keep in mind that the ability to make sense out of video conventions is an acquired skill. When do children learn to handle flashbacks, dissolves, jump cuts, and so on? Unfortunately, we know very little about when and how children learn to make sense of video's manipulation of reality, and much research on the matter remains to be done.

Video is not alone in its reliance on accepted conventions for interpretation and appreciation. Flashback techniques are regularly used in literature and usually accepted by readers. Playgoers readily go along with the theatrical convention of the aside. The following anecdote about Picasso illustrates how a new artistic convention may seem to the uninitiated as merely a distortion of reality rather than, as intended, a particular and valid view of reality. It also illustrates how a convention (in this case a convention of photography) can become so readily accepted and commonplace that we are amusingly surprised at being reminded it exists.

Picasso showed an American soldier through his villa one day, and on completion of the tour the young man felt compelled to confess that he didn't "dig" Picasso's weird way of painting, because nothing on the canvas looked the way it really is. Picasso turned the conversation to more acceptable matters by asking the soldier if he had a girlfriend back in the States. The boy proudly pulled out a wallet photograph. As Picasso handed it back, he said, "She's an attractive girl, but isn't she awfully small?" (Forsdale & Forsdale, 1966, p. 609).

VIDEO FORMATS

Like most media, video is generated in both digital and analog formats. Digital is the most popular form of video. Technically speaking, digital video signals are in the form of 1s and 0s that are displayed via light and color intensity of fixed dots, whereas analog video signals are produced as waves that are displayed by a series of scans. Digital is the newer technology, with many advantages over analog, but both formats are widely available.

DIGITAL VIDEO

Digital video images can be manipulated, stored, duplicated, sent from one computer to another, and replayed without loss of quality. DVDs provide approximately 500 lines of resolution, which is double that of an analog videocassette. The digital camcorder has decreased in cost and increased the ease and portability of video recording. It allows video production to be taken into the field, wherever that might be: the science laboratory, the classroom, the counseling office, the athletic field, the factory assembly line, the hospital, the neighborhood, and even the home. Equally important, the simplicity of the system has made it feasible for nonprofessionals, teachers, and students alike to create their own video materials.

Another advantage of digital video is that editing can be done on a computer using software that makes it easy to manipulate the sequence of images. The quality of the video image will not degrade during editing and copying, as happens with videocassettes. Digital video can also be viewed at varying speeds, allowing students to study images from very slow to accelerated motion. Still images can also be captured from digital video files and inserted into a digital video. Finally, it is quick and easy to transfer large video files to the computer using a high-speed connection. Common digital video formats include DVD, Blu-ray Discs, computer-based files, and Internet video.

DVD. A digital videodisc (DVD) is a medium offering digital storage and playback of full-motion video. DVDs did for movies what the CDs did for music. The disc is the same physical size as an audio CD but can hold enough data for nine hours of video with high-quality soundtracks. Like CDs, DVDs have instant random access and are highly durable. There is no distortion when you watch a DVD in slow motion. DVDs provide superior sound and picture quality compared to standard videocassettes, and, unlike videotape, DVDs do not deteriorate over time.

Blu-ray Disc. **Blu-ray Discs** (also known as BD) store high-definition video, games, and other data on discs noted with

Figure 10.3
Blu-Ray Logo
Source: http://vectorlogo.blogspot.com/ 2009/03/blu-ray-disc-logo-eps.htm

the BD Logo (Figure 10.3). The name comes from the blue laser used to read the disc, meaning BDs can only be viewed on BD video players (which can also play DVDs). Although BDs are the same size as standard DVDs, they store almost ten times more data than a DVD.

Computer-Based Video. Students can prepare video reports, class presentations, and digital portfolios on computers. Starting with video sequences or images from materials they have recorded or from DVDs, they can use video editing software such as iMovie or Movie Maker to manipulate the images and sounds similarly to rearranging information in word processing or presentation software. For example, students can employ a multimedia approach when creating an oral report. Students begin by researching a topic with books, databases, videos, CDs, and other media. Relevant content is "captured" on video, edited, and student narration added before presenting the final report. Remember that copyright laws also apply to the use of video created by others. See Copyright Concerns: Video on page 245.

Digital videos are also an important component in computer-based student portfolios as the videos capture actual student reflections and performance over time. This enables the students, teachers, and others to follow student progress through the archived videos.

Internet Video. Many websites now offer Internet broadcasts of events or activities at their sites, including newsworthy stories, scientific activities, and cultural presentations. Some of the broadcasts are live and others are recorded. "Live cams" can "take" students to a museum, a national park, zoo, historical landmark, or an aquarium to observe activities in real time (Figure 10.4). These Internet broadcasts use compressed video or streaming video.

Compressed Video. Compressed video saves data space by recording only the moving or changing parts of each frame. The parts of the picture that are not changing are not recorded; hence less data are needed to reproduce the image, resulting in smaller video files. Compressed video is used to upload and download video files over the Internet.

Streaming Video. Video also can be delivered over the Internet using streaming video. *Streaming* means that the file doesn't have to be completely downloaded before it starts playing. Instead, as soon as the user clicks on a link that contains streaming video, the content begins to play. The video content is actually downloading to the user's computer in a series of small information packets that arrive shortly before the viewer sees the material. Any video materials can be delivered over the Internet using the streaming technique. The content is not stored on your computer. It "flows" into your active memory, is displayed (or played), and then is erased.

ANALOG VIDEO

Many schools and media resource centers still have a library collection of videos in all subject areas stored on videocassettes. Most classrooms have ready access to a large-screen TV or digital projector connected to a VCR. It is also common to see classrooms equipped with ceiling-mounted TVs that are connected to a central station that will play a requested video at a designated time. These same systems are used for students to create and present a morning information (news) broadcast that is distributed schoolwide.

Figure **10.4**

Monterey Bay Aquarium

The Monterey Bay Aquarium website offers eight live web cams to observe kelp, underwater kelp, sea otters, wading birds, penguins, the outer bay, aviary, and Monterey Bay.

Source: www.montereybayaquarium.org/efc/cam_menu.aspx. © 2010, Monterey Bay Aquarium. Reprinted by permission.

ADVANTAGES

- *Motion.* Moving images have an obvious advantage over still visuals in portraying concepts and processes in which motion is essential to learning (such as Newton's Laws of Motion, erosion, metamorphosis).
- *Risk-free observation.* Video allows learners to observe phenomena that might be too dangerous to view directly, such as an eclipse of the sun, a volcanic eruption, or warfare.
- *Dramatization.* Dramatic recreations bring historical events and personalities to life. They allow students to observe and analyze human interactions.
- *Affective learning.* Because of its great potential for emotional impact, video can be useful in shaping personal and social attitudes, such as "going green." Documentary and propaganda videos have often been found to have a measurable impact on audience attitudes.
- *Problem solving.* Open-ended dramatizations are frequently used to present unresolved situations, leaving it to the students to discuss various ways of dealing with the problem.
- *Cultural understanding.* We develop a deep appreciation for other cultures by seeing depictions of everyday life in other societies. The whole genre of ethnographic video serves this purpose. Feature-length ethnographic

ASSURE Case Study Reflection

Review the ASSURE Classroom Case Study and video at the beginning of the chapter. What are the advantages for Scott James and his class in using digital or analog video for the lesson on natural disasters? How could you use video in your teaching?

videos include *The Hunters, The Tribe That Hides from Man, The Nuer,* and *River of Sand.*

- *Establishing commonality.* By viewing video programs together, a dissimilar group of students can build up a common base of experience to discuss an issue effectively.

LIMITATIONS

- *Fixed pace.* Although videos can be stopped for discussion, this is not usually done during group showings. Because the program runs at a fixed pace, some students may fall behind while others are waiting impatiently for the next point.
- *Talking head.* Many videos, especially local productions, consist mostly of close-ups of people talking. Video is not a great oral medium—it is a visual medium! Use audio recordings for verbal messages.
- *Still phenomena.* Although video is advantageous for concepts that involve motion, it may be unsuitable for other topics in which detailed study of a single visual is involved (e.g., a map, a wiring diagram, or an organization chart).
- *Misinterpretation.* Documentaries and dramatizations often present a complex or sophisticated treatment of an issue. A scene intended as satire might be taken literally by a young or naive student. The thoughts of a main character may be interpreted as the attitudes and values of the producer.

- *Abstract, nonvisual instruction.* Video is poor at presenting abstract, nonvisual information. The preferred medium for words alone is text. Philosophy and mathematics do not lend themselves well to video unless the specific concepts discussed lend themselves to illustration using historical footage, graphic representation, or stylized imagery.

INTEGRATION

We are now teaching a video generation. Consequently, the use and creation of video can greatly enhance student learning. As emphasized in the ASSURE model, student viewing or production of videos should directly support achievement of the lesson standards and objectives while building video literacy knowledge and skills.

One approach is to strategically integrate segments of video that align with the lesson. Keep in mind that students have grown up with TV programs that utilize short segments rather than 30-minute programs. For example, "Sesame Street" changes topics every few minutes. Video segments that are a few minutes in length provide maximum flexibility for the teacher to promote learning specifically related to student needs. Many educational videos are available as "short, concise segments that teachers can assemble in a variety of ways to support a variety of utilization scenarios" (Nugent, 2005, p. 61).

Video can also help in adapting lessons to meet the special needs of students. Video-based courses with multiple

TECHNOLOGY
for Diverse Learners

Adapting Video Features

Video offers different options for meeting the needs of diverse learners.

Video technology helps students with hearing impairments. Captioning is readily available on TV and other video formats as a way to assist students with learning disabilities and hearing impairments. Captioning consists of text at the bottom of the viewing area. The text provides students the opportunity to read what others are hearing through the audio channel of the video.

Video technology also helps students with visual impairments. Descriptive video is a technique in which a soft-spoken voice describes the scenes on the video to help students with visual impairment grasp the idea of what is being presented visually by hearing the description. This service is available for

many TV programs and instructional videos. For more information see The Development of the Descriptive Video Services by Cronin and King (2007), available at the National Center to Improve Practice in Special Education through Technology, Media, and Materials (http://www2.edc.org/NCIP/library/v&c/cronin.htm).

Video technology can be used by gifted students. Gifted students can be challenged to explore videos for higher-order concepts, generate questions for further research, or present summary points to share in groups of mixed ability students. In addition, students gifted with different aspects of video production can provide peer tutoring to build the skills of all students.

WHEN to USE Video

Use when student learning will be enhanced by . . .

Guidelines	Example
motion	High school students watch video clips of various chemical reactions to determine the environmental impact of using gasoline engines.
processes	Elementary students watch a video that shows each step of the recycling process to learn how aluminum cans are recycled.
risk-free observation	Middle school students view a video of a Hawaiian volcano eruption.
dramatization	Elementary children watch a video showing the evolution of transportation.
skill learning	Art students in a middle school view a video that shows step-by-step techniques used to draw shadows.
affective learning	Kindergarten students watch a video to better understand the feelings and challenges of children with disabilities.
problem solving	Middle school students in an interdisciplinary gifted class view documentaries explaining the overpopulation concerns of some large U.S. cities and then discuss possible solutions.
cultural understanding and establishing commonality	High school students in a school with a growing population of English language learners from multiple ethnic backgrounds view videos that highlight the commonalities between ethnicities.

soundtracks can be aimed at different types of learners. Text can be displayed in multiple languages and used to subtitle or annotate video content. DVDs offer many tools for adaptation and access, including index searching by title, chapter, track, or time-code for quick navigation. As another example, barcodes are often added to text materials to access specific video segments on a DVD. Some DVDs even offer the ability to view an object from different angles with up to nine different camera views that can be selected in real time during playback.

There are multiple benefits for integrating student production of video into instruction. Understandably, increased student engagement and motivation are at the top of the list because is it is fun to create videos. Additional benefits include use of higher-order skills to solve ill-defined but authentic problems through the collaborative production of a video that demonstrates a solution for a real audience (Schuck & Kearney, 2008). Student creation of video also aligns and supports achievement of the six NETS for Students.

When planning lessons, keep in mind the prominent features of video that will help to enhance student learning—depicting motion, showing processes, offering risk-free observations, providing dramatizations, and supporting skill learning. Scenarios portrayed in videos are tools to build affective learning, introduce open-ended problem solving vignettes, and develop cultural understanding and establish commonality. See When to Use Video for examples of each guideline.

SELECTING VIDEO

As seen, there are many advantages for integrating video into PK–12 instruction. The first step to integrating these useful resources is to locate videos that are directly aligned to and support achievement of your lesson objectives. The second step is to evaluate the selected video to ensure that it *actually* aligns to your objectives and will meet the needs of your students.

Locating Videos. In most educational settings, teachers have access to numerous educational videos from a variety of sources. As mentioned in the introduction, school districts totaling more than one million teachers provide online access to over 80,000 Discovery Education digital videos. The Internet also offers vast educational video options, with most being freely available for classroom viewing. School library media specialists are a key resource for locating video owned by the school, district, or regional resource center. They also assist with locating other providers of sponsored videos.

Private companies, associations, and government agencies sponsor videos for a variety of reasons. Private companies may make videos to promote their products or to enhance their public image. Associations and government agencies sponsor videos to promote causes, such as better health habits, conservation of natural resources, and proper use of park and recreation areas. Many of these sponsored videos are worthwhile instructional materials that have the advantage of being free or inexpensive.

A certain amount of caution, however, is called for in using sponsored videos for instructional purposes. Some privately produced materials may be too flagrantly self-serving. Or they may deal with products not suitable for instructional settings, for example, the manufacturing of alcoholic beverages or cigarettes. Some association and government materials may contain a sizable dose of propaganda or special pleading for favorite causes. You *must always preview* sponsored materials. When properly selected, many sponsored materials can be valuable additions to classroom instruction. Modern Talking Picture Service is one of the major distributors of sponsored videos.

Evaluating Video. After you have located some potentially useful videos, use an evaluation tool to assess alignment with your lesson. Some schools and online teacher websites offer standard evaluation forms from meticulous evaluations involving numerous factors to others that are much more perfunctory. A good appraisal form is brief enough not to be intimidating but complete enough to help teachers choose materials that will enhance student learning. In some cases, evaluation results help decide on purchase or rental of specific titles.

The Selection Rubric: Video at the end of this chapter includes the most commonly used criteria, particularly those

Video

Abraham Lincoln: Animated Hero Classics

www.nestfamily.com/Animated-History-Biographies-C1518.aspx

This video biography of Abraham Lincoln is a "Kids First" award winner that presents highlights of Lincoln's personal and political life. The story, targeted for age 7 to 12 students, depicts the human side of Lincoln and his passion for civil liberties for all Americans. (Nest Family Entertainment)

Math . . . Who Needs It?

www.fasestore.org/default.asp

This video is aimed at parents and their kids. It gives a perspective on the rewards and opportunities open to anyone with good math skills. It challenges myths about math, pokes fun at society's misconceptions of the subject, and provokes viewers to think and talk about math in a more positive way. (FASE Productions)

The Supreme Court

www.ambrosevideo.com/items.cfm?id=1217

A winner of eight prestigious awards, including the 2008 Parents' Choice Gold Award, this four-part video series about the Supreme Court is appropriate for high school history and social studies classes. The videos use archival footage, interviews with the justices, and digital graphics to explore and personalize the history and impact of the Supreme Court. (Ambrose Video Publishing, Inc.)

One Woman, One Vote

www.pbs.org/wgbh/americanexperience/films/OneWomanOneVote

Witness the 70-year struggle for women's suffrage, from fledgling alliances to a sophisticated mass movement. This video documents the history of the women's suffrage movement from the Seneca Falls Convention in 1848, when Elizabeth Cady Stanton demanded the right for women to vote, to the last battle for passage of the 19th Amendment in 1920. (PBS Video)

Are You Addicted?

www.hrmvideo.com/items.cfm?action=view&item_id=2307&search_keywords=Are%20You%20Addicted%3F

An award-winning video, directed toward adolescents, focuses on three young people dealing with addictions. Two medical experts provide a definition of addiction and guide students through the signs and symptoms that can lead to an addiction. The end of the video emphasizes recovery. (Human Relations Media)

The following tips apply to the enhancement of video presentations to students:

- *Sightlines.* Check lighting, seating, and volume control to be sure that everyone can see and hear the presentation.

- *Light control.* When using digital video projection, dim or turn off lights if dimming is not available. When viewing with a TV, use normal room lighting and dim the lights above and behind the monitor if possible.

- *Mental set.* Briefly review prior content and ask questions about the current topic to get students mentally prepared for use of video.

- *Advance organizer.* List and introduce the main points to be covered in the presentation.

- *Vocabulary.* Preview any new vocabulary.

- *Short segments.* Show only 8 to 12 minutes of a video at any one time (even shorter for younger students). Rather than showing a 30-minute video from start to finish, increase viewer learning and retention by using the following technique: Introduce the first segment and show about 10 minutes of the video, stopping at a logical breaking point. Discuss the segment and then introduce the second segment, tying it to the first. Show the second 10-minute segment and repeat the procedure. Keep in mind that all video segments should directly align with lesson objectives.

- *Role model.* Most important, get involved in the program yourself. Watch attentively and engage learners at appropriate times during the video.

- *Follow-up.* Reinforce the video content with meaningful follow-up activities.

that have research-based evidence of effectiveness. Specific areas of importance in evaluating video are pacing and the use of cognitive learning aids, such as an overview or summary. Cues are another aid, pointing learners to important aspects of the video, such as a flashing arrow pointing to parts of a flower as each is being presented. In evaluating videos, you also have the opportunity to make notes for class discussion of the key topics as well as areas that need further explanation or emphasis to enhance student learning.

PRODUCING VIDEO

Student video production promotes learning by engaging critical thinking about cultural, political, scientific, financial, and environmental issues. At the same time, creating videos helps to build technology literacy skills. Students' passion for technology can fuel active exploration of their world. Combining these two characteristics can ignite a passion for learning because the experience is creative and fun. Student video production aligns with and supports ISTE NETS-S in encouraging student awareness, the development of creativity, the potential for engagement, and a bridge to life outside the classroom. Teachers can also produce video by customizing visual materials for their lessons. Remember, you and your students must follow copyright guidelines when producing video.

Videography, or the creation of video, enables students to explore any curriculum subject through the active process of making a video about it. In addition to video production skills,

students learn problem solving, scheduling, analysis, research, planning, imagination, and communication—all real-world skills required for 21st century careers. They become better thinkers, better communicators, and better problem solvers.

Once the video equipment (cameras, microphones, computers, and software) has been purchased, the production of in-house video is inexpensive when compared to educational benefits such as the following:

- Dramatization of student stories, songs, and poems
- Immediate feedback to improve performance
- Skills training (e.g., how to use digital science probes)
- Interpersonal techniques (e.g., how to work cooperatively)
- Student documentaries of school or neighborhood issues
- Preservation of local folklore
- Demonstrations of science experiments and safety drills
- Replays of field trips for in-class follow-up

PLANNING

As with all media production, preproduction planning is necessary. Actively involve students in designing videos they are to produce. Planning can involve storyboarding, scripting, and preparing outlines for recording and revising their video productions. To provide each student with a variety of experiences, rotate roles among writers, editors, camera operators, and on-camera "talent."

Video

The Copyright Act of 1976 did not cover educational uses of video copies of copyrighted broadcasts. A negotiating committee composed of representatives from industry, education, and government agreed on a set of guidelines for video recording of broadcasts for educational use. The following guidelines apply only to nonprofit educational institutions.

You may do the following:

- Ask your media/technology specialist to record the program for you if you lack the equipment or expertise. The request to record must come from a teacher.
- Retain the recording of a broadcast (including cable transmission) for a period of 45 calendar days, after which you must erase the program.
- Use the recording in class once per class during the first 10 school days of the 45 calendar days, and a second time if instruction needs to be reinforced.
- Have professional staff view the program several times for evaluation purposes during the full 45-day period.
- Make a limited number of copies to meet legitimate needs, but you must erase these copies when erasing the original recording.

- Use only a part of the program if instructional needs warrant.
- Enter into a licensing agreement with the copyright holder to continue use of the program.

You may *not* do the following:

- Record premium cable services such as HBO without express permission.
- Alter the original content of the program.
- Exclude the copyright notice on the program.
- Record a program in anticipation of use.
- Retain the program, and any copies, after 45 days.

Remember that these guidelines are not part of the copyright act but are rather an agreement between producers and educators. You should accept them as guidelines in good faith.

For general information on copyright, see the copyright section on pages 13 through 15 in Chapter 1. Suggested resources (print and websites) on copyright appear at the end of Chapter 1.

Students begin the process of video production by creating a series of storyboards to facilitate planning and production of video. The storyboards include a rough sketch of the scene, script, and any notes for the camera operator, such as "zoom in for close-up of face." Graphic organizer software, such as Kidspiration and Inspiration, provide useful tools for creating storyboards. When a group of students are cooperatively involved in designing a video, storyboarding is particularly helpful to organize and represent multiple viewpoints.

ASSURE Case Study Reflection

Review the ASSURE Classroom Case Study and video at the beginning of the chapter. How does Scott James use script writing to support student learning? In what ways does Mr. James engage students in the production of digital video? What role does Mr. James play during video production?

RECORDING

Handheld cameras usually come with a built in microphone. This microphone has an automatic level control that adjusts the volume to keep the sound at an audible level; in other words, the camera "hears" as well as "sees." The problem is that along with the sounds you want these microphones amplify all audio within their range, including shuffling feet, coughing, street noises, and equipment racket. You may therefore want to bypass the built-in microphone by plugging in a separate microphone better suited to your particular purpose.

The lavaliere, or neck mike, is a good choice when recording a single speaker. It can be clipped to a tie or dress, hung around the neck, or even hidden under lightweight clothing. A desk stand may be used to hold a microphone for a speaker or several discussants seated at a table. For situations in which there is unwanted background noise or the speaker is moving, a highly directional microphone is best.

EDITING

Digital video editing refers to the means by which video can be taken apart and put back together using a computer and editing software. With some digital camcorders there is no videotape; others use specialized videotape to record in a digital mode. After shooting video, you can watch it on the camera's built-in LCD monitor or connect the camcorder to a TV or computer to view the footage or to transfer the file to a computer. There are several methods for storing video on a computer. One format is QuickTime, for use with Mac and Windows operating systems. Many applications, such as Compton's Multimedia Encyclopedia, incorporate QuickTime "movies." The transferred video file is then edited using software such as the applications that come with iMovie for Apple computers and Windows Movie Maker for PCs. The editing software not only provides tools to delete and rearrange content, but also to add titles, music, photos, and special transitions.

A high definition camcorder offers a variety of technology tools in addition to recording HD video.

Shutterstock

ASSURE Case Study Reflection

PEARSON
myeducationkit™

Review the ASSURE Classroom Case Study and video at the beginning of the chapter. What recording and editing equipment did students use to create digital videos on natural disasters? Which strategies did Mr. James use to assist students who experienced trouble when creating their videos?

INNOVATION on the HORIZON

HIGH DEFINITION VIDEO PRODUCTION COMES TO SCHOOLS

Among the new technology devices that are smaller, more efficient, and less expensive are camcorders that produce high definition (HD) video. For example, Genius offers a pocket size G-Shot camcorder HD520 that sells for around $150. The G-Shot provides a variety of tools that reduce the need for additional classroom technology, such as voice recorder, digital still camera, HDMI TV/Audio-out, web camera, and brightness control for low light or backlit environments with specialized "Z Lighting."

SUMMARY

Today's students are accustomed to learning through Internet videos, TV, and other motion media. There are many exciting applications of video in the classroom. Video provides special applications in learning—particularly involving motion. Producing video engages students in higher-order thinking while reinforcing content area knowledge and skills; teacher-produced video can present material that enhances learning beyond the textbook. This chapter presented the specific attributes of video along with its advantages and limitations. It also described how to select, produce, and integrate video into student learning.

PEARSON
myeducationkit™

To check your comprehension of the content covered in Chapter 10, go to the **MyEducationKit** for your book and complete the Study Plan for Chapter 10. Here you will be able to take a chapter quiz, receive feedback on your answers, and then access resources that will enhance your understanding of the chapter content.

ASSURE Lesson Plan

The following ASSURE Lesson Plan provides a detailed description and analysis of the lesson in the ASSURE Classroom Case Study and video at the beginning of the chapter. To review the video again, go to the MyEducationKit for your text and click on the ASSURE Video under Chapter 10. This video, based on an interdisciplinary lesson created by Scott James, shows Mr. James implementing the lesson in his fifth-grade classroom and providing his insights for achieving successful use of student-created video.

Analyze Learners

General Characteristics. The students in Scott James's fifth-grade class are of mixed ethnicities and from low- to middle-income homes. They are fairly equally distributed with regard to gender and are either 9 or 10 years old. Student reading ability ranges from below to above grade level. Student behavior problems increase when completing traditional seatwork.

Entry Competencies. The students are, in general, able to do the following:

1. Conduct online research
2. Use iMovie software to edit digital video

Learning Styles. Mr. James's students learn best when engaged in activities that are relevant to the content and provide self-selection of topics. Their interest and motivation increase when they use technology. The students vary greatly in their comfort level with speaking and acting for the digital video news broadcasts. Differences are also seen with regard to use of graphics and sound, some using a traditional approach while others attempt more creative and fun methods for their final products.

State Standards and Objectives

Curriculum Standards. National Council of Teachers of English 4: Students adjust their use of spoken, written, and visual language (e.g., conventions, style, vocabulary) to communicate effectively with a variety of audiences and for different purposes. National Science Education Standards for 5–8—Earth and Space Science: Structure of the earth system. Global patterns of atmospheric movement influence local weather. Oceans have a major effect on climate, because water in the oceans holds a large amount of heat.

Technology Standards. National Educational Technology Standards for Students 1— Creativity and Innovation: Students demonstrate creative thinking, construct knowledge, and develop innovative products and processes using technology.

Learning Objectives

1. Using content from conducting Internet and library research on a student-selected natural disaster, the fifth-grade students will write a script for a news anchor and an "on the scene" reporter.

2. Using the student-written scripts, the students will create storyboards that include segments for a news anchor and an "on the scene" reporter and meet the lesson criteria for storyboards.
3. Using their student-created storyboards and scripts, each student records their portion (news anchor or "on the scene" reporter) of the news broadcasts with digital video.
4. Using the digital video of their news broadcast, students will work in iMovie to produce a final edit of their news broadcast that meets the lesson criteria.

Select Strategies, Technology, Media, and Materials

Select Strategies. Scott James selects teacher- and student-centered strategies for the natural disaster lesson. The teacher-centered strategies involve providing a detailed description of the lesson objectives and how the student pairs will conduct their research and create their news broadcasts. The student-centered strategies include conducting Internet and library research, writing scripts, developing storyboards, planning, recording, and editing their news broadcast video.

Select Technology and Media. This lesson involves student use of computers, a digital camcorder, microphones, a green screen, and iMovie to edit their natural disaster videos. Mr. James uses the following guidelines to assess his technology and media selections:

1. *Alignment with standards, outcomes, and objectives.* The library, Internet sites, and iMovie software provide the necessary tools for students to meet the learning objectives.
2. *Accurate and current information.* Students research text-based and Internet resources to find information on natural disasters.
3. *Age-appropriate language.* Students examine websites and books that are appropriate for fifth-grade students. Mr. James provides assistance and job aids for student use of iMovie.
4. *Interest level and engagement.* Students choose a natural disaster of interest to them and create a personalized news broadcast, which increases student interest and engagement.
5. *Technical quality.* Both the Internet sites and iMovie have high technical quality.
6. *Ease of use.* Student use of iMovie requires initial training and support, but is fairly easy for fifth-grade students to use after basic skills training.
7. *Bias free.* Students use multiple references for their research to better ensure bias-free content. iMovie software is bias-free.
8. *User guide and directions.* The online help features of iMovie are not very easy for fifth-grade students to follow. Therefore, students frequently ask each other or Mr. James for assistance with technical difficulties.

Select Materials. Scott James selects "kid-friendly" Internet sites and library materials for students to conduct research.

Utilize Technology, Media, and Materials

Preview the Technology, Media, and Materials. Scott James selects and previews the "kid-friendly" Internet sites, library materials, and iMovie software to ensure they have the needed features.

Prepare the Technology, Media, and Materials. Mr. James prepares an assignment sheet that describes the lesson requirements and criteria used to assess the final student products.

Prepare the Environment. Mr. James tests the Internet connections on the lab computers and ensures that iMovie is installed on each one. He also tests the digital video camera to ensure that it is working and downloads to the computers.

Prepare the Learners. The students have experience with Internet research and iMovie; thus the lesson begins with an overview of technical skills and an introduction to natural disasters.

Provide the Learning Experience. Mr. James guides student learning during video production and presentation of final videos to the class.

Require Learner Participation

Student Practice Activities. The students in Scott James's class use computers, the Internet, library materials, and iMovie to complete their natural disaster news broadcasts. Student pairs select a natural disaster and then conduct Internet and library research to find information about the topic. With this information students write the news anchor and "on the scene" reporter scripts and storyboards. Students then team to record news broadcasts on digital video, which they edit on iMovie to create a final cut of a video that is presented to the class.

Feedback. Scott James provides continuous feedback as students conduct their research, write their scripts, create storyboards, edit videos, and present their news broadcasts.

Evaluate and Revise

Assessment of Learner Achievement. Mr. James assesses learner achievement in two ways. First is demonstration of content knowledge, as seen in student scripts, storyboards, and iMovie presentations. The second is demonstration of technology skills, which is assessed according to the assignment criteria as stated in the learning objectives.

Evaluation of Strategies, Technology, and Media. Mr. James evaluates the lesson strategies through continuous communication with the students. He also examines student products to determine if the strategies were effective. Evaluation of the technology and media involves noting technical problem that occur during the lesson. This requires examining the functionality of the various software applications, Internet and library resources, and the digital camcorder.

Revision. After reviewing the evaluation results collected from student achievement measures and assessing the lesson strategies, technology, and media, Mr. James concludes that the lesson worked well, with one minor exception. He thought three weeks was too much time to devote to the designated standards and objectives. Therefore, Mr. James revised the lesson by borrowing digital video cameras from a regional media center to decrease the time needed to record all students.

CONTINUING MY PROFESSIONAL DEVELOPMENT

Demonstrating Professional Knowledge

1. Define video literacy and list the five core concepts of viewing and producing video.
2. Explain how student learning is enhanced by the application of video in each instructional domain—cognitive, affective, psychomotor, and interpersonal.
3. List and describe how the four types of educational video support student learning.
4. Describe three attributes of video and how they impact classroom instruction.
5. Compare and contrast digital versus analog video formats.
6. Outline the process for selecting and evaluating video for classroom use.
7. Describe techniques for video production by students and teachers.

Demonstrating Professional Skills

1. Preview a video and appraise it using the Selection Rubric: Video. (ISTE NETS 2.C)
2. Observe a classroom in which students are creating video to enhance content area learning and critique the classroom practices based on video production guidelines. (ISTE NETS 5.C)
3. Plan a lesson for a subject area of your choice in which you incorporate the use of a video. For that video, brainstorm a variety of assessment techniques to measure student learning of the content. (ISTE NETS-T 2.B & 2.D)
4. Create a digital video to support and enhance a topic you teach as a way to model creative and innovative thinking for your students. (ISTE NETS-T 1.A)

Building My Professional Portfolio

- *Creating My Lesson.* Using the ASSURE model, design a lesson for a scenario from Appendix A or create a scenario of your own design. With one of the instructional strategies described in Chapter 4 and information from this chapter, integrate video into your instruction. Be sure to include information about the audience, the objectives, and all other elements of the ASSURE model.
- *Enhancing My Lesson.* With the lesson just designed, consider your audience again. Assume that some of your students have special needs, such as physical or learning difficulties. Also consider that several students are identified as gifted. How will you change your lesson design to ensure that these students are recognized and supported to allow them to succeed in achieving the lesson objectives?
- *Reflecting on My Lesson.* Reflect on the process used to design your lesson and meet student needs. What have you learned about aligning audience, content, strategies, and materials? What could be done to better develop your students' higher-order thinking or creativity skills? In what ways did the selected materials and hands-on activities enhance the learning opportunities for your students?

SUGGESTED RESOURCES

Print

Abrams, A., & Hoerger, D. (2009). *Award winning digital video projects for the classroom*. Eugene, OR: Visions Technology in Education.

Chenail, R. J. (2008). YouTube as a qualitative research asset: Reviewing user generated videos as learning resources. *The Weekly Qualitative Report, 1*(4), 18–24.

Theodoskis, N. (2009). *The director in the classroom: How filmmaking inspires learning* (Version 2.0). British Columbia, Canada: Author.

Watson, L. (2010). *Teach yourself visually: Digital video*. New York: Wiley.

Web Links

To easily access web links from your browser, go to the MyEducationKit for your text, then go to Chapter 10 and click on the web links.

Library Video Company

http://libraryvideo.com

A distributor of educational videos, DVDs, and audio books to schools nationwide, the company stocks over 18,000 titles covering a diverse range of topics for all ages and grade levels. Each program has been carefully reviewed and selected for content that is appropriate for the classroom setting.

neoK12

www.neok12.com/

This site provides a collection of free online educational videos, lessons, games, Web 2.0 tools, and quizzes for PK–12 students. Topic areas include physical, life, earth, and space science, social studies, math, English, and the human body. The American Library Association recognized neoK12 as a "Great Web Site for Kids 2009."

TED: Ideas Worth Spreading

www.ted.com

TED is a small nonprofit organization devoted to "Ideas Worth Spreading" regarding Technology, Entertainment, and Design (TED). The award-winning site has a collection of more than 500 free talks from the world's most fascinating thinkers and doers, who are challenged to give the talk of their lives (in 18 minutes). All of the talks feature closed captions in English, and many offer subtitles in various languages. These videos are released under a Creative Commons license, so they can be freely shared and reposted.

$ FREE & INEXPENSIVE
Videos

TeacherTube

www.teachertube.com

The TeacherTube site provides free instructional videos for teachers, students, schools, and home learners. The video collection includes teacher-posted videos designed to help students learn new knowledge and skills and professional development videos with teachers teaching teachers. Members of the site use a video rating system to provide feedback and suggestions to assist other teachers interested in using the videos. To create a safe venue, TeacherTube uses a flagging system to alert staff to remove inappropriate materials.

KidsKnowIt

www.kidsknowit.com/index.php

KidsKnowIt offers free educational movies featuring Avatar-type characters who teach basic knowledge and skills such as adjectives, acids and bases, Lewis and Clark, telling time, and tornados. Each movie ends with an interactive online quiz. New movies are added weekly.

SqoolTube

http://sqooltube.com

This site offers a wide variety of free online videos in the following categories: book related, character education, early childhood, holidays, math, music, reading and communication arts, safety, science, social studies, and Spanish.

Selection Rubric: VIDEO

Complete an evaluation and add it to your Professional Development portfolio using the Selection Rubric: Video. A version of this rubric is available at the MyEducationKit website. To download and complete this rubric for your own use, go to the MyEducationKit for your text, then go to Chapter 10 and click on Selection Rubrics.

Search Terms Used to Locate Resources

_____

_____

_____

Title _____

Source/Location _____

© Date _____ Cost _____ Length _____ minutes

Subject Area _____ Grade Level _____

Instructional Strategies _____

Format

_____ DVD

_____ Blu-Ray

_____ Computer-based

_____ Internet

_____ Compressed

_____ Streaming

_____ Videocassette

Brief Description

Standards/Outcomes/Objectives

Prerequisites (e.g., prior knowledge, reading ability, vocabulary level)

Strengths

Limitations

Special Features

Name _____ Date _____

Rating Area	High Quality	Medium Quality	Low Quality
Alignment with Standards, Outcomes, and Objectives	Standard/outcome/objective addressed and use of video should enhance student learning.	Standard/outcome/objective partially addressed and use of video may enhance student learning.	Standard/outcome/objective not addressed and use of video will likely not enhance student learning.
Accurate and Current Information	Information correct and does not contain material that is out of date.	Information correct but does contain material that is out of date.	Information is not correct and does contain material that is out of date.
Age-Appropriate Language	Language used is age appropriate and vocabulary is understandable.	Language used is nearly age appropriate and some vocabulary is above/below student age.	Language used is not age appropriate and vocabulary is clearly inappropriate for student age.
Interest Level and Engagement	Topic is presented so that students are likely to be interested and actively engaged in learning.	Topic is presented to interest students most of the time and engage them in learning.	Topic is presented so as not to interest students and not engage them in learning.
Technical Quality	The material represents best available media.	The material represents media that are good quality, although there are some problems.	The material represents media that are not well prepared and are of very poor quality.
Ease of Use (Student or Teacher)	Material follows easy to use patterns with nothing to confuse the user.	Material follows patterns that are easy to follow most of the time, with a few things to confuse the user.	Material follows no patterns and most of the time the user is very confused.
Bias Free	There is no evidence of objectionable bias or advertising.	There is little evidence of bias or advertising.	There is much evidence of bias or advertising.
User Guide and Directions	The user guide is excellent resource to support a lesson. Directions should help students use the material.	The user guide is good resource to support a lesson. Directions may help students use the material.	The user guide is poor resource to support a lesson. Directions do not help students use the material.
Pacing Appropriate	The video material is presented so most students can understand and process the information.	The video material is presented so some students start to understand and process the information.	The video material is presented so most students cannot understand and process the information.
Use of Cognitive Learning Aids (Overviews, Cues, Summary)	The video material is well organized and uses cognitive learning aids.	The video material is fairly well organized and uses some cognitive learning aids.	The video material is not well organized and does not use cognitive learning aids.

Recommended for Classroom Use: _____ Yes _____ No

Ideas for Classroom Use:

CHAPTER ELEVEN

Using Multimedia to Engage Learners

Knowledge Outcomes

This chapter addresses ISTE NETS-T Standard 2.

1. Discuss media literacy, including the aspects of consuming and producing media.

2. Discuss the advantages, limitations, and instructional applications of multimedia in learning.

3. Discuss four types of learning centers and describe one specific example of each.

4. Describe instructional applications that are especially appropriate for manipulatives.

5. Compare the advantages and limitations of various types of display surfaces.

6. Describe instructional applications that are especially appropriate for field trips, displays, and dioramas.

Goal

Select, integrate, and use multimedia to promote student learning.

The ASSURE Classroom Case Study for this chapter describes how Phil Ekker, a first-grade teacher, selects media experiences for his classroom of approximately 20 students. The school in which Mr. Ekker teaches is located in a suburban neighborhood of middle- to high-income families. His students vary in their reading, writing, and mathematics abilities. This makes it difficult for Phil to use whole-class instructional approaches for these subject areas. To address this concern, Mr. Ekker would like to integrate multimedia and learning centers into his instructional strategies. However, he is not sure how to select the appropriate multimedia materials and learning center strategies to meet the individual learning needs of his students.

To view the **ASSURE Classroom Case Study** *video for this chapter, go to the MyEducationKit for your text and click on the ASSURE Video under Chapter 11 to explore how Mr. Ekker uses multimedia to achieve 21st century learning environments.*

Throughout the chapter you will find reflection questions that relate to the ASSURE Classroom Case Study. At the end of the chapter you will be challenged to develop your own ASSURE lesson that incorporates use of these strategies, technology, media, and materials for a topic and grade level of your choice.

PEARSON
myeducationkit™

INTRODUCTION

A variety of media can make your lessons more realistic and engaging. This chapter describes how you and Mr. Ekker can use multimedia and learning centers to involve 21st century students. Although many of the media and materials discussed in this chapter are so common that instructors are inclined to underestimate their instructional value, you need to be able to use whiteboards, flip charts, bulletin boards, and other display formats confidently.

Objects and models bring "the real thing" into the classroom. Students can construct displays and dioramas themselves as part of learning activities. Materials don't have to be digital or expensive to be useful. Small can indeed be beautiful, and inexpensive can be effective!

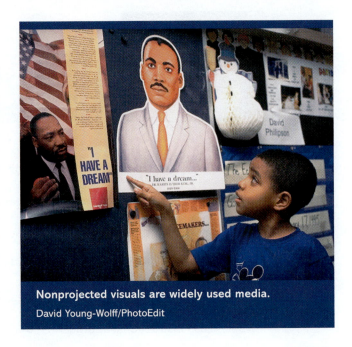

Nonprojected visuals are widely used media.
David Young-Wolff/PhotoEdit

MEDIA LITERACY

Today's students must be good consumers and producers of a wide variety of media, including text, audio, visuals, video, real objects, and/or models. Many of these media are combined to form multimedia. Even textbooks combine text and visuals. Computer programs can include the six types of media listed previously. Understanding how the various types of media produce meaning is called **media literacy**.

CONSUMING MEDIA

To be "media literate," students must be able to consume or interpret media in all formats—text, audio, visuals, and video. To learn to "read" and understand the forms of media students should be taught critical thinking skills in order to properly analyze and question the various messages from media. Is the photograph real or has it been manipulated to distort reality? Is the message on television fact? Students should be taught to question different sources of news and information on television and the Internet.

PRODUCING MEDIA

Students should also be able to generate media in these same formats and in various combinations. Teachers can encourage students to produce media in all four formats as part of class projects and reports. Students must be able to communicate successfully regardless of the type of media used. For example, to develop an accurate video they need to understand how to communicate with their audience and produce visuals that capture the essence of a narrative.

MULTIMEDIA

Multimedia is the sequential or simultaneous use of a variety of media in a presentation or self-study program. Computers are often involved in multimedia presentations that incorporate text, audio, and still or animated images.

An example is Anne Frank House, a House with a Story (Anne Frank House Museum), a tour on CD-ROM of Anne Frank's hiding place in Amsterdam. Here students can visit a digital recreation of the annex where Anne and her family hid from the Nazis when Holland was invaded. Students can **navigate** (use the keyboard and mouse to move around) the rooms, viewing them three-dimensionally as they appeared when she lived there from 1942 to 1944. They can view video and hear audio of people who lived during that period. They can study pages from Anne's diary, which document her plight during that period.

One common method of integrating media is with a **multimedia kit,** a collection of teaching/learning materials involving more than one type of medium and organized around a single topic. Kits often include real objects, models, and mock-ups. They may also include computer programs, audio and video materials, worksheets, charts, graphs, or booklets. Some multimedia kits are designed for the teacher to use in classroom presentations. Others are designed for use by individual students or small groups.

Commercial multimedia kits are available for a variety of educational subjects. They normally include student worksheets and a teacher's manual. Teachers or media specialists

Multimedia kits provide varied sensory experiences. They give the concrete referents needed to build a strong foundation for more abstract mental abilities.

Bob Torrez/PhotoEdit

- *Individualization.* Multimedia allow students to oversee the rate and sequence of their learning, giving them more control over the outcomes.
- *Special needs.* Multimedia are effective with special learners—at-risk students, student with diverse ethnic backgrounds, students with disabilities, and gifted and talented students. Multimedia accommodate student needs by allowing them to proceed through the instruction at an appropriate pace for each individual learner.
- *Information management.* Multimedia can cover a growing knowledge base associated with the information explosion. Multimedia can manage all types of information—text, graphic, audio, and video—to put more information at the instructor's and student's disposal.
- *Multisensory experiences.* Multimedia provides diverse learning experiences. These can employ a variety of instructional strategies suitable for basic instruction, remediation, or enrichment.

can also prepare multimedia kits. The main purpose of a kit is to give learners a chance at firsthand learning—to touch, to observe, to experiment, to wonder, and to decide (see When to Use Multimedia).

ADVANTAGES

- *Interactive.* Multimedia engage learners to make choices about moving within the material in meaningful ways, thus fulfilling the requirement of learner participation (the R of the ASSURE model).

LIMITATIONS

- *Availability and cost of materials.* Materials can be difficult to obtain or priced too high to permit their use.
- *Storage of materials.* Finding storage space for a wide variety of multimedia materials can pose problems.

INTEGRATION

Including multimedia in classrooms is only part of the task. The ultimate value of multimedia in education depends on

WHEN to USE Multimedia

Use when student learning will be enhanced by . . .

Guidelines	Examples
practicing what they have just studied in class	Students who need extra help with a skill or task can work with multimedia materials to practice skills or reinforce their understanding.
enhancing learning opportunities for gifted students	Gifted students can be challenged to expand or enhance their learning by using multimedia or computer software that introduces them to extended problems associated with the classroom activities.
working collaboratively with other students	Students can work together to navigate through instructional materials to help each other understand the information.
reaching a student who is having difficulty in learning	Students can use media materials in a way that is meaningful for them as part of their learning, navigating through the material as appropriate to their style of learning.
challenging students to present information in a new way	Students can create their own multimedia to share their knowledge with others in the class or school.

Multimedia Materials

Rainforest Researchers

www.tomsnyder.com

This combination of CD-ROM, video, and printed materials virtually puts students in the middle of the Indonesian rainforest. They work as teams of scientists and through collaborative problem solving explore the diverse and mysterious web of life in this rich ecosystem. Students work in cooperative teams of four, each taking the role of a chemist, ethnobotanist, taxonomist, or ecologist. Teams watch video and use onscreen displays to guide them in analyzing information, collaborating, and making decisions. (Tom Snyder Productions)

Neighborhood MapMachine

www.tomsnyder.com/products/products .asp?Subject=SocialStudies

Neighborhood MapMachine is a hands-on social studies program in which students can create and navigate community maps. While engaged in generating their maps, students learn concepts related to location, scale, distance, and compass navigation. Students can add pictures, movies, and links to websites on their customized community maps. In addition, students can use their writing and mathematics skills as they share their maps with others. (Tom Snyder Productions)

Diorama Designer

www.tomsnyder.com

It is easy for students to create dioramas on the computer using the Diorama Designer program. They can design original dioramas, print them in color, and assemble them to demonstrate understanding of historical periods for interdisciplinary units in social studies, language arts, or other classes. Students can select from a variety of backgrounds and decorative elements. People and furniture can be printed separately as 3D elements to place inside the diorama. Dioramas can be printed in different sizes, from small enough to fit in a shoebox to a puppet-sized stage. Options include making posters, puppets, and masks. (Tom Snyder Productions)

A variation of this is Rainforest Designer, which lets students design, build, and print 3D rainforest habitats.

Science Court Explorations

www.tomsnyder.com

An exciting science CD-ROM series that combines the power of technology with the effectiveness of hands-on manipulatives is available in an all-in-one, easy-to-use kit. Science Court

Mary Kate Denny/Getty Images/Stone Allstock

Explorations, designed for grades 2 to 4, is an extension of Tom Snyder Productions' award-winning Science Court series.

Science Court Explorations comes with a hybrid Mac/ Win CD-ROM, a class set of manipulatives (enough for six cooperative learning teams), and a comprehensive teacher's guide with reproducible worksheets and take-home activities.

Science Court Explorations introduces and reinforces the scientific method and fundamental science concepts for young students. A funny and compelling animated story on CD-ROM introduces a scientific question. The CD-ROM then walks students step by step through the scientific process and illustrates how to set up the hands-on experiment. Working in teams, students use the experiment to test hypotheses and answer questions.

Titles include "Pendulums," "Rockets," "Flight," "Heat Absorption," "Magnets," and "Friction." (Tom Snyder Productions)

PBS for Kids

http://pbskids.org

PBS Kids is an interactive website with many types of activities for kids, involving language arts and math experiences developmentally appropriate to the age groups. The themes of the activities relate to popular children's PBS shows such as *Arthur, Sesame Street,* and *Reading Rainbow.* A separate link connects parents and teachers to resources they can use to supplement student learning.

how fully and seamlessly they are integrated into the curriculum. Results need to be measurable against a clear set of objectives—the second step in the ASSURE model. Multimedia should promote problem solving, cultivate creativity, facilitate collaboration, and emphasize the value of lifelong learning.

Multimedia materials are valuable for tasks that must be shown rather than simply described. For example, printed materials and lecture alone cannot present some instruction adequately, such as how to test the pH of soil, erosion patterns, or the dynamics of a presidential debate. If the learner needs to interact with the instruction through the handling of virtual or visual manipulatives, viewing a video of ice formations at slow speed, or controlling a web cam to view different angles of the Golden Gate Bridge, multimedia is an appropriate choice. See When to Use Multimedia for other classroom examples. When you and your students are creating new multimedia materials to fit learning needs, be certain to follow copyright guidelines (see Copyright Concerns: Multimedia Materials).

LEARNING CENTERS

A combination of instructional media and materials, the **learning center** is a self-contained environment designed to promote individual or small-group learning focused on a

Multimedia Materials

The advent of new technologies, such as the Internet, the World Wide Web, CDs, and DVDs, have made it necessary to reexamine the copyright laws in view of multimedia capabilities. In 1996, a U.S. House of Representatives Subcommittee on Courts and Intellectual Property adopted a set of fair use guidelines for the production and use of multimedia in educational settings. These guidelines include the following allowances:

- When creating multimedia programs, students and teachers may legally use the following copyrighted materials:

  Text: up to 10% or 1,000 words, whichever is less

  Audio: up to 10%, but not more than 30 seconds, provided the excerpt does not comprise a part of the whole that would constitute a performable unit such as a section, movement, or aria

  Images: not more than 5 images by the same artist or photographer and up to 10%, but not more than 15 images from a single collection

  Video: up to 10% or 3 minutes, whichever is less

  Numerical data: up to 10% or 2,500 fields or cell entries, whichever is less

- Students and teachers may possess three copies. Two may be placed in service, only one of which may be placed on reserve, with a third as a backup in case the original is lost, damaged, or stolen.

- Students and teachers may retain multimedia projects for personal portfolios to be used later for assessment of learning, tenure review, and job interviews. Beyond that period they must acquire permission of the holders of each copyrighted portion.

- Students and teachers are advised to include at the opening of their multimedia project and in any accompanying print material a notice that certain materials are included under the fair use exemption of the U.S. copyright law. It is always best to give credit for the sources of any materials used.

- Students may use their educational multimedia projects and materials only for the duration of the course for which it was prepared.

- Teachers may use their multimedia projects and materials for educational purposes for a period of up to two years after the first instructional use in class. Beyond that period they must acquire permission of the holders of each copyrighted portion.

For general information on copyright, see the Copyright Concerns on pages 13 and 15 in Chapter 1. Suggested resources (print and web links) on copyright appear at the end of Chapter 1.

Teacher-Made Multimedia Kits

An elementary teacher developed a series of separate multimedia kits on science topics for use with her third-grade class. She incorporated real objects, such as musical instruments, magnets, small motors, rocks, harmless chemicals, and insect specimens in the kits. She also gathered pictures associated with each topic from magazines and old textbooks. A study guide, prepared for each unit, required students to inquire about the topic, make hypotheses, and conduct investigations. References were included for books and computer-based information on the topic. Audiotapes were prepared for use at school and at home for students who had access to audiocassette players.

For a unit on sound, the teacher prepared a multimedia kit that included several musical instruments, cassette recordings of common noises for listeners to identify, anatomical models of the human ear, books about how humans hear, and educational videos explaining how animals like bats, dogs, and dolphins hear and use sound.

The students enjoyed taking the kits home to work on the experiments. The response from parents was very positive. Several parents reported that they, too, learned by working through the activities with their children. Students often preferred to stay in at recess and work on the multimedia kits in the science corner.

Michael Newman/PhotoEdit

specific topic. A learning center may be as simple as some chairs and a table around which students discuss or as sophisticated as organizing several networked computers for collaborative research and problem solving.

An individual teacher may use one learning center within a classroom as a way of breaking the class into small groups to perform hands-on activities (e.g., in a science class with a laboratory-type learning center). Or a whole school may be organized to incorporate learning centers into the daily mix of activities, as in the Project CHILD schools (see Taking a Look at Technology Integration: Project CHILD).

Learning centers should encourage active participation rather than allowing students to simply sit and read text on a computer screen or in a book. Most learning centers provide students practice with feedback through individualized activities. They tend to be designed for use by individuals; however, they can be arranged for pairs or triads.

Learning centers may be set up in any suitable and available classroom space. They are also commonly found in school media centers. Learning center materials may include any or all of the technology and media mentioned in this text. Teachers or media specialists may purchase center materials and software from commercial producers or can create their own products.

Although students may perform simple learning center activities at their desks or some other open space, it is advisable that learning centers be confined to a clearly identifiable area and that they be at least partially enclosed to reduce distractions. Learning carrels, or booths, which may be purchased from commercial sources or made locally, provide a clearly defined enclosure. You can make carrels by placing simple cardboard dividers on classroom tables.

SKILL CENTERS

Skill centers can provide students with opportunities to do additional practice, typically to reinforce a skill previously taught through other media or strategies. Basic skills that are built up through drill-and-practice lend themselves to the skill center approach. For example, you might design a skill center to give practice in using prefixes for students who are learning word skills. Skill centers could also provide math manipulatives to engage students in constructing concrete examples of math problems completed on a worksheet.

Project CHILD

Project CHILD (Changing How Instruction for Learning is Delivered) is an innovative instructional system for the elementary school. The CHILD model differs from the traditional single-grade classroom with one teacher covering all subjects. In Project CHILD, teachers form cross-grade cluster teams (primary clusters for grades K–2 and intermediate clusters for grades 3–5). The CHILD cluster teachers each choose a core subject (reading, writing, or mathematics) as their specialty.

Students rotate to each of the three classrooms in their cluster and spend 60 to 90 minutes working at a variety of learning stations focused on the core subject. Each CHILD classroom has six learning stations:

- *Computer* for learning with instructional software
- *Teacher* for small-group tutorials
- *Textbook* for written work
- *Challenge* for learning in a game-like format
- *Exploration* for hands-on activities and projects
- *Imagination* for creative expression

Students stay with the same team of cluster teachers for three years. In addition to having more time to work with students, each teacher receives special training in applying technology and cooperative learning techniques in his or her designated specialty area. The teachers still cover the school's required curriculum and use their basic texts and other school resources. The change with Project CHILD comes through the delivery method

Project CHILD

that moves beyond lecture and seatwork, now enhanced with technology and hands-on active learning.

Numerous evaluations have shown the following results for CHILD students:

- Significantly higher performance on standardized tests
- Fewer discipline problems
- Highly satisfied parents

For additional information on this topic, go to the Institute for School Innovation (www.ifsi.org/projectchild).

INTEREST CENTERS

Interest centers can stimulate new interests and encourage creativity. For example, you might set up a get-acquainted center on insect life before actually beginning a unit on specific insects. Or prior to a lesson covering the impact of Native Americans on our culture, you could create a display of photos and artifacts representing various aspects of Native American culture.

REMEDIAL CENTERS

Remedial centers can help students who need additional assistance with a particular concept or skill. A student who has difficulty determining the least common denominator of a group of fractions, for example, could receive the needed help in a remedial learning center. The center could include

fun-to-do computer activities, flashcards, and magnetic number boards.

ENRICHMENT CENTERS

Enrichment centers can offer stimulating learning experiences for students who have completed required classroom activities. You might, for example, allow students who have finished their assigned geometry activities to go to a video center that features a DVD showing geometric shapes in bridges.

Computers can provide skill reinforcement and remedial instruction through the use of carefully selected drill-and-practice software. Interest and enrichment centers can be created from CD reference materials and child-safe Internet resources to allow students to explore topics on their own or to expand their exploration of topics covered in the

TECHNOLOGY
for Diverse Learners

Learning Centers

Learning centers facilitate learning by diverse students with materials and activities implemented using a variety of technology and media. You can often find existing materials, units, and modules that are appropriate for a learning center. If you are designing your own learning center, components may already be available from web-based and other sources. Be sure to follow copyright guidelines.

You cannot assume that technology will automatically engage students. The technology and media must match each student's learning style and ability. Some students prefer to work in pairs or small groups. Others prefer working by themselves.

Be sure to select appropriate technology for the diverse students in your classroom. Students with special needs can use adaptive technologies to meet their learning needs. For example, a student with motor-skill impairment can type on a large keyboard or students with visual impairments can employ print-to-voice or large-font software. Meeting the needs of your regular and gifted students requires using resources at their level.

Provide students with a variety of self-paced modules from which they can select. Adding elective units—often enriching experiences—allows students to engage in making decisions about their own learning. The "curriculum" varies for each individual student depending on his or her learning abilities. This ensures that students are mastering requirements and at the same time provides opportunities for alternative learning activities.

Assessment of each student's accomplishments can be measured and recorded through a variety of approaches. Technology may be used as a tool to administer tests or self-assessments. In addition, the students may use computer software to develop an artifact demonstrating mastery of the topic in the learning center.

---

classroom. Learning centers may also use a computer station for learning with instructional software or for student production of work.

ADVANTAGES

- *Self-pacing.* Learning centers encourage students to take responsibility for their own learning and allow them to learn at their own pace, thus minimizing the possibility of failure and maximizing the likelihood of success.
- *Active learning.* Learning centers provide for student participation in the learning experience, for student response, and for immediate feedback to student responses.
- *Teacher role.* Learning centers allow the teacher to play more of a coaching role, moving around the classroom and providing individual help for students when they need it (see Technology for Diverse Learners: Learning Centers).

LIMITATIONS

- *Cost.* A great deal of time must be spent in planning and setting up centers and in collecting and arranging for center materials. The equipment and materials used in the center, too, entail costs. Storage of materials not in use can also pose a problem.

- *Management.* Teachers who use learning centers must be very good at classroom organization and management.
- *Student responsibility.* Any form of independent study will be successful only insofar as students are able and willing to accept some responsibility for their own learning.

INTEGRATION

You can arrange learning centers for a number of specialized purposes. Computers can be used for information retrieval, construction of knowledge, problem solving, and multimedia learning. When computers are part of a learning center, it is a good idea to provide headphones or earbuds so the audio does not distract other students (see When to Use Learning Centers). Position the computers to prevent glare on the screens and so that students are not facing windows (Morrison & Lowther, 2010).

 MANIPULATIVES

Manipulatives are objects that can be viewed and handled in a learning setting. They are often included in learning centers and instructional modules (discussed earlier in this

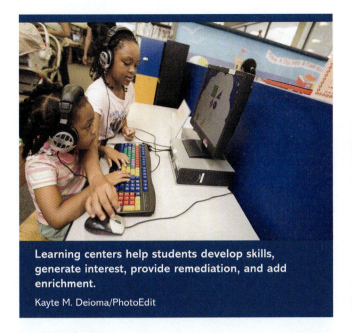

Learning centers help students develop skills, generate interest, provide remediation, and add enrichment.

Kayte M. Deioma/PhotoEdit

There is no substitute for the real thing when learning some content.

Richard Hutchings/PhotoEdit

chapter). Field trips, displays, and dioramas (discussed later in this chapter) may include manipulatives. They attract student attention and promote learning because students can handle and inspect them. There are three types of manipulatives: real objects, models, and mock-ups.

REAL OBJECTS

Real objects—such as coins, tools, artifacts, plants, and animals—are some of the most accessible, intriguing, and involving materials in educational use. The gerbils that draw a crowd in kindergarten, the terrarium that introduces middle school students to the concept of ecology, and the collection of Colonial-era coins displayed in a high school social studies class are just a few examples of the potential of real objects to elucidate the obscure and to stimulate the imagination.

Real objects are especially appropriate for learners who are encountering a subject about which they have had little direct experience in their daily lives. Educators have understood for many years the dangers of plunging into abstract concepts and principles without building a foundation in concrete experience. To avoid verbalism, or parroting words without meaningful understanding, it is important for learners

WHEN to USE Learning Centers

Use when student learning will be enhanced by . . .

Guidelines	Examples
the teacher serving as coach/facilitator during active student participation in stimulating experiences	Students use a series of tests to identify unknown rocks in a "Geology Skill Center."
self-paced learning experiences	Students move at their own pace through a "History Enrichment Center" display of a photo timeline depicting how their town center has changed over the past 100 years.
practice and feedback after direct instruction	Students go to the "Mathematics Bar-Graph Center" and use computer software to practice creating and interpreting bar graphs.
students working collaboratively in a small group	The "Language Arts Skill Center" is used by students to construct correct sentences from word cards.
an introduction to a new concept or topic	The "American History Interest Center" is used to present civil rights materials (e.g., magazine articles, video of Martin Luther King).

to build an understanding that has meaning and relevance in their lives. This can be accomplished by providing a base of concrete experiences that involves the manipulation of real objects associated with the content to be learned.

Real objects may be used as is, or you may modify them in different ways to enhance instruction, as in the following examples:

- *Cutaways*. Devices such as machines with one side cut away to allow close observation of their inner workings
- *Specimens*. Actual plants, animals, or parts thereof preserved for convenient inspection
- *Exhibits*. Collections of artifacts, often of a scientific or historical nature, brought together with printed information to illustrate a point

Besides their obvious virtues as a means of presenting information, raising questions, and providing hands-on learning experiences, real objects can also play a valuable role in the evaluation phase of instruction. They can be displayed in a central location where learners can identify, classify, or describe them; explain their function or utility; or compare and contrast them. Such testing emphasizes the real-world application of the topic of study, aids transfer of training, and helps transcend the merely verbal level of learning.

An anatomical model, being three-dimensional, is a more concrete referent than a photograph, drawing, or even a videotape.

T. Hubbard/Merrill

MODELS

Models are three-dimensional representations of real objects. A model may be larger, smaller, or the same size as the object it represents. It may be complete in detail or simplified for instructional purposes. Indeed, models can provide learning experiences that real objects cannot offer. For example, important details can be accented with color or models can be constructed for easy disassembly to provide interior views not possible with the real thing.

Models of almost anything—from airplanes to zebras—can be purchased for classroom use. Providing collections of models is a standard service of most media centers. School districts and regional media centers and museums often loan artifacts and models, usually as part of multimedia kits (described earlier in this chapter).

A variety of hobby kits are also available for you or your students to assemble. Assembly itself can be instructional. Classroom construction of model kits appeals to children of all ages and can stimulate inquiry and discovery while helping to sharpen both cognitive and psychomotor skills.

MOCK-UPS

Mock-ups are simplified representations of complex devices. By highlighting essential elements and eliminating distracting details, mock-ups clarify the complex. They are sometimes constructed as working models to illustrate the basic operations of a real device, allowing individuals or small groups to manipulate the mock-up at their convenience and work with the subject matter until they comprehend it. For example, a mock-up of a laptop computer might have the internal components spread out on a large board with the components labeled and the circuit diagrams printed on the board. The

Artifacts and models provide hands-on experiences.

Bonnie Kamin/PhotoEdit

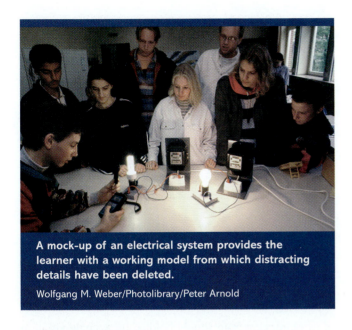

A mock-up of an electrical system provides the learner with a working model from which distracting details have been deleted.

Wolfgang M. Weber/Photolibrary/Peter Arnold

most sophisticated type of mock-up, the simulator, is a device that allows learners to experience the important aspects of a real-life activity without the risks.

ADVANTAGES

- *Realism.* Manipulatives provide realism and illustrate concepts that involve three dimensions. They enhance identification of objects by size, shape, or color and provide hands-on experience and laboratory practice.
- *Interest.* Manipulatives arouse interest because they are multisensory. Everyone likes to touch and manipulate real objects—to inspect unusual specimens up close.
- *Cooperation.* Manipulatives can be ideal mechanisms for stimulating small-group project work. Cooperative

learning activities can revolve around experiments, problem solving, role-playing, or other types of hands-on practice.

LIMITATIONS

- *Expense.* Manipulatives are often more expensive than other, more conventional materials.
- *Storage.* It can be difficult to find storage space for manipulatives and to remember where they are when you want to use them.
- *Fragility.* Some manipulatives are easily broken or damaged and may then become unusable.

INTEGRATION

Manipulatives are particularly well suited to content for which discovery learning is preferred (see Using Manipulatives in the Classroom). You can pose questions to guide learners' explorations and conclusions. Science topics are well suited to this approach. For example, a unit on magnetism might include several types of magnets, iron filings, and metal objects that may or may not be attracted to magnets. In mathematics, a unit on measurement might involve a folding meter stick and directions for measuring various objects and dimensions around the school or at home. Virtual mathematics manipulatives are provided by teachers to help students gain a deeper understanding of abstract concepts and improve problem-solving skills (Moyer, Salkind, & Bolyard, 2008). When to Use Manipulatives presents guidelines and examples for including manipulatives.

An exciting science CD-ROM series designed for grades 2 to 4 combines the power of technology with the effectiveness of hands-on manipulatives. Science Court Explorations introduces and reinforces the scientific method

USING
Manipulatives
in the Classroom

- Familiarize yourself with the object or model before using it in classroom instruction.
- Practice your presentation. If your object or model is a working one, be sure you know how it works and what might go wrong.
- Be sure your students do not get the wrong impression of the size, shape, or color of the real object, if the model differs from it in these respects.

- Whenever feasible, encourage students to handle and manipulate the objects and models under study.
- Store objects out of sight when not using them for instruction. Left standing around, they are likely to take students' attention away from other classroom activities.

Use when student learning will be enhanced by . . .

Guidelines	Examples
encountering a subject for which they have had little direct experience	Using sand trays for younger students to practice writing letters.
using concrete objects to build a foundation for understanding abstract concepts	Building an algebra problem with base-10 blocks for gifted elementary students.
engaging in real-world applications of knowledge and skills	Using a mock-up of a traffic light to test electrical circuits.
engaging in experiences not possible without the use of models	Examining a 3D model of a plant cell.

and fundamental science concepts for young students. A funny and compelling animated story introduces a scientific question. The software then walks the students step-by-step through the scientific process and illustrates how to set up the hands-on experiment. Working in teams, students use the manipulatives included in the kit to experiment with possible answers. When they feel they have resolved the problem, they enter the information into the computer for confirmation. This seems to be the best of both worlds: efficient use of a computer and authentic learning experiences for students.

ASSURE Case Study Reflection

Review the ASSURE Classroom Case Study and video at the beginning of the chapter. What types of manipulatives could Phil Ekker's first-grade students use to reinforce basic mathematics and language arts skills? How would manipulatives benefit student learning?

DISPLAY SURFACES

If you are going to provide visuals such as photographs, drawings, charts, graphs, or posters, you need a way to show them. Visuals may be displayed in the classroom in a variety of ways, ranging from simply holding up a single visual in your hand to constructing elaborate exhibits for permanent display. Classroom surfaces commonly used for display of visuals include whiteboards, bulletin boards, cloth boards, magnetic boards, and flip charts (see When to Use Display Surfaces).

WHITEBOARDS

The most common display surface in the classroom is the **whiteboard**. Interactive or **electronic whiteboards** can print copies of the information written on them and can often be connected to whiteboards at different locations for distance learning.

Although the whiteboard is most commonly employed to support verbal communication, you can use it as a drawing

Whiteboards are common in educational institutions.
David Young-Wolff/PhotoEdit

WHEN to USE Display Surfaces

Use when student learning will be enhanced by . . .

Guidelines	Examples
Whiteboards	
viewing text and/or visuals that support the verbal presentation of information	Elementary students diagram a sentence while describing the function of each part.
capturing brainstorming ideas on an interactive whiteboard and digitally downloading to printed material for use in other activities	Middle school social studies students record and print copies of class ideas for increasing voter turnout rate and then use the ideas in a letter to the mayor.
sharing interactive whiteboard information during videoconferencing between two or more distant sites	High school students from two neighboring schools collaboratively design a recycling center for a local park.
Bulletin Boards	
actively engaging with the bulletin board content through reading and answering questions and/or directly interacting with "moveable" features	Elementary students sequence diagrams in the correct order (e.g., the water cycle) or create complete sentences with word cards and pockets.
creating a bulletin board that depicts designated knowledge and skills	Students display unlabeled digital photos that represent the weekly vocabulary words. Other students match the photos with the words by placing them in pockets under each photo.
Cloth and Magnetic Boards	
viewing illustrations of stories, poems, and other reading materials that can be moved to emphasize key learning points	Students illustrate growth of a flower from a seed; how the shape of an object changes by adding sides; how characters interact during a story.
demonstrating knowledge and skills through verbal descriptions and manipulation of cloth board pictures, shapes, or objects	Students place pictures of food on the correct section of the Food Pyramid. Students create a rainbow by correctly arranging color bars.
Flip Charts	
viewing limited verbal/visual messages in a sequential order	High school students name the main components of a business letter.
visual cues that assist in creating relationships between concepts and information	Students view step 1 of cell division on page 1 of flip chart and step 2 on page 2 of flip chart, etc.
viewing diagrams and lists of brainstormed ideas as thoughts are generated	Students suggest ideas on how to increase recycling at the school.
using group-produced ideas to guide further discussion and decision making	Student groups create a family history interview form from ideas recorded on a flip chart during a class discussion.

surface to help illustrate instructional units. The white surface is also suitable for projection of video, PowerPoint slides, and overhead transparencies. Materials cut from thin plastic, such as objects and letters, will adhere to the surface when rubbed in place. Some of these boards have a steel backing and can be used as magnetic boards (see pages 269–270). Using a whiteboard effectively requires conscious effort (see Using Whiteboards in the Classroom).

The most common writing materials for whiteboards are dry erase markers, available in a variety of colors and tip widths. Because their solvent base dries quickly, store the markers in a horizontal position with the cap tight to prevent drying out. If a marker dries out, fasten the cap, turn it upside down, and shake vigorously for 20 seconds. Leaving the marker stored overnight with the tip end down may also help.

A whiteboard will provide many years of service if cared for properly. Do not use permanent felt-tip markers that may damage the surface beyond repair. Completely erase the whiteboard with a felt eraser after each use. Do not let the marks remain on the board overnight, as the longer they

- Organize in advance what you plan to write on the board and where you plan to write it. You can draw your planned layout on a sheet of paper and use it as notes during the lesson.

- Put extensive drawing or writing on the board before class. Taking too much time to write or draw creates restlessness and may lead to discipline problems.

- Cover material such as a test or extensive lesson materials with wrapping paper, newspaper, or a pull-down map until you are ready to use it.

- Eye contact with students is important! Face the class when you are talking. Do not talk to the board. Do not turn your back to the class unless it is absolutely necessary.

- Vary your presentation techniques. Do not overuse or rely entirely on the board. Use handouts, PowerPoint, flip charts, and other media during instruction when appropriate.

- Print neatly rather than using script. For a 32-foot-deep classroom, the letters should be $1\frac{1}{2}$ to 2 inches high and the line forming the letters should be $\frac{1}{4}$ inch thick.

- Check the visibility of the board from several positions around the room to be sure there is no glare on the surface. In case of glare, move the board (if portable) or close blinds.

- Use color for emphasis, but don't overuse it. Two or three different colors at a time work best.

- Move around so you do not block what you have written on the board. Do not stand in front of what you have written.

- Use drawing aids such as rulers, stencils, and patterns to save time and improve the quality of your drawings.

stay, the more difficult they are to erase. You can remove old marks by tracing over them with a black erasable marker and erasing immediately.

For general cleaning, simply wipe the board clean with a soft, damp cloth. If further cleaning is necessary, use a commercial mild spray cleaner. You can also apply a soapy detergent solution and rub briskly with a soft, clean cloth. Always rinse thoroughly with clean water and dry with a soft towel after cleaning.

Interactive whiteboards allow you to "capture" digitally anything written on them and interact with the information. They work in conjunction with a computer to create a file into which screens are fed and from which the screens can be edited, printed, faxed, or emailed. You can make as many copies of each screen as you like. After copying the information, you are free to erase the board and continue without losing valuable time or ideas. Whiteboards are sometimes known by the brand name Smart Boards (www.smarttech .com). Another brand name is Promethean ActivBoard (www .Prometheanworld.com).

Many interactive whiteboards enable the user to access multiple screens or frames that can be scrolled forward and backward. You can prepare content beforehand on any or all of the screens. During your presentation you can reveal the screens one at a time and add new information as desired. You can also move the image forward or backward to a desired frame quickly and easily.

With interactive whiteboards, you can capture your work or save your notes directly into different software applications.

This feature is especially valuable for brainstorming sessions and for summarizing group discussions. Copies could be particularly helpful for students who miss class. You can include complex drawings without having students hand copy them. The computer and interactive whiteboard configuration lets you run software programs, surf the Web, review documents, and toggle between items as you would on a desktop computer. Interactive whiteboards allow data and information sharing during a videoconference. You can write, erase, and perform mouse functions with your finger or a pen. Recent

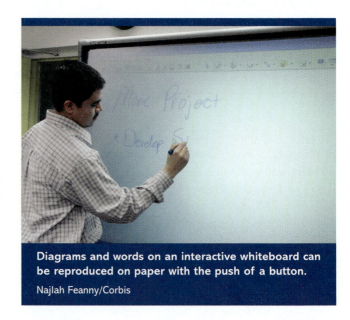

Diagrams and words on an interactive whiteboard can be reproduced on paper with the push of a button.

Najlah Feanny/Corbis

research indicates that interactive whiteboards are frequently used to increase student interactivity and participation and increase the efficiency and professionalism of multimedia delivery (Salton & Arslan, 2009).

BULLETIN BOARDS

With all the modern technology available, classrooms still need **bulletin boards.** Bulletin boards are surfaces of various sizes and shapes made of materials that hold pins, thumbtacks, and other sharp fasteners without damage to the board. One way to attract attention to your bulletin board is to lead off with a catchy headline, one that communicates the main theme, perhaps with a question, a challenge, or a humorous phrase. In practice, bulletin board displays tend to serve three broad purposes: decorative, motivational, or instructional.

The decorative bulletin board is very common in schools. You might have a bulletin board that displays the colors and designs associated with a special holiday or a season. Or you might have one showing books that students might be interested in reading for pleasure.

Displaying student work exemplifies the motivational use of bulletin boards. The public recognition offered by such displays can play an important role in the life of the classroom. It fosters pride in achievement, reinforcing students' efforts to do a good job. It is also relatively easy for you to create a display of student work.

The third broad purpose of bulletin boards is instructional, complementing the educational objectives. Rather than merely presenting static informational messages, you may design displays that actively invite participation. Such displays ask questions and give students some means of manipulating parts of the display to verify their answers, such as flaps, pockets, dials, or movable parts.

Another form of learner participation is taking part in the actual construction of the display. For example, to introduce a unit on animals, an elementary teacher might ask each student to bring in a picture of a favorite animal. The students would then make a bulletin board incorporating all the pictures. Or a geometry teacher might divide the class into five groups and assign each group a different geometric shape. As the class studies each shape, the appropriate group would construct a bulletin board about that shape.

Materials for production of bulletin boards may be available through the school media center. Most schools have workrooms with large tables where you can construct items for your bulletin board and consider various layouts. These workrooms often are equipped with a popular letter-cutting device called the Ellison Prestige die cutter, which allows large letters or other shapes to be cut quickly and neatly from construction paper. The media center may also store the components for bulletin board displays so that teachers can share and easily access materials.

CLOTH AND MAGNETIC BOARDS

Cloth boards are constructed of cloth stretched over a sturdy backing material such as plywood, Masonite, or heavy cardboard. The cloth used for the board may be of various types, including flannel, felt, or hook-and-loop (e.g., Velcro) material.

Pieces of flannel stick together when gentle pressure is applied. You can draw with felt-tip markers on visuals cut from flannel or back still pictures and graphics with pieces of flannel to put on a flannel board. Coarse sandpaper also

Bulletin boards have many important functions in the classroom.

Matthew Steigbigel/Taxi/Getty Images

Cloth boards are often used to involve students in storytelling.

Robin L. Sachs/PhotoEdit

Magnetic boards allow quick manipulation of letters and other materials.

Scott Cunningham/Merrill

works to attach visuals to a cloth board. Pipe cleaners, available in a variety of colors, and fuzzy yarns stick to the flannel and can be attached to form lines and letters. If adhesion is less than desired, slant the board slightly back at the top to prevent materials from slipping.

Reading teachers often use the cloth board to illustrate stories, poems, and other reading materials. For example, they may depict characters and scenes in a story and move them around as the story unfolds. Use this approach to encourage your students' creativity by allowing them to manipulate cloth board materials. Shy children may profit from this kind of activity. It encourages them to speak through the visual representations of story characters as they move the illustrations on the board.

Magnetic boards serve much the same purpose as cloth boards. Visuals are backed with magnets and then placed on the metal surface of the board. Magnetic boards, magnets, and flexible strips of magnetic materials for backing are available commercially. Plastic lettering with magnetic backing can be purchased from teacher supply stores and used for captioning visuals.

Any metal surface in the classroom to which you can attach a magnet can serve as a magnetic board. For example, some whiteboards are backed with steel and thus attract magnet-backed visuals. Use whiteboard markers for captioning or to depict lines of association between visuals. You can also use steel cabinets and metal walls and doors as magnetic boards.

The major advantage of magnetic boards is that maneuvering visuals is easier and quicker than with cloth boards. For example, physical education instructors often use them to demonstrate rapid changes in player positions. Magnetic boards also have greater adhesive quality. Visuals displayed on a magnetic board are not likely to slip or fall. They move only when you move them.

FLIP CHARTS

A **flip chart** is a pad of large paper fastened together at the top and typically mounted to an easel. The individual sheets hold a limited verbal or visual message and usually are arranged for sequential presentation to a small group. You may write key words extemporaneously while talking or you can prepare them in advance to be revealed one at a time.

Easel-sized Post-it chart pads are available from 3M. These 25-by-30-inch self-sticking easel sheets come in plain white or with a blue outline grid. The easel pads have a built-in handle, a sturdy backing, and a cover flap to protect the sheets from damage or flapping while in transit. The universal slots on the backing attach to most easel stands. Each sheet peels off for quick posting on a nearby wall, or it can be flipped over the top of the pad.

You can use poster software such as PosterPrinter to produce flip chart pages. Commercially produced materials are also available in this format. Prepared visual sequences are especially useful for instruction involving sequential steps in a process. The diagrams or words can serve as cues, reminding you of the next point in your presentation.

The most common use of flip charts, though, is for the extemporaneous drawing of key illustrations and key words to supplement a presentation. The flip chart is an extremely versatile, convenient, and inexpensive media format. It is portable, requires no electrical power, has no moving parts to wear out, can be used in a range of lighting conditions, and requires only a marking pen. But don't let the flip chart's simplicity fool you. Using it professionally takes some practice (see Using Flip Charts in the Classroom).

The PosterPrinter can convert a notebook-size original into a poster or banner that is many times larger.

Image provided by HP: www.hp.com/go/designjet

USING
Flip Charts
in the Classroom

- Position the flip chart at an angle so everyone can see it. Place it in the left front corner (as you face the audience) if you are right-handed and in the right front corner if you are left-handed.

- Be sure the easel is properly assembled and the pages are securely fastened so the flip chart will not fall apart during your presentation.

- Prepare lettering and visuals in advance or outline their shape using a light blue pencil; then trace them during your presentation.

- For group-generated responses, draw lettering guidelines with a blue pencil.

- Keep lettering and visuals simple but large enough for everyone to see.

- Use more than one color, but not more than four.

- Use broad-tip marking pens that provide contrast but will not bleed through to the next sheet.

- Print rather than use cursive writing.

- Keep words short or use well-understood abbreviations.

- Include simple drawings, symbols, and charts.

- Talk to the audience, not to the flip chart.

- Avoid blocking the audience's view of the flip chart.

- Be sure your materials are in proper sequence.

- Have a blank sheet exposed when not referring to the flip chart.

- Reveal pages only when you are ready to discuss them, not before.

- Put summary points on the last sheet rather than paging back as you make your summary.

ADVANTAGES

- *Visual stimulation.* Display surfaces can provide colorful and dynamic displays for instruction and interaction requiring learner participation.
- *Variety of instructional strategies.* Display surfaces can be incorporated into all levels of instruction—basic, remediation, or enrichment.

LIMITATIONS

- *Lack of attention to proper use.* Display surfaces are so common that teachers often neglect to give them the attention and respect they require.
- *Need for careful thought and planning.* An effective display, whether done by a teacher or students, should focus on one main topic or objective.

INTEGRATION

Display surfaces allow you to present prepared visuals or visuals you create as you are discussing the topic. Common in most classrooms, whiteboards can display written, drawn, or projected visuals. Bulletin boards can enhance the atmosphere of the classroom and motivate students to learn. Cloth boards and magnetic boards allow easy manipulation of instructional materials. Flip charts provide convenient writing surfaces for small groups of students. They can also be used to show prepared materials. Don't neglect the multiple uses and value of display surfaces in the classroom. See When to Use Display Surfaces for possible uses of various display surfaces.

ASSURE Case Study Reflection

Review the ASSURE Classroom Case Study and video at the beginning of the chapter. What considerations does Phil Ekker need to address when selecting display surfaces for use with his first-grade students? How do these considerations vary when using different types of displays, such as whiteboards, bulletin boards, cloth or magnetic boards, or flip charts?

EXHIBITS

Exhibits are collections of various objects and visuals designed to form an integrated whole for instructional purposes. Any visuals, real objects, models, or mock-ups can be included in an exhibit. Any of the display surfaces discussed in this chapter can contribute to an exhibit. Exhibits

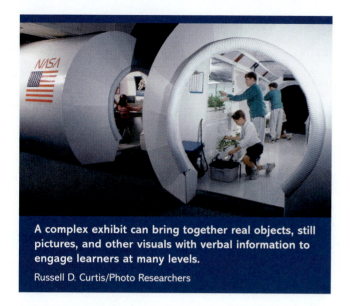

A complex exhibit can bring together real objects, still pictures, and other visuals with verbal information to engage learners at many levels.

Russell D. Curtis/Photo Researchers

can generally be used for the same instructional purposes and in the same ways as their individual components.

Exhibits provide a display format incorporating a variety of materials such as real objects and models along with visuals (see When to Use Exhibits). Often area museums or historical societies will lend items. How you display the materials will depend on a number of factors, including type of audience, the nature of your objects and visuals, the instructional setting, and, of course, the availability of the various display surfaces.

Exhibit locations are readily available in most classrooms. You can set up simple exhibits on a table, shelf, or desk. More complex exhibits may require considerable floor space and special structures (a booth or bookcase, for example). The school media center is a convenient location for student-produced exhibits, displays, and dioramas.

There are three types of exhibits—field trips, displays, and dioramas. Field trips provide an exhibit of real objects in their natural environment. A display is a collection of materials, whereas a diorama shows a three-dimensional scene.

FIELD TRIPS

The **field trip,** an excursion outside the classroom to study real processes, people, and objects, often grows out of student need for firsthand experiences. It makes it possible for students to encounter phenomena that cannot be brought into the classroom for observation and study.

Examples of field trips include a visit of a few minutes into the schoolyard to observe a tree, a trek across the street to see construction work, or a longer trip of several days to tour historical locations. Popular field trip sites include zoos, museums, public buildings, and parks. The school media specialist can increase the chances for a successful field trip experience by maintaining a local resource file listing possible sites to visit. Usually the file includes the names, addresses, and phone numbers of people to contact. A good resource file will also include notes regarding the value of previous trips. Some district media centers and

WHEN to USE Exhibits

Use when student learning will be enhanced by . . .

Guidelines	Examples
Field Trips	
firsthand experiences (seeing and hearing) with phenomena that cannot be brought into the classroom for observation or study	A class visits a city council meeting to learn about governmental processes, or goes to the schoolyard to collect leaf samples.
virtual experiences of phenomena that cannot be visited during a field trip due to distance or safety issues	Students explore a space station by viewing live video broadcasts on the Internet.
Displays	
viewing and studying, or creating, a collection of labeled objects, visuals, printed materials, and perhaps audio recordings that have an instructional intent	Students create a "Countries of Our Classroom" corner by displaying artifacts that represent the cultural heritage of each student and a map depicting the country of each student's ancestors.
Dioramas	
viewing or creating three-dimensional representations of past, present, or future events or settings	Student groups build a four-part diorama to show how a tree changes with the four seasons.

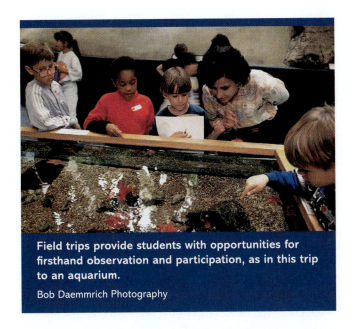

Field trips provide students with opportunities for firsthand observation and participation, as in this trip to an aquarium.

Bob Daemmrich Photography

public libraries maintain a local resource file as part of their electronic catalog.

Virtual field trips are an extension of actual field trips. Often the expense or the time to travel to an interesting location is not possible. But, using computers, students may experience the sights and sounds of a faraway location from their home or school. In addition to virtual field trips based on computer technology, videoconferencing can also be used. Teachers with videoconferencing equipment can take their students to any location that has videoconference capabilities, such as manufacturing facilities. Some of these trips are offered at predetermined dates and times and are available on a first-come, first-served basis. The only charge is for network time—no transportation or other fees.

For example, the Cincinnati Zoo (www.cincyzoo.org) offers virtual field trips in which students get to interact live with zookeepers. Their program "Nobody Likes Me," for example, introduces students to frogs, toads, bats, bugs, and snakes.

For any field trip to be justified, it should grow out of and be directly related to the regular course of study. You should devise lead-in as well as follow-up (including evaluation) activities to first prepare students for the field trip and then to help them reflect on the experience and integrate it into their understanding.

The follow-up is a vital aspect of a field trip. If the purpose for making the trip is to get additional factual information, the evaluation will be more formal. If the objectives involve attitudes and appreciation, follow-up activities might include discussion, role playing, or creative art projects. Whatever form it takes, follow-up activity should measure the success of the trip. Students and teachers should address content as well as possible ways to improve future trips.

DISPLAYS

A **display** is an array of objects, visuals, and printed materials (e.g., labels and descriptions). Most displays include descriptive information about the objects or visuals shown. Instructional displays are not only used in the classroom but also in museums and many other settings.

Student assembly of a display can be a motivating learning experience, fostering retention of subject matter and sharpening visual skills. For a lesson on transportation, one sixth-grade teacher had each student bring in a replica of a vehicle. Some students made their own vehicles from construction paper. Others brought in toys from home or contributed vehicles assembled from hobby kits (e.g., boats, cars, trucks, trains, space ships). The teacher set up tables and other classroom furniture along a wall to provide a "shelf" on which to arrange the three-dimensional objects. On the wall above the display surface, the teacher placed a long sheet of paper with a timeline illustrating forms of transportation from the past (humans and beasts), through the present (trains, cars, planes), and into the future (space vehicles). The display was a great success!

DIORAMAS

A **diorama** is a static display consisting of a three-dimensional foreground and a flat background to create a realistic scene. Dioramas are usually designed to reproduce scenes and events from the past or present or to depict future scenarios.

Students may design their own dioramas as a follow-up activity to instruction. Scenes from history are often portrayed with model figures and photographs or drawings from the time period as background images. Animals can be shown in their natural habitats for a biology class. Scenes including towns and landscapes from various parts of the world make stimulating dioramas for geography instruction. Prehistoric landscapes and geologic formations are also popular topics.

ADVANTAGES

- *Actual materials.* Students go to the materials during field trips. Displays and dioramas bring materials into the school.
- *Multisensory experience.* Displays can provide sight, sound, touch, and sometimes taste.
- *Access to materials not available in the classroom.* Field trips and displays off campus allow students to experience sights, sounds, and materials that cannot be brought into the classroom.

LIMITATIONS

- *Expense of field trips.* Taking students on field trips can be expensive and time-consuming.
- *Storage of materials.* Displays and dioramas in the school often cause storage problems between uses.
- *Space required.* Space to exhibit displays and dioramas is often limited in classroom and media centers.

INTEGRATION

Integrating exhibits into your instruction adds variety and real-world experiences that increase student engagement and opportunities for learning. If you are studying Paris, France, it would be nearly impossible for the whole class to go there. However, with a few simple clicks of a mouse, the whole class can see and hear the city through a virtual field trip. Although it is not exactly the same as being there, it certainly makes it possible to learn about a location with some authenticity to the experience.

Displays are commonly used to provide hands-on experiences for students. For elementary students studying musical instruments, a teacher collected scale-model plastic instruments that his students could handle and classify by describing the function of each instrument. During a field trip, middle school students visited a historical museum that included a scale-model diorama of their community in the early 1930s. The students took pictures of the diorama and compared them to recent pictures of the same areas when they returned to their classroom.

Middle school students could create a display of arts and crafts they construct from recycled materials. A high school English class might display political cartoons depicting opinions on a current issue. As a way to extend understanding of a Shakespeare play, student groups could build a diorama depicting a key scene from each act of the play. Groups then could compare the dioramas to see which scenes were selected and how they were depicted.

ASSURE Case Study Reflection

Review the ASSURE Classroom Case Study and video at the beginning of the chapter. What types of exhibits would be effective to use with first graders? What types might Mr. Ekker develop to reinforce math skills? What type could his first-graders construct to build their reading skills?

INNOVATION on the **H**ORIZON

3D INTERACTIVE CUBE DISPLAY
Tabletop Display Gets Rid of the Glasses

A cube-shaped device offers all the thrills of 3D without those annoying glasses. The device, called "pCubee," has five LCD screens—one on each side and another on the top of the cube. The viewer can pick it up and see virtual objects from four sides and the top. The viewer can shake the cube, tilt it, and even interact with objects in the cube using a virtual stylus. Just think of the advantages of using the 3D cube in the classroom to show different objects without having to store the many objects between uses.

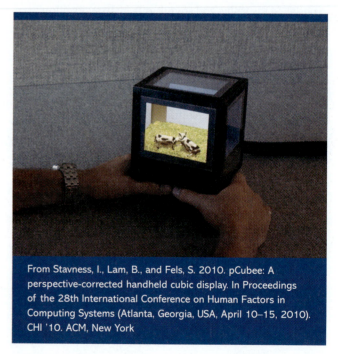

From Stavness, I., Lam, B., and Fels, S. 2010. pCubee: A perspective-corrected handheld cubic display. In Proceedings of the 28th International Conference on Human Factors in Computing Systems (Atlanta, Georgia, USA, April 10–15, 2010). CHI '10. ACM, New York

SUMMARY

Multimedia materials come in a variety of formats, from real objects to printed materials that can be displayed in a variety of ways. They can be effective tools for engaging students and facilitating learning if used properly. This chapter explored the use of these materials in learning centers, instructional modules, and integrated learning systems. We have discussed their advantages and limitations as well as when and how to use them effectively. Various types of manipulatives and display surfaces were described. The chapter concluded with a discussion of exhibits, including field trips, displays, and dioramas.

ASSURE Lesson Plan

The ASSURE Classroom Case Study is based on an interdisciplinary lesson created by Phil Ekker using multimedia materials and experiences to meet the individual needs of his first-grade students. His insights for achieving successful use of instructional materials and displays integrated into learning centers are provided. Go to Chapter 11 of MyEducationKit to view the Chapter 11 "Multimedia" Video.

Analyze Learners

General Characteristics. The students in Phil Ekker's first-grade class are from middle- to high-income homes. There is little variation with regard to ethnicity, gender, and age of the children. Student reading ability ranges from below to above grade level. Student behavior problems are minimal when they are engaged in hands-on activities.

Entry Competencies. The students are, in general, able to do the following:

- Operate a player to listen to audio books.
- Use educational software on a desktop computer
- Complete assignments requiring basic first-grade-level writing skills
- Independently move among and complete learning center activities

Learning Styles. Phil's students learn best when engaged in a variety of activities that last from 15 to 20 minutes each. Their level of interest and motivation increases when they use technology or hands-on materials. Differences are seen in student learning styles with regard to working with other students, some preferring cooperative learning groups and others preferring to work alone. There are also differences in student need for reinforcement from the teacher or fellow students.

State Standards and Objectives

Curriculum Standards. National Council of Teachers of Mathematics 1—Numbers and Operations 1.6: Understand numbers, ways of representing numbers, relationships among numbers, and number systems; understand and represent commonly used fractions, such as $\frac{1}{4}$, $\frac{1}{3}$, and $\frac{1}{2}$. National Council of Teachers of English 3: Students apply a wide range of strategies to comprehend, interpret, evaluate, and appreciate texts; and 5: Students employ a wide range of strategies as they write and use different writing process elements appropriately to communicate with different audiences for a variety of purposes.

Technology Standards. National Educational Technology Standards for Students 1: Students apply existing knowledge to generate new ideas, products, or processes.

Learning Objectives. The learning objectives for this lesson are as follows:

1. Given mathematics drill-and-practice software for fractions, students will successfully progress through the five levels.
2. Given audio books and a player, students will successfully follow along as the book is read.
3. Given alphabet practice sheets, students will correctly write the designated letter and draw a picture that represents the same letter.
4. Given a book and a reading buddy, students will read the book to their buddy and provide corrective feedback as they listen to their buddy reading.

Select Strategies, Technology, Media, and Materials

Select Strategies. Phil Ekker selects teacher- and student-centered strategies for the learning centers lesson. The teacher-centered strategies involve conducting small reading groups or buddy reading with students. Mr. Ekker also provides feedback and guidance to students as they work in the various learning centers. The student-centered strategies consist of the following learning center activities: books on tape, fractions software, handwriting, story writing, group reading, and buddy reading.

Select Technology and Media. Mr. Ekker selects two types of technology for this lesson: computers and audiotape players. The media include the fractions software, books on tape packets, storybooks, and the letter "H" handwriting/drawing sheet. Phil uses the following guidelines to assess the appropriateness of his technology and media selections:

- *Alignment with standards, outcomes, and objectives*. The fractions software, books on tape packets, storybooks, and the letter "H" handwriting/drawing sheet were selected because they are directly aligned to the learning objectives.
- *Accurate and current information*. The lesson materials have accurate information. The currency of the materials is not of concern for this lesson as it focuses on basic skills.
- *Age-appropriate language*. Mr. Ekker selects materials appropriate for the varying reading, writing, and mathematics ability levels of his students.
- *Interest level and engagement*. The storybooks, books on tapes, and fractions software were selected because they were written to appeal to young children and keep them engaged.
- *Technical quality*. The audiotapes for books on tape are of high quality as is the fractions software.
- *Ease of use*. Both the books on tape and the fractions software were developed to be used by young children. Mr. Ekker shows the students how to use the audiotape player and software at the beginning of the year. Afterward the children are able to use them with little or no assistance.

- *Bias free*. Prior to including materials in a learning center, Mr. Ekker reviews all storybooks and software to ensure they are bias free.
- *User guide and directions*. Mr. Ekker reviews the software user guide prior to including it in the learning center.

Select Materials. Phil Ekker uses the preceding guidelines for selecting all learning center materials.

Utilize Technology, Media, and Materials

Preview the Technology, Media, and Materials. As mentioned, Phil Ekker previews all technology, media, and materials before including them in the learning centers. He reads the storybooks, listens to the books on tapes, and completes the fractions software to ensure they are aligned with his standards and learning objectives.

Prepare the Technology, Media, and Materials. Phil ensures that the fraction software is loaded and functioning on the two desktop computers. He tests the tape players to ensure they are working. He then prepares copies of the letter "H" handwriting sheet and organizes learning center cards so students will know which activities to complete.

Prepare the Environment. The learning center lesson requires desks to be arranged for handwriting, story writing, and listening to books on tapes; floor space to be available for buddy reading; and the computer area to be readily accessible.

Prepare the Learners. Students in Mr. Ekker's class have experience working in learning centers and know how to check the learning center cards to see which activities they are to complete and in which order they are to be completed.

Provide the Learning Experience. The learning experience occurs in each learning center and is provided as the students rotate through their designated activities.

Require Learner Participation

Student Practice Activities. Each learning center requires students to practice reading, writing, or math skills. In the Buddy Reading center students practice reading to each other; in the writing center students practice their handwriting by completing an "H" page. Students also practice by writing a story about a topic of their choice. When students go to the small reading groups, they work with Mr. Ekker on their reading skills and comprehension. And, the computer center provides students practice with fractions.

Feedback. Feedback for learning center work is provided immediately in the computer center as the fractions software lets students know the correctness of their response with each action. It also provides instructional feedback to help them improve their performance. In the small reading groups, students receive immediate feedback on their reading skills from Mr. Ekker. While buddy reading, students receive feedback from each other; however, the accuracy of the feedback cannot be ensured. Students receive feedback for the remaining activities when Mr. Ekker returns their corrected learning center work.

Evaluate and Revise

Assessment of Learner Achievement. Phil assesses learner achievement in two ways. First is a casual assessment completed while students are working. The second is assessment of student work that is submitted at the conclusion of the learning center activities.

Evaluation of Strategies, Technology, and Media. Phil evaluates the lesson strategies through continuous observation of students working in the centers and from feedback he receives from students while in the centers. He also examines student products to determine if the strategies are effective. Evaluation of the technology and media involve noting technical problems that occur during the lesson. He also gauges student interest and ability to complete the fractions software.

Revision. After reviewing the evaluation results collected from student achievement measures and evaluation of the lesson strategies, technology, and media, Phil concludes that the learning centers worked well. However, he feels students need an additional creative writing activity. Therefore, Mr. Ekker revises the lesson by adding an activity in which students write captions for cartoons with the wording removed.

CONTINUING MY PROFESSIONAL DEVELOPMENT

Demonstrating Professional Knowledge

1. Discuss media literacy, including the aspects of consuming and producing media.
2. Discuss the advantages, limitations, and instructional applications of multimedia in learning.
3. Discuss four types of learning centers and describe one specific example of each.
4. Describe instructional applications that are especially appropriate for manipulatives.
5. Compare the advantages and limitations of various types of display surfaces.
6. Describe instructional applications that are especially appropriate for field trips, displays, and dioramas.

Demonstrating Professional Skills

1. Generate two ideas for using learning centers in your own teaching. (ISTE NETS-T 2.A & 3.B)
2. Develop an instructional module for a topic and audience of your choice. (ISTE NETS-T 2.A & 3.B)
3. Obtain an example of a manipulative(s) that you could use for instruction. Submit the manipulative(s) and a description of how you would use it, including an objective. (ISTE NETS-T 2.C & 3.B)
4. Plan a lesson that would include a field trip (real or virtual). Locate at least one site on the World Wide Web that could be a place to visit as a virtual field trip in your lesson. (ISTE NETS-T 2.A).

Building My Professional Portfolio

- *Creating My Lesson.* Using the ASSURE model, design a lesson for a scenario from the table in Appendix A, or create a scenario of your own design. Use the information from this chapter related to learning centers, manipulatives, display surfaces, and exhibits. Be sure to include information about the audience, the objectives, and all other elements of the ASSURE model. Be certain to match your intended outcomes to state or national learning standards for your content area. (ISTE NETS-T 2.A & 2.B)

- *Enhancing My Lesson.* Using the lesson you've just designed above, consider your audience again. You might wish to consider that some of your students have special needs, such as physical or learning disabilities. You might also consider those students who are identified as gifted. How will you change your lesson design to ensure that these students are recognized and supported to allow them to succeed in your lesson? (ISTE NETS-T 2.B & 2.D)
- *Reflecting on My Lesson.* Reflect on the process you have used in the design of your lesson and your efforts at enhancing that lesson to meet student needs within your class. What have you learned about matching audience, content, instructional strategy, and materials? What can you have done to develop your students' higher-order thinking or creativity skills? In what ways did the materials you selected for your lesson enhance the learning opportunities for your students? (ISTE NETS 5.C)

SUGGESTED RESOURCES

Print

Alvarado, A. E., & Herr, P. R. (2003). *Inquiry-based learning using everyday objects: Hands-on instructional strategies that promote active learning in grades 3–8.* Thousand Oaks, CA: Sage.

Bender, W. N. (2005). *Differentiating instruction for students with learning disabilities: A multimedia kit for professional development.* Thousand Oaks, CA: Corwin Press.

Butzin, S. (2005). *Joyful classrooms in an age of accountability: The Project CHILD recipe for success.* Bloomington, IN: Phi Delta Kappa International.

Cambre, M., & Hawkes, M. (2004). *Toys, tools, & teachers: The challenges of technology.* Lanham, MD: Scarecrow Press.

Counts, E. L. (2003). *Multimedia design and production for students and teachers.* Boston: Allyn & Bacon.

Cummings, J. P., Sayers, D., & Brown, K. (2006). *Literacy, technology, and diversity: Teaching for success in changing times.* Boston: Allyn & Bacon.

Ivers, K. S., & Barron, A. E. (2006). *Multimedia projects in education: Designing, producing, and assessing* (3rd ed.). Westport, CT: Libraries Unlimited.

Karnes, F. A., & Bean, S. M. (2001). *Methods and materials for teaching the gifted.* Waco, TX: Prufrock.

Ruffin, M. F. (2009). *Designing and creating virtual field trips: A systematic approach with Microsoft PowerPoint 2007* (2nd ed.). Boston: Pearson Learning Solutions.

Stainfield, J., Fisher, P., Ford, B., & Solem, M. (2000). International virtual field trips: A new direction? *Journal of Geography in Higher Education, 24*(2), 255–262.

Web Links

To easily access these web links from your browser, go to the MyEducationKit for your text, then go to Chapter 11 and click on the web links.

Project CHILD

www.ifsi.org/projectchild

The Institute for School Innovation is the organization that developed Project CHILD. Refer to their website for more information about the research and developments related to the project.

Smart Boards

www.smarttech.com

Smart Technology is one of the companies that produces interactive whiteboards. They refer to their product as "Smart Boards."

Cincinnati Zoo

www.cincyzoo.org

The Cincinnati Zoo & Botanical Garden is dedicated to creating experiences that foster a sense of wonder, share knowledge, and advocate active involvement with wildlife and wild places. The Cincinnati Zoo & Botanical Garden is proud to offer programs for children and adults, school groups, and families.

Selection Rubric: MULTIMEDIA

 To download and complete this rubric for your own use, go to the MyEducationKit for your text, then go to Chapter 11 and click on Selection Rubrics.

Search Terms Used to Locate Resources

_____

_____

_____

Title _____

Source/Location _____

© Date _____ Cost _____ Length _____ minutes

Subject Area _____ Grade Level _____

Instructional Strategies _____

Format

_____ text

_____ audio

_____ still visual

_____ moving images

_____ real object(s)

_____ model(s)

Brief Description

Standards/Outcomes/Objectives

Prerequisites (e.g., prior knowledge, reading ability, vocabulary level)

Strengths

Limitations

Special Features

Name _____ Date _____

Rating Area	High Quality	Medium Quality	Low Quality
Alignment with Standards, Outcomes, and Objectives	Standards/outcomes/objectives addressed and use of media should enhance student learning.	Standards/outcomes/objectives partially addressed and use of media may enhance student learning.	Standards/outcomes/objectives not addressed and use of media will likely not enhance student learning.
Accurate and Current Information	Information is correct and does not contain material that is out of date.	Information is correct, but does contain material that is out of date.	Information is not correct and does contain material that is out of date.
Age-Appropriate Language	Language used is age appropriate and vocabulary is understandable.	Language used is nearly age appropriate and some vocabulary is above/below student age.	Language used is not age appropriate and vocabulary is clearly inappropriate for student age.
Interest Level and Engagement	Topic is presented so that students are likely to be interested and actively engaged in learning.	Topic is presented to interest students most of the time and engage most students in learning.	Topic is presented so as not to interest students and not engage them in learning.
Technical Quality	The material represents best available media.	The material represents media that are good quality, although there may be some problems using it.	The material represents media that are not well prepared and are of very poor quality.
Ease of Use (Student or Teacher)	Media are easy to use with nothing to confuse the user.	Media are easy to use most of the time, with a few things to confuse the user.	Media are not easy to use and most of the time the user is very confused.
Bias Free	There is no evidence of objectionable bias or advertising.	There is little evidence of bias or advertising.	There is much evidence of bias or advertising.
User Guide and Directions	The user guide is an excellent resource to support a lesson. Directions should help teachers and students use the media.	The user guide is good resource to support a lesson. Directions may help teachers and students use the media.	The user guide is poor resource to support a lesson. Directions do not help teachers and students use the media.
Variety of Media	Most students like the variety of media and are not confused.	Some students find the media interesting and some are confused.	Most students do not find the media interesting and many are confused.
Multisensory Experience	The media incorporate the appropriate number of senses to promote learning.	The media incorporate some senses to promote learning.	The media incorporate few of the senses to promote learning.

Recommended for Classroom Use: _____ Yes _____ No

Ideas for Classroom Use:

CHAPTER TWELVE

Preparing
for Tomorrow's Challenges

1. Describe how the ASSURE model supports 21st century learning as described in the National Education Technology Plan.

2. Discuss the characteristics of a 21st century teacher who is technologically competent, information literate, and committed to professional growth and engagement.

3. List ways that 21st century environments use technology for inclusion, to connect schools and homes, and to offer the choice of online education.

4. Describe the types of technology grants available for 21st century learning and briefly explain the basic components included when writing a grant proposal.

Goal

Understand factors influencing the advancement of 21st century teaching and learning

INTRODUCTION

Today's schools and teachers must continually advance 21st century learning as our society transitions to innovative digital tools for work, communication, and entertainment. This advancement can be supported with use of the ASSURE model and technology-focused professional development to guide teacher implementation of 21st century learning environments. Technology grants can assist schools in increasing student access to cutting-edge technology and media that build 21st century knowledge and skills.

THE ASSURE MODEL AND 21ST CENTURY LEARNING

The ASSURE model is structured to help teachers achieve 21st century classrooms. By following the step-by-step ASSURE model, teachers receive the support and guidance to develop, implement, evaluate, and revise lessons that integrate technology to increase student learning and prepare them for future careers. The ASSURE model directly supports the following learning goal in the National Educational Technology Plan (NETP) (US DOE, 2010):

> Goal: All learners will have engaging and empowering learning experiences both in and outside of school that prepare them to be active, creative, knowledgeable, and ethical participants in our globally networked society. (p. 9)

The first step in the ASSURE model, *Analyze learners*, asks teachers to identify the needs of all learners to better ensure that they have the resources and individualized support to participate in learning experiences. The next four steps help teachers to strategically plan technology integration lessons:

2. *State standards and objectives*
3. *Select strategies, technology, media, and materials*
4. *Utilize technology, media, and materials*
5. *Require learner participation*

These steps guide teachers in strategically planning and implementing learning experiences that align with key strategies in the NETP goal—engaging and empowering activities that encourage active, creative, and knowledgeable interaction.

The final ASSURE model step, *Evaluate and revise*, involves assessment of both student progress and the instructional process to determine what worked well and what needs to be revised before implementing the lesson again. Application of the ASSURE model enables 21st century teachers to continually engage students in activities that increase 21st century knowledge and skills and better prepare them for successful careers.

21ST CENTURY TEACHERS

The role of a teacher will always include the foundational responsibility of enabling students to learn. However, differences have been seen over time in *how* teachers accomplish this goal. The role of the 21st century teacher still is to improve student learning, but it requires the teacher to have broader capabilities than content knowledge, the ability to use pedagogy in the classroom, and basic computer skills. They also need to be technologically competent and information-literate.

TECHNOLOGICAL COMPETENCE

Teachers in the 21st century need to go beyond computer literacy to attain **technological competence** (Morrison & Lowther, 2010). This means not only knowing the basics of computer literacy, but more importantly, how and when to use technology to enhance student learning. For example, technologically competent teachers seamlessly integrate rich multimedia experiences into classroom activities that engage students in meaningful learning. To individualize instruction, teachers can base expectations on data collected from digital records of daily performance. For assessment, teachers can use digital tools such as e-portfolios that maintain PK–12 archives of student-created digital audio, video, and other documents in individual student portfolios.

INFORMATION LITERACY

Teachers in the 21st century require a high degree of capability with regard to **information literacy.** To prepare for a class, teachers need to locate materials from a variety of online sources and ensure the material is accurate, appropriate, easily accessible, and useable according to copyright guidelines. Teachers should model information literacy skills to their students by demonstrating the following skills:

- Accessing information
- Verifying data
- Appropriately acknowledging information sources
- Following copyright regulations

To keep students and parents informed of learning expectations and activities and regularly communicate with parents through email and discussion boards, 21st century teachers should develop and maintain a classroom website. They also need to exemplify a willingness to explore and discover new technological capabilities that enhance and expand learning experiences. This involves an openness to learn from and ask students for their thoughts about applying innovative technologies to examine and solve real-world problems—thus better preparing students to demonstrate these abilities in their future careers. Teachers should also regularly participate in opportunities to increase their experience in using technology and media for learning.

TECHNOLOGY-FOCUSED PROFESSIONAL DEVELOPMENT

As with any profession, long-term and consistent professional development is necessary for teachers to maintain proficiency and to have a positive impact on student learning. The same is true for teacher professional development focused on effective use of technology, which consists of six components (ISTE, 2009b) (see Figure 12.1):

1. Preservice technology training aligned to inservice expectations
2. Modeling of technology use by trainers and experienced teachers
3. Communities of practice

4. Professional engagement
5. School and district leadership in (and modeling of) technology use
6. Online learning (both the type and topic of professional development) (p. 8)

The National Educational Technology Standards for Teachers (NETS-T) describe classroom practices, lesson development, and professional expectations for 21st century teachers (ISTE, 2008). The content and activities of technology-focused professional development (PD) should address the NETS-T through face-to-face or virtual sessions in the following modalities:

- District or school-provided inservice vendor sessions
- Workshops or webinars at educational conferences
- Graduate coursework

Virtual PD also includes teacher communities of practice, in which teachers with common interests share best practices, solutions, and often join advocacy initiatives.

Figure **12.1**

Components of Professional Development for Effective Technology Use

ISTE's model for Professional Development for Effective Technology Use includes six components dependent on long-term, consistent professional development implementation.

Source: ISTE Policy Brief, "Technology and Teacher Quality—The Indelible Link," p. 9. Copyright 2009.

NETS-T 1: Facilitate and Inspire Student Learning and Creativity. Engage teachers in activities that demonstrate how new and innovative uses of technology and media can advance student learning and creativity in face-to-face and virtual environments. PD facilitators can achieve this goal by having teachers assume the role of students while they model a variety of ways to help, facilitate, and inspire learning during the hands-on activities. For example, teachers could create interactive digital posters that demonstrate content and skills to be learned by their students (see Figure 12.2).

NETS-T 2: Design and Develop Digital-Age Learning Experiences and Assessments. This standard requires teachers to participate in ongoing hands-on activities facilitated by technology coaches or similar PD staff. Teachers should design, develop, and evaluate authentic learning and assessment experiences that require students to use technology and media. The goals of the PD for teachers are to produce lessons that foster student achievement of learning objectives and to meet the NETS for Students standards of technology implementation.

Figure 12.2

Creating Interactive Digital Posters

The education version of Glogster provides online tools to create interactive digital posters that can include video, audio, hyperlinks, photos, text, images, and more.
Source: http://edu.glogster.com. Reprinted by permission.

NETS-T 3: Model Digital-Age Work and Learning. As mentioned, it is important for 21st century teachers to be competent users of technology and media. To achieve this goal, many teachers will require PD to help them gain the knowledge and skills to apply digital solutions for modeling digital-age work and learning processes needed in a global and digital society. PD topics can include how to create and maintain a class website, use social networking tools, participate in webinars, and apply digital tools to manage teacher responsibilities.

NETS-T 4: Promote and Model Digital Citizenship and Responsibility. For teachers to gain an understanding of the legal and ethical issues associated with digital citizenship, they need to be provided PD in which they study and practice applying copyright regulations, district acceptable use policies, and other general guidelines such as netiquette rules offered by many different sources. Within these areas it is critical to prepare teachers with knowledge and tools to address digital issues concerning their students, including Internet safety for students, such as never sharing personal information, and cyberbullying, which is student use of "the Internet, cell phones, or other devices to send or post text or images intended to hurt or embarrass another person" (National Crime Prevention Council, 2010).

NETS-T 5: Engage in Professional Growth and Leadership. It is important to provide teachers PD about how to become lifelong learners and how to serve as leaders in the effective use of technology by modeling these skills in their schools, districts, and community. Teachers can also be introduced to technology and media associations and journals as additional options for achieving professional growth and engagement.

PROFESSIONAL ENGAGEMENT

The 21st century is an exciting time for teachers as the opportunities to expand teaching and learning are becoming more and more pervasive in formal and informal education each year. Associated with this growth are the increasing numbers of professional organizations that support educators interested in application of technology and media to improve learning.

Professional Organizations. Whether your interest is in instructional technology and media in general or you intend to specialize in this area of education, it is important to be familiar with some of the major organizations dedicated to its advancement.

Association for Educational Communications and Technology (AECT). AECT (www.aect.org) is an international organization representing educational technology professionals working in schools, colleges, and universities, as well as the corporate, government, and military sectors. Its mission is to provide leadership in educational communications and technology by linking professionals holding a common interest in the use of educational technology and its application to the learning process. AECT has ten divisions designed around areas of special interest represented within the membership: design and development, distance learning, graduate student assembly, international, multimedia production, research and theory, school media and technology, systemic change, teacher education, and training and performance.

The association maintains an active publications program, including *Tech Trends* and *Educational Technology Research and Development,* both published six times during the academic year, as well as a large number of books and videos. AECT sponsors an annual conference that features over 300 educational sessions and workshops focusing on how teachers are using new technologies and teaching methods in the classroom. It also hosts a summer professional development conference and a biannual research symposium.

Association for the Advancement of Computing in Education (AACE). AACE (www.aace.org) is an international educational and professional organization dedicated to the advancement of the knowledge, theory, and quality of learning and teaching at all levels with information technology. AACE disseminates research and applications through publications and con-

ferences. Journals published by AACE include *Journal of Computers in Mathematics and Science Teaching (JCMST),* *Journal of Interactive Learning Research (JILR),* *Journal of Educational Multimedia and Hypermedia (JEMH),* *Journal of Technology and Teacher Education (JTATE),* *AACE Journal (AACEJ),* and *Contemporary Issues in Technology & Teacher Education (CITE).*

American Library Association (ALA). ALA (www.ala.org) is the largest library association in the world. Over 60,000 members represent all types of libraries—public, school, academic, state, and special libraries serving persons in government, commerce, the armed services, hospitals, prisons, and other institutions. The association has 11 divisions focusing on various types of libraries and services. The American Association of School Librarians (AASL), one of the divisions, holds national conferences focusing on the interests of school media specialists. AASL also publishes *School Library Media Research,* which presents research that pertains to the uses of technology for instructional and informational purposes. Special issues have dealt with such themes as communications, technology, and facility design for learning environments that require a great deal of technology.

Global SchoolNet Foundation (GSN). GSN (www.globalschoolnet.org) was founded by teachers with a mission to support 21st century learning through content-driven collaboration among teachers and students in order to improve the academic performance of our students. GSN brings together online youth from 194 countries to explore community, cultural, and scientific issues that prepare them for the workforce and help them to become responsible and literate global citizens. Global SchoolNet's free membership program provides project-based learning support materials, resources, activities, lessons, and special offers from its partners.

International Society for Technology in Education (ISTE). The mission of ISTE (www.iste.org) is to improve education through the use of technology in learning, teaching, and administration. ISTE members include teachers, administrators, computer coordinators, information resource managers, university faculty, and educational technology specialists. The organization maintains regional affiliate memberships to support and respond to grassroots efforts to

improve the educational use of technology. Its support services and materials for educators include books, courseware, conferences, and a variety of publications.

ISTE publishes *Learning and Leading with Technology,* *Journal of Research on Computing in Education,* *Journal of Digital Learning in Teacher Education, ISTE Daily Leader, ISTE Update,* books, and courseware packages. Of particular interest to teachers is *Leading and Learning with Technology,* which focuses on technology integration in PK–12 classrooms. Many of the articles are written by teachers, sharing what they have accomplished using computers in their classrooms with children of all ages and abilities.

The International Technology and Engineering Educators Association (ITEEA).

ITEEA (www.iteea.org) is the professional organization for technology, innovation, and  design in engineering education. Its mission is to promote technological literacy by supporting the teaching of technology and promoting the professionalism of those engaged in this pursuit. ITEEA strengthens the profession through leadership, professional development, membership services, publications, and classroom activities.

ITEEA publishes two peer-reviewed scholarly journals, *Technology and Engineering Teacher* and the *Journal of Technology Education*. Another journal is *Children's Technology and Engineering* (CTE), which is a useful, engaging tool for K–6 teachers interested in technological literacy. ITEEA also provide *Science, Technology, Engineering, and Mathematics (STEM) Connections,* a free online newsletter to keep teachers current on the latest STEM strategies and resources.

International Visual Literacy Association (IVLA).

IVLA (www.ivla.org) is dedicated to exploring the concept of visual literacy—how we use visuals for communication and how we interpret these visuals. It is particularly concerned with the development of instructional materials designed to foster skills in interpreting visuals. The organization draws its members from a variety of disciplines and professions, including public schools, higher education, business and communication, professional artists, production specialists, and design specialists.

United States Distance Learning Association (USDLA).

USDLA (www.usdla.org) promotes the development and application of distance learning for education and training.  The 20,000 members and sponsors represent PK–12 education, higher education, continuing education, corporate training, telemedicine, and military and government training. The association has become a leading source of information and recommendations for government agencies, the U.S. Congress, industry, and those involved in the development of distance learning programs. USDLA has chapters in all 50 states. It is a sponsor of annual USDLA National Conferences and provides a variety of online resources. In addition, USDLA holds regular meetings with leaders of distance learning programs in Australia, Europe, India, Japan, and the United Kingdom.

State Organizations. Several of the national professional organizations have state and/or local affiliates (AECT, ALA, ISTE, USDLA). By joining one or more of these, you will quickly make contact with nearby professionals who share your particular interests. As a teacher, you will want to be active in at least one local or state organization in addition to active participation in at least one national organization. If you are a full-time student, you can join many organizations at a reduced rate.

Professional Journals. As seen, a key contribution of professional organizations in instructional technology and media is to publish journals of interest to their members. Various other print and electronic periodicals are targeted to educators interested in using educational technology and media. Electronic journals are quickly becoming the journal of choice as they are "green" products that provide teachers with current information that includes interactive links to additional information. Examples of highly-respected journals are noted in the following list.

- *Educational Technology* has been the leading periodical for five decades and is read by educators in over 100 countries. The magazine addresses both teachers and educational technologists, providing articles on a range of topics, from theoretical to practical (www.asianvu.com/bookstoread/etp).

- *T.H.E. Journal* is dedicated to informing and educating PK–12 practitioners to improve and advance the learning process through the use of technology. It has over 90,000 subscribers to a variety of resources, including a monthly print and digital magazine, two websites, and five newsletters (http://thejournal.com).

- *eSchool News* in both print and online publication provides "Technology News for Today's K–20 Educator" covering education technology in all its aspects—from legislation and litigation to case studies and new products. The newspaper has over 300,000 subscribers and the website has over 500,000 unique visitors each month (www.eschoolnews.com).

- *Media and Methods* highlights new software and hardware to assist schools with purchase decisions (www.mediamethods.com).

- *Tech & Learning* (www.techlearning.com) provides district technology coordinators with practical resources and expert strategies for transforming education through integration of digital technologies. The magazine is also used as a professional development tool to help educators learn about the newest technologies and products in order to best prepare students for the global digital workforce.

Through regular reading of educational technology journals, teachers can expand their professional knowledge and growth by staying informed of new technology and media that have positive impacts on student learning. Teachers can use this knowledge and growth to better create and implement a variety of 21st century learning environments.

21ST CENTURY LEARNING ENVIRONMENTS

Going beyond the traditional classroom, which is dependent on the teacher and textbooks as the primary sources of information, 21st century learning environments expand into "global" classrooms that use technology for inclusion, connecting schools and homes, and offering the choice of online education.

THE GLOBAL CLASSROOM

Our world, through the use of a complex satellite system, is connected with an invisible digital network that truly makes today's classrooms global. Students now learn from a multitude of resources that range from textbooks to live videoconferences with people geographically separated by thousands of miles. Teachers use resources such as ePals LearningSpace (https://learningspace.epals.com), which has supported cross-cultural learning activities through connections among 600,000 teachers and their students in over 200 countries. Teachers can plan lessons with one or two teachers or engage their students in one of the many large interactive research projects involving children from around the globe. Sample projects include *Digital Storytelling, The Way We Are, Global Warming,* and *Maps* (see Figure 12.3).

The world is also opened to students through live, streamed video that

begins playing before the entire file is downloaded from the Web. Students can see live shots from the South Pole, the streets of Vienna, Kenya game reserves, the Eiffel Tower, the Bavarian Forest, Mt. Fuji, a cathedral in Florence, a city market in Hong Kong, or the Olivetti Research Laboratory at Cambridge.

Many of these sites have user controls on the cameras so students can freely explore the distant site from multiple viewpoints. By visiting different countries through live video, student awareness of differences in time is increased as the video may show the sun rising when it is afternoon in the student's classroom. Viewing the world "as it happens" opens student eyes to differences and similarities found in the world's cultures by seeing what people are wearing, driving, eating, and doing.

TECHNOLOGY FOR INCLUSION

In the midst of increased technology access in today's schools, there are still underserved students who experience "digital exclusion" due to disparities in socioeconomic status, ethnicity, geographic location, gender, primary language, and disabilities (Pew Internet & American Life Project, 2007). In particular, low-income and minority learners,

Figure 12.3

ePals Global Community

National Geographic's ePals Global Community provides resources to engage students in interactive projects, such as "The Way We Are," which include collaboration with students from around the world.
Source: www.epals.com/projects/info.aspx?DivID=TheWayWeAre_overview. Reprinted by permission.

English language learners, and learners with disabilities tend to have less access and use of technology in schools (US DOE, 2010). An ISTE report (Davis, Fuller, Jackson, Pittman, & Sweet, 2007) recommends five strategies to address "Digital Equity" challenges:

1. Legitimize the significant role culture plays in students' educational experience.
2. Continue to challenge perceptions about the role of technology in education.
3. Encourage others to recognize the critical link between technology professional development and classroom practice.
4. Create opportunities for students to access technology outside of the classroom.
5. Continue to seek funding for technology in spite of challenges (pp. 11–13).

Low-Income and Minority Learners. Because students from low-income and/or minority families often have limited access to technology at home as well as to others who regularly use technology, it is important to provide increased opportunities for these students at school. Time at the computer may need to be personalized and include extra remediation on computer skills to put these learners on a more equal footing with students who have home computers and access to family and friends who regularly use computers. Teachers may also want to encourage student participation in after-school and summer programs in which students use technology as a learning tool in community centers, libraries, churches, and so on (Gray, Thomas, & Lewis, 2010).

English Language Learners. Today's schools are faced with growing numbers of English language learners (ELL), English as a second language (ESL), or limited English proficient (LEP) students whose native languages can vary among a multitude of possibilities (National Clearinghouse for English Language Acquisition, 2010). Teachers of English language learners find that technology and media offer useful support and interventions. For example, software that provides audio narration of the content, such as certain tutorials, drill-and-practice, and word processing programs, help students learn correct pronunciation of English words as they read content from the computer screen. Mobile media players, such as iPods, also allow students access to audio recordings in English. Other digital tools that are useful for ELL students are social networking sites, which provide ELL students the opportunity to interact with others who not only speak their native language but also speak English. Teachers can use a combination of technology tools to meet the individualized needs of ELL students.

Learners with Disabilities. The Individuals with Disabilities Education Improvement Act (IDEA) (2004) and the No Child Left Behind (NCLB) (US DOE, 2002) legislation mandate that students with disabilities be taught to the same high standards as students without disabilities. In 2008, this impacted approximately seven million PK–12 students identified as having special needs (Institute of Educational Sciences, 2009).

Innovative advances in technology assist teachers to better meet the special needs of students with learning or physical disabilities. For example, teachers can use specialized software and digital tools to create, maintain, and report student individualized education programs (IEPs) for special needs learners as well as to provide overall special education management support. Iowa provides teachers with Electronic Filemaker IEP software (www.iowa-iep.net), whereas other states and school districts choose to use commercial IEP programs such as Case e special education case management solutions (www.msb-services.com/case-e). Special Education Automation Software (SEAS) provides another management option (www.computerautomation.com).

Advantages of using digital support tools for students with special needs include instant access to digital copies of all required forms. Digital forms use auto-fill capabilities to enter key student data, thus saving time and better ensuring accuracy of information. Teachers can generate and email current reports to parents and other staff. Research-based intervention strategies are readily accessible through digital databases. Records can be directly transferred to district, state, and federal reports. These advances increase the amount of time teachers have to work with and instruct students with special needs because they decrease the time needed for teachers to plan individualized instruction and fulfill compliance reporting requirements.

New technologies also increase teacher capability to adapt classrooms to accommodate learners with special needs. Learning stations can be specially equipped with **assistive technology,** or digital devices and software designed specifically for those with learning or physical disabilities. The assistive technology enables students to control the rate of speech delivery, augment the audio signal in the classroom, enlarge information on a computer screen so they can read the results of a database search better, use a voice synthesizer to have a printed page read to them, or take notes in class through an electronic storage device that will later print out the document in Braille. Some web pages accommodate these needs by offering user-selected graphic and text design options. Interestingly, it often happens that the techniques and alternatives that we use with special needs learners, such as providing handouts and notes for learners with hearing impairments and using audio recordings for learners with visual impairments, can improve the learning of *all* students.

TECHNOLOGY CONNECTS SCHOOLS AND HOMES

As computers become increasingly popular in today's homes, teachers have greater opportunities to communicate with students and parents. Many teachers maintain class websites that contain teacher contact information, calendars, assignment sheets, parent notices, links to Internet resources, and social networking tools to encourage ongoing communication. Class websites are often supported by a school or district server or by one of the free or inexpensive web hosting services, such as Wikispaces for educators (www.wikispaces.com/site/for/teachers) (see Free and Inexpensive Class Websites at the end of the chapter).

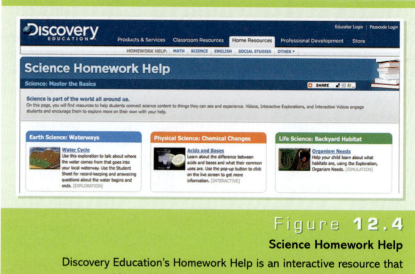

Figure 12.4
Science Homework Help

Discovery Education's Homework Help is an interactive resource that provides students with homework help in a variety of subjects.

Source: http://school.discoveryeducation.com/homeworkhelp/homework_help_home.html

Common links on teacher websites include basic skills practice, online demonstrations, or content-specific reference information. For example, PK–12 students can be directed to the National Library of Virtual Manipulatives for interactive math tools to solve homework problems for numbers and operations, algebra, geometry, measurement, data analysis, and probability (http://nlvm.usu.edu). The Internet also offers students help to complete their work. For example, over 10,000 students visit Discovery Education's Homework Help every day to research questions about their homework and to use the content area resources available on the website (see Figure 12.4).

Assistive technology extends the learning opportunities for students with disabilities.

Courtesy of Flaherty family and at4Learning

Through technology, parents stay informed about homework requirements.

Masterfile RF

Another useful site, Infoplease Homework Center, provides students access to resources categorized by subject area and skills (writing, research, speaking, listening, studying) (www.infoplease.com/homework). The site also has links to searchable references (almanacs, atlas, dictionary, encyclopedia, and biographies), tools (conversion calculator, distance calculator), practice tools (math flashcards, spelling bee), and links to current events by year.

With this increased communication between school and home, it is possible to lengthen the time devoted to learning. Technology permits teachers to send homework and assignments over networks to homes. Parents, students, and teachers are able to interact about the assignment. Students can access their personal data files from home and also connect to instructional materials housed on the school's computer. However, as mentioned, teachers who assign technology-based homework need to assist underserved students in finding alternative ways of accessing digital resources to ensure equitable learning opportunities.

THE CHOICE OF ONLINE EDUCATION

According to the 2010 International Association for K–12 Online Learning (iNACOL) "Fast Facts about Online Learning" report, there has been explosive growth of online learning opportunities in PK–12 environments. Specifically, in 2000, there were approximately 50,000 students enrolled in K–12 online education as compared to 320,000 in 2009 (iNACOL, 2010). Florida Virtual School (FLVS) has grown from being the first state-run Internet-based high school in 1997 to a nationally recognized e-learning model with over 71,000 students enrolled globally in 2009. FLVS reaches beyond Florida by providing customized eLearning Solutions for schools in approximately 40 countries. FLVS is the only public school whose state funding is tied directly to student performance (www.flvs.net). FLVS offers online students multiple resources such as a virtual library, information sessions, student clubs, Facebook updates, and a tour of an online course for new users. Typically, statewide programs are free of cost to residents and often target students in rural, high-poverty, or low-performing schools (see Figure 12.5).

Online courses are often provided on school campuses as a way for students to have access to computers with high-speed Internet access. Scholarships and computer donation programs assist students from low-income families who need to complete online courses at home.

Students of tomorrow will have multiple distance education opportunities because online learning bridges the gap of distance, poverty, and limited course offerings in small schools. However, Watson (2005) cautions educators to carefully examine their distance education programs to ensure that the benefits match those of public schools, especially with regard to ensuring equitable access to all students. States must recognize and support distance education initiatives with policies and funding if future programs are to be sustainable and of high quality.

Overall, 21st century learning environments provide new opportunities for teachers to expand student learning opportunities by creating "global classrooms." They also use technology and media to address the diverse needs of students, to improve communication with students and parents, and to explore online learning options to better meet the individual learning requirements of students.

Figure **12.5**

Virtual School Website

The Florida Virtual Schools website offers online students multiple resources such as a virtual library, information sessions, course tours, student clubs, and Facebook updates.

Source: www.flvs.net

TECHNOLOGY GRANTS FOR 21ST CENTURY LEARNING

Even though PK–12 access to technology is continually increasing, many teachers prefer to have a class set of computers rather than limiting student use to one or two days a week in the computer lab or bringing in a laptop cart. To solve this dilemma, districts, schools, and teachers apply for technology grants to provide hardware, software, and professional development to use the technology. Computers and other digital devices can also be acquired with grants focused on areas such as core content, social behavior improvement, and career training, if technology is integrated as a program component.

TYPES OF GRANTS

There are two basic types of technology grants: government grants funded at the federal, state, district, or school level and organization grants from businesses and corporations or nonprofit organizations such as foundations, groups, or associations.

Government Grants. The U.S. Department of Education's Office of Educational Technology and other departments offer several grant programs that are listed in the Federal Register of Education grants (http://www2.ed.gov/news/fedregister/announce/index.html). The grants range from statewide funding for longitudinal data systems to program-specific initiatives such as funding to improve the provision of assistive technology to individuals with disabilities. Of interest to districts, schools, and teachers are the "Enhancing Education Through Technology" or EETT grants, which are focused on improving elementary and secondary student achievement through the use of technology. Specifically, the EETT grant recipients are charged with meeting the following goals: (1) helping all students become technologically literate by the end of the eighth grade, (2) integrating technology into teacher training and core curriculum, and (3) establishing research-based instructional methods that can be widely implemented (US DOE Office of Educational Technology, 2010).

Government grants can provide substantial funding, but frequently require the submission of a lengthy, detailed proposal and budget; collaborative partnerships between districts, universities, and community organizations; and matching funds from the districts and partners. Thus, federal grants are normally awarded to districts or regions rather than to schools or teachers. However, the General Services Administration of the federal government sponsors the "Computers For Learning" (CFL) as a way to promote the reuse of government computers scheduled for replacement. The CFL program transfers excess computers and technology equipment to high-needs schools that complete the application and meet the program requirements (http://computersforlearning.gov).

Organization Grants. Grants from nongovernment organizations and foundations often involve a less extensive proposal process that is flexible enough to award funding to individual schools or teachers as well as to districts and collaborative partnerships. In addition, most schools can typically meet the requirements of grants sponsored by well-known organizations such as AT&T, Kellogg Foundation, and Cisco Systems Virtual Schoolhouse. However, please note that some grants have a very targeted focus. For example, the Lockheed Martin Corporation Philanthropy only funds K–16 science, technology, engineering, and math initiatives in schools located in communities where Lockheed Martin has employees.

Numerous websites provide lists of organizations that offer PK–12 technology grants. Examples include Top Teaching Resource (www.topteachingresources.com) and School-Grants (http://k12grants.org). The Fund$Raiser Cyberzone (www.fundsraiser.com) offers fundraising ideas, such as silent auctions, raffles, and donations. For further examples, see Free and Inexpensive Technology Grant Resources at the end of the chapter.

WRITING A GRANT PROPOSAL

Writing a successful grant proposal begins with a clear and structured process to describe how the funds will be used to achieve the overall purpose of the grant. It is critical to follow the specific guidelines in the Request for Proposal (RFP), as most proposals have a strict page limit and require information to be presented in a designated order. Many grants use an outline similar to the following:

- *Title page.* Select a title that is concise and clearly states the intent of the project. Avoid the use of clever or cute titles. Include the funder name and the names of the key people involved with the project.

- *Project Abstract.* Typically a one-page description of the project that includes overall goal/purpose, description of the project and how it will be implemented, who will benefit from the project, key staff, evaluation plans, overall costs, and timeline. Avoid overuse of academic jargon.

- *Statement of the Problem.* The intent of this section is to convince the funder that your proposed project will benefit students. Your argument should be supported with data and research. It is important to include data about your current situation by providing information such as the student-to-computer ratio and a description of student and teacher needs. For example, will the project focus on students who are from low-income families, who are English language learners, or who have special learning needs—including providing advanced studies for gifted students? Show how your project will use research-based approaches to guarantee successful outcomes.

- *Project Description.* The project description includes the goals and outcomes, target population, methods, project staff, and timeline.

  - Goals and Outcomes. Begin this section with clearly stated goals and measurable outcomes that will be achieved at the end of the project.
  - Target Population. Describe who will benefit from the project. Include descriptions of the students by grade level and subject areas that will be emphasized and the teacher(s) who will implement the project.
  - Methods. Provide clear and concise descriptions of the methods that will be used to implement the project. How and what type of technology will be provided to the targeted population? How will teachers be prepared? How will the project change classroom practices and learning opportunities?
  - Project Staff. Most grants designate the lead project staff as the Principal Investigator or PI and secondary lead staff as Co-PIs. So begin your list with the PI and Co-PIs and then list other key staff: professional development facilitators, technology coaches, and technical assistants. It is not necessary to list those who provide accounting or secretarial support. Include names and a brief description of qualifications for the assigned roles of every staff member.
  - Timeline. Use a timeline to depict when each major activity will take place and the staff responsible for the activity. A table works well to display the information by using the following columns: Date, Activity, and Person(s) Responsible. It is sometimes helpful to outline how the project will continue in the future to demonstrate how you plan to sustain the project beyond the grant-funded time period.

- *Resources.* Describe the available resources that will be used to support the project (e.g., facilities, personnel, and equipment: printers, projectors, interactive whiteboards, etc.). Then describe resources that will be purchased with project funds. Include a rationale for each purchase.

- *Evaluation Plan.* Provide a clear description of the methods and procedures for evaluating the degree to which the project goals and outcomes have been met. Describe which participants will be included in the evaluation, the evaluation instruments to be used, how the results will be analyzed, and how the findings will be shared.

- *Appendices.* The RFP typically limits the appendices to specific types of content and number of pages. Common information in an appendix includes detailed descriptions of professional development models, example student work, data collection instruments, and staff curriculum vitas.

One way to improve technology grant proposals is to review past proposals submitted by your school or district, which often have descriptions of your student population and local setting that can be adapted for your proposal. It is also useful to review proposals submitted by other schools and districts, such as those provided by SchoolGrants (www.k12grants.org/samples/samples_index.htm).

SUMMARY

This chapter discusses the need to advance 21st century learning in our schools and describes how the ASSURE model can help teachers reach this goal. Specifically, today's teachers must integrate innovative uses of technology and media to implement and enrich 21st century learning environments. Teachers need to continually engage in professional growth activities, such as technology-focused professional development and national and local educational technology organizations. It is also important for teachers to stay informed of current research and technology grant opportunities that may increase student access to digital devices and resources. These combined efforts will not only benefit student learning, but also benefit our society by better preparing students to successfully contribute to the 21st century workforce.

CONTINUING MY PROFESSIONAL DEVELOPMENT

Demonstrating Professional Knowledge

1. Describe how the ASSURE model supports 21st century learning as described in the National Education Technology Plan.

2. Discuss the characteristics of a 21st century teacher who is technologically competent, information literate, and committed to professional growth and engagement.

3. List ways that 21st century environments use technology for inclusion, to connect schools and homes, and to offer the choice of online education.

4. Describe the types of technology grants available for 21st century learning and briefly explain the basic components included when writing a grant proposal.

Demonstrating Professional Skills

1. Review ASSURE lesson plans that you have developed or other technology integration lessons and describe how each lesson aligns with the NETP goals for learning and in what ways the lesson can be modified to address goals not included in the lesson. (ISTE NETS-T 2.A & 2.C)

2. Conduct a self-reflection to assess the ways in which you demonstrate technological competence and other traits of a 21st century teacher. Address the following questions in your self-assessment: What are your strengths and weaknesses in how you use technology to support your teaching? What are the strengths and weaknesses of how your students use technology and media to improve learning? How could you address the weaknesses? (ISTE NETS-T 5.C)

3. Interview two or more teachers who integrate various types of technology and media into their instruction or select two or more MyEducationKit videos of teacher interviews to learn how the teachers create 21st century learning environments. In a three- to five-page paper, compare and contrast how each teacher uses technology for inclusion or to interact with parents and what their thoughts are about using online learning as a learning option. (ISTE NETS-T 5.C)

4. Analyze the technology needs of the school in which you work or would like to work and locate a grant that would help the school address the identified needs. Use the grant proposal outline to write a brief description of how you would write each section of the proposal. (ISTE NETS-T 5.B)

Building My Professional Portfolio

- *Enhancing My Portfolio.* Select a technology integration lesson from MyEducationKit, the Web, or one that you have developed. After citing the source of the lesson, analyze it according to topics discussed in this chapter. Specifically, take note how or if the lesson addresses 21st century learning by examining: (1) use of technology and media for inclusion (e.g., ELL students, learning disabled and/ or gifted students), (2) types of technology and media used to communicate outside the classroom, (3) types of technology skills required for the teacher and the

student, and (4) how the lesson could be improved if grant funding provided students greater access to technology. (ISTE NETS-T 4.B & 5.C)

- *Reflecting on My Learning.* Reflect on the need to advance to 21st century teaching, as described in this chapter, and write a description of how you think this need will impact your teaching. What do you think will be the most rewarding aspects of 21st century teaching and why do you think so? List what you think will be the most challenging aspects and explain why. (ISTE NETS-T 2.A & 5.C)

SUGGESTED RESOURCES

Print

Andio, L. (2006). An observatory for e-learning technology standards. *Advanced Technology for Learning, 3*(2), 99–108.

Orey, M., Jones, S., & Branch, R. M. (Eds). (2010). Graduate programs in educational technology. Educational Media and Technology Yearbook *(35)*. New York: Springer.

Powell, A. (2006). Online support for teacher community of practice. In C. Crawford et al. (Eds.), *Proceedings of Society for Information Technology and Teacher Education International Conference 2006, 2633–2638.* Chesapeake, VA: AACE.

Reiser, R. A., & Dempsey, J. V. (2011). *Trends and issues in instructional design and technology* (3rd ed.). Upper Saddle River, NJ: Merrill/Prentice Hall.

Schlager, M. S., & Fusco, J. (2004). Teacher professional development, technology, and communities of practice: Are we putting the cart before the horse? In S. Barab, R. Kling, and J. Gray (Eds.), *Designing virtual communities in the service of learning.* New York: Cambridge University Press.

Technology Grant News (2010). *Winning at IT: Grant writing for technology grants.* New York: Technology Grant News Publication.

Web Links

To easily access these web links from your browser, go to the MyEducationKit for your text, then go to Chapter 12 and click on the web links.

Discovery Education

http://education.discovery.com

Through its public service initiatives, products, and partnerships, Discovery Education reaches over 90,000 schools across the United States, serving 1.5 million teachers and their 35 million students each year. The site provides free lesson plans, *Kathy Schrock's Guide for Educators*, Teaching Tools, Curriculum Center, Brain Boosters, Clip Art, Puzzlemaker, Science Fair Central, Discovery Student Adventures, and more.

Edutopia

www.edutopia.org

Edutopia is a site supported by the George Lucas Educational Foundation (GLEF) that provides more than a hundred video segments of classroom practices and expert interviews, as well as free instructional modules that include articles, videos, blogs, PowerPoint presentations, discussion questions, and class activities. They draw from GLEF's archives of best practices and correlate with ISTE/NCATE NETS standards.

Eduscape

http://eduscapes.com

Eduscape, a site developed by Annette Lamb and Larry Johnson, includes multiple resources for teachers:

42eXplore—a weekly project section that contains multiple resources; Multimedia Seeds—ideas and resources to improve the use of multimedia; Teacher Tap—a professional development resource that helps teachers address common technology integration questions; and *Activate E-Journal*—a nonperiodic online publication with articles aimed at developing technology-rich learning environments.

National Center for Technology Innovation

www.nationaltechcenter.org

The National Center for Technology Innovation (NCTI), funded by the U.S. Office of Special Education Programs (OSEP), advances learning opportunities for individuals with disabilities by fostering technology innovation. The website provides resources and information to promote partnerships for the development of tools and applications by developers, manufacturers, producers, publishers, and researchers.

Study Guides and Strategies

www.studygs.net/index.htm

This is a public service site developed by Joseph Landsberger that provides study guides and strategies for multiple topics. Example topics are time management, problem solving, learning, learning with others, studying, classroom participation, online learning communication, thinking, memorizing, reading, research, project management, presenting projects, writing basics, taking tests, math, science and technology, and the teaching corner.

$ FREE & INEXPENSIVE
Class Websites

TeacherWeb

http://teacherWeb.com

A popular site that, for a nominal yearly fee, provides teachers a wide variety of tools to create an interactive class website. Sample tools include pages to post announcements, homework, links, teacher information, calendar, frequently asked questions, WebQuests, and teacher-created interactive tests.

Assign-A-Day

http://assignaday.4teachers.org

A free site hosted by 4Teachers that has an easy-to-personalize calendar for teachers to post homework assignments.

School Rack

www.schoolrack.com

An easy-to-use site that allows teachers to quickly set up a site that offers posting of digital files, assignments, parent notices, and more.

Class Homepage Builder

http://teacher.scholastic.com/homepagebuilder

This site provides tools for K–8 teachers to build a password-protected Class Homepage that offers space for recommending books, showcasing student work, communicating with parents, and archiving handouts. The site supports importing images and videos and the use of Google Calendar.

Funding Your Technology Dreams

www.cpsb.org/Scripts/abshire/grants.asp

Multiple listings of ongoing sources of technology grants, funding opportunities, and creative solutions to obtain technology resources for your class. The site also includes resources to help write grants.

Kathy Schrock's Grant Sources for Educators

http://school.discoveryeducation.com/schrockguide/business/grants.html

This site provides links to federal and foundation grant listings as well as tips for grant writing, how to locate grants on the Internet, and ideas for classrooms, schools, and districts to obtain technology funding.

SchoolGrants

www.schoolgrants.org

A variety of information and resources on grant writing, grant opportunities, and sample grant proposals. Also provided are newsletters and an index of links, including one for technology resources.

Foundation Center: Proposal Writing Short Course

http://foundationcenter.org/getstarted/tutorials/shortcourse/index.html

This short online course provides step-by-step guidance through the proposal writing process for grants funded by foundations and corporate donors.

Teacher Tap: Grants and Grant Writing

www.eduscapes.com/tap/topic94.htm

Professional development resources for teachers and librarians focused on grant resources starting points, exploring grant possibilities, getting started, identifying the need and your solution, goal setting, and writing a grant proposal.

Appendix A   Lesson Scenario Chart

Scenario	Content	Students	Goal
Mr. Wilson wants his preschool children to have a better understanding of the weather cycles.	Weather/Seasons	Preschool-aged children, 4–5 years old, with little instruction in weather patterns	At the end of the lesson, the children will have a general understanding of the seasons and the weather patterns associated with them.
Mrs. Harris plans to introduce the concept of simple addition to her K–1 class.	Mathematics	Students, 5–6 years old, with knowledge of number concepts.	At the end of the lesson, the students will be able to complete simple addition problems with sums less than 10.
Mr. Martinez wants to reinforce his students' understanding of prepositions.	Language Arts	Elementary students, 7–8 years old, who are building their vocabulary skills.	At the end of the lesson, students will be able to place graphics in the location specified in given prepositions.
Ms. Eller's class expresses interest in the states surrounding their own.	U.S. Geography	Students, 8–9 years old, with limited knowledge of the influence of geography on states' development.	At the end of the lesson, the students will be able to identify the geographic factors that influence the states' economic, social, and political histories.
Mr. Cheon wants to introduce his students to art forms made from natural stone.	Art	Upper elementary students, 9–10 years old, who have limited knowledge about using stone for artwork.	At the end of the lesson, the students will be able to identify several types of artwork that are created with natural stone.
Mr. James wants to introduce his students to the concept of life cycle by studying the life cycle of a frog.	Life Science	Students, 11–12 years old, with strong physical science and limited biological science background.	At the end of the lesson, the students will be able to identify the stages in the life cycle of the frog and be able to describe the relationships among the stages in the development of the frog.
Mr. Heller's class is interested in issues related to health, especially related to eating a balanced diet.	Nutrition	Middle school/junior high students, 13–14 years old, with knowledge of the Food Pyramid.	At the end of the lesson, the students will be able to select a balanced menu covering three meals per day for one week.
Ms. Galloway has decided to collaborate with the world history teacher's lesson on World War II by introducing her students to the literature of the period.	World Literature	High school, college-bound students, 16–17 years old, who have an interest in reading and exploring period literature.	At the end of the lesson, students will be able to discuss the relationship between international events during World War II and the literature produced in that period.
Mr. Wasileski's high school English class is ready to begin learning to write a research paper.	English Writing	High school students who have limited experience writing a research paper.	At the end of the lesson, students will be able to write a paper that includes appropriate use of references, following the pattern of introduction, research questions, analysis and discussion, and conclusions.

Appendix B Equipment Safety and Setups

INTRODUCTION

Most users of technology are not—and do not expect to become—electronic wizards, but they want to be able to use the equipment safely and effectively. The most fundamental elements of effective technology use are simply getting the equipment properly set up, keeping it running, and being ready to cope with "glitches," which always seem to occur at the most inopportune times. This appendix provides guidelines for safe care, proper setup, and handling of media equipment and computer hardware.

EQUIPMENT SAFETY

Safety is the paramount concern whenever teachers and students are using technology. Accidents involving heavy pieces of equipment can be serious, even fatal. The U.S. Consumer Product Safety Commission has noted deaths of children and serious injuries resulting from top-heavy projection carts that tipped over, dumping a heavy object onto the child. The carts often had a TV monitor on the top shelf. Particularly hazardous are carts over 50 inches (127 centimeters) high. With the number of TV monitors being used in schools, this hazard is a concern.

MOVING AND LIFTING

All educators must be aware of their responsibility—and legal liability—regarding students' exposure to hazardous conditions. The operating rule should be to *NEVER allow children to move carts with heavy equipment on them.*

Adults, too, can sustain injuries from mishandling equipment. Many back injuries occur when people attempt to lift heavy objects by simply bending over, grasping the object, and pulling directly upward. This puts a strain on the lower back. The recommended procedure is to bend at the hips and knees, and lift upward with the *legs* providing upward spring, as shown in Figure B.1.

CARTS

Carts come in many different sizes and shapes for different types of equipment. Carts are designed both for inside-only use and inside/outside use. You take a great risk in moving equipment outside the building on a cart designed for inside-only use. The small wheels can catch in cracks in the pavement and cause the cart to tip over. For this reason, even for exclusive indoor use it is wise to purchase carts with 5-inch wheels.

Figure **B.1**
Lifting Equipment
The wrong way (left) and the correct way (right) to pick up heavy equipment.

Manufacturers normally offer power outlet cord assemblies for their carts. These are worthwhile investments. You plug your equipment into the outlet on the cart and the cord on the cart into the wall outlet. If someone should trip over the power cord, the cart moves and the computer, projector, or monitor does not crash to the floor. In addition, the cord on the cart is considerably longer than the typical power cord furnished with the equipment. You can lay the longer cord on the floor along the wall, thereby reducing the risk that someone will trip over it.

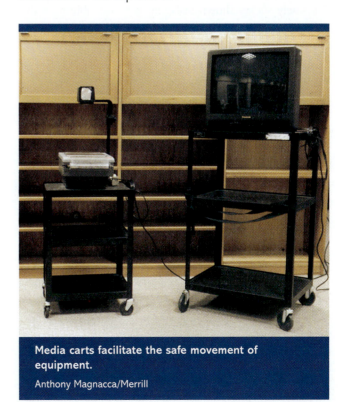

Media carts facilitate the safe movement of equipment.
Anthony Magnacca/Merrill

To minimize the number of people stepping over the power cords, use extension cords so that the power cords can run along the wall to the outlet rather than across the center of the room. Any cord that lies where someone might trip over it should do so only temporarily, and you should firmly tape it down during that time.

With laptops, projectors, document cameras, television monitors, and media players affixed to movable carts, moving equipment from classroom to classroom is much easier. Carts help to organize and transport equipment. They also provide easy storage for equipment. They can be pushed to a locked room for security when not in use.

Schools equip the carts to meet the needs of their students. Specialized carts are available for videoconferencing, presentation hardware, or classroom laptops. To use equipment on a cart, the teacher simply plugs it into an ordinary electrical outlet and into the computer network, if necessary. Many schools have instructional technology staff to visit classrooms and help students and teachers if they experience problems.

EXTENSION CORDS

Extension cords are made to serve different purposes—indoor and outdoor, higher and lower power capacity. Whenever using an extension cord, be sure that you are not exceeding its power capacity. If in doubt, consult a media specialist.

All educators must recognize their special responsibility to serve as role models for safe practices when using technology. They have to know and follow good safety habits. The safety sticker shown in Figure B.2, available from the International Communications Industries Association (ICIA), should be on all media carts.

CARE AND HANDLING OF EQUIPMENT

The proper care and handling of all media equipment is very important. Damage from mishandling can be very expensive to repair.

DIGITAL PROJECTORS

Television monitors are well suited to individual or small-group viewing, but large groups require multiple monitors for adequate viewing. Playing a video recording also requires wires to connect the video player to each of the monitors. A better option in such cases is the digital projector. In addition to being used for showing video images, they can also be used for showing computer data, text, and graphics.

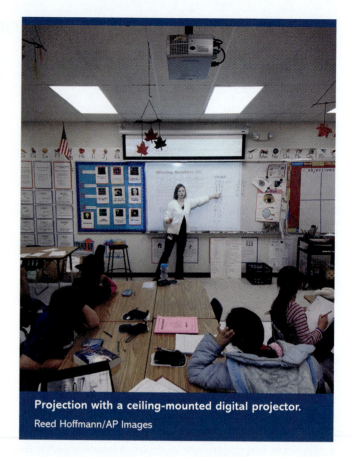

Projection with a ceiling-mounted digital projector.
Reed Hoffmann/AP Images

Digital projectors can project an image large enough to fill a variety of screen sizes from small classroom screens to larger-than-life models used in auditoriums. Units may be permanently mounted at ceiling level or placed on low carts for larger screens. Observe the following rules of thumb for optimal viewing:

- Watch in dim light, not darkness. Turn off the lights over the screen, if possible.
- Seat audiences as close as possible to the centerline of the screen.
- Make sure that all can see the image clearly.
- Place projector on "stand-by" when not in use for short periods to extend the life of the expensive projector bulb.

OVERHEAD PROJECTORS

The overhead projector, still found in most schools, is a simple piece of equipment with few components. Reliable as it is, however, you should not take it for granted. Rather, take a few basic precautions to ensure that the projector keeps putting on a bright performance.

Keep the overhead projector as clean as possible. The horizontal glass, called the stage, tends to gather dust, fingerprint smudges, and marking-pen traces. Clean it regularly with spray window cleaner or a mild solution of soap and water. The lens in the head (or top) assembly should also be kept free of dust and smudges. Clean it periodically with lens tissue and

FOR YOUR SAFETY

Only adults should move this unit

Apply moving force on narrow dimension

Never apply force at top—always push near middle

Push, don't pull

GUIDE FOR EQUIPMENT SAFETY AND SETUPS

Safely Moving and Using Audiovisual Equipment

Loading Projection Carts

- *Prohibit children from moving carts.* Only adults should be allowed to move loaded carts. A safety sticker showing the ICIA warning (shown above) should be placed on all carts.
- *Lock casters.* Be sure to engage caster locks before loading a cart.
- *Unplug cords.* Disconnect all power cords from wall outlets and wrap them around the equipment.
- *Use lower shelves.* Place equipment on the lower shelves before moving. Disconnect VCR from TV monitor before moving units to lower shelves.

Moving Projection Carts

- *Unlock casters.* Disengage all caster locks before moving the cart.
- *Push, don't pull.* Always push the cart, applying force on the narrow dimension, and watch where you're going. Never pull the cart.
- *Elevator angle.* When entering or leaving an elevator, push the cart at an angle so that one caster at a time passes over the gap between building and elevator.
- *Strap for ramp.* If a cart is to be moved up or down a ramp, use a strap to secure equipment to the cart.

Using Equipment

- *Lock casters.* Engage the caster locks as soon as the projection cart is in place.
- *Center on shelf.* Make sure equipment is centered on the cart shelf, with nothing protruding over the edge.
- *Check power cords.* Inspect for frayed cords and loose plugs. When unplugging, pull the plug, not the cord.
  - Secure cords.
  - Keep power and speaker cords out of traffic lanes; leave a lot of slack.
  - Wrap the power cord around the bottom of a leg of the cart so that if someone does trip on the cord, the cart (not the equipment) is pulled.
  - Use duct tape to cover cords that could be a tripping hazard.

Figure B.2

Safety Sticker and Equipment Guidelines

This safety sticker, available from the International Communications Industries Association (ICIA), should be on all carts.
Source: Adapted from guidelines provided by the International Communications Industries Association (ICIA). Additional information, including safety warning stickers for carts, is available from ICIA, 3150 Spring Street, Fairfax, VA 22031.

a proper lens-cleaning solution. The Fresnel lens under the stage may also need cleaning eventually, but this procedure is better left to the technology or media specialist. The lens is a precision optical element requiring special care. In addition, some disassembly of the unit is required to get to the lens.

The best way to prolong the life of the expensive lamp in the overhead projector is to allow it to cool before moving the projector. Move the projector with care. Keep it on a cart that you can roll from one location to another. When moving the equipment, hold onto the body of the projector, not the thin arm of the head assembly. The head assembly arm is not intended to be a carrying handle; used as such, it can easily be twisted out of alignment, thus distorting the projector's image.

PROJECTOR SETUPS

The proper setup of screens and projectors is very important in the use of projected media. We have all been distracted by the distorted or off-screen images of a misaligned screen and projector.

SCREEN ALIGNMENT

The first requirement in projector placement is to align the projection lens perpendicular to the screen (i.e., it must make a 90-degree angle with the screen). Thus, the lens of the projector should be about level with the middle of the screen. If the projector is too high, too low, or off to either side, a distortion of the image will occur, referred to as the **keystone effect** (see Figure B.3). The effect takes its name from the typical shape of a keystoned image—wide at the top, narrower at the bottom, like a keystone. To remedy this situation, move either the projector or the screen to bring the two into a perpendicular relationship.

The keystone effect is especially prevalent with the overhead projector because it is ordinarily set up very close to the screen and lower than the center of the screen to allow the instructor to write on its stage.

Figure **B.3**

The Keystone Effect

The "keystone effect" describes a projected image that resembles the architectural keystone, the wedge-shaped stone at the top of a rounded arch that locks its parts together.

PROJECTOR DISTANCE

Once you have properly aligned the projector and screen, consider the distance between them. If the distance is too long, the image may spill over the edges of a given screen. If it is too short, the image will not fill the same screen properly. Your goal is to fill the screen as fully as possible with the brightest image attainable. The principle to remember here is that the image becomes larger and less brilliant with an increase in distance between the projector and screen. Follow these simple rules of thumb:

- If the projected image is *too large* for your screen, push the projector closer.
- If the image is *too small,* pull the projector back.

LAMPS

When handling a lamp, *never* touch the clear glass bulb. The oil from your fingers can shorten the life of the lamp. Always manipulate the lamp by its base. Incandescent lamps and tungsten halogen lamps (without exterior reflector) are supplied with a piece of foam or paper around the lamp. Use this material or a cloth to hold the lamp when inserting it into the projector.

When removing a burned-out lamp, wait until the lamp has cooled to prevent burning your fingers. It is wise to always use a cloth when removing a lamp. Even a lamp that burns out when the projector is first turned on will be hot enough to burn you.

Lamps for equipment are expensive. They usually cost about 20 times the cost of a household light bulb. To increase lamp life, turn off projectors when not using them. If the projector offers a low lamp setting, use it if possible to increase the life of the lamp. Try not to jar a projector when the lamp is on, as this can cause a premature burnout of the lamp. You should *not* leave the fan on for cooling after use unless the projector is going to be moved immediately, as this also will shorten the life of the bulb.

SCREENS

Arranging a proper environment for viewing projected visuals involves screen size and placement. For everyday teaching situations your classroom will often be equipped with a screen of a certain type attached in a fixed position.

A rule of thumb for the relationship between screen size and viewer seating is called the *two-by-six rule:* No viewer should be seated closer to the screen than *two* screen widths or farther away than *six* screen widths.

This means that in the case where the farthest viewer could be 30 feet from the front of the room, a screen about

5 feet wide (60 inches) would be required to ensure that this farthest-away viewer is within six screen widths of the screen ($30 \div 6 = 5$). A square screen is generally preferable because you can use it to show rectangular images (digital projectors) as well as square images (overhead projectors). Thus, in this case a screen measuring 60 by 60 inches is recommended (see Figure B.4).

In most cases placement of the screen centered in the front of the room will be satisfactory. In some cases, however, it may not be. Perhaps light from a window that you cannot fully cover will wash out the projected image (sunlight is much brighter than any artificial light), or maybe you wish to use the board during your presentation and a screen position in the center front will make it difficult or impossible for you to do so. Also, the screen should not be at center stage if it will attract unwanted attention while nonprojection activities are going on. An alternative position is in a front corner of the room. In any case, nowhere is it written in stone that the screen must be placed front and center. Position your portable screen wherever it will best suit your purpose.

In general, adjust the height of the screen so that the bottom of the screen is about level with the heads of the seated

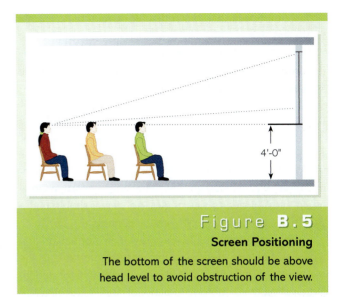

Figure B.5
Screen Positioning
The bottom of the screen should be above head level to avoid obstruction of the view.

viewers. The bottom of the screen should be at least 4 feet above the floor to prevent excessive head interference (see Figure B.5). Other inhibiting factors aside, this arrangement will allow reasonably clear sight lines for the most viewers. In general, the higher the screen is placed, the greater is the optimal viewing area. Of course, you must take care that viewers can see the screen without uncomfortably straining their necks.

VIDEO SETUPS

Before students can learn from any material presented on a video screen or monitor, they first have to be able to see and hear it! This means providing proper seating arrangements, placement of the monitor, lighting, and volume control.

For group showings, an ideal seating arrangement may sometimes be difficult to achieve. In some cases there are simply not enough monitors available to seat all students in the most desirable viewing area. It may be possible to have students move closer together to get more people into the desirable viewing area. Try to stagger the seats to reduce blocked sight lines.

The following are some basic rules of thumb for seating:

- The total number of viewers should be no more than the number of inches of screen size. For example, for a 23-inch monitor, the largest number of viewers would be 23.
- Seat no one closer than twice the *inches* of screen size. For example, for a 23-inch monitor, the closest viewer would be 46 inches (or about four feet) from the screen.

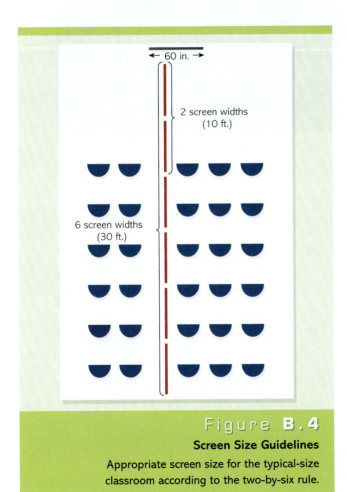

Figure B.4
Screen Size Guidelines
Appropriate screen size for the typical-size classroom according to the two-by-six rule.

- Seat no one farther *in feet* than the size of the screen in inches. For example, for a 23-inch monitor, the farthest viewer would be 23 feet away. The maximum viewing distance would be much smaller if the video included details that were critical to learning.

In addition to distance from the screen, you must consider viewing angles—both up and down and side to side. As shown in Figure B.6, the monitor placement should require no more than 30 degrees of head tilt. In general, a 54-inch-high monitor provides a good viewing angle for group viewing. In terms of side-to-side angles, no viewer should be located more than 45 degrees from the centerline.

Video monitors should be viewed in normal or dim light, not darkness. Besides being more comfortable to the eye, normal illumination provides necessary light for student participation (e.g., referring to handouts and taking notes).

Locate the monitor so that harsh light from a window or light fixture does not strike the screen and cause glare. Do not place the monitor in front of an unshaded window that will compete with light from the television screen and make viewing difficult.

The rules of thumb for lighting conditions for video monitors are as follows:

- View in normal or dim light.
- Avoid direct light on the screen, causing glare.
- Avoid sunlight behind monitor.

For proper loudness levels, set the volume of the monitor loud enough to be heard clearly in the rear of the viewing area but not so loud that it "deafens" those in the front. Normally this happy middle ground is not difficult to achieve if your seating arrangement is within acceptable bounds and your monitor's speaker mechanism is functioning properly.

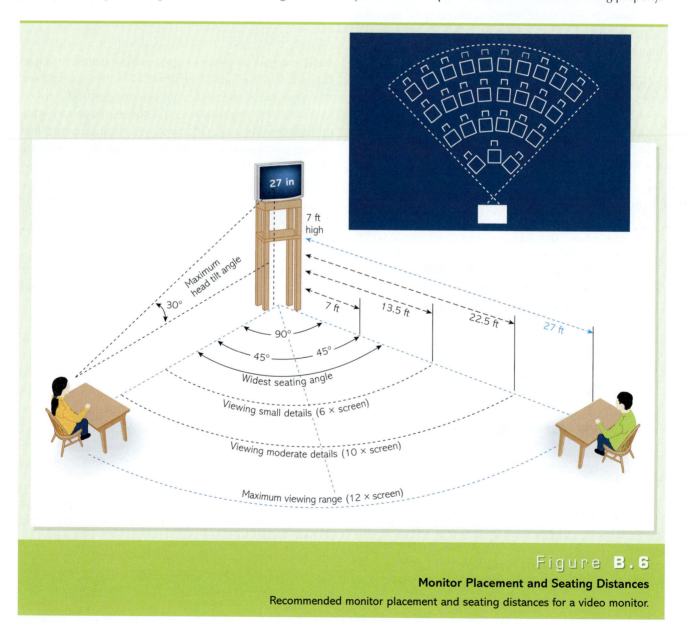

Figure **B.6**

Monitor Placement and Seating Distances

Recommended monitor placement and seating distances for a video monitor.

AUDIO SETUPS

Just as proper projector setups are important for the use of video materials, audio setups are equally important for learning. If students cannot hear the content, they cannot learn from it!

SPEAKER PLACEMENT

Most audiovisual equipment intended for use in educational settings comes equipped with a built-in speaker system. This type of unit is suitable for many but not all instructional purposes. Playing a CD or DVD on a portable player or a video on a computer is particularly troublesome when used in an average-size classroom. Even under the best conditions, the sound quality of portable players is severely limited by their undersized speakers. If you use such a unit to play back material in which audio fidelity is essential (e.g., a musical composition), use an auxiliary speaker if possible. You may be able to plug a high-efficiency speaker—for instance, one having a six- or eight-inch diameter—into the external speaker or earphone jack of the player to provide better fidelity.

Another problem with built-in speakers is that they are often built into the side of the machine containing the controls. This is fine when the operator of the equipment is also the listener. But if the apparatus is placed on a table or desk and operated by an instructor for the benefit of an audience, the speaker will be aimed away from the audience. The simple remedy for this situation is to turn the machine around so that the speaker faces the audience and operates the controls from the side of the machine.

Be sure nothing obstructs the sound waves as they travel from the speaker toward your audience. Classroom furniture (e.g., desks, chairs) and the audience itself may present physical obstructions to sound. To avoid such interference, place the speaker on a table or some other kind of stand so that it is at or above the head level of your seated audience.

If you are using multiple speakers for stereo or surround sound playback from CDs, DVDs, iPods, or other MP3 devices, the left and right speakers should be far enough apart so that the sound is appropriately balanced between the two. Typically the distance between the speakers should equal the distance from each speaker to the middle of the audience. Thus, in the average 22-by-30-foot classroom, place stereo speakers about 15 feet apart, or nearly in the corners of the room.

The rules of thumb for speaker placement can be summarized as follows:

- Face speaker toward the center of the audience.
- Raise speaker to head level of seated audience.

MICROPHONE HANDLING AND PLACEMENT

Microphones should be placed at least six inches (15 centimeters) from the presenter's mouth. Placed closer to the mouth, the microphone is likely to pick up "pops" and "hisses" when the presenter says words with plosive or sibilant sounds. As shown in the accompanying photos, you should place the microphone below the mouth so that the presenter

A handheld microphone should be held at a 45-degree angle and below the mouth.

Michael Littlejohn/Prentice Hall

Clip a lavaliere microphone to the presenter's clothing below the mouth.

Sharon Smaldino

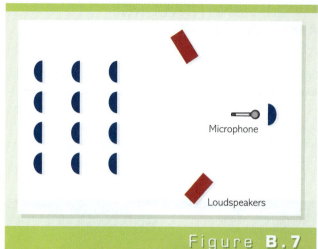

Figure B.7

Microphone Placement

To avoid feedback, keep the microphone behind the speakers.

LISTENING CENTERS

Many classrooms, especially at the elementary level, are arranged in a more open form with flexible furnishings to allow diverse yet simultaneous activities. In such a classroom, learning centers are a common format for learning. One popular type of learning center is a listening center, an area especially arranged for audio media. Listening centers can be set up to accommodate either an individual student or a small group.

You should situate a listening center away from noisy areas or at least partially enclose it to reduce visual and auditory distractions. If intended for an individual, you can probably equip it with an audio player having a headset. For a small group, the listening center would typically contain an audio player and should be equipped with a multiple headset device.

talks across it rather than into it. The rule of thumb for microphone placement, then, is to place the microphone *below* and at least six inches *away from* the mouth.

Feedback is that annoying squeal that sometimes intrudes when using public address systems. The usual cause is simple: the signal coming out of the loudspeaker is fed back into the microphone. The most direct remedy is to make sure to set up the speakers in front of the microphone, as shown in Figure B.7.

If you experience feedback, try the following solutions:

- Place the microphone behind the speaker(s) or move the speaker(s) in front of the microphone.
- If neither step is possible, adjust the volume and tone controls to reduce the interference.

A quiet corner of a classroom may be set aside as a listening center.

Scott Cunningham/Merrill

Selection Rubric: AUDIOVISUAL EQUIPMENT

Type _____   Price _____

Manufacturer _____   Model _____

Audio

Speaker Size _____   Amplifier Output _____

Inputs _____   Outputs _____

_____

Sound Controls _____   Audio Format _____

_____

Other Features _____

Projector

Lamp _____ Wattage _____   Exciter Lamp _____

Power Controls _____   Lamp Level Control _____

_____

Lens _____

Additional Features _____

Strengths _____

Limitations _____

Recommended for Classroom Use: _____ Yes _____ No

Name _____   Date _____

Rating Area	High Quality	Medium Quality	Low Quality
Sound Quality	Clear and distinct with excellent range of volume and tone	Some distortion, but good range of volume and tone	Static and distortion in range of volume and tone
Picture Quality	Clear and distinct image with excellent color and resolution	Some distortion to image, but acceptable color and resolution	Blurred image with color distortion and poor resolution
Ease of Operation	Easy to use without referring to manual	Use is fairly obvious, requiring some referral to manual	Difficult to use, requiring frequent referral to manual
Price Range	Excellent value per dollar spent compared to other models	Fair value per dollar spent compared to other models	Poor value per dollar spent compared to other models
Durability	Appears very durable; other users report high dependability	Questionable durability; other users report moderate dependability	Does not appear durable; other users report low dependability
Ease to Maintain	Low-level maintenance; very little servicing required	Medium-level maintenance; some servicing required	High-level maintenance; frequent servicing required
Ease to Repair	Parts easily accessible and replacement parts readily available	Parts fairly accessible and replacement parts somewhat available	Parts difficult to access and replacement parts not readily available

Selection Rubric: COMPUTER HARDWARE

Manufacturer _____

Model _____

Monitor _____ Graphics _____

Sound _____ Memory _____ Expandable _____ Hard Drive _____

Peripherals _____

Other Features _____

Strong Points _____

Weak Points _____

Recommended Action _____

Name _____ Date _____

Rating Area	High Quality	Medium Quality	Low Quality
Ease of Operation	Easy to use without referring to manual/help screens	Use is fairly obvious, requiring some referral to manual/help screens	Difficult to use without referring frequently to manual/help screens
Durability and Reliability	Appears very durable; other users report high dependability and reliability	Questionable durability; other users report some problems	Does not appear durable; other users report low dependability and reliability
Availability of Software	Can utilize most of the software that is currently available and will be purchased	Can utilize some of the software that is currently available and will be purchased	Cannot utilize most of the software that is currently available and will be purchased
Display Quality	Image resolution is clear and crisp; colors are accurate; moving images display with little or no jerkiness or distortion	Image resolution is mostly clear and crisp; colors are reasonably accurate; moving images display with minimal jerkiness or distortion	Image resolution is not clear and crisp; colors are not accurate; moving images display with jerkiness or distortion
Keyboard Layout and Touch	Size of keyboard and location of keys appropriate for intended users	Keyboard useable by intended users, but "feel" is not the best	Size of keyboard too large or too small for intended users
Compatibility	Compatible with previously purchased hardware and peripherals	Some compatibility problems with purchased hardware and peripherals	Not compatible with previously purchased hardware and peripherals
Expandability	Can be upgraded to meet future needs; has ports and slots for expansion	Allows for some upgrade to meet future needs; has some ports and slots for expansion	Cannot be upgraded to meet future needs; has few ports and slots for expansion
Documentation	User's manual and help screens easy to understand; includes index and table of contents	User's manual and help screens lack completeness; includes limited index and table of contents	Confusing user's manual and help screens; lacks good index and table of contents
Service	Vendor support and maintenance readily available; service is quick and dependable	Vendor support and maintenance is available, but takes time and is not always dependable	Vendor support and maintenance is lacking; service is slow and undependable

Glossary

A

Acceptable Use Policy (AUP) An agreement among students, parents/guardians, and school administrators regarding appropriate use of the Internet.

Acetate A transparent plastic sheet associated with overhead projection.

Advance organizer An outline, preview, or other such preinstructional cue used to promote retention of verbal material, as proposed by David Ausubel. Also known as *preinstructional strategies.*

Affective domain The domain of human learning that involves changes in interests, attitudes, and values and the development of appreciation.

Alt-tag Alternative textual descriptions to provide brief descriptions of graphics or images.

Analogical visuals Visuals that convey a concept or topic by showing something else and implying a similarity.

Analogous colors Any two colors that lie next to one another on the color wheel. Contrasted with complementary colors.

Animation A technique in which the artist gives motion to still images by creating and juxtaposing a series of pictures with small, incremental changes from one to the next.

Applications Games, simulations, tutorials, problem-solving programs, productivity software, and graphic software programs.

Arrangement The overall look or pattern of a visual.

Assistive technology Devices and software designed specifically for those with learning or physical disabilities.

Asynchronous Not at the same time.

Audio literacy Understanding the role of hearing and listening in learning.

Audio teleconference A teleconference involving transmission of voices only. The voices are amplified at each end by a speaker system.

Auditory fatigue The process by which attention to a sound gradually decreases because of the monotony of the sound.

Augmented reality (AR) Combining real-world data with virtual data.

Authentic assessment Evaluation that is usually performance based and that requires students to demonstrate their learning in a natural context.

B

Balance A psychological sense of equilibrium.

Behaviorism A theory that equates learning with changes in observable behavior; with this theory, there is no speculating about mental events that may mediate learning.

Bit An acronym for binary digit; the smallest unit of digital information. The bit can be thought of as a 1 or a 0 representing a circuit on or off, respectively.

Blended instruction A combination of e-learning with live, face-to-face instruction.

Blog Web log serving as a publicly accessible personal journal for an individual.

Bridge An electronic system that joins telephone calls from all participating locations in an audio teleconference, equalizes the sound levels, filters out extraneous noises, and takes care of disconnections.

Bulletin board Computer system used as an information source and message posting system for a particular interest group.

Byte The number of bits required to store or represent one character of text (a letter or number); most commonly, but not always, made up of eight bits in various combinations of 0s and 1s.

C

Cable modem A television cable connection that provides very high-speed access to the Internet.

Cartoon Line drawing that is a rough caricature of real or fictional people, animals, or events.

Central processing unit (CPU) The core element of a computer that carries out all the calculations and controls the total system.

Chart Visual representation of abstract relationships.

Clip art Prepared visual images (drawings and digital pictures) that can be inserted into digital documents and presentations.

Cloth board A display surface made of fabric for temporarily adhering materials with cloth or sandpaper backing.

Cloud computing System in which applications are available through networked computers to distribute greater access to processing power and applications.

Cognitive domain The domain of human learning involving intellectual skills, such as assimilation of information or knowledge.

Cognitivism A theory according to which mental processes mediate learning and learning entails the construction or reshaping of mental schemata.

Collaborative A sharing or cooperative nature of an experience.

Community of practice A group of educators from across the nation and around the world who have common goals and share ideas and resources.

Complementary colors Any two colors that lie directly opposite one another on the color wheel. Contrasted with analogous colors.

Compressed video Video images that have been processed to remove redundant information, thereby reducing the amount of bandwidth required to transmit them. Because only changes in the image are transmitted, movements appear jerky compared with full-motion video.

Computer-assisted instruction (CAI) Instruction delivered directly to learners by allowing them to interact with lessons programmed into the computer system.

Computer conferencing Connecting two or more computers together for textual and/or graphical information exchange.

Computer laboratory A room set apart from regular classrooms and furnished with multiple computers, usually established in schools that do not have computers in individual classrooms.

Computer-managed instruction (CMI) The use of a computer system to manage information about learner performance and learning resources and to then prescribe and control individual lessons.

Computer platform Different types of computer operating systems, such as Mac OS, Unix, or Windows.

Consistency Characteristic of a series of visuals that have a similar arrangement of elements.

Constructivism A theory that considers the engagement of students in meaningful experiences as the essence of learning.

Cooperative learning An instructional configuration involving small groups of learners working together on learning tasks rather than competing as individuals.

Copyright Regulations that describe the manner in which an original work can be used and copied. Copyright laws regulate the manner in which authors or artists can be reimbursed for their creative work.

Course Management Tool (CMT) Software designed to make it easier for teachers to use resources in the distance learning system, such as the discussion board, test options, and grade book.

Courseware Lessons delivered via computer, consisting of content conveyed according to an instructional design controlled by programmed software.

Cyberlearning The use of Web 2.0 networked computing and communication technologies to support learning.

Cyberlearning literacy The knowledge and skills necessary to successfully use technology tools.

D

Database A collection of related information organized for quick access to specific items of information.

Decode To comprehend information that is presented.

Digital image An image that is not stored on film or processed like film, but rather stored on disk or on a computer using digital numbers to represent the image.

Digital recording A recording process in which analog information is encoded in binary form before being saved onto the recording medium.

Digital subscriber line (DSL) A telephone line that provides very-high-speed access to the Internet.

Digital video Video recording technology that stores video images as strings of binary numbers.

Digital video editing Taking apart and putting back together video segments using a computer and associated software.

Diorama A static display employing a flat background and three-dimensional foreground to achieve a lifelike effect.

Discovery A teaching strategy that proceeds as follows: immersion in a real or contrived problem situation, development of hypotheses, testing of hypotheses, and arrival at conclusion (the main point).

Discussion A teaching strategy involving the exchange of ideas and opinions.

Display An array of objects, visuals, and printed materials.

Distance education Any instructional situation in which learners are separated in time or space from the point of origination, characterized by limited access to the teacher and other learners.

Distance learning An instructional situation in which students learn via telecommunications.

Documentary A video program that deals with fact, not fiction or fictionalized versions of fact.

Document camera A video camera mounted on a copy stand to show documents, pictures, graphics, and real objects to groups.

Download To transfer programs or data files from a computer to another device or computer; to retrieve something from a network.

Drawing Graphic arrangement of lines to represent persons, places, things, and concepts.

Drill-and-practice A teaching strategy in which learners are led through a series of exercises or problems and given feedback.

DVD *See* Digital videodisc.

E

Educational gaming A competitive environment in which learners follow prescribed rules as they strive to attain a challenging goal.

Electronic learning (e-learning) Internet-based learning. Components can include content delivery in multiple formats, management of the learning experience, and a networked community of learners, content developers, and experts. E-learning provides faster learning at reduced costs, increased access to learning materials, and clear accountability for all participants in the learning process.

Electronic mail (email) Transmission of private messages over a computer network; users can send mail to a single recipient or broadcast it to multiple users on the system.

Electronic portfolio (e-portfolio) A digital collection of student work that demonstrates progress in learning as shown in student self-reflections of the portfolio contents.

Electronic whiteboard A display surface that "captures" digitally anything written on it.

Emoticon An email symbol generated from punctuation marks.

Encode To express an idea to others.

Enrichment centers An area that offers stimulating learning experiences for students who have completed required classroom activities.

Entry tests Assessments, both formal and informal, to determine if students possess desired identified prerequisites.

Exhibit A display incorporating various media formats (e.g., realia, still pictures, models, graphics) into an integral whole intended for instructional purposes.

F

Fair use Basic criteria by which an educator may determine if it is appropriate to use copyrighted materials in a classroom setting.

Feedback (electronic) The regeneration of sound caused by a system's microphonic pickup of output from its own speakers, causing a ringing sound or squeal. In communication, signals sent from the destination back to the source that provide information about the reception of the original message.

Feedback (learner) Information provided to the learner regarding correctness of performance and suggestions for improvement.

Fiber optics A transmission medium using spun silicon shaped into threads as thin as human hair. It transmits more signals with higher quality than can metal cables.

Field trip An excursion outside the classroom to study real processes, people, and objects.

File server In local area networks, a station dedicated to providing file and mass data storage services to the other stations on the network.

Firewall Intranet software that prevents external users from accessing a proprietary network, while allowing internal users access to external networks.

Flash drive USB minidrive; a form of removable storage device that allows the user to store files outside the computer.

Flip chart A pad of large paper fastened together at the top and mounted on an easel.

G

Gateway A computer that interconnects and makes translations between two different types of networks. Also called a portal.

General literacy The ability of a student to comprehend or decode information and to use, transform, and create new information.

GB *See* Gigabyte.

Gigabyte (GB) Approximately one million bytes, or 1,000 megabytes.

Graph Visual representation of numerical data.

H

Hardware The mechanical and electronic components that make up a computer; the physical equipment that makes up a computer system, and, by extension, the term that refers to any audiovisual equipment.

Hearing A physiological process in which sound waves entering the outer ear are transmitted to the eardrum, converted into mechanical vibrations in the middle ear, and changed in the inner ear to nerve impulses that travel to the brain.

HTTP *See* Hypertext transfer protocol.

Hybrid instruction *See* Blended instruction.

Hypertext transfer protocol (HTTP) The web protocol that ensures compatibility before transferring information.

I

Iconic Any referent that resembles the thing it represents.

ILS *See* Integrated learning system.

Informal learning An instructional setting that provides students with opportunities to learn from experiences outside of the classroom.

Information Knowledge, facts, news, comments, and content as presented in memos, lectures, textbooks, or websites.

Information literacy The ability to use a range of critical thinking and problem-solving skills to effectively participate in today's society.

Information processing Approaches used to learn information.

Instruction Deliberate arrangement of experience(s) to help learners achieve a desirable change in performance; the management of learning, which in education is primarily the function of the teacher.

Instructional material Specific items used within a lesson that influence student learning.

Instructional technology Hardware, software, and/or processes to facilitate learning.

Integrated learning system (ILS)   A set of interrelated computer-based lessons organized to match the curriculum standards.

Integrated Services Digital Network (ISDN)   A network that provides high-speed access to the Internet using digital communication.

Interest center   A type of learning center that stimulates new interests and encourages creativity by exposing students to new topics that will be covered in later class lessons.

Internet radio   A system used for broadcasting online programs over the Internet.

Interpersonal domain   The domain of learning that involves interaction among people and the ability to relate effectively with others.

Interpretive visuals   Visuals that illustrate theoretical or abstract relationships.

K

KB   *See* Kilobyte.

Keystone effect   The distortion (usually creating a wide top and narrow bottom) of a projected image caused when the projector is not aligned at right angles to the screen.

Kilobyte (KB or K)   Approximately 1,000 bytes; more precisely, 1,024 bytes.

L

Learning   A general term for a relatively lasting change in capability caused by experience; also, the process by which such change is brought about. *See also* Behaviorism and Cognitivism for different interpretations of learning.

Learning center   A self-contained environment designed to promote individual or small-group learning around a specific task.

Learning communities   Student and teacher use of electronic connectedness to share ideas, engage in inquiry, and search for additional information.

Learning objective   *See* Objective.

Learning style   A cluster of psychological traits that determine how a person perceives, interacts with, and responds emotionally to learning environments.

Link   An association between two (or more) nonsequential concepts. In hypermedia, a direct connection between two asynchronous items of data.

Listening   A psychological process that begins with someone's awareness of and attention to sounds or speech patterns, proceeds through identification and recognition of specific auditory signals, and ends in comprehension.

Listening center   A learning center especially designed for audio media.

Log-on   The process of entering a specific name and password to access online materials.

M

Magnetic board   A display surface made of metal for temporarily adhering materials with magnetic backing.

Manipulative   Object that can be viewed and handled in a learning setting.

MB   *See* Megabyte.

Media   *See* Medium.

Media centers   School facilities that offer traditional library reading resources as well as a variety of information technology assets.

Media format   The physical form in which a message is incorporated and displayed. Examples include flip charts, photographic prints, audio, video, and computer multimedia.

Media literacy   The ability to interpret and produce a wide variety of media, including text, audio, visuals, and video, which are often combined to form multimedia.

Medium   A means of communication. Derived from the Latin *medium* ("between"), the term refers to anything that carries information between a source and a receiver. Plural: *media*.

Megabyte (MB or M)   Basic unit of measurement of mass storage.

Memory   Element of a computer that stores information for manipulation by the CPU.

Metacognition   Knowledge of and thinking about one's own thinking process.

Mock-up   Representation of a complex device or process.

Model   A three-dimensional representation of a real object; it may be larger, smaller, or the same size as the thing represented.

Motivation   An internal state that leads people to choose to pursue certain goals and experiences.

Motor skill domain   The category of human learning that involves athletic, manual, and other physical action skills.

MP3 (MPEG Audio Layer 3)   A format for compression of audio files to reduce them into more manageable size, especially when using the Internet.

Multimedia   Sequential or simultaneous use of a variety of media formats in a given presentation or self-study program. *See also* Computer multimedia.

Multimedia kit   A collection of teaching-learning materials involving more than one type of medium and organized around a single topic.

Multiple intelligences   Theory developed by Howard Gardner that suggests humans have multiple methods of learning: verbal/linguistic (language), logical/mathematical (scientific/quantitative), visual/spatial, musical/rhythmic, body/kinesthetic (dancing/athletics), interpersonal (understanding other people), intrapersonal (understanding oneself), naturalist, and existentialist.

Musical Instrument Digital Interface (MIDI) Technology that allows students to create music by focusing on musical ideas rather than the mechanics of playing an instrument or learning musical notation.

N

National Education Technology Standards for Students (NETS-S) A document that specifically outlines expectations for student use of technology to guide their learning.

Navigate To move about at will within a hypermedia environment by means of buttons and other onscreen devices.

Netiquette Guidelines relating to email and other interactions on the Web.

Network A communication system linking two or more computers.

O

Objective A statement of the new capability the learner should possess at the completion of instruction. A well-stated objective names the intended audience, then specifies (1) the performance or capability to be learned, (2) the conditions under which the performance is to be demonstrated, and (3) the criterion or standard of acceptable performance.

Online learning The result of instruction that is delivered electronically using computer-based media.

Open source Websites that offer free productivity suites (e.g., word processing, spreadsheets, presentation software).

Operating system Software that functions as the computer's interface with the user.

Optical disc A type of disc storage device that records and reproduces digital information using a laser beam, e.g., CD and DVD.

Oral history Historical documentation of a time, place, or event by means of recording the spoken recollections of participants in those events.

Organizational visuals Visuals that show the qualitative relationships among various elements.

Overhead projection Projection by means of a device that produces an image on a screen by transmitting light through transparent acetate or a similar medium on the stage of the projector. The lens and mirror arrangement in an elevated housing creates a bright projected image over the head or shoulder of the operator.

Overlay One or more additional transparent sheets with lettering or other information that can be placed over a base transparency.

P

Persistence of vision The psychophysiological phenomenon that occurs when an image falls on the retina of the eye and is conveyed to the brain via the optic nerve. The brain continues to "see" the image for a fraction of a second after the image is cut off.

Personal response system Handheld wireless devices (similar to TV remotes) used to collect and graphically display student answers to teacher questions.

Pictures Photographic (or photograph-like) representations of people, places, and things.

Place-shift Experiencing instruction at some place away from the live teacher.

Podcast Internet-distributed multimedia file formatted for direct download to mobile devices.

Podcasting Distribution of recorded audio files in MP3 format over the Internet.

Portable digital audio player Device that allows users to take digital audio files with them, such as an Apple iPod.

Portal *See* Gateway.

Portfolio An integrated collection of student work including a variety of media to demonstrate progress and accomplishments.

Poster A visual combination of images, lines, color, and words.

Practice Learner participation that increases the probability of learning.

Prerequisites Competencies that learners must possess to benefit from instruction.

Presentation An instructional strategy in which a source tells, dramatizes, or disseminates information to learners.

Presentation software Computer software used to create attractive graphic displays without specialized production skills and to display visuals with a digital projector.

Problem-based learning A process in which students actively seek solutions to structured or ill-structured problems situated in the real world.

Problem-solving skills Reaching a solution to a novel problem using higher-order thinking skills such as defining the problem, considering alternatives, and logical reasoning.

R

RAM *See* Random access memory.

Random access memory (RAM) The flexible part of computer memory. The particular program or set of data being manipulated by the user is temporarily stored in RAM, then erased to make way for the next program.

Read-only memory (ROM) Control instructions that have been "wired" permanently into the memory of a computer. Usually stores instructions that the computer will need constantly, such as the programming language(s) and internal monitoring functions.

Realistic visuals Visuals that show the actual object under study.

Real object Not a model or simulation but an example of an actual object used in instruction.

Relational visuals Visuals that communicate quantitative relationships.

Remedial center A type of learning center that helps students who need additional assistance with a particular concept or skill.

Removable-storage device High-capacity portable computer storage unit that allows the user to store information and move it from one computer to another.

ROM *See* Read-only memory.

Rubric A tool used to provide a more comprehensive assessment of student performance through the use of performance criteria, a rating scale, and level of performance descriptors.

S

Scaffold To build on prior knowledge as part of the learning process.

Scanner A computer device that converts an image on a piece of paper into an electronic form that can be stored in a computer file.

School media center An area of the school where a variety of media are organized and made available to students and teachers.

Search engine A program that identifies Internet sites that contain user-identified keywords or phrases.

Simulation An abstraction or simplification of some real-life situation or process.

Site license Provides unlimited use of software at specified locations by licensing agreement.

Skill center A type of learning center that provides students with opportunities to do additional practice, typically to reinforce a skill previously taught through other media or strategies.

Social psychology The study of the effects of the social organization of the classroom on learning.

Standard Stated expectations of what students should know and be able to do as established at the school district, state, and/or national level.

Storyboarding An audiovisual production and planning technique in which sketches of the proposed visuals and verbal messages are put on individual cards or into a computer program; the items are then arranged into the desired sequence on a display surface.

Strategy A way of doing something; in instruction a way of involving learners in a particular teaching-learning activity.

Streamed Transmission method by which an audio file itself stays on a network server, but the file is available to listeners on an audio device.

Streaming audio Audio sent in packets to allow listening to portions of a file before all portions are downloaded.

Streaming video A video file downloaded from the Internet that starts playing before it is completely downloaded.

Student-centered strategies A type of learning experience in which the learners are involved in the direction of the experience.

Study print A photographic enlargement printed in a durable form for individual or group examination.

Surf Exploring websites on the Internet in order to find information.

T

TB *See* Terabyte.

Teacher-centered strategies A type of learning experience in which the teacher directs the learners in the experience.

Technology (1) A process of devising reliable and repeatable solutions to tasks. (2) The hardware and software (i.e., the product) that result from the application of technological processes. (3) A mix of process and product, used in instances where the context refers to the combination of technological processes and resultant products or where the process is inseparable from the product.

Technological competence Knowing not only the basics of computer literacy, but also how and when to use technology to enhance student learning.

Telecommunications A means for communicating over a distance; specifically, any arrangement for transmitting voice and data in the form of coded signals through an electronic medium.

Terabyte (TB) Approximately one million megabytes.

Text literacy The ability to use text as a means to gather information or to communicate.

Thematic unit Instruction organized around a topic or theme.

Time-shift Experiencing instructions at some time after the live lesson.

Transformational visuals Visuals that illustrate movement or change in time and space.

Transparency The large-format (typically 8 by 10 inches) film used with the overhead projector.

Tutorial   A teaching strategy in which content is presented, questions posed, responses given, and feedback provided.

U

Uniform resource locator (URL)   The address for an Internet site or World Wide Web page containing the protocol type, the domain, the directory, and the name of the site or page.

URL   *See* Uniform resource locator.

USB (universal serial bus)   A hardware interface technology that allows the user to connect a device without having to restart the computer.

V

Vidcast   A type of podcast that allows students to see and hear the information being presented.

Video   The storage of visuals and their display on a television-type screen.

Videography   The creation of video.

Video literacy skills   The ability to understand and evaluate video messages and to create video that appropriately achieves the intended outcomes.

Virtual field trip   A type of field trip in which the students do not leave the classroom setting; instead they use media to provide the experience of "being there."

Virtual reality   A computer-controlled environment in which users experience multisensory immersion and interact with certain phenomena as they would in the physical world.

Visual literacy   The learned ability to interpret visual messages accurately and to create such messages.

Visual pointer   An item that draws the learner's attention and thinking to relevant parts of a visual.

W

WAN   *See* Wide area network.

WAV   The digital version of analog audio created by using a computer sound card and software to convert and store files in a digital format.

Web   See World Wide Web.

Web pages   Documents that make up the World Wide Web. *See* Website.

WebQuest   A set of steps that provide guidance when seeking information about a simulated problem.

Website   A collection of web pages available on the Internet that provide information about products, services, events, materials, etc.

Web 2.0 tools   Available online resources that provide students with many types of learning opportunities beyond simple information access.

Whiteboard   A display surface, also called multipurpose board or marker board, for visual and textual communication using special felt-tip markers.

Wide area network (WAN)   A communications network that covers a large geographic area, such as a state or country.

Wiki   A web-based document subject to edit by any of its users.

Wireless network   Computers connected by radio frequency, microwave, or infrared technology instead of wires.

World Wide Web (the Web)   A graphical environment on computer networks that allows you to access, view, and maintain documents that can include text, data, sound, graphics, and video.

References

Barrett, H. (2009). *ePortfolios with GoogleApps*. Retrieved March 14, 2010, from http://sites.google.com/site/eportfolioapps/Home

Bausell, C. V. (2008). Tracking U.S. trends. *Education Week: Technology Counts, 27*(30), 39–42.

Becker, G. H. (2003). *Copyright: A guide to information and resources* (3rd ed.). Lake Mary, FL: Gary H. Becker (P.O. Box 951870, Lake Mary, FL 32795-1870).

Black, P., & William, O. (1998). Assessment and classroom learning. *Assessment in Education, 5*(1), 7–73.

Bloom, B. S., Engelhart, M. D., Furst, E. J., Hill, W. H., & Krathwohl, D. R. (Eds.). (1956). *Taxonomy of educational objectives: The classification of educational goals. Handbook 1: Cognitive domain.* New York: David McKay.

Bowes, K. A., D'Onofrio, A., & Marker, E. S. (2006). Assessing technology integration: Its validity and value for classroom practice and teacher accountability. *Australasian Journal of Educational Technology, 22*(4), 439–454.

Bransford, J., Brown, A., & Cocking, R. (Eds.). (2000). *How people learn: Brain, mind, experience, and school.* Washington, DC: National Research Council.

Branzburg, J. (2009, May). *Use Google Maps mashups in K–12 education*. Retrieved July 17, 2009, from www.techlearning.com/articles/5760

Butler, K. A. (1986). *Learning and teaching style: In theory and in practice* (2nd ed.). Columbia, CT: Learner's Dimension.

Carter, D. (2010, May). Ed-tech officials: Video will make schools more "efficient." *eSchool News*. Retrieved May 14, 2010, from www.eschoolnews.com/2010/05/05/ed-tech-officials-video-will-make-schools-more-efficient/2/?_login=cb81edbc3b?_login=cb81edbc3b

Center for Applied Special Technology (CAST). (2009). *Universal design for learning.* Retrieved August 21, 2009, from www.cast.org/about/index.html

Clark, R. C., & Lyons, C. (2004). *Graphics for learning.* San Francisco: Pfeiffer.

Cooper, C., & Varma, V. (Eds.). (1997). *Processes in individual differences.* London: Routledge.

Crandell, C. C., Smaldino, J. J., & Flexer, C. (2005). *Sound field amplification: Applications to speech perception and classroom acoustics* (2nd ed.). Clifton Park, NY: Thompson/Delmar Learning.

Cronin, B. J., & King, S. R. (2007). *The development of the descriptive video services.* National Center to Improve Practice in Special Education through Technology, Media, and Materials. Retrieved May 15, 2010, from www2.edc.org/NCIP/library/v&c/cronin.htm

Dabbagh, N., & Bannan-Ritland, B. (2005). *Online learning: Concepts, strategies, and application.* Columbus, OH: Merrill/Prentice Hall.

Dale, E. (1969). *Audio-visual methods in teaching* (3rd ed.) New York: Holt, Rinehart, & Winston.

Davis, T., Fuller, M., Jackson, S., Pittman, J., & Sweet, J. (2007). *A national consideration of digital equity*, www.iste.org/digitalequity. Washington, DC: International Society for Technology in Education.

DeLoache, J. S. (2005). Mindful of symbols. *Scientific American, 33*(3), 73–77.

Dick, W., Carey, L., & Carey, J. O. (2009). *The systematic design of instruction* (7th ed.). Boston: Allyn & Bacon.

Discovery Education. (2010). *About us.* Retrieved May 14, 2010, from www.discoveryeducation.com/aboutus

Dodge, B. (1999). *The WebQuest page.* Retrieved from http://webquest.org/index.php

Donovan, M. S., & Bransford, J. D. (2005). Introduction. In M. S. Donovan & J. D. Bransford (Eds.), *How students learn: Mathematics in the classroom*. Washington, DC: National Academies Press.

Driscoll, M. P. (2005). *Psychology of learning for instruction* (3rd ed.). Boston: Allyn & Bacon.

Dunn, R., & Dunn, K. (1992). *Teaching elementary students through their individual learning styles: Practical applications for grades 3–6.* Boston: Allyn & Bacon.

Dwyer, F. M. (1978). *Strategies for improving visual learning.* State College, PA: Learning Services.

Farmer, D. (2009, May 18). *Digital information growth outpaces projections, despite down economy.* EMC Corporation. Retrieved August 21, 2009, from www.emc.com/about/news/press/2009/20090518-01.htm

Flynn, J., & Russell, J. (2008). Personal response systems: Is success in learning just a click away? *Educational Technology, 48*(6), 20–23.

Forsdale, J. R., & Forsdale, L. (1966). Film literacy. *Teachers College Record, 67*(8), 608–617.

Gagné, R. M. (1985). *The conditions of learning* (4th ed.). New York: Holt, Rinehart & Winston.

Gagné, R. M., Briggs, L. J., & Wager, W. W. (1992). *Principles of instructional design* (4th ed.). Fort Worth, TX: Harcourt Brace Jovanovich.

Gardner, H. (2006). *Multiple intelligences: New horizons.* New York: Basic Books.

Gee, J. (2005). Good video games and good learning. *Phi Kappa Phi Forum, 85*(2), 33–37.

Gray, L., Thomas, N., & Lewis, L. (2010). *Educational technology in U.S. public schools: Fall 2008 (NCES 2010–034).* U.S. Department of Education, National Center for Education Statistics. Washington, DC: U.S. Government Printing Office.

Gronlund, N. E. (2009). *Writing instructional objectives for teaching and assessment* (8th ed.). Upper Saddle River, NJ: Merrill/Prentice Hall.

Hightower, A. E. (2009, March). Tracking U.S. trends: States earn B average for policies supporting educational technology use. *Education Week: Technology Counts, 28*(26), 30–33.

Individuals with Disabilities Education Improvement Act (IDEA). (2004). Special Education and Rehabilitation Services, U.S. Department of Education. Retrieved October 23, 2006, from www.ed.gov/policy/speced/guid/idea/idea2004.html

Institute of Educational Sciences. (2009). *Digest of education statistics: 2009 tables and figures,* Table 50. Retrieved June 26, 2010, http://nces.ed.gov/programs/digest/d09/tables/dt09_050.asp

International Association for K–12 Online Learning (iNACOL). (2010). *Fast facts about online learning.* Retrieved June 27, 2010, from www.inacol.org

International Society for Technology in Education (ISTE). (1998). *National educational technology standards (NETS) for students.* Retrieved August 21, 2009, from www.iste.org/Content/NavigationMenu/NETS/ForStudents/1998Standards/NETS_for_Students_1998.htm

International Society for Technology in Education (ISTE). (2007). *National educational technology standards for students (NETS-S)* (2nd ed.). Eugene, OR: ISTE. Retrieved August 21, 2009, from http://cnets.iste.org/students/index.html

International Society for Technology in Education (ISTE). (2008). *National educational technology standards for teachers (NETS-T).* Eugene, OR: ISTE.. Retrieved August 21, 2009, from www.iste.org/Content/NavigationMenu/NETS/ForTeachers/NETS_for_Teachers.htm

International Society for Technology in Education (ISTE). (2009). *ISTE policy brief: Technology and teacher quality—the indelible link.* Washington, DC: ISTE Advocacy.

Jeng, H., Chandler, P., & Sweller, J. (1997). The role of visual indicators in dual sensory mode instruction. *Education Psychology, 17*(3), 329–343.

Johnson, D. W., & Johnson, R. T. (1999). *Learning together and alone: Cooperative, competitive, and individualistic learning.* Boston: Allyn & Bacon.

Johnson, L., Levine, A., & Smith, R. (2009). *The 2009 horizon report.* Austin, TX: The New Media Consortium.

Jolls, T. (2008). *Literacy for the 21st century: An overview and orientation guide to media literacy education.* Retrieved May 11, 2010, from www.medialit.org/reading_room/article540.html

Jonassen, D. H., Howland, J., Marra, R., & Crismond, D. (2008). *Meaningful learning with technology* (3rd ed.). Upper Saddle River, NJ: Merrill/Prentice Hall.

Jonassen, D. H., Howland, J., Moore, J., & Marra, R. M. (2003). *Learning to solve problems with technology: A constructivist perspective.* Upper Saddle River, NJ: Merrill/Prentice Hall.

Keegan, D. (1980). On defining distance education. *Distance Eduction, 1*(1), 13–16.

Keller, J. (1987). The systematic process of motivational design. *Performance and Instruction, 26*(9), 1–8.

Keller, J. M., & Suzuki, K. (1988). Use of the ARCS motivation model in courseware design. In D. H. Jonassen (Ed.),

Instructional designs for microcomputer courseware. Hillsdale, NJ: Lawrence Erlbaum.

Mager, R. F. (1997). *Preparing instructional objectives: A critical tool in the development of effective instruction* (3rd ed.). Atlanta, GA: The Center for Effective Performance.

Marzano, R. J., Pickering, D. J., & Pollock, J. E. (2001). *Classroom instruction that works: Research-based strategies for increasing student achievement.* Alexandria: VA: Association for Supervision and Curriculum Development (ASCD).

Maslow, A., & Lowery, R. (Eds.). (1998). *Toward a psychology of being* (3rd ed.). New York: John Wiley & Sons.

Mayer, R. E., & Moreno, R. (2003). Nine ways to reduce cognitive load in multimedia learning. *Educational Psychologist, 38*(1), 43–52.

Morrison, G. R., & Lowther, D. L. (2010). *Integrating computer technology into the classroom* (4th ed.). Upper Saddle River, NJ: Merrill/Prentice Hall.

Moursund, D. (2006). *Introduction to using games in education: A guide for teachers and parents.* Eugene, OR: Author.

Moyer, P., Salkind, G., & Bolyard, J. J. (2008). Virtual manipulatives used by K–8 teachers for mathematics instruction: The influence of mathematical, cognitive, and pedagogical fidelity. *Contemporary Issues in Technology and Teacher Education, 8*(3), 202–218.

National Clearinghouse for English Language Acquisition. (2010). National Clearinghouse for English Language Acquisition & Language Instruction Educational Programs. Retrieved June 26, 2010, from www.ncela.gwu.edu

National Crime Prevention Council (NCPC). (2010). *Cyberbullying.* Retrieved August 7, 2010, from www.ncpc.org/newsroom/current-campaigns/cyberbullying

Nelson, T. A. (1992). *Metacognition.* Boston: Allyn & Bacon.

Newby, T. J., Ertmer, P. A., & Stepich, D. A. (1995). Instructional analogies and the learning of concepts. *Educational Technology Research and Development, 43*(1), 5–18.

Newby, T. J., Stepich, D. A., Lehman, J. D., & Russell, J. D. (2010). *Educational technology for teaching and learning* (4th ed.). Upper Saddle River, NJ: Merrill/Prentice Hall.

Nielsen Company. (2010, January 22). *Led by Facebook, Twitter, global time spent on social media sites up 82% year over year.* Retrieved March 8, 2010, from http://blog.nielsen.com/nielsenwire/global/led-by-facebook-twitter-global-time-spent-on-social-media-sites-up-82-year-over-year

Nugent, G. C. (2005). Using and delivery of learning objects in K–12: The public television experience. *TechTrends, 49*(4), 61–66.

Paine, S. (2009, May). Profile. *T.H.E. Journal.* Retrieved July 22, 2010, from http://thejournal.com/articles/2009/05/01/profile--steven-paine.aspx?sc_lang=en

Papert, S. (1993a). *The children's machine: Rethinking school in the age of the computer.* New York: Basic Books.

Papert, S. (1993b). *Mindstorms: Children, computers, and powerful ideas.* New York: Basic Books.

Partnership for 21st Century Skills. (2009). *Framework for 21st century learning.* Retrieved August 6, 2009, from www.p21.org/index.php?option=com_content&task=view&id=254&Itemid=119

Partnership for 21st Century Skills. (n.d.). *Learning for the 21st century: Report and mile guide for 21st century skills.* Retrieved October 2, 2008, from www.p21.org

Pew Internet and American Life Project (2007). *Information searches that solve problems.* Retrieved June 26, 2010, from www.pewinternet.org/pdfs/Pew_UI_LibrariesReport.pdf

Pew Internet and American Life Project. (2009). *Demographics of internet users.* Retrieved August 7, 2009, from www.pewinternet.org/Trend-Data/Whos-Online.aspx

Pfaffman, J. (2007). It's time to consider open source software. *TechTrends, 51*(3), 38–43.

Prensky, M. (2006, December/January). Adopt and adapt: 21st century schools need 21st century technology. *Edutopia,* 43–45.

Robertson, K. (2008). *Preparing ELLs to be 21st-century learners.* Retrieved February 15, 2010, from www.colorincolorado.org/article/21431

Robinson, F. P. (1946). *Effective study.* New York: Harper & Row.

Salton, F., & Arslan, K. (2009). A new teacher tool, interactive white boards: A meta analysis. In I. Gibson et al. (Eds.), *Proceedings of Society for Information Technology & Teacher Education International Conference 2009* (pp. 2115–2120). Chesapeake, VA: AACE.

Schuck, S., & Kearney, M. (2008). Classroom-based use of two educational technologies: A sociocultural perspective. *Contemporary Issues in Technology and Teacher Education, 8*(4). Retrieved May 15, 2010, from www.citejournal.org/vol8/iss4/currentpractice/article2.cfm

Shaffer, D., Shaffer, K., Squire, R., & Gee, J. (2005). Video games and the future of learning. *Phi Delta Kappan, 87*(2), 105–111.

Simonson, M., Smaldino, S., Albright, M., & Zvacek, S. (2006). *Teaching and learning at a distance: Foundations of distance education* (3rd ed.). Upper Saddle River, NJ: Merrill/Prentice Hall.

Slavin, R. E. (1989–1990). Research on cooperative learning: Consensus and controversy. *Educational Leadership, 47*(4), 52–54.

Solomon, G., & Schrum, L. (2007). *Web 2.0: New tools, new schools.* Eugene, OR: ISTE.

Stansbury, M. (2009). Groups push for media literacy education. *eSchool News.* Retrieved May 15, 2009, from www.eschoolnews.com/resources/measuring-21st-century

Thoman, E., & Jolls, T. (2004). Media literacy: A national priority for a changing world. *American Behavioral Scientist, 48*(1), 18–29.

U.S. Department of Education (USDOE). (2002). *No Child Left Behind Act of 2001.* Retrieved October 21, 2006, from www.ed.gov/admins/lead/account/nclbreference/page_pg28.html#ii-d1

U.S. Department of Education (USDOE). (2010). *National Education Technology Plan (NETP).* Retrieved July 5, 2010, from www.ed.gov/technology/netp-2010

U.S. Department of Education Office of Educational Technology. (2010). *Grant programs.* Retrieved June 28, 2010, from www2.ed.gov/about/offices/list/os/technology/edgrants.html

Wagner, T. (2008). *The global achievement gap: Why even our best schools don't teach the new survival skills our children need—and what we can do about it.* New York: Basic Books.

Watson, J. (October, 2005). *Keeping pace with K–12 online learning: A review of state-level policy and practice.* Naperville, IL: North Central Regional Educational Lab at Learning Point Associates.

Weinstein, P. (2005). Assessments unplugged. *Technology and Learning, 25*(6), 8–12.

Wikipedia. (2009). *Computer literacy.* Retrieved September 9, 2009, from http://en.wikipedia.org/wiki/Computer_literacy

Wood, C. (2005, April/May). Highschool.com: Online learning comes of age. *Edutopia,* 32–37.

Zawilinski, L (2009). HOT blogging: A framework for blogging to promote higher order thinking. *The Reading Teacher, 62*(8), 650–661.

Name Index

Subject Index

ABCD objectives checklist, 43
Abstract random learners, 22
Abstract sequential learners, 22
Acceptable use policies (AUPs), 155
Acetate, 198
Adobe Illustrator, 179, 197
Affective domain, 235
Affective learning, 240
Age appropriateness, 73, 83
Alt-tags, 101
American Association of School Librarians (AASL), 286
American Library Association (ALA), 286
Analog audio, 216–217
Analogical visuals, 183
Analogous colors, 193
Analog video, 240
Animation, 238
Animoto, 128
Anne Frank House Museum, 256
Anxiety, in presentation, 51
Apple iPod, 127, 218
Applications, 108
Arctic Stories website, 236
Askkids.com, 164
Assessment
    authentic, 55–59
    basis for, 41
    conditions and, 42
    of learner achievement, 55–59
    portfolio, 55, 57
    of prior knowledge, 25–26
Assessment data, 7
Assessment tools, mobile, 7
Assistive technology, 3, 289, 290
Association for Advancement of Computing in Education (AACE), 286
Association for Educational Communications and Technology (AECT), 286
ASSURE lesson plans, 63, 89, 116, 136, 166, 201, 223, 275
ASSURE model, 1, 8
    analyzing learners in, 38, 39, 50, 63, 89, 117, 136, 201, 224, 247, 275, 283
    benefits of, 6, 8
    evaluating and revising in, 39, 55–63, 92, 119, 139, 169, 204, 227, 249, 278, 283
    learning objectives in, 39
    previewing technology, media, and materials, 47
    requiring learners' participation in, 39, 52–55, 72, 91, 119, 138, 168, 203, 226, 249, 277
    selecting strategies for technology, media, and materials in, 39, 45, 64, 90, 117, 137, 167, 202, 225–226, 248, 276

stating standards and objectives in, 39, 45, 64, 90, 117, 136–137, 166–167, 201–202, 224, 247, 275
    and 21st century learning, 283
    utilizing strategies, technology, media, and materials in, 39, 47–51, 52, 64, 91, 118, 138, 168, 226, 248–249, 277
    see also Case studies
Asynchronous settings, 85
Attitude scale, 55, 57
Audacity software, 214
Audio, 208–233
    accessing, 217–219
    in the classroom, 213–214
    copyright concerns with, 220
    creating, 219–223
    for diverse learners, 213
    how students can use, 214
    how teachers can use, 213–214
    setups, 305–306
    streaming, 217
    when to use, 222
Audiobooks, 221
Audiocassette recorders, 220
Audiocassette tapes, 216–218
Audio CDs, burning, 215
Audio compression, 215–216
Audio downloads, 127
Audio files, 217, 218
Audio formats, 215–217
Audio literacy, 11, 210–213
Audio materials, 214
    selection rubric for, 230–231
Audio media, 210, 220
Audiometric hearing tests, 212
Audio podcasts, 134
Audio recorder, 218–219
Audio storybook, 56
Audiotapes, 220
Audio technology, 148
Audio teleconference, 148
Audio Theatre Production Kit, 221
Audiovisual equipment, 301
    selection rubric, 307
Auditory fatigue, 211
Augmented reality (AR), 165
Authentic assessment, 55–59

Bar graphs, 179, 180
Behavior, objectives and, 42
Behaviorist perspective, 23
Bias, 86
Bias free, 87
Bit, 111

Credits

pp. 27, 45, 52–53, 90, 117, 137, 167, 201, 224, 247, 276: Reprinted with permission from *National Educational Technology Standards for Students* © 2007, ISTE (International Society for Technology in Education, www.iste.org). All rights reserved; pp. 45, 56, 66, 276: Standards for the English Language Arts, by the International Reading Association and the National Council of Teachers of English, Copyright 1996 by the International Reading Association and the National Council of Teachers of English. Reprinted with permission. www.ncte.org/standards; p. 90: National Center for History in the Schools, http://nchs.ucla .edu; p. 166: National Council for the Social Studies, Expectations of Excellence: Curriculum Standards for Social Studies (Washington, DC: NCSS, 1994); pp. 201, 275: Principles and Standards for School Mathematics by NCTM. Copyright 2000 by the National Council of Teachers of Mathematics. Reproduced with permission of the National Council of Teachers of Mathematics via Copyright Clearance Center; p. 285: Reprinted with permission from *National Educational Technology Standards for Teachers: Preparing Teachers to Use Technology* © 2008, ISTE (International Society for Technology in Education, www.iste.org). All rights reserved; p. 286: Copyright 2010 by the Association for the Advancement of Computing in Education (AACE), www.aace.org. Included here by permission; p. 286: Reprinted by permission of Global SchoolNet; p. 286: Reprinted by permission of International Society for Technology in Education; p. 287: Used with permission of ITEEA (www.iteea.org); p. 287, Reprinted by permission of United States Distance Learning Associates.